PERSPECTIVES ON SCHOLARLY
MISCONDUCT IN THE SCIENCES

Perspectives on Scholarly Misconduct in the Sciences

Edited by
JOHN M. BRAXTON

Ohio State University Press
Columbus

Earlier versions of chapters 1, 3, 4, 7, 10, 11, and the Conclusion originally appeared as part of a special issue of the *Journal of Higher Education* entitled Perspectives on Research Misconduct (vol. 65, May/June 1994).

Copyright © 1999 by The Ohio State University.
All rights reserved.

Library of Congress Cataloging-in-Publication Data

Perspectives on scholarly misconduct in the sciences / edited by John M. Braxton.
    p.   cm.
    Includes bibliographical references and index.
    ISBN 0-8142-0815-0 (alk. paper)
    1. Scientists—Moral and ethical aspects.   2. Self-control.   3. Scientists—Discipline.   4. Research—Social aspects.   I. Braxton, John M.
Q147.P47   1999
174'.95—dc21   98-50039
                                                                                     CIP

Text and jacket design by Paula Newcomb.
Type set in Minion by Wilsted & Taylor Publishing Services.
Printed by Thomson-Shore, Inc.

The paper used in this publication meets the minimum requirements of the American National Standard for Information Sciences—Permanence of Paper for Printed Library Materials. ANSI Z39.48–1992.

9 8 7 6 5 4 3 2 1

CONTENTS

INTRODUCTION: Exercising Responsibility for Scholarly Misconduct
John M. Braxton   1

PART I   Historical Overviews

1   A Foundation of Trust: Scientific Misconduct, Congressional Oversight, and the Regulatory Response
Marcel C. LaFollette   11

2   From Denial to Action: Academic and Scientific Societies Grapple with Misconduct
David Johnson   42

3   Research Universities and Scientific Misconduct: History, Policies, and the Future
Nicholas H. Steneck   75

PART II   Theoretical Perspectives

4   A Social Control Perspective on Scientific Misconduct
Edward J. Hackett   99

5   Universities and the Regulation of Scientific Morals
Stephen Turner   116

PART III   Policy and Law Perspectives

6   Toward a Guiding Framework for Self-Regulation in the Community of the Academic Profession
John M. Braxton   139

7 Scientific Misconduct and Editorial and Peer Review Processes
  Mary Frank Fox 162

8 Including Ethics in Graduate Education in Scientific Research
  Stephanie J. Bird 174

9 Legal Aspects of Scholarship Misconduct
  Barbara A. Lee 189

PART IV Empirical Treatments

10 Disciplinary and Departmental Effects on Observations of Faculty and Graduate Student Misconduct
   Melissa S. Anderson, Karen Seashore Louis, and Jason Earle 213

11 Perceptions of Research Misconduct and an Analysis of Their Correlates
   John M. Braxton and Alan E. Bayer 236

12 Understanding the Potential for Misconduct in University-Industry Relationships: An Empirical View
   Teresa Isabelle Daza Campbell and Sheila Slaughter 259

13 Uncovering the Covert: Research on Academic Misconduct
   Melissa S. Anderson 283

CONCLUSION: Self-Regulation and Social Control of Scientific Misconduct: Roles, Patterns, and Constraints
Mary Frank Fox and John M. Braxton 315

CONTRIBUTORS 331

INDEX 335

INTRODUCTION

Exercising Responsibility for Scholarly Misconduct

John M. Braxton

Society expects professions to be self-regulating (Goode, 1969). *Self-regulation* refers to a profession's assumption of responsibility for ensuring that its members perform their professional roles in a competent and ethical manner. However, well-publicized incidents of scientific misconduct (e.g., Baltimore, Bruening, Benvenista, Borer, Darsee, Gallo, Imanishi-Kari, Slutsky, Stricker, and Summerlin) during the past two decades have led the lay public to question the effectiveness of self-regulation by the scientific community.

Such public skepticism emanates from both the perception that misconduct is not as rare as scientists contend and the lethargic response of the scientific community to allegations of wrongdoing. It raises a rudimentary question: Where does the locus of responsibility for addressing misconduct reside? Self-regulation requires social control. Social control pertains to various mechanisms designed to induce conformity to normative or ethical standards (Clark & Gibbs, 1965; Horowitz, 1990; Parsons, 1951; Pitts, 1961). Such mechanisms serve to delineate and respond to acts of wrongdoing (Horowitz, 1990). More specifically, Zuckerman (1977, 1998) asserted that the social control of scientific improprieties requires mechanisms of deterrence, detection, and punishment. Although the lay public expects the scientific community to assume responsibility for such mechanisms, Chubin (1983) has cast a broader net of "collective responsibility" that includes not only individual scientists but also governmental agencies and legislatures, academic societies, academic journals, and universities.

Fox and Braxton (1994) described these various loci of responsibility as constituting a "trans-scientific community." They posited that the trans-scientific community lacks stability and that alliances among its segments depend on the issues and interests pertinent to a given aspect of the process of self-regulation. This characterization raises an important question: What part do the various segments of the trans-scientific community play in deterring, detecting, and sanctioning scientific wrongdoing?

This question has received some scholarly treatment in the burgeoning literature on scientific misconduct (Braxton, 1994; Cheney, 1993; Chubin, 1983; LaFollette, 1992; Pallone & Hennessy, 1995; Penslar, 1995; Teich & LaFollette, 1992). In particular, Braxton's (1994) edited collection concentrated on the responsibilities of the various segments of the trans-scientific community to deter, detect, and sanction scientific improprieties. Specifically, it focused on the reaction of the federal government to wrongdoing, the role of editors and peer reviewers for academic journals, the response of universities to scientific malfeasance, the advancement of a set of guidelines for universities to follow in handling allegations of misconduct, the effects of graduate school departments on scientific wrongdoing, and the attitudes and perceptions of individual scientists toward taking action for incidents of scientific misbehavior.

The current volume also explores the above issues, but it extends Braxton's (1994) work by attending to the following significant questions that were neglected by it: Why have universities been slow to respond to incidents of misconduct? Why is self-regulation in the best interests of the academic profession? Do the roles of the various segments of the academic profession—for example, individual scientists, department chairs and laboratory directors, journal editors, professional associations—vary according to research misconduct associated with the various stages of the research process? What role do academic and scientific societies play in deterring, detecting, and sanctioning scientific wrongdoing? How might graduate departments include research ethics into their curricula? Do collaborative relationships between university researchers and industry have a potential for misconduct? What are the legal issues associated with addressing misconduct? What kind of research is needed to increase our knowledge and understanding of scholarship misconduct?

Because the scholarship of this volume takes a diversity of forms—historical overviews, theoretical perspectives, policy/law perspectives, and empirical treatments—the forms themselves provide the basis for the book's organization, an organization that facilitates the readers' use of this volume. In addition to this introductory chapter and a concluding chapter, the book has four parts.

Part I, "Historical Overviews," consists of three chapters. In chapter 1, LaFollette provides a historical account of the relationship between the oversight function of Congress and its reaction to incidents of misconduct. From this historical account, she offers explanations for the lay public's deep concern about scientific malfeasance. LaFollette also suggests ways for the scientific community to respond to the exercise of social control by the lay public.

Academic and scientific societies have begun to exercise responsibility for misconduct. In chapter 2, David Johnson offers a historical overview of these efforts. These efforts include the development of procedures that universities can use to handle allegations of wrongdoing, the facilitation of dialogue on misconduct-related issues, development and enforcement of codes of conduct, and the formulation of uniform policies for use by academic journals to control scientific misconduct.

Universities shoulder a major responsibility for exercising control over scholarship misconduct. They also possess the authority to develop policies and procedures for handling allegations of misconduct and the power to hire, promote, and reward faculty. Thus, they hold much power and authority to deter, detect, and sanction wrongdoing. In chapter 3, Nicholas H. Steneck describes, from a historical perspective, the slow response of universities to charges of misconduct. He also posits a set of basic considerations and principles for universities to follow in their development of policies and procedures for handling allegations of scholarship misbehavior.

Two chapters make up Part II, "Theoretical Perspectives." In chapter 4, Edward J. Hackett offers explanations for why social control of scientific malfeasance has been exercised by the lay public. Hackett also suggests means for the scientific community to respond to the exercise of such social control. Stephen Turner, in chapter 5, augments Steneck's discussion of the sluggish response of universities to allegations of misconduct by presenting a set of theoretical formulations to account for why universities have been hesitant to exercise responsibility for misconduct.

Part III, "Policy and Law Perspectives," consists of four chapters that advance perspectives on the development of policy for the exercise of responsibility for scientific wrongdoing by various levels of the trans-scientific community. In chapter 6, John M. Braxton offers a guiding framework for self-regulation by the community of the academic profession: individual scientists, laboratories, academic departments, universities, academic journals, and professional associations and scientific societies. This framework is predicated on the contention that self-regulation serves the self-interests of the community of the academic profession. The framework also apportions responsibility to the various levels of the community of the academic profession for deterring, detecting, and sanctioning misconduct associated with the four stages of the research process—production, reporting, dissemination, and evaluation—delineated by Chubin (1983). Braxton suggests that this framework can be used by the community of the academic profession to guide its self-regulatory processes, as well as by scholars and public policy makers to assess the efficacy of self-regulation by the academic community.

Mary Frank Fox, in chapter 7, appraises the capability of editors and peer reviewers of academic journals to detect and sanction scientific wrongdoing. She identifies several aspects of the role of the editor and the journal peer review process that work against the detection of misconduct. Fox proffers some remedies for the improvement of the review process.

Zuckerman (1977, 1988) asserted that the doctoral socialization process is an important mechanism for the deterrence of scholarship misconduct. Universities, academic departments, and individual faculty members all share some responsibility for ensuring that the doctoral socialization process inculcates ethical standards in aspirants to the academic profession. Some guidelines for the teaching of research ethics are needed by graduate departments. In chapter 8, Stephanie J. Bird describes various possible formats for the teaching of appropriate research conduct, such as courses, seminars, integration of ethics content into all courses, and mentoring programs. She also suggests some approaches and materials that can be used in the teaching of research conduct. Moreover, Bird delineates the elements of an effective program for the teaching of research conduct to guide the development of such efforts.

The law represents social control by governmental agencies (Black, 1976). Law as social control prevails when less formal types of social control are weak (Black, 1976). Thus, the use of law to exercise responsibility for scholarly improprieties is a compensatory mechanism for ineffective self-regulation through other means. Barbara A. Lee, in chapter 9, describes the various legal remedies that individuals and universities may employ to sanction scholarship misconduct. She also discusses the application of laws to protect both whistle-blowers and accused individuals from unfair or trivial charges. The law in these situations offers a vehicle for effective self-regulation.

Zuckerman (1988) pointed to the lack of basic evidence on the "incidence, distribution, and effectiveness of various controls of deviant behavior in science" (p. 526). Thus, we lack a knowledge base concerning the exercise of responsibility for scientific wrongdoing. The four chapters of Part IV, "Empirical Treatments," assist in the development of such a needed knowledge base by offering the findings of empirical studies and recommendations for research on scholarship misconduct. As previously indicated, the doctoral socialization process plays an important role in the exercise of responsibility for scientific wrongdoing. In chapter 10, Melissa S. Anderson, Karen Seashore Louis, and Jason Earle describe the results of their empirical tests of the influence of departmental structure, departmental climate, and academic discipline on the observation of wrongdoing by graduate students. They also suggest some of their findings' implications for the design of the graduate school socialization process.

Academic associations and societies, academic journals, and universities rely on individual scholars to report scholarly wrongdoing. Chubin (1983) asserted that individual scientists bear the ultimate responsibility for taking action when misconduct is suspected. John M. Braxton and Alan E. Bayer, in chapter 11, identify a set of attitudes and beliefs regarding the taking of action for suspected wrongdoing. They also focus on the effects of intraprofessional status, departmental cohesion, institutional pressure for grants, and professional solidarity on these attitudes and beliefs.

Individual scientists also shoulder responsibility for their own research conduct (Braxton, 1990). However, attitudes and beliefs regarding taking action for misconduct influence the actions that individual academics take. The types of relationships that individuals have with organizations and individuals external to the academic community can also influence action. In chapter 12, Teresa Campbell and Sheila Slaughter offer an empirical perspective on the pressures for inappropriate research behavior derived from collaborative research between university scientists and business and industry. Their research identifies some possible forms of scientific impropriety that are likely to result from such pressures.

What do we need to know about misconduct in order to develop policies and procedures to deter, detect, and punish offenders? In chapter 13, Melissa S. Anderson advances recommendations for a research agenda on misconduct and associated issues. These recommendations serve two basic functions. First, they furnish scholars with research ideas on misconduct. Second, they provide insight into the various difficulties and issues connected with exercising responsibility for misconduct.

How well does social control of scholarship misconduct work? In the conclusion to this volume, Fox and Braxton appraise the effectiveness of the various segments of the trans-scientific community in discharging responsibility for scholarship misbehavior. The previous chapters of this volume supply a foundation for this assessment. Fox and Braxton also identify limits on social control and offer some recommendations for policy on the deterrence, detection, and sanctioning of scholarship misconduct.

Although this book is organized according to the scholarly forms described above, it may also be viewed as a handbook or desk reference for use by various segments of the trans-scientific community: public policy makers, journal editors, officers of academic and scientific societies, university central administrators (presidents, chief academic affairs officers, research grant administrators), academic deans, members of university research integrity committees, laboratory directors, academic department chairs, individual scientists, and scholars of scientific misconduct. Individual scientists and scholars of scientific misconduct will find most of the chapters to be of interest. The conclusion will be of interest to all segments of the trans-scientific community. However, specific chapters will be of special value to particular segments of the community. The following list recommends specific chapters for use by these various segments:

Public policy makers	1, 3, 4, 5, 9
Journal editors	2, 6, 7
Officers of academic and scientific societies	2, 6
University central administrators and academic deans	3, 5, 6, 9, 12
University research integrity committees	3, 6, 9, 11
Laboratory directors and department chairs	6, 8, 10

CONCLUSION

Research and scholarship begotten through misconduct mislead members of the academic community and practitioners who apply the findings of research. Thus, failures in executing responsibility for wrongdoing by the various segments of the trans-scientific community erode the public trust and support for academic work. Such deterioration in trust and support could lead to further social control by the lay public. Such social control might restrict the autonomy of the academic community to engage in scholarship and hinder future contributions to knowledge. Consequently, this edited book is devoted to the exercise of effective self-regulation by the trans-scientific community.

REFERENCES

Black, D. (1976). *The behavior of law.* New York: Academic Press.

Braxton, J. M. (1990). Deviancy from the norms of science: A test of control theory. *Research in Higher Education, 31,* 461–476.

Braxton, J. M. (Ed.). (1994). Perspectives on research misconduct [Special issue]. *Journal of Higher Education, 65*(3).

Cheney, D. (Ed.). (1993). *Ethical issues in research.* Frederick, MD: University Publishing Group.

Chubin, D. E. (1983). Misconduct in research: An issue of science policy and practice. *Minerva, 23,* 175–202.

Clark A., & Gibbs, J. (1965). Social control: A reformulation. *Social Problems, 12,* 398–415.

Fox, M. F., & Braxton, J. M. (1994). Misconduct and social control in science: Issues, problems and solutions. *Journal of Higher Education, 65,* 373–383.

Goode, W. J. (1969). The theoretical limits of professionalization. In A. Etzioni (Ed.), *The semi-professions and their organization* (pp. 266–313). New York: Free Press.

Horowitz, A. V. (1990). *The logic of social control.* New York: Plenum.

LaFollette, M. C. (1992). *Stealing into print: Fraud, plagiarism and misconduct in scientific publishing.* Berkeley: University of California Press.

Pallone, N. J., & Hennessy, J. J. (Eds.). (1995). *Fraud and fallible judgment: Varieties of deception in the social and behavioral sciences.* New Brunswick, NJ: Transaction.

Parsons, T. (1951). *The social system.* New York: Free Press.

Penslar, R. L. (Ed.). (1995). *Research ethics: Cases and materials.* Bloomington: Indiana University Press.

Pitts, J. R. (1961). Social control: The concept. In D. L. Shils (Ed.), *International encyclopedia of the social sciences* (Vol. 14, pp. 381–396). New York: Macmillan.

Teich, A. H., & LaFollette, M. C. (Eds.). (1992). Understanding scientific misconduct: What do we know? [Special section]. *Knowledge: Creation, Diffusion and Utilization, 14*(2).

Zuckerman, H. E. (1977). Deviant behavior and social control in science. In E. Sagarin (Ed.), *Deviance and social change* (pp. 87–138). Beverly Hills, CA: Sage.

Zuckerman, H. E. (1988). The sociology of science. In N. J. Smelser (Ed.), *Handbook of sociology* (pp. 511–574). Newbury Park, CA: Sage.

PART I

Historical Overviews

CHAPTER ONE

A Foundation of Trust: Scientific Misconduct, Congressional Oversight, and the Regulatory Response

Marcel C. LaFollette

> *At the base of our investment in research lies the trust of the American people and the integrity of the scientific enterprise.*
> —Albert Gore, Jr.

> *The foundation of public support for science... is trust... that scientists and research institutions are engaged in the dispassionate search for truth.*
> —John Dingell

For the last half-century, since the scientific community summarized its proposals for postwar research funding in the "Bush report" (*Science: The Endless Frontier,* Bush, 1945; see also U.S. House, Committee on Science and Technology, 1986b), regulation of federally funded scientific research in the United States has been under the influence of a political attitude that has brought scientists close to the seat of power and left them "on tap" but not "on top." The key to this wary acceptance of science has been trust. In the Bush report, the scientific community argued that wartime research success could be duplicated through extensive funding of university science and graduate education, and they attempted to link investment in fundamental research explicitly to economic prosperity and social progress—to "pay envelopes on a peacetime Saturday night" (Bush, 1945, p. 10). By further asserting that intellectual as well as managerial independence was essential to innovation and by promising unassailable trustworthiness in return, they established idealistic political expectations that probably no bureaucracy could ever meet.

In the intervening decades, vigorous debates over such issues as the use of animals in experimentation, the safety of biological materials, laboratory waste disposal, and national security controls on scientists' communications have regularly tested the strength of this arrangement. Each controversy has resulted in new regulatory mechanisms governing researchers' conduct or has reshaped and tightened the old ones. None of these episodes, however, have exposed the system's structural flaws and idealistic assumptions as clearly as the "scientific integrity" and "scientific misconduct" controversies of the 1980s and 1990s. From the perspective of legislative oversight of research, the issue of scientific misconduct, which often is discussed solely in terms of the personalities involved or the sensational accusations against them, can be seen more clearly as an indicator of ongoing change in how the U.S. government manages and regulates university-based scientific research and how the U.S. Congress uses its oversight authority to communicate to science.

MUTUAL ASSURANCE

The Bush report was compiled in 1945 by Vannevar Bush, head of the U.S. Office of Scientific Research and Development, from the recommendations of four scientific committees. Without the usual rhetorical obfuscation of government reports, it bluntly states the assumptions and demands of the scientific community's leadership and supporters. Perhaps because of this clarity, the report has since become a touchstone for every reassessment of federal policy (see, e.g., Brown, 1992; U.S. House, Committee on Science, Space, and Technology, 1992).

In 1945, the time was ripe for exploitation of a national resource that had been steadily proving its relevance during the war. Science, the Bush report stated, has been waiting "in the wings" and now "should be brought to the center of the stage" (p. 12). Although the Manhattan Project and many military research programs remained classified in July 1945, the Bush committees pointed out major accomplishments, such as penicillin, sulfa drugs, and successful treatments for dysentery, typhoid, cholera, and tetanus, and alluded to many others. They believed that these results proved that scientists could be organized and managed to serve the national interest but that without immediate action, science could easily demobilize and return to its previous uncoordinated state (and, obviously, to prewar funding levels). Creation of a new research agency would allow the government to increase its "scientific capital" via investment in university-based basic research, encouragement of industrial applied research, and "development of scientific talent" (Bush, 1945, pp. 6, 7). Scientists needed more than money, however; they also required congenial work environments, sufficient equipment, relaxed and indulgent management, and preservation of their freedom of inquiry.

Bush and his supporters were enthusiastic boosters of higher education: "publicly and privately supported colleges and universities and the endowed research institutes" would offer the best home for basic research in medicine, science, and engineering (Bush, 1945, p. 19) because academic settings would nurture creativity. In addition to training future researchers, academic institutions would "provide the environment . . . most conducive to the creation of new scientific knowledge and least under pressure for immediate, tangible results" (p. 6). Linking higher education's training role to the receipt of investments in research placed the universities in the role of managing the research.

By locating basic research in the ivory tower rather than in the commercial sector, the planners hoped to insulate science from the negative values associated with business during that era. Any university's standards, whether scientific or moral, were assumed to be higher than those of any industrial research group. Someone had to turn the dreams of basic scientists into practical products, however. Therefore, the report encouraged universities and industry to act cooperatively, to think like team members in a relay race rather than competitors (Bush, 1945, p. 11). The report also treated the products of such cooperative ventures as common property, implying that knowledge would be freely shared. It recommended that the federal government hold the licenses for any patents resulting from federally supported basic research, yet it assumed that the private sector would be able to use such licenses without royalties and that all rights would not need to be assigned to the government. Once basic researchers passed the baton of knowledge, American industry would win the race for everyone. Industry would convert academic science into marketable products and thereby put demobilized soldiers back to work and stimulate the postwar economy. Inherent in this dream was also an assumption that science can be automatically transformed into technology through some linear process of knowledge transfer. Government's role was to facilitate the transfer and then to stand back and let the market work its magic.

The key to maintaining creativity and productivity in the university setting would be not a desire for profit but an atmosphere of intellectual freedom: "As long as [colleges and universities] are vigorous and healthy and their scientists are free to pursue the truth wherever it may lead, there will be a flow of new scientific knowledge to those who can apply it to practical problems in Government, in industry, or elsewhere" (Bush, 1945, p. 12). Nowhere in the document is there any explicit discussion of the *responsibility* of the individual investigators or their institutions, however; it was simply assumed that scientists (and universities) were, as historian Bruce L. R. Smith (1996) phrased it, a "community of truth-seekers operating within a set of internally generated norms who seek to govern themselves in accordance with those high standards" (p. 47). The Bush report does mention that the new agency for science would be "responsible to the President and the Congress" (Bush, 1945, p. 33). Questions about managerial authority became a flashpoint in the subsequent political debate and resulted in President Harry S. Truman's veto of the initial legislation establishing the National Science Foundation (NSF) (England, 1982; U.S. House, Committee on Science and Technology, 1986c), but no one appears to have raised questions about how the trustworthiness of individual investigators would be monitored or ensured.

Support of the Bush plan was not unanimous, even within the scientific community. Few questioned *whether* the federal government should fund basic research; instead, disagreement centered on management policies at both the agency and laboratory levels, with some politicians concerned that there were insufficient controls and some scientists arguing that there were too many (Price, 1954, pp. 48–64). University scientists were accustomed to pursuing their work without significant bureaucratic oversight. Large-scale federal support would alter that independence. Inside the Manhattan Project and other military programs, the situation had been different, of course, but censorship, classification, and even the heavy hand of military supervision had been temporary, the controls had seemed endurable for a short time, and the goals had seemed noble. Personal as well as professional autonomy had been willingly sacrificed to the war effort. The conditions likely to accompany peacetime funding of nonmilitary research and the dependency implicit in such funding would be different, and that made many scientists uncomfortable.

Diminished scientific autonomy was not the only concern. Frank Jewett, president of the National Academy of Sciences (and a former president of Bell Laboratories), warned in 1945 that the proposed arrangement contained a number of hidden dangers: "Every direct or indirect subvention by Government is not only coupled inevitably with bureaucratic types of control, but likewise with political control and with the urge to create pressure groups seeking to advance special interests" (quoted in England, 1982, p. 35). The Bush report attempted to allay such fears by suggesting that university administrators and the agency program managers would buffer political interference. The "scientific worker" need not worry, the report explained, because individual researchers would retain "a substantial degree of personal intellectual freedom" (Bush, 1945, p. 19) and because bureaucrats friendly to science would shield the universities from congressional micromanagement or special-interest pressures.

By the 1950s, the political opposition had been overcome and the new NSF had been established, converting Bush's dreams into reality. By the 1950s, it was also apparent that Jewett's instincts had been correct. In lectures presented at Columbia University in 1953, political scientist Don K. Price (1954) outlined the new pressures on scientists: legitimate and predictable differences among the goals of academic freedom, acquisition of research funding, and national security had created new and serious tensions as restrictions were placed on scientific information. Many scientists, Price observed, had begun to perceive the relationship between government and science as "an unhappy shotgun marriage" (p. 2) consummated out of fear (Cold War concerns about nuclear proliferation) and greed (the belief that science fueled capitalism).

Because the model for the relationship had been unconventional, some of the tension can be attributed to organizational adjustment. But the research system envisioned in the Bush report had also assumed a "top-down" management scheme and had paid little attention to coordination of institutional research policies. Government was being asked to support scientists in their search for knowledge but to leave "internal control of policy, personnel, and the method and scope of research to the institutions" that employed the scientists and were becoming dependent on their grants (Bush, 1945, p. 9). Crucial to the success of such an arrangement were mutual assurances of trustworthiness and accountability. Universities must administer federal grants and contracts responsibly; the funding agencies must be accountable to Congress and the president; and scientists must be honest, conducting their research as promised. This last assumption, while the most crucial, was also the least easily verified. It rested on a pervasive public image of science: the belief that scientists could be trusted because they were interested in accumulating truth, not wealth or power. (As Dingell, 1993, p. 1610, would later express this assumption, "The foundation of public support for science . . . is trust . . . that scientists and research institutions are engaged in the dispassionate search for truth.")

Investigator autonomy was linked directly to institutional accountability and indirectly to scientific productivity. No one proposed establishment of comprehensive mechanisms for monitoring or certifying nonfiscal accountability at the institutional or laboratory level. Such bureaucratic encumbrances would have been regarded as unseemly or insulting, as simply unnecessary for *scientists*. If a scientist said that he or she had collected the data, run the experiment, or written the paper, then who would ever suspect the opposite?

A NEW ENVIRONMENT

Forty years later, the contours of science's extensive regulatory environment are well defined, shaped in part by events and political change that influenced all American life, as well as by the response to discovery of abuse. "Ever since Benjamin Franklin and Thomas Jefferson, Americans have been inclined to put their faith in a combination of democracy and science as a sure formula for human progress" (Price, 1965, p. 1), but Americans have also been inclined to put their faith in federal regulation as a way to keep progress on the right moral and ethical track. Federal regulations, implemented primarily via the funding relationship with higher education, now affect researchers' agendas, communications, and laboratory processes (U.S. House, Committee on Science and Technology, 1986c, 1986d). They determine such aspects as how (or whether) human subjects are used in experiments, how laboratories must dispose of each vial of chemical and biological waste, who can or cannot be hired on university research grants, and how institutions must investigate allegations of plagiarism in published work derived from government grants. Since the 1950s, the trend has been toward more, not fewer, regulations—a tightening, not a loosening, of federal control.

Congress has participated actively at each stage of construction of this regulatory framework, sometimes taking the lead but most often responding only after the discovery of abuse or after vigorous lobbying by an advocacy group, and never seeming to relish the role. Where science is concerned, congressional criticisms have tended to focus on such issues as how to stimulate innovation, foresight, and strategic planning—that is, on *what* scientists accomplish, not on their moral integrity as they attempt to accomplish it.

Throughout the 1950s and 1960s, the White House and executive agencies dominated national science planning, and relations between Congress and the research universities were described as friendly, almost cozy. When scientists came to Capitol Hill, it was usually as expert advisors (Golden, 1993; Smith, 1992), and they were treated with respect.

A new "scientific estate" was emerging, and scientists' political capital rose with every new discovery. Scientists frequently exercised political influence "in concert with Congressional committees" that shared their "specialized interest" (Price, 1965, p. 216). If members of Congress did find fault, it was more likely to be with an agency's proposed level of funding for a favorite project, or with the performance of executive branch officials, than with the conduct of the individual scientists or institutions who received the funds. Publications, discoveries, and Nobel prizes flooded from university science in a seemingly unlimited stream, the work was regarded as vital to the national interest, and the mission agencies appeared to be monitoring research progress and performance thoroughly and conscientiously.

When federal regulations of scientific research were proposed in the 1960s to cover the use of human subjects, questions were quickly raised about whether such controls might actually impede scientific progress. There were debates among legal scholars and philosophers about the constitutionality of federal regulation of research. The assumption was that regulation, not freedom of inquiry, required justification. By the 1970s, the supportive tone shifted slightly. Controversy over the safety of university-based recombinant DNA research prompted local governments to assert their right to monitor potentially hazardous research conducted in their neighborhoods, and questions were raised about who would profit from commercialization of university-based research. In the 1970s and 1980s, Congress also began to inquire more aggressively about rising indirect cost rates, and there were fights over "pork barrel" project funding. Even the long-standing rationale for funding scientific research through the universities began to be questioned, at the same time that universities' cooperation with industry was encouraged (Armstrong, 1993; Brown, 1992; U.S. House, Committee on Science, Space, and Technology, 1992). Senators and representatives investigated university management processes and began to voice constituents' complaints about the rising costs of higher education as universities pled for additional funding.

Throughout this time, Americans have never seemed to lose faith in science altogether (National Science Board, 1996, chap. 7). They have embraced science and incorporated it into their cultural myths, social goals, popular entertainment, and national dreams (LaFollette, 1990). They have leaned on science's intellectual authority and exploited the word *scientific* as high praise for all sorts of things. Ironically, the controversy over misconduct in scientific research has also made scientists appear to be more susceptible to human faults (and thus perhaps more human). It has drawn laboratory squabbles, and the darker aspects of a highly competitive enterprise, into the light of intense mass media attention where nothing ever looks better and no one is automatically treated with respect.

Why did the issue of professional ethics among scientists, and such matters as coauthorship practices, plagiarism, note taking, and data averaging, become part of a political controversy involving high-profile congressional investigations? Similar problems, we now know, have occurred in a number of countries (Lock & Wells, 1996), but only in the United States have the private sorrows of scientists been paraded so sensationally on the stage of national politics. To understand the politics of scientific misconduct in the United States, one must first look at the peculiar context in which the issue was played out, that of legislative oversight.

LEGISLATIVE OVERSIGHT: GOALS AND MECHANISMS

The twin responsibilities of *authorization* and *appropriation*—that is, the organization of government activities and the allocation of money to carry them out—traditionally demand the greatest attention from the U.S. Congress. They attract the most news coverage and tend to be the congressional actions with which citizens are most familiar. Congress's third responsibility—*oversight* of government actions and policies—is an ongoing but imprecise process, involving the monitoring of government programs and the investigation of possible problems or abuse (Aberbach, 1990; Foreman, 1988; Keefe & Ogul, 1977; Maas, 1983; Ogul, 1990; Thurber, 1991).

Despite its importance, the oversight process is the least visible to outside observers, in part because it can occur after the fact, or behind the scenes, and because it regularly employs both formal *and* informal information gathering. Although oversight can stimulate legislation, it does not have legislation as its goal. As a congressman boasted in the 1940s, "Our business is to be a spotlight, not to recommend legislation. Our reports are for information. Our real weapon is publicity" (Dos Passos, 1944, p. 202). Moreover, neither the forms nor the procedures of legislative oversight are prescribed, so they vary widely among committees and issues. Legislative oversight is most noticeable when it generates political heat and stimulates headlines, but political scientists counter that it is most effective when it is low key, comprehensive, continuous, and directed at identifying small problems *before* they erupt into scandal.

In theory, as part of the balance of power among the three branches of government, the entire Congress is responsible for monitoring executive branch activities, but in practice, particular committees and subcommittees are assigned responsibility for monitoring particular government sectors, with each group identifying its issues, determining the form and timing of its investigations, and deciding which questions to raise (Davidson, 1981, p. 117). In theory, Congress is expected to exercise "continuous watchfulness" over *all* federal policies and programs, but in practice, this is an impossible task, given the size of government. Consequently, members and committees tend to choose issues that are "ripe" for investigation, are related to their constituencies' concerns, or are simply too visible to be ignored. Choice of one topic invariably results in the neglect of equally important others and in calls for more oversight.

The organization and structure of congressional oversight groups have changed continually over the years, with much of that change being a response to the growth in the federal bureaucracy, of which science has been only a part. In 1946, Congress passed the Legislative Reorganization Act, streamlining the committee system in both chambers, reducing the number of standing committees, clarifying responsibilities, increasing staff, and expressing "the first formal congressional endorsement of oversight" by directing full committees to maintain "'continuous watchfulness' over the activities of the executive agencies" under their jurisdiction (Aberbach, 1990, p. 22). Each new Congress or new leadership has tinkered with the system. In 1994, for example, responding to the electorate's call for greater accountability in government, the House of Representatives reorganized its committee structure. It abolished several committees altogether, transferring and reassigning some responsibilities to a new Committee on Government Reform and Oversight directed to "review and study on a continuing basis the operation of Government activities at all levels with a view to determining their economy and efficiency" (Rules of the U.S. House of Representatives, Rule 10, Clause 2(a)(2)). Each standing committee was also required to review laws or regulations within their jurisdictions and to note "any conditions or circumstances which may indicate the necessity or desirability of enacting new or additional legislation within the jurisdiction of that committee . . . and . . . undertake future research and forecasting" (Rules of the U.S. House of Representatives, Rule 10, Clause 2(b)(1)).

Whatever the current organization, legislative oversight inquiries tend to cluster around four issues: money, personnel, structure, and policy (Keefe & Ogul, 1977, pp. 389–390). The most visible type is *review of expenditures*—for example, whether appropriations for a particular program were spent prudently, efficiently, and legally. *Oversight of personnel,* a second type of inquiry, centers on the qualifications of government officials and how they perform in office. In the third type, *oversight of bureaucratic structures,* committees may investigate the executive's plans to establish or abolish programs: Congress has monitored, for example, establishment of the National Institutes of Health (NIH) Office of Scientific Integrity (now called the Office of Research Integrity) and has debated whether it should be moved elsewhere within the Department of Health and Human Services (DHHS). Finally, Congress may review *policies* set by the executive branch (e.g., selection criteria for research project awards, or the implementation of ethics regulations). Although review of organizational or budgeting issues might seem their most important responsibility, Griffith (1961) argued that congressional oversight investigations are actually far better suited to review "those situations in which no law has been violated, but in which there has been an apparent betrayal of public trust" (p. 115). He claimed that "by focusing on ethics rather than legality," Congress "crystallize[s] opinion on what things are or are not 'done'" (p. 115). This was the case for the issue of scientific misconduct.

To carry out oversight, committees and subcommittees use various investigative techniques (Keefe & Ogul, 1977, p. 408; Maas, 1983, pp. 203–215). The most frequently used, and the one considered most effective in provoking immediate change, is the one least visible, least "on the record," and most difficult for historians or political scientists to trace—namely, direct communication with agency personnel by either telephone, mail, or electronic communication (Aberbach, 1990). The most visible mechanisms—congressional hearings and reports—are actually considered (by both members and staff) to be the least efficient and effective (Aberbach, 1990, pp. 14, 66); such activities do, however, place evaluations and criticisms on the public record and attract media attention because they offer prime visual and audio content (Cook, 1989; Hess, 1991). Another technique especially well suited for the assessment of science and engineering research problems is the evaluation report, which Congress requests from the Congressional Budget Office, the Congressional Research Service, the General Accounting Office, or, before its dismantling in 1995, the Office of Technology Assessment. These reports can involve close accounting of program expenditures or analyses of a broad topic like patent policy. Because evaluation reports are requested by members or committees, rather than initiated by the support agencies themselves, their steady growth in recent years is a useful indicator of growing oversight attention to science and technology *and* of the legislators' increased need for technical evaluations. From the 94th through the 100th Congresses, there was an almost threefold increase in all OTA reports, and from the 89th through the 98th Congresses, there was about a fourfold increase in CRS science policy reports.[1]

When media coverage accompanies release of a formal report, the oversight process can appear to have actually done something about a problem. When the problem then continues, oversight can appear to have been ineffectual. At the committee level, however, the oversight process is not intended as a route to action; instead, it is a review process, gathering information for possible action by the Congress as a whole (e.g., for subsequent legislation). An oversight investigation's greatest power lies in the information placed on the record (and in the collateral press coverage), which may itself pressure a reluctant agency, institution, or group to correct the problem. Oversight therefore serves as a form of indirect communication: both the initiation and accomplishment of oversight are intended to convey the message (or possibly the threat) that unless there is suitable response, corrective legislation or regulation will follow. In the late twentieth century, congressional committees have occasionally employed such pressure to micromanage agency affairs. "Congress, constitutionally, has at least as much to do with executive administration as does an incumbent of the White House" (Neustadt, 1965, p. 103), for Congress not only creates the executive departments and agencies but also has the power to organize, finance, and investigate them, sometimes by redirecting agency resources (Ogul, 1990, p. 421).

This same power has, from time to time, been turned on nongovernmental groups or organizations—for example, in hearings on questionable banking practices, intended to pressure change among private banks, or on television violence, intended to persuade Hollywood producers to select different content. This was, in fact, the tactic chosen by the congressional committees concerned with scientific misconduct, although many scientists had difficulty in seeing this intent or in acknowledging congressional authority to conduct oversight investigations. Accustomed to good relations with the Congress, some scientists perceived the antagonistic (and occasionally overdramatized) style of oversight as an insult and an invasion of professional privacy, rather than as a stylized technique for gathering information on how public money was spent. The perpetuation of that misperception within the scientific community was an important factor in delaying institutional change and in fueling the controversy that erupted in the 1980s.

SPECIAL OVERSIGHT FOR SCIENCE

In 1945, the Bush report had observed that there was "no body within the Government charged with formulating or executing a national science policy" and that there were "no standing committees of the Congress devoted to this important subject" (Bush, 1945, p. 12). Despite the establishment of NSF, a presidential science advisor, and even a congressional science committee, responsibility continues to be dispersed, and this fragmentation inhibits the development of comprehensive, anticipatory oversight. There is simply too much to watch over, with too many overlapping activities. As government science and technology agencies like NSF, NIH, and the Atomic Energy Commission were created and expanded to thousands of employees, multimillion-dollar budgets, and thousands of external grants and contracts, they required new levels of legislative attention (U.S. House, Committee on Science and Technology, 1986b). Responding in part to the launch of *Sputnik* (U.S. House, Committee on Science and Technology, 1986b, pp. 41–44) and to the creation of the U.S. space program, the House of Representatives established in 1958 a Committee on Science and Astronautics as the select committee on science and technology oversight. Under House rules, this group (renamed the Committee on Science during the 104th Congress) is assigned responsibility for reviewing, on a continuing basis, the laws, programs, and government activities involving nonmilitary research and development (R&D), including that on energy, environment, space, and oceans (Rules of the U.S. House of Representatives, Rule 10, Clause 1(n)). NSF and the National Aeronautics and Space Administration fall under this committee's jurisdiction, for example, but military R&D is watched over by the Committee on National Security, biomedical research (i.e., NIH) by the Committee on Commerce, and agricultural R&D by the Committee on Agriculture.

In the Senate, attention to science is similarly scattered, organized not by scientific discipline but by research application. The Committee System Reorganization Amendments of 1977 transformed the Senate Commerce Committee into the Committee on Commerce, Science, and Transportation and granted it "comprehensive jurisdiction over national policy in science, engineering, and technology, including research and development in those fields" and including nonaeronautical and space science policy (U.S. Senate, 1978, p. 11). But, as in the House, many types of research are monitored elsewhere—for example, energy R&D falls under the jurisdiction of one committee and military R&D under another (Rules of the U.S. Senate, Rule 25, "Standing Committees").

The pluralistic nature of congressional attention to science has prompted, from time to time, the suggestion that committee activities be consolidated, and there have been similar proposals to create a single Department of Science and Technology in the executive branch (U.S. House, Committee on Science and Technology, 1986b, pp. 44–45). The pluralism in fact reflects the history (and, one might argue, the true nature) of the federal government's relationship to science. From the national geological and botanical surveys in the nineteenth century to the Human Genome Initiative in the twentieth, Americans have never been willing to support science for science's sake alone, or even for the sake of the knowledge produced. Instead, they have valued it for the promise of useful products, progress, or benefits and for its contributions to solving society's current problems (LaFollette, 1990, 1997). Although overlapping committee jurisdictions and a lack of coordination may appear to be evidence of congressional inattention to (or misunderstanding of) science, the situation actually mimics the evolving rationale for public support. Americans like science and underwrite scientific activities for many reasons, all of them related to the results, not to the nobility of effort.

Compared to the scrutiny given other government activities, congressional investigation of science has been, in fact, tame. The Bush report had linked scientific progress directly to "millions of pay envelopes on a peacetime Saturday night which are filled because new products and new industries have provided jobs for countless Americans" (Bush, 1945, p. 10). America's postwar prosperity and growth steadily reinforced confidence in scientists' ability to deliver on that promise. Science basked in the glory of extraordinary technological and medical achievements and happily took credit for them: life-saving vaccines, astronauts jumping on the moon, microminiaturization, and electronic computers were all attributed to "science."

Until the 1980s, there was also little scandal involving science. Episodes of fraud were kept quiet, and there seemed little cause for questioning scientific accountability. The nature of the activities being funded encouraged arm's-length evaluation. The Bush report had cautioned against political impatience: "Important discoveries have come as a result of experiments undertaken with very different purposes in mind," and "the results of any one particular investigation cannot be predicted with accuracy" (Bush, 1945, p. 19). Whenever scientists assured the Congress that federal investments in research would pay off eventually, no one really expected (or demanded) quantitative proof of progress. And few members of Congress or their staff had the special expertise to question further.

Formal investigations assisting comprehensive oversight disturb the status quo; they pit the various interests against each another, and legislators naturally prefer not to be caught in the crossfire. Significant conflicts can even serve to neutralize oversight, especially if a university in a member's home state is involved. Constituents expect their legislators to act positively but prudently: they expect them to encourage government action but to monitor government performance, to appropriate money but to control spending, and to solve new problems but to raise taxes only as a last resort. Scientists form a secondary, nonelectorate constituency for the science committees, and universities all expect Congress to fight *for* research, not to criticize or impede it. Indeed, by the time any research program is in place, considerable political as well as personal capital has been invested in its success. Huntington (1965) has long argued that such investment of political capital and time ultimately cripples the process: "Congress can assert its power or it can pass laws; but it cannot do both" (p. 6). Other political scientists take a more moderate view, believing that those activities can coexist effectively. No one, however, appears to believe that the long-standing tensions between advocacy and scrutiny are likely to dissipate.

As a result of these circumstances, the oversight units of the committees concerned with science have rarely engaged in confrontational politics. They have focused on ensuring sufficient R&D funding to meet national needs; they have unabashedly promoted federal investment in basic research; they have engaged in partisan squabbling over projects; but they have been always supportive of science overall (Aberbach, 1990; Huntington, 1965, p. 20).

Two organizational changes within the Congress in the 1970s helped to encourage closer scrutiny. The Legislative Reorganization Act of 1970 (amending the 1946 act) and the 1974 Select Committee on Committees (the Bolling Committee) gave more oversight power to standing committees such as the House Science Committee (Aberbach, 1990, p. 27). Both chambers also began to assign special responsibilities for oversight to work groups separate from the regular committee structure, and, as a result, the full committees established "oversight and investigations" subcommittees to conduct such monitoring. And Congress initiated annual authorization for some research programs, subjecting them to yearly review apart from the normal appropriations cycle for that agency.

Another indicator of a changing political climate was passage of the Inspector General Act of 1978 (Pub. L. No. 95452), part of a larger effort at government reform (Light, 1993, p. 11). Every agency was required to establish a separate unit for conducting independent audits and ensuring thorough investigation of financial mismanagement or nonperformance of duties by government employees, grantees, or contractors. When NSF created its Office of the Inspector General in 1989 (following Pub. L. No. 100504), the

Inspector General was assigned responsibility for investigating fraud and misconduct allegations involving NSF-sponsored research (Buzzelli, 1993). For NIH-funded research, however, such investigations are conducted by an office housed within the Public Health Service (PHS) administration that is devoted to allegations of research misconduct alone, despite continual attempts to move the office under the control of the DHHS Inspector General (Goodman, 1996b; U.S. DHHS, 1996). This difference reflects the fact that NIH's investigations of misconduct have been at the center of the congressional firestorm on this issue, offering a tempting target for micromanagement.

THE MISCONDUCT ISSUE

Heightened sensitivity to all types of sloppy federal management and wasteful spending undoubtedly influenced the congressional response in the 1980s to a flurry of reports of scientific misconduct in government-funded research. American voters were already expressing their disgust at fraud, waste, and abuse throughout government. If federal funds were misspent or work was not completed as promised, then congressional committees were under pressure to investigate; they could not treat scientists and universities any differently than they were treating defense contractors or banks. Support for basic research was only one of many demands on federal or state funds, neither an "entitlement" nor exempt from budget reductions. Scientists who pled for more money in front of one committee could not reasonably expect immunity from oversight by another.

Because the first highly publicized cases, and consequent congressional attention, were concentrated in the biological sciences, many people jumped to the conclusion that those fields had special ethical problems. Federal funding for biology and medicine had accelerated in the postwar era, and by then it represented a major component of university-based research. Competition for NIH grants was keen, so "competition" was also assumed to be driving much of the misconduct. When misconduct allegations involved clinical research or emotional topics such as cancer or heart disease, the prospect of tainted or discredited data naturally intensified media attention.

In retrospect, one of the most remarkable aspects of the misconduct issue is the dramatic shift in the tone of congressional inquiries over the space of a few years from the relatively benign, skeptical but polite questioning in 1981 to antagonism, grandstanding, and threats of subpoena in 1988. The first formal oversight attention to scientific misconduct took place in the House Committee on Science and Technology. Two subcommittee hearings, held on March 31 and April 1, 1981, responded to publicity over the John

Darsee case at Harvard University and to other sensational cases (U.S. House, Committee on Science and Technology, 1981). In his opening statement, subcommittee chairman Albert Gore, Jr., who was then a representative from Tennessee, spoke of the national "investment" in research and pointed to science's "integrity" and society's "trust": "We need to discover whether recent incidents are merely episodes that will drift into the history of science as footnotes, or whether we are creating situations and incentives in the biomedical sciences, and in all of 'Big Science,' that make such cases as these 'the tip of the iceberg,'" Gore observed (U.S. House, Committee on Science and Technology, 1981, pp. 1–2).

The testimony of senior NIH officials and other government advisors in that hearing typified how the leaders of the scientific community had begun responding to the issue. Philip Handler, President of the National Academy of Sciences, dismissed recent news coverage of the Darsee case and other fraud in science as "grossly exaggerated"; he was supported in this characterization as NIH officials vehemently denied that fraud was widespread in the biomedical research community (Broad, 1981). Members of the subcommittee questioned that assessment, however. They also expressed surprise at learning that NIH was continuing to fund scientists who had been accused of wrongdoing. NIH representatives countered by explaining that investigations took a long time and that their policy avoided the danger of "blacklisting" someone who might later be acquitted of charges (even though it might also continue to reward someone who might be later proven to be guilty). As the hearing progressed, further testimony revealed that *no* scientist was being disqualified from eligibility for NIH funding, even after an admission of guilt. Several Congressmen criticized that policy, pointedly remarking that there is no political "entitlement" to uninterrupted federal funding, even for an honest scientist.

The 1981 hearing had no other purpose than communication. It sought to convey an unambiguous message to the scientific community: Congress is concerned about the issue and it has a legitimate reason to investigate, but it wants the academic institutions and scientific associations to try to fix the problem first. To the politicians, this seemed a simple matter: scientists should do everything possible to prevent unethical conduct in their ranks, but if fraud did occur, it should be investigated and resolved quickly by scientists, lest it deter scientific progress. And scientists should not, in the name of progress, sweep problems under the rug. Legislation (i.e., regulation of research and publication practices, or requirements for how allegations should be handled) should be proposed only if attempts at self-correction failed.

This "two-minute warning" was emphatically and repeatedly stated in subsequent hearings, yet the scientific leadership seemed unwilling to acknowledge its intrinsic logic at the time. And in their dismissal of congressional concern, the scientists followed a pattern of behavior first described by Price (1965): they perceived themselves as a "professional peerage," above the demands of messy democratic politics and therefore not required to respond to the complaints of nonscientists with whom they disagreed, even if those nonscientists were members of a Congress that was delegated the authority to express such complaints.

During the 1980s, the investigation and resolution of cases seemed to drag on endlessly; the pace of regulatory rule making was even slower. In 1981, responding to congressional pressure, the NIH began to develop formal policies on how its institutes and its grantee institutions should conduct investigations. Under the Health Research Extension Act of 1985 (42 U.S.C. 289b, Section 493(a)), the secretary of DHHS was directed to develop regulations that would apply to all institutions seeking grants, contracts, and cooperative agreements, requiring them to establish administrative processes for reviewing all allegations of fraud in biomedical and behavioral research and for reporting investigations to DHHS (U.S. House, Committee on Science, Space, and Technology, 1990, pp. 707–709). NIH published its agency guidelines in 1986 and its institutional guidelines in 1989 (42 C. F. R. Part 50) (U.S. House, Committee on Science, Space, and Technology, 1990, pp. 710–816). Final regulations governing research sponsored or conducted by NSF were published in 1987 (45 C. F. R. Part 689) (*Scientific Fraud*, 1990, pp. 817–884). Universities, too, gave the appearance of dragging their heels in following up allegations or developing procedures for ethics training. Many institutions did not even begin to develop comprehensive internal ethics procedures until 1989 or 1990, and only then in response to federal mandate. A similar pattern of procedural changes, policy making, and argument has followed the 1996 recommendations of the NIH Commission on Research Integrity (Goodman, 1996c; U.S. DHHS, 1996).

Not all the blame for delay can or should be placed on the scientific community. The political climate of the 1980s also undoubtedly played a role. The Republican administrations of Presidents Ronald Reagan and George Bush emphasized deregulation, not regulation; they denounced all types of "federal interference" in private sector activities. This ideological distaste for regulation undoubtedly influenced policies and actions within the agencies, albeit in ways that are hard to document. Although strong forces among Congress may have pulled toward tougher misconduct rules, the speed and extent of regulatory enforcement ultimately depended on the willingness of officials in the executive branch to act, and to act swiftly.

Science itself had also changed. "International competitiveness" had become a favored theme for science and technology policy, and universities were being encouraged to engage in interdisciplinary, multi-institutional research, often with industrial partners. Each collaborator brought a different set of expectations and sometimes different disciplinary or managerial standards. When disputes or allegations arose, merely sorting out the "who, what, where, and when" of actions and responsibilities exposed the weaknesses in existing ethics rules and in the assumptions being made about "normal" scientific conduct. By the 1980s, a scientist could, over the course of a career, expect to conduct research in many different institutions and to collaborate or coauthor with perhaps dozens of colleagues around the world. In addition, the potential financial or professional rewards from research were (or seemed to be) higher than in the Bush days. Neither accountability nor autonomy could be assumed, therefore, and maintaining each was beginning to require a substantial bureaucracy and to suggest the need for policies conforming to the changed social context of research.

As agencies, universities, and scientific associations argued about the various policy changes, the number and types of publicized cases continued to grow (LaFollette, 1992). By 1988, Congress had been urging action for over seven years, yet little action seemed to have taken place. At NIH, administrators (who were themselves mostly scientists by training, per the Bush model) still argued that the notion of fraud in the biomedical sciences was "a maliciously constructed illusion" and "a trivial matter gone berserk" (Greenberg, 1988b, p. 4; also see Greenberg 1988a). In response to such attitudes, several congressional subcommittees began to use their oversight authority to break the impasse.

April 1988 represents a watershed, a point at which the issue gained political momentum and began to receive attention from the general news media as well as the scientific press. On April 11, 1988, at a hearing of the House Committee on Government Operations, Human Relations and Intergovernmental Relations Subcommittee, chaired by Rep. Ted Weiss (D-New York), scientists who had "blown the whistle" on fraudulent research described how they had been vilified by colleagues and senior administrators and how the investigations prompted by their allegations had been repeatedly delayed at all institutional levels (*Scientific Fraud and Misconduct and the Federal Response,* 1988). The very next day, the House Committee on Energy and Commerce's Subcommittee on Oversight and Investigations, chaired by John Dingell, opened its inquiry into one of the most high-profile and sensational cases examined to date. During the hearing, biologists Margot O'Toole and Charles Maplethorpe testified about NIH-supported research conducted in the MIT laboratory of Thereza Imanishi-Kari and later reported in a paper coauthored by Imanishi-Kari with Nobel laureate David Baltimore and other scientists (*Scientific Fraud and Misconduct in the National Institutes of Health,* 1988). O'Toole, who had been an NIH postdoctoral fellow in Imanishi-Kari's lab, recounted how Imanishi-Kari, Baltimore, and a sequence of MIT administrators had rebuffed her allegations about the data and discouraged her from raising the questions formally or publicly. Maplethorpe had been a graduate student during this time and had apparently believed that his degree would be jeopardized if he supported O'Toole's allegations; he testified, "I felt that if I pursued the case at MIT and nothing happened then I would be the one to suffer" (*Scientific Fraud and Misconduct in the National Institutes of Health*, 1988). The "Baltimore case" (as it came to be known, even though the formal accusations of misconduct were lodged against Imanishi-Kari) showed that even well-known scientists and institutions were not immune from harsh congressional questioning.

When Dingell told the hearing audience that congressional inquiries would continue, he put the entire scientific community on notice: "We are going to be visiting again about these matters," he promised (Greenberg, 1988b, p. 6). Other members of Congress shared Dingell's resolve, to the point of introducing legislation to criminalize the knowing misreporting or misrepresentation of scientific data to the federal government (Zuckoff, 1988; Zurer, 1988a). Then on April 15, 1988, psychologist Stephen J. Breuning (who had first been accused of misconduct in 1983) was indicted in federal court and charged with falsifying research project reports to the National Institutes of Mental Health (NIMH). The coincidence of this indictment with the ongoing investigation of Imanishi-Kari stimulated further press coverage because this was the first such criminal action to reach the courts (Roman, 1988; Valentine, 1988; Wheeler, 1988; Zurer, 1988b).

Breuning pled guilty a few months later. His case, however, delivered an important message: science does not always "self-correct," as scientists had so often claimed in their attempts to forestall regulation. Breuning's fabricated research data had been, in fact, both widely reported and widely used. From 1980 to 1983, his published papers represented at least one-third of all scientific articles on the topic, and citation analysis has shown that from 1981 to 1985, his "impact on the literature was meaningful" (Garfield & Welljams-Dorof, 1991; Roman, 1988, p. 53). Moreover, the conclusions of his drug "experiments" (many of which were never conducted) were used to justify treatment plans for hundreds of hyperactive children. Although there is no evidence that any patient was harmed by use of the data, the episode demonstrated that fraudulent science could be accepted by mainstream science, could persist in the literature, and could adversely affect innocent parties. The illusion that science and the universities had things under control was brutally dispelled.

No group, institution, or profession ever welcomes close legislative scrutiny. Scientists are no exception. The editors of the *New England Journal of Medicine* articulated widespread sentiments in the biomedical community when, in a June 1988 editorial, they argued against establishment of *any* federal ethics oversight system and asserted that Congress was simply laboring under a false impression and should back off (Angell & Relman, 1988). "The biomedical-research community is willing and able to police itself and is taking steps to do so more effectively," they wrote. "Let us hope that Congress will give this process time to work" (Angell & Relman, 1988, p. 1463). Baltimore initially took an even more aggressive approach, issuing public statements in response to Dingell hearings and offering himself for interviews with journalists (Sarasohn, 1993), but his criticism of Dingell and the Congress gradually softened as the investigations continued and resistance proved ineffective.

For the next few years, an annual round of oversight hearings became commonplace. On June 28, 1989, the House Committee on Science and Technology, Subcommittee on Investigations and Oversight, summoned testimony from representatives of NIH, NSF, and various universities; questioned journal editors about the peer review process and the integrity of the published literature; and later published a 1,455-page compendium of the day's testimony and several hundred other documents on the subject of scientific misconduct and the integrity of scientific publications (U.S. House, Committee on Science, Space, and Technology, 1990). Committee chairman Robert A. Roe stated bluntly that "scientific misconduct is a general problem that threatens the health of the scientific enterprise at all levels," and he appealed to scientists to act: "There will be no greater force for maintaining the integrity of scientific research than the science community itself" (U.S. House, Committee on Science, Space, and Technology, 1990, pp. 3–4). "But the science community needs help in this endeavor," he continued. "The federal government cannot fund science at ever greater levels and then turn its back on the problem of scientific misconduct" (U.S. House, Committee on Science, Space, and Technology, 1990, p. 4). In 1989 and 1990, further hearings on the "Baltimore case" included testimony by Secret Service document experts asked to evaluate, as forensic evidence, laboratory notebooks and data tapes from Imanishi-Kari's lab (*Scientific Fraud*, 1990; *Scientific Fraud and Misconduct*, 1989). In his opening statement to the 1990 hearing, John Dingell criticized how NIH and several academic institutions had handled various cases of "proven misconduct." After a sober summary of events in the investigation of Imanishi-Kari, he noted that Congress was still expecting the community of scientists "to police itself," that his subcommittee had been "severely disappointed by the response of the scientific community," and that the "reluctance by prominent scientists to deal fully and frankly with the problems of scientific fraud and misconduct" had "greatly complicated" attempts to investigate and resolve ongoing cases (*Scientific Fraud*, 1990).

The "Baltimore case" dragged on for many more years, as NIH and Imanishi-Kari questioned every finding at every stage. Finally, in 1996, Imanishi-Kari won a form of vindication when a departmental Appeals Panel cleared her of all charges and NIH officials chose not to pursue the matter further (Goodman, 1996a). O'Toole had first raised her questions in

1986. The length and bitterness of this case took its toll; no one really won, and everyone lost something. It has served as a harsh lesson in how *not* to conduct an investigation, and in the limited ability of congressional oversight to effect behavioral change when a group simply refuses to hear the message.

Subsequent congressional attention has been low key and more focused. Hearings have concentrated on the management of NIH's ethics office and on the effectiveness of proposed whistle-blower protections. Meanwhile, the implementation and enforcement of regulations continues. As part of the NIH Revitalization Act of 1993, Congress mandated establishment of the Commission on Research Integrity, which reported its findings in 1996 and was promptly subjected to intense adverse criticism from within the scientific community (Goodman, 1996c). Following one of the commission's recommendations, however, the President's National Science and Technology Council established a committee to write a definition of misconduct that would apply across all agencies of the federal government and bring some consistency to federal policy (Goodman, 1996b). One hopeful sign is that more colleges and universities have begun to develop comprehensive administrative procedures for handling investigations, to create ethics training programs, and, on some campuses, to encourage faculty to address these issues directly in their classes and laboratories before problems arise (Steneck, 1994).

LESSONS TO BE LEARNED

The congressional misconduct hearings neither accelerated nor forestalled the implementation of regulations. A less obstructionist response to such hearings from scientists and universities might have delayed the implementation of federal regulation, however, and avoided the cumbersome rules that are now in place. Such an outcome would have required academic institutions to agree on a strategy and on the ability of the research fields themselves, through their professional associations, to establish ethics codes articulating their common expectations for conduct. Given the lack of incentives to coordinate and the lack of administrative linkages among these groups, it seems unlikely that such unity could ever have been achieved quickly enough to stem the tide of congressional criticism, although it probably would have resulted in regulations that incorporated such feedback and were thus more finely tuned to scientists' laboratory norms.

The hearings did affect science's public image and professional reputation, but not to the extent that many scientists assume. Sensational accusations made about prominent people and institutions attracted attention from parts of the mass media normally uninterested in science policy.

Stories in the mainstream press and on television were far less kind to scientists, and, as I have described elsewhere (LaFollette, 1992, pp. 151–153), tended to justify the coverage in terms of its political or public policy relevance rather than as part of "science" news. When these reports were placed alongside accounts of fraud, waste, and abuse in other types of institutions and occupations, the juxtaposition made science seem less special and may then have stimulated additional attention from investigative reporters. These circumstances lent credence to the belief among scientists that they were being unfairly singled out and to their embarrassment at having science's "dirty linen" aired on television. To the extent that news coverage included negative images, therefore, it may have muddied science's public face. Nevertheless, data from the public attitude surveys conducted by NSF over the years (e.g., National Science Board, 1996, 1998) continue to show little long-term damage: Americans still seem to hold science and universities in reasonably high esteem, compared to other occupational groups and institutions, and science still retains its ability to spark the public imagination and to inspire hope for the future.

Science is neither immune nor especially vulnerable to ideological influence over its political fortunes. No one would discount the role that personal ambition or partisan politics plays in all legislative activities. On the other hand, there is no evidence that these factors disproportionately influenced the misconduct investigations. Ideological differences over when human life begins, for example, shape contemporary biomedical research policy (such as policy over whether such research may use tissue obtained from a human fetus), but they are the same social and moral attitudes that influence health care spending, welfare reform, and other contemporary political issues.

What lessons, then, might we draw from this episode of extended oversight? Should the scientific community, for example, welcome legislative oversight or do everything possible to prevent it? Contrary to what the objects of such scrutiny might argue, Congress most often errs in neglecting its oversight responsibilities rather than in indulging in too much oversight: it fails to oversee an agency's performance, for example, or fails to address a problem until it has adequate publicity value or has become the source for scandal or disaster. Congressional committees that had been overly sympathetic to (and therefore insufficiently skeptical of) science clearly missed the warning signs of an impending ethical crisis or gave it only perfunctory and intermittent attention. Scientists and the academic institutions should be concerned less with how much oversight takes place and more with how comprehensive, efficient, and thorough it is. Low-key, continuous attention to the state of the research system as a whole is better for all concerned. It helps to detect problems as they are emerging (and controllable) and to avoid creating crises where none really exist (a tempting option in a political setting because it draws attention away from negligence even as it obscures the real issues and inhibits change).

Lessons about Who Should Initiate or Conduct Oversight of Scientific Research

During the height of the misconduct controversy, some scientists complained that the matters at stake were "technical" and that therefore neither congressional committee members nor their staffs had sufficient expertise to investigate or understand whether the behavior had been fraud, error, or just normal deviation from standard practices in that field. The scientists seemed often to be asserting that they should be exempt from oversight and were entitled to be left alone, as when a prominent biologist stated that "government intervention is inappropriate for concerns regarding errors in collecting and interpreting data, incompetence, poor laboratory procedures, selection of data, authorship practices, and multiple publications" (Schachman, 1993, p. 148). After all, he and others claimed, how could someone trained as a lawyer know anything about how biologists keep their laboratory notebooks?

The issues at stake in oversight on scientific misconduct are, of course, not really the "scientific" ones at all. They are political. Have federal funds been misused? Has the public trust been betrayed? Knowledge of the federal government or the political system is far more useful in such an inquiry than is skill as a molecular biologist. Congressional committees also have easy access to expert advice on every imaginable subject, including standard laboratory practice. Over 20 years ago, the scientific associations themselves established a successful program of congressional fellowships (Stine, 1994), and legislative staffs now include many people trained and experienced in science and engineering. At the legislative support agencies, there are other well-trained people whose sole task is to provide technical help or locate data needed for the work of the Congress. One lesson for the future, then, is to concentrate more on improving information flow and less on the personalities engaged in the dispute.

Because oversight tends to be more reactive than proactive, political scientists sometimes argue that a "fire alarm" mentality dominates the process: rather than continuously patrolling or gathering information, the committees and their staffs respond only to crises (Neustadt, 1965). Aberbach (1990) concluded that Congress intuitively chooses the alarm strategy: that is, it "structures the situation so that information can come its way" and so that it can then choose "whether or not to respond" (p. 97). This posture encourages interest groups to bring their complaints to the Hill and, more importantly, to do the legwork beforehand. That strategy can backfire, however, if the complaints are driven primarily by ideology and partisan politics or by individuals with a grudge.

For the issue of scientific fraud and misconduct, for example, the role played by Walter Stewart and Ned Feder, two NIH scientists who had taken on the misconduct issue as a private crusade, led to the charge that they had single-handedly created the controversy. When they assisted the Dingell subcommittee during 1988 and 1989 (on detail from their NIH jobs), they apparently did play some role behind the scenes in encouraging continuation of the congressional investigation of Imanishi-Kari. Their participation added color to the media coverage. But congressional concern had, in fact, been raised years before, and one should not conclude that, without considerable existing interest on the part of the subcommittee members and their staff, any gadfly could have arranged for the hearings or investigations to have gone forward.

Others have tended to pin the blame on Representative Dingell, saying that he must have had some grudge against science or that this was a personal vendetta against David Baltimore. Such accusations can be traced in part to the extensive press coverage of the Dingell investigations, which gave disproportionate attention to this one politician. Because committee chairs wield considerable power within the congressional system, most have the propensity and skill to attract media attention whenever they initiate investigations. John Dingell is no exception to this rule. Yet a closer look reveals that his performance in the misconduct hearings was consistent with how he has always acted in his congressional career. As the son of a noted congressional reformer and as a former prosecutor, Dingell has an adversarial style that comes naturally—and differs little from that employed by other members of Congress through the years (Sarasohn, 1993, pp. 46–57). Moreover, he has frequently been an advocate *for* science and *for* adequate funding of university research, and the record shows that his quarrels in the misconduct hearings were not with science per se but with the failings of particular institutions.

When oversight seems to falter—for example, because of insufficient evidence or premature public statements—such failures are often attributed to an eager, aggressive staff. Certainly, the investigation of a prominent scientific personality offers more excitement than the routine activities of congressional staff work, and there are data showing that the rise in all types of oversight after 1950 coincided with an explosive growth in congressional staff (Malbin, 1980). However, Aberbach (1990) concluded that additional staff members produce only "a marginally greater (but not statistically significant) amount of oversight" (p. 75), insufficient to account for a rise in oversight in any area, including science. The radical reductions in legislative staff during the 104th Congress offer an opportunity to test this linkage between staff and oversight, especially if there appears to be no proportionate decrease in such trackable oversight activities as the number of oversight hearings and number of requests for evaluation reports.

Lessons about How to Respond to Oversight

As an issue explored through congressional oversight, scientific misconduct has, to date, been characterized more by gray areas and lack of agreement than by any coordinated response from the community with most at stake. No one has sat at a witness table and stated confidently, "I come here representing the views of most American scientists." No one has really seemed to represent the interests of all science, only his or her particular institution or scientific discipline. As Sanford Lakoff observed, the question of "Who speaks for science?" is perennial in American politics and transcends the congressional process or any single issue: "It's really that the scientific community is a house divided, . . . full of people pursuing special interests, without trying to coordinate them or to see where the fundamental interests of the country's scientific progress lie" (Atkinson & Blanpied, 1989, pp. 45–46). The scientific community's response to oversight has included establishment defenders and radical critics as well as more moderate voices. Usually the moderate view prevails because of Congress's historical tendency to protect the interests of the science they know. "To the extent that [committees] are boosters for the programs they sponsor," Davidson (1981) wrote about Congress in general, "vigorous questioning of those programs may be frowned on by members and outside clientele. Raising questions, it is argued, will only weaken a program's support and hamper the implementing agencies" (p. 112). Such attitudes have in the past "cooled down" congressional oversight of science and technology, and probably helped to moderate the hearings held after 1988. Once the crisis-driven momentum dies down, the likelihood of coordinated response grows smaller.

Lessons about How to Improve the Quality of Oversight

The significant errors in congressional oversight for science—especially for the issue of scientific misconduct—have tended, I believe, to be ones of neglecting the long view—of paying insufficient attention to systemic problems in programs or policies. Studies of congressional oversight units have shown that when committees routinely "patrol" the agencies under their jurisdiction, the overall result can be more effective than if they respond only to alarm or crisis (Aberbach, 1990, pp. 90–93). In the current political and economic environment for science, encouraging better oversight—that is, continuous, low-key *monitoring and action* rather than crisis-driven *reaction*—would benefit all parties concerned: the scientists, the institutions, and the public. It would be far more likely to result in a balanced view when controversies do arise and to avoid the collateral damage associated with scandal and sensation.

Failing to set science and technology policy problems in their national and international contexts (e.g., by concentrating only on one research field or institution) has historically resulted in oversight that is too narrow to be effective. Despite Albert Gore's reference in 1981 to "situations and incentives," the subsequent oversight activities on misconduct tended to examine only specific cases. To use the metaphor popular at the time, they essentially reinforced attention to the rotten apples while neglecting the changing composition and context of the barrel (U.S. House, Committee on Science and Technology, 1987). Had this truly been a matter of the discovery of rotting fruit in a warehouse, we would have been remiss if we had not first asked about the warehouse conditions (too hot? too humid? infested or contaminated?) before we cut down the orchard. Only two hearings of the House Committee on Science, Space, and Technology—those of May 14, 1986 (U.S. House, Committee on Science and Technology, 1987) and June 28, 1989 (U.S. House, Committee on Science, Space, and Technology, 1990)—could be said to represent such attempts to look at how the misconduct issue was affecting all science, and they appear to have had little impact in cooling down a controversy fueled by other factors at that point.

Lessons about How to Listen to Oversight

When tough oversight inquiries did occur on the misconduct issue, the universities and the scientific community seemed often to misunderstand their goals and to overlook subtle but crucial political undercurrents, while concentrating on narrow issues or disputes or questioning the Congress's authority to conduct oversight. On the surface, for example, the misconduct issue appeared free of partisan politics, but the "deregulatory" messages of the Reagan and Bush administrations undoubtedly affected how agencies responded to congressional queries. The scientific community sometimes interpreted agency resistance as proof that Congress had overstepped its authority (even though it is not unusual for committees to use oversight for such legislative battles over programmatic goals)[2] (Foreman, 1988; Ornstein, 1981, pp. 372–373). When prominent scientists then reacted with hostility to congressional inquiries or questioned John Dingell's right to investigate this issue, rather than merely voicing their disagreement with his stand, they inadvertently gave credence to the arguments of critics and gadflies who were calling for harsher penalties.

For O'Toole, Imanishi-Kari, Baltimore, and all those caught up in the 1988 and subsequent hearings, the oversight process must seem an overwhelmingly negative political instrument, fueled by unsubstantiated allegations, destructive of privacy and career, and beneficial only to politicians. Yet oversight *can* play a useful role. In times of economic and social change, the oversight process provides institutions with a valuable barometric reading of the political environment for science, and listening to that message carefully is a crucial part of the process.

THE REGULATORY FUTURE

Americans disturbed by economic uncertainty and politicians wanting to tap that concern still turn to science as the answer: they still point to a linkage between scientific knowledge and paychecks at the end of the week (Bush, 1945; LaFollette, 1996). But does that mean that either the Bush model for organizing science or its rationales and assumptions are unchanged or unchallenged? No. Universities are no longer regarded as the only suitable places to conduct basic research. Creativity has been shown to flower in nonacademic settings. Autonomy has become a social luxury. Accountability demands appropriate extensive mechanisms for monitoring it.

The people in the hearing rooms today are also different. Members of Congress are more likely to have been born after 1945, so their political philosophies reflect postwar prosperity, not fear of economic depression. Their faces turn toward the next century and its problems, not the obligations of the last. No assumption is unquestionable. No entitlement or activity is automatically immune from scrutiny, just as no public figure or occupation is exempt from satire. Deficit spending, social security, street crime, disease, drugs, poverty, pollution, illiteracy, and terrorism all can (and do) push science news off the front page. While science itself may not be pushed back into the wings, it *is* being pressed to play a different role, one with far more externally imposed direction and far less opportunity for improvisation in the laboratory.

All parties would profit from better public understanding of the conditions under which research is conducted today. Educating science's public constituency should be a top priority because more realistic public expectations of scientific progress and better understanding of the true nature of the research process and its occasional lack of perfection require a much more sophisticated, honest approach to public communication strategies. It rejects reliance on "gee-whiz" popular science and the promotion of scientists as universal experts (LaFollette, 1997). Politicians and policy makers alike need to be better informed about what scientists regard as their emerging problems and to engage in honest discussions about development of public policies that nourish creativity and intuitive insight, preserve intellectual independence, *and* encourage and reward responsible conduct.

As economic competitiveness dominates U.S. domestic and international political choices, increased attention is being given to "the whole set of processes ... by which new knowledge gets converted to economic wealth" (Armstrong, 1993, p. 5). Accordingly, Congress has become more concerned with how well research programs work and with eliminating any impediments (including fraud, waste, and abuse) to their success. As these changes continue, oversight investigations of science will continue to probe into what happens inside labs, how and to whom scientists communicate their ideas, and the standards and expectations for professional behavior. The "logic of the situation," Smith (1996) concurred, is that "science will most likely be conducted under more restrictive conditions.... Scientific activity will become more regulated even as resources decrease" (p. 54). In the Bush model, science was proposed as a way to preserve democracy; today's revised model says that preservation of democracy (including its economic viability and moral consensus) cannot be sacrificed for the sake of science (Bozeman, 1977, p. 60).

As the story of legislative oversight on scientific misconduct demonstrates, the scientific community's anticipatory concern about such public policy issues could help to avoid repeating past damaging controversies, in which the outcomes have not necessarily alleviated the original problem and yet the regulatory burden on investigators has increased further. Legislative oversight can be perceived as an intrusion on science's sacred autonomy, or it can be received as part of the governmental mechanisms necessary to ensure that publicly funded research remains at highest quality. Construing oversight as the latter—and assisting legislators to improve its quality and effectiveness—would be a sign that the scientific community has truly claimed an essential role on the stage of American life and has achieved the mature role imagined for it in 1945.

NOTES

This chapter is a revised and expanded version of my article "The Politics of Research Misconduct: Congressional Oversight, Universities, and Science" that appeared in the *Journal of Higher Education*. The historical interpretations were first presented at the National Air and Space Museum, Smithsonian Institution, Washington, D.C., and I thank seminar participants for their comments. The sections on congressional oversight draw on background papers that I wrote for the Carnegie Commission on Science, Technology, and Government. Finally, I thank the following people for comments on drafts: Donald Buzzelli, Nancy Carson, Christopher Foreman, Jr., Patricia Garfinkel, James Paul, and Jeffrey K. Stine.

1. Based on data reported in U.S. House of Representatives, Committee on Science and Technology (1986a) and Carson (1989, table 1).

2. I am grateful to Christopher Foreman, Jr., for bringing this interpretation to my attention.

References

Aberbach, J. D. (1990). *Keeping a watchful eye: The politics of congressional oversight.* Washington, DC: Brookings Institution.

Angell, M., & Relman, A. S. (1988). A time for congressional restraint. *New England Journal of Medicine, 318,* 1462–1463.

Armstrong, J. A. (1993). Research and competitiveness: Problems of a new rationale. *Bridge, 23*(1), 3–10.

Atkinson, R. C., & Blanpied, W. A. (Eds.). (1989). *Science, technology, and government: A crisis of purpose. Proceedings of a symposium held at the University of California, San Diego, March 1988.* San Diego: UCSD Extension.

Bozeman, B. (1977). A governed science and a self-governing science: The conflicting value of autonomy and accountability. In J. Haberer (Ed.), *Science and technology policy: Perspectives and developments* (pp. 55–66). Lexington, MA: Lexington.

Broad, W. J. (1981). Congress told fraud issue "exaggerated." *Science, 212,* 421.

Brown, G. E., Jr. (1992). Rational science, irrational reality: A congressional perspective on basic research and society. *Science, 258,* 200–201.

Bush, V. (1945). *Science: The endless frontier. A report to the president on a program for postwar scientific research.* Washington, DC: Government Printing Office.

Buzzelli, D. E. (1993). The definition of misconduct in science: A view from NSF. *Science, 259,* 584–585, 647–648.

Carson, N. (1989, November). *Process, prescience, and pragmatism: The Office of Technology Assessment.* Paper presented at the 11th Annual Research Conference of the Association of Public Policy Analysis and Management, Arlington, VA.

Cook, T. E. (1989). *Making laws and making news: Media strategies in the House of Representatives.* Washington, DC: Brookings Institution.

Davidson, R. H. (1981). Subcommittee government: New channels for policy making. In T. E. Mann & N. J. Ornstein (Eds.), *The new Congress* (pp. 91–133). Washington, DC: American Enterprise Institute for Public Policy Research.

Dingell, J. D. (1993). Shattuck Lecture: Misconduct in medical research. *New England Journal of Medicine, 328,* 1610–1615.

Dos Passos, J. (1944). *State of the nation.* Boston: Houghton Mifflin.

England, J. M. (1982). *A patron for pure science: The National Science Foundation's formative years, 1945–57.* Washington, DC: National Science Foundation.

Foreman, C. H., Jr. (1988). *Signals from the Hill: Congressional oversight and the challenge of social regulation.* New Haven, CT: Yale University Press.

Garfield, E., & Welljams-Dorof, A. (1991). The impact of fraudulent research on the scientific literature: The Stephen E. Breuning case. In *Peer review in scientific publishing: Papers from the First International Congress on Peer Review in Biomedical Publication, Chicago, Illinois, 10–12 May 1989* (pp. 197–204). Chicago: Council of Biology Editors.

Golden, W. T. (Ed.). (1993). *Science and technology advice to the president, Congress, and judiciary.* Washington, DC: AAAS Press.

Goodman, B. (1996a). Decision in Imanishi-Kari appeal spurs call for changes in system. *Scientist, 10*(16), 1, 6–7.

Goodman, B. (1996b). HHS panel issues proposals for implementing misconduct report. *Scientist, 10*(15), 3, 6.

Goodman, B. (1996c). Scientists are split over findings of Research Integrity Commission. *Scientist, 10*(2), 1, 8–9.

Greenberg, D. S. (1988a, April 15). Fraud inquiry: Harsh treatment for NIH on Capitol Hill. *Science and Government Report, 18,* 1–6.

Greenberg, D. S. (1988b, May 1). Fraud inquiry: NIH on the Capitol griddle (continued). *Science and Government Report, 18,* 3–6.

Griffith, E. S. (1961). *Congress: Its contemporary role* (3rd ed.). New York: New York University Press.

Hess, S. (1991). *Live from Capitol Hill! Studies of Congress and the media.* Washington, DC: Brookings Institution.

Huntington, S. P. (1965). Congressional responses to the twentieth century. In D. B. Truman (Ed.), *The Congress and America's future* (pp. 5–31). Englewood Cliffs, NJ: Prentice Hall.

Keefe, W. J., & Ogul, M. S. (1977). *The American legislative process: Congress and the states* (4th ed.). Englewood Cliffs, NJ: Prentice Hall.

LaFollette, M. C. (1990). *Making science our own: Public images of science, 1910–1955.* Chicago: University of Chicago Press.

LaFollette, M. C. (1992). *Stealing into print: Fraud, plagiarism, and other misconduct in scientific publishing.* Berkeley: University of California Press.

LaFollette, M. C. (1996). Paycheques on a Saturday night: A brief history and analysis of the politics of integrity in the United States. In S. Lock & F. Wells (Eds.), *Fraud and misconduct in medical research* (2nd ed., pp. 1–13). London: British Medical Journal Books.

LaFollette, M. C. (1997). Why "more" is not necessarily better: Strategies for communication of science to the public. *Accountability in Research, 5,* 1–15.

Light, P. C. (1993). *Monitoring government: Inspectors General and the search for accountability.* Washington, DC: Brookings Institution.

Lock, S., & Wells, F. (Eds.). (1996). *Fraud and misconduct in medical research* (2nd ed.). London: British Medical Journal Books.

Maas, A. (1983). *Congress and the common good.* New York: Basic Books.

Malbin, M. J. (1980). *Unelected representatives: Congressional staff and the future of representative government.* New York: Basic Books.

McCubbins, M. D., & Schwartz, T. (1984). Congressional oversight overlooked: Police patrols versus fire alarms. *American Journal of Political Science, 2,* 165–179.

National Science Board. (1996). *Science and engineering indicators—1996.* Washington, DC: Government Printing Office.

National Science Board. (1998). Science and engineering indicators—1998. Washington, DC: Government Printing Office.

Neustadt, R. E. (1965). Politicians and bureaucrats. In D. B. Truman (Ed.), *The*

Congress and America's future (pp. 102–120). Englewood Cliffs, NJ: Prentice Hall.

Ogul, M. S. (1990). Legislative oversight of bureaucracy. In D. C. Kozak & J. D. Macartney (Eds.), *Congress and public policy* (2nd ed., pp. 417–424). Prospect Heights, IL: Waveland.

Ornstein, N. J. (1981). The House and the Senate in a new Congress. In T. E. Mann & N. J. Ornstein (Eds.), *The new Congress* (pp. 363–384). Washington, DC: American Enterprise Institute for Public Policy Research.

Price, D. K. (1954). *Government and science: Their dynamic relation in American democracy.* New York: New York University Press.

Price, D. K. (1965). *The scientific estate.* Cambridge, MA: Harvard University Press.

Roman, M. B. (1988, April). When good scientists turn bad. *Discover,* pp. 50–58.

Sarasohn, J. (1993). *Science on trial: The whistle-blower, the accused, and the Nobel laureate.* New York: St. Martin's.

Schachman, H. K. (1993). What is misconduct in science? *Science, 261,* 148–149, 183.

Scientific fraud: Hearing before the Subcommittee on Oversight and Investigations of the House Committee on Energy and Commerce, 101st Cong., 2d Sess. (1990).

Scientific fraud and misconduct: The institutional response: Hearing before the Subcommittee on Oversight and Investigations of the House Committee on Energy and Commerce, 101st Cong., 1st Sess. (1989).

Scientific fraud and misconduct and the federal response: Hearing before the Subcommittee on Human Resources and Intergovernmental Relations of the House Committee on Government Operations, 100th Cong., 1st Sess. (1988).

Scientific fraud and misconduct in the National Institutes of Health biomedical grant programs: Hearing before the Subcommittee on Oversight and Investigations of the House Committee on Energy and Commerce, 100th Cong., 1st Sess. (1988).

Smith, B. L. R. (1992). *The advisers: Scientists in the policy process.* Washington, DC: Brookings Institution.

Smith, B. L. R. (1996). The accountability of science. *Minerva, 34,* 45–56.

Steneck, N. H. (1994). Research universities and scientific misconduct: History, policies, and the future. *Journal of Higher Education, 65,* 310–330.

Stine, J. K. (1994). *Twenty years of science in the public interest: A history of the Congressional Science and Engineering Fellowship Program.* Washington, DC: American Association for the Advancement of Science.

Thurber, J. A. (Ed.). (1991). *Divided democracy: Cooperation and conflict between the president and Congress.* Washington, DC: CQ Press.

U.S. Department of Health and Human Services, Public Health Service. (1996). *Integrity and misconduct in research: Report of the Commission on Research Integrity.* Washington, DC: Government Printing Office.

U.S. House of Representatives, Committee on Science and Technology, Subcommittee on Investigations and Oversight. (1981). *Fraud in biomedical research.* Washington, DC: Government Printing Office.

U.S. House of Representatives, Committee on Science and Technology, Task Force on Science Policy. (1986a). *Bibliography of studies and reports on science policy and related topics, 1945–1985* (Science Policy Study Background Rep. No. 2, Part A). Washington, DC: Government Printing Office.

U.S. House of Representatives, Committee on Science and Technology, Task Force on Science Policy. (1986b). *A history of science policy of the United States, 1940–1985* (Science Policy Study Background Rep. No. 1). Washington, DC: Government Printing Office.

U.S. House of Representatives, Committee on Science and Technology, Task Force on Science Policy. (1986c). *The regulatory environment for science* (Science Policy Study Background Rep. No. 10). Washington, DC: Government Printing Office.

U.S. House of Representatives, Committee on Science and Technology, Task Force on Science Policy. (1986d). *Science and the regulatory environment* (Science Policy Study Hearings, Vol. 15). Washington, DC: Government Printing Office.

U.S. House of Representatives, Committee on Science and Technology, Task Force on Science Policy. (1987). *Research and publication practices* (Science Policy Study Hearings, Vol. 22). Washington, DC: Government Printing Office.

U.S. House of Representatives, Committee on Science, Space, and Technology. (1990). *Maintaining the integrity of scientific research.* Washington, DC: Government Printing Office.

U.S. House of Representatives, Committee on Science, Space, and Technology. (1992). *Report of the Task Force on the Health of Research.* Washington, DC: Government Printing Office.

U.S. Senate, Committee on Commerce, Science, and Transportation. (1978). *A brief history of the Senate Committee on Commerce, Science, and Transportation and its activities since 1947.* Washington, DC: Government Printing Office.

Valentine, P. W. (1988, April 16). Drug therapy researcher is indicted. *Washington Post,* pp. A1, A14.

Wheeler, D. L. (1988, April 27). Researcher is indicted for falsifying data and impeding investigation of his work. *Chronicle of Higher Education 39,* A4, A12.

Zuckoff, M. (1988, April 12). Health agencies hinder research-fraud probes, House committee told. *Boston Globe,* p. 12.

Zurer, P. S. (1988a, April 18). Research fraud as criminal offense argued. *Chemical and Engineering News,* p. 6.

Zurer, P. S. (1988b, April 25). Researcher criminally charged with fraud. *Chemical and Engineering News,* p. 5.

CHAPTER TWO

From Denial to Action: Academic and Scientific Societies Grapple with Misconduct

David Johnson

Academic associations (i.e., those associations that represent the interests of universities and colleges) and scientific societies whose purpose is to satisfy certain interests of the scientists who are their members have each taken some responsibility for the control of scientific misconduct. Each, however, has taken a different role. The academic associations have helped provide the framework within which universities and the federal government attempt to prevent misconduct, or, failing that, receive, investigate, and rule on allegations of misconduct. Scientific societies have helped build the knowledge base that constitutes current understanding of misconduct and its prevention and control. They have also kept alive a dialogue on misconduct through their scientific journals and meetings and through publication of research on misconduct. Moreover, they have developed ethical codes to instruct their members in proper conduct. Sometimes those codes are accompanied by mechanisms for enforcement. The academic associations and scientific societies adopted their roles in part because pressure from Congress and the American public thrust it upon them. While scientists and academicians agree that scientific misconduct must be controlled, there remains a good deal of debate over the magnitude of the problem and thus over the elaborateness of the mechanisms needed to achieve control. This chapter is a roughly chronological examination of how the associations and societies have responded to misconduct over the past 16 years and of the forces that led to those responses.

CONGRESS PRESSES SCIENTISTS TO CONTROL MISCONDUCT

Reluctantly, scientific societies and academic associations began an odyssey on March 31, 1981. On that day, these representatives were summoned to testify before the Oversight Subcommittee of the U.S. House of Representatives Science and Technology Committee, chaired by then-Representative Al Gore (D-TN) (*Fraud in Biomedical Research,* 1981). The topic was fraud in science. Congressional interest stemmed from a series of cases beginning in 1974 with William Summerlin, a dermatologist at the Sloan-Kettering Institute for Cancer Research, who used a felt-tip pen to blacken a portion of a white mouse's fur to make it appear that an experiment on preventing rejection of foreign skin grafts had been successful. By 1980, there were at least three more cases receiving national coverage.

While scientists knew a few famous cases of fraud—Piltdown man, for example—in 1981 few of them believed there was a large problem here, appearances notwithstanding. Phillip Handler, then president of the National Academy of Sciences, voiced most scientists' sentiments when he told the Gore subcommittee, "The matter of falsification of data, I contend, need not be a matter of general societal concern. It is, rather, given the size of the total research effort, a relatively small matter which is generated within and is normally effectively managed by that smaller segment of the large society, which is the scientific community itself" (*Fraud in Biomedical Research,* 1981, p. 10). That view still anchors one side of debate and is justification for measured responses toward misconduct.

The opposing view was voiced by both Al Gore and Robert Walker (D-PA), then ranking minority member of the Oversight Subcommittee. Gore's political career has been associated with strengthening science and using it for public good. Walker became ranking minority member, then chair, of the full Science Committee. Their view has justified aggressive action against misconduct. Gore stated the position thus: "At the base of our investment in research lies the trust of the American people and the integrity of the scientific enterprise. If that trust is threatened—as it is when leading scientists are discovered falsifying their data—then not only are the people placed at potential risk, but the welfare of science itself is undermined" (*Fraud in Biomedical Research,* 1981, p. 1). Walker's opening comments on day two of the hearing underscored the consequence of treating misconduct as a small problem internal to science: "We believe that allowing these problems to become buried in the scientific bureaucracy may well create the ultimate loss of public support which is essential for the continued funding of publicly supported research.... I still believe that it is only through a careful self-examination that science will be able to carry out that biblical mandate, 'Physician, cure thyself.' I hope that our attention will help to bring about that searching examination" (*Fraud in Biomedical Research,* 1981, p. 112).

Those congressional views became strong goads to the scientific community. They moved it from regarding misconduct as a minor, private, internal problem to treating it as a major public problem, regardless of its frequency—a problem whose resolution sometimes must be widely known because the public has a stake in the outcome. Congress has maintained pressure on the scientific community as, periodically, new cases have arisen. Two more rounds of hearings were held in 1989, leading to creation of offices at the National Institutes of Health (NIH) and the National Science Foundation (NSF) to ensure appropriate responses by the scientific community to allegations of misconduct (*Fraud in Grant Programs,* 1989; *Is Science for Sale?* 1989; *Maintaining the Integrity of Scientific Research,* 1989; *Scientific Fraud,* 1989; *Scientific Fraud, Part 2,* 1990; U.S. House of Representatives, 1990).

Fifteen years of adverse public attention have made scientists painfully aware that Gore and Walker were right: the financial health of science, not to mention scientific freedom itself, is dependent on the good will of the public. That good will is not guaranteed. Public trust in, and support of, science can be dangerously shaken if the public perceives that the scientific community has been unjust, lax, or self-serving in its treatment of misconduct. It matters little to the public that the notorious cases of misconduct represent a vanishingly small fraction of all the research conducted. Worse, the damage caused by public perception that misconduct is pervasive has spread beyond science to one important institution in which scientists work—the university.

The allegation that universities have used tax dollars meant for research overhead for other purposes has helped erode confidence in universities. That has adversely affected their forms and levels of support: caps have been placed on the reimbursements universities can receive for the cost of federally sponsored research. And state legislatures such as that of Virginia have apparently come to regard research and teaching as incompatible. They have considered withholding funds to public research universities not able to document that their faculty members meet a specified standard for contact hours with students. Many influences figure into these changes in the treatment of research universities. But loss of public trust in scientists and their institutions must be counted among the more significant of them. Scientists have paid a high price to understand that they must control misconduct. It is against this backdrop of public perception and its consequences that scientists, through their societies, academic associations, and other institutions, have been considering and implementing actions to control misconduct.

ACADEMIC ASSOCIATIONS DEVISE MISCONDUCT CONTROL PROCEDURES

Would scientists have dealt formally and forcefully with misconduct in the absence of public scrutiny? A comment by one of the witnesses at the 1981 hearing is telling. Dr. Philip Felig had coauthored a paper with a scientist,

Dr. Vijay Soman, whose reported research was discovered to be partly plagiarized and partly fraudulent. Representative Gore asked about the response of the scientific community to misconduct. Dr. Felig answered, "For reasons that I don't think that we all understand, despite a history of data fraud that has existed in science including what was considered classical work over 100 years ago, such mechanisms that both safeguard the data and the quest for truth, and safeguard the rights of the individuals who may be challenged have not been in place. In other words, we didn't know how to react" (*Fraud in Biomedical Research,* 1981, p. 194).

If the scientific community did not know how to react—that is, lacked formal mechanisms for responding to allegations of misconduct—it agreed at least on where such mechanisms should be located. Donald S. Fredrickson, then-director of NIH, put it this way to the Gore subcommittee:

> It is technically true that the institutions are the ones that receive NIH grants, rather than the individual scientists, but the role of the university or similar institutions in the maintenance of scientific ethics is greater and older than their fiduciary relationships to Government, or to any of the newly required guidelines to which they must bear obedience.... Control of their staff appointments, their tenure, their promotions is really the main power of the university for the preservation of scientific ethics, and I think the principal responsibility must go along with the ultimate power. (*Fraud in Biomedical Research,* 1981, p. 28)

Given this consensus, it is appropriate that university associations were among the first professional organizations to attempt formulation of practical means to address allegations of misconduct. Most cases attracting congressional and press attention occurred in biomedical research. Officials at institutions where these cases arose sometimes made errors and misjudgments in treating allegations, including punishing the person making the allegation before doing an adequate investigation. So it was doubly urgent that the biomedical research community take action.

The Association of American Medical Colleges (AAMC) created an Ad Hoc Committee on the Maintenance of High Ethical Standards in the Conduct of Research in January 1982. Chaired by Julius R. Krevans, M.D., a dean at the University of California, San Francisco, the committee was charged with creating guidelines that medical college and teaching hospital officials could use in designing institutional procedures to respond to misconduct allegations.

The AAMC represents all accredited medical schools in the United States and Canada and is associated with 91 academic and professional societies. Its reach in biomedicine is far. Relevance of the guidelines, however, has not been limited to biomedical research institutions because they treat each logical stage in *any* institutional effort to deal with misconduct. One sees in the committee's recommendations the beginnings from which thinking about how institutions should address misconduct has developed.

At about the time that the AAMC created its working group, the Association of American Universities (AAU) created a Committee on the Integrity of Research, chaired by William Danforth, longtime chancellor of Washington University. While the AAMC recommendations guided *institutions* in creating misconduct control mechanisms, the AAU report, entitled *Report of the Association of American Universities Committee on the Integrity of Research* (1982), emphasized *individual* responsibility. The committee, for example, declared that "it is our opinion that a positive attitude of intellectual honesty does more to prevent dishonesty than any other single factor" (AAU, 1982, p. 2). Like the AAMC, the AAU recognized that an important incentive to engage in misconduct is the relentless pressure to publish. And like the AAMC, the AAU recommended that universities emphasize quality over quantity. To ease pressures on individuals, some institutions, such as Harvard and NSF, acted consistently with the recommendations by limiting the number of articles that could be considered in promotion and tenure decisions or in research proposal citations. It has proven difficult, however, to achieve universal adherence to a principle of quality over quantity.

The AAU report was reflective of the view Handler expressed to the Gore subcommittee—namely, that misconduct should be dealt with internally, mainly through incentives to comply with principles of good science. Openness with colleagues, adherence to well-established research protocols, and giving credit where credit is due were cited as means to control misconduct. In treating an allegation of misconduct, the AAU counseled that "a researcher under suspicion should be treated as a colleague whose cooperation in providing access to data and procedures is expected" (AAU, 1982, p. 4). Further upholding collegiality and the value of a scientist's reputation, the report noted that "the mere suspicion of wrongdoing, even if totally unjustified, is potentially damaging to an investigator's career. . . . Thus, information concerning any investigation should be available only to those who need to know" (AAU, 1982, p. 4). The recommendations of the AAU were approved by the Joint Committee on Health Policy, which, together with the AAU, included the American Council on Education and the National Association of State Universities and Land-Grant Colleges. While embraced officially by most of the country's research universities, the AAU recommendations did not provide the practical guidance universities needed to deal with misconduct. Instead, the AAU report referred the reader to the AAMC report for such guidance.

The AAMC committee recommendations were published in June of 1982, a little more than a year after the Gore hearings, in a booklet entitled

The Maintenance of High Ethical Standards in the Conduct of Research (AAMC, 1982). Its introduction echoed and linked the themes struck in the hearings:

> The responsibility of the scientific community to the public is acknowledged. The maintenance of public trust in this pursuit is vital to the continuing vigor of the biomedical research enterprise. Loss of this trust because of isolated instances of dishonest behavior on the part of a few researchers could cause great harm by calling into question in the mind of the public the validity of all new knowledge and the integrity of the scientific community at large. In short, it is in the best interest of the public and of academic medicine to prevent misconduct in research and to deal effectively and responsibly with instances where misconduct is suspected. (AAMC, 1982, p. 1)

The AAMC recognized that institutions have two distinct responsibilities: to try to prevent misconduct and to deal effectively with allegations. The guidelines break the response to an allegation into three stages: discovery, in which it is determined whether there are grounds for a formal investigation; formal investigation, which is entered when there are sufficient grounds; and a concluding stage in which action may be taken, if warranted, against the accused, or in which measures should be taken to reinforce the honest reputation of the scientist when no misconduct has been found. This view that universities are responsible for both preventing and investigating misconduct and the three-step procedure for treatment of an allegation of misconduct have become standard at research universities. The elements of the investigatory process have become part of federal regulations governing the conduct of institutions receiving research support from the Public Health Service.

Besides its framework for addressing misconduct, the AAMC guidelines raised, and took a particular stance toward, key issues related to methods to prevent misconduct and to the investigatory process after an allegation has been made. That the AAMC raised these issues is to its credit: experience has shown them to be critical issues. But the debates among scientists, government officials, and university administrators in the years since the guidelines were issued have demonstrated much less consensus on the proper stance with respect to many of these issues than the AAMC's presentation suggested. Among the most critical issues has been how to approach misconduct. That is, should scientists examine the work of accused scientists within the framework of scientific traditions, or should the approach have characteristics of a courtroom? The AAMC and the AAU favored the scientific framework.

It had been the intention of scientists, academic administrators, and many federal officials to model processes to address misconduct on peer review rather than on legal proceedings. Legal proceedings are public and adversarial. Many scientists felt such a process would erode the bond of trust essential to developing new knowledge. Moreover, scientists were cognizant of the importance of reputation. A legalistic approach might irreparably damage the reputation of a scientist simply by making it publicly known that the individual had been accused of misconduct. So the community preferred a quiet, low-key, collegial approach to dealing with misconduct. Thus, the first recommendation of the AAMC with regard to processing initial reports of fraud stated, "From the outset, institutions should protect rights and reputations for all parties involved including the individual(s) who report perceived misconduct in good faith" (AAMC, 1982, p. 4). Not until and unless a panel of faculty peers with no conflict of interest in investigating the particular allegation of misconduct had determined that grounds existed for a formal investigation did the AAMC recommend that the accused be told that an allegation had been made. The secrecy was meant to protect accuser and accused for as long as possible.

Similarly, while the AAMC recommended keeping the accused informed of the progress of the formal investigation, there was no recommendation that the accused be informed of the accuser, the nature of the allegation, or the evidence in support of the allegation. This paralleled the peer review system, in which a researcher submits proposed or completed work to a panel of anonymous peers who judge the submission and deliver a decision, perhaps with a summary of considerations weighed in the decision, only after all deliberations have been completed. It departed markedly from a legal proceeding, in which the accused is confronted by the accuser in a public setting and both sides examine the evidence and prepare arguments and counterarguments based on that evidence.

The post-formal investigation actions recommended by the AAMC were like a legal proceeding in that, if found guilty, the guilty party was to be punished. If the accuser was found to have brought the accusation in bad faith, then action could be taken against the accuser. But in its 1982 document, the AAMC did not recommend a process of appeal, as would be the case in the legal system. Rather, the concern was for the scientific community: journals in which the individual published were to be informed of an adverse finding, as were institutions where the individual has worked and funding agencies that had supported the work. When the misconduct might have some public impact, as when the benefits of a new drug were falsely reported, then the public was to be informed of the finding of misconduct as well.

Those who designed these guidelines, and many other scientists who have helped build the system we have today, believe that scientists want their conduct reviewed in a framework consistent with the institutions and practices of science. It is now clear that this is not precisely what all scientists want. The equivalent of case law has been building as experience in dealing with misconduct accumulates. The result is that the scientific and the legal systems have begun to blend. Today's practices still have some of the adherence to confidentiality and preservation of trust prized by scientists, but many aspects of due process, including an appeals system, have also become part of the system. The system is still undergoing evolution. Change comes continually as the values of science clash with the values of law to produce hybrid practices. Now, for example, there is sometimes allowance for the accused to prepare a defense, but often not until an initial finding of misconduct has been made.

The AAMC's work was seminal in this evolution. It gave the scientific community a way to begin the process of discovery. Experience, however, has taught much since the AAMC issued its guidelines, and much is yet to be learned. The AAMC has tried to keep the academic and scientific communities up to date as thinking has developed. In 1988, it helped form an interassociation working group to further develop ways to deal with allegations of misconduct. Besides the AAMC, the group included the Association of Academic Health Centers, the AAU, the American Council on Education, the American Society for Microbiology, the Council of Graduate Schools, the Council on Government Relations, the Federation of American Societies for Experimental Biology, the National Association of College and University Attorneys, and the National Association of State Universities and Land Grant Colleges. Funding came from the American Association for the Advancement of Science (AAAS)–American Bar Association (ABA) Council on Law and Science. It was, in other words, a group broadly representative of the scientific and academic communities.

The working group formed as Congress's attention turned again to scientific misconduct and to the alleged misuse by universities of public funds meant to support the indirect costs of federally sponsored research. Those hearings influenced the Department of Health and Human Services and NSF to create offices to ensure proper use of public funds for research. Together with these offices, new regulations, based on legislation passed in 1985 (Pub. L. No. 99–158), were produced to augment those already in place to govern university handling of misconduct allegations (see 45 C. F. R.). In their deliberations, the working group took account of the proposed new regulations that were issued in final form between the publication of the first (March 1989) and second (February 1990) editions of the group's report. The AAMC published the report as a booklet entitled *Framework for Institutional Policies and Procedures to Deal with Misconduct in Research* (1990). The Association of American Universities published it in slightly different form as *Framework for Institutional Policies and Procedures to Deal with Fraud in Research* (1989).

These documents did not address prevention as a means to deal with misconduct, as did the earlier AAMC and AAU documents. Rather, they concentrated on procedures to follow after an allegation had been made. Reflecting development in thinking, the documents added to the basic steps of informal inquiry, formal investigation, and concluding actions recommended in 1981 an appeal process presided over by a university official not involved in the deliberations of the original investigative body. Provision was made for even further review of the appeal decision by the institution's "chief executive officer or designee" (AAMC, 1990, p. 10). After that final review, it was suggested that "the institution should note that the decision of the review is final" (AAMC, 1990, p. 10).

In practice, such a decision has not always been final. At its discretion, the Public Health Service's Office of Research Integrity may undertake further investigation and review and may make its own decision, and the accused may further appeal that decision. The discrepancy between the recommendation and the practice underscores the evolutionary nature of the effort to control misconduct. The evolution has often been difficult, with change coming as the result of bitter challenges to existing procedures or policies. Academic societies have not foreseen all the pitfalls their recommendations would encounter, but they have laid an invaluable groundwork, giving everyone involved a common starting point for dealing fairly and effectively with misconduct.

SCIENTIFIC SOCIETIES PROMOTE THINKING AND DEVELOP UNDERSTANDING REGARDING MISCONDUCT

It seemed that everyone agreed that the first responsibility for controlling misconduct fell to institutions in which scientists work. So it was appropriate for academic associations to design the means to control misconduct. It was less clear what role the scientific societies should play. Certainly, they should have some role; nearly every scientist in the country belongs to one or more scientific societies. Already, many societies had statements of proper conduct for members, and some had detailed codes of ethics and sanctions for violating the code. Also, societies control many scientific journals, the means by which research, honest or fraudulent, becomes known.

But the role of societies in the misconduct "crisis" was not clear, in large part because societies lack what universities have—namely, the direct power to affect the career of a scientist who has engaged in misconduct. True, societies can expel a member. This is the most serious sanction they can employ. But there are many societies to which a scientist may belong. Loss of membership in even a major one need not be an overwhelming impediment. Some scientists even choose not to join scientific organizations, and that places their conduct well beyond the ability of societies to control. It is also true that societies control the major scientific journals. But no one society controls all the journals of a scientific discipline. Prohibition from publishing in one journal does not preclude publishing in another. Consequently, the direct power of societies to control conduct is limited.

Their indirect influences, however, can be considerable, and here societies have made significant contributions. As the scientific community, along with the rest of the country, grew in awareness of misconduct, it became clear that awareness and understanding were not the same thing. Knowing that a problem exists is not the same as knowing its solution. Understanding misconduct and its possible solutions turned out to be an ideal challenge for the largest of the scientific societies, the AAAS. It and several other scientific societies have been building the knowledge base to deal intelligently with misconduct.

In June 1982, section K (Social, Economic and Political Sciences) of the Pacific Division of AAAS held a symposium on misconduct at its 63rd annual meeting. The proceedings were published in a book entitled *The Dark Side of Science* (Kilbourne & Kilbourne, 1983). AAAS has since hosted many discussions of misconduct at its annual meetings. These have been a means for authorities to think out loud about the nature of misconduct and about ways to control it. Much soul searching has occurred in these symposia. Cases of misconduct from Galileo to the present time have been examined. Shortcomings of the peer review approach to dealing with misconduct have been discussed. The effects of power relations have been noted, including the tendency of authorities to punish junior faculty or postdoctoral fellows mercilessly while treating senior faculty, especially ones who bring in large grants, less harshly. The prevalence of misconduct has been estimated, and a myriad of methods to detect or prevent it have been suggested.

The symposia have been one device for building understanding. But AAAS eventually hit on a more systematic way to undertake the needed examination. In 1974, it entered into a partnership with the ABA to form the AAAS-ABA National Conference of Lawyers and Scientists. Its purpose is to examine issues at the intersection of science and law. Misconduct fits the bill. With a grant from the Alfred P. Sloan Foundation, the conference sponsored a series of three workshops between September 1987 and February 1989. The proceedings, published in three volumes entitled *Project on Scientific Fraud and Misconduct* (AAAS-ABA, 1988, 1989a, 1989b), are the most thorough examination currently available of the range of issues surrounding misconduct.

Volume 1 presents many of the themes to be treated further in volumes 2 and 3: the prevalence of misconduct, the nature of efforts to address it, and gaps to be found in those procedures; the role of due process in misconduct proceedings; and treatment of whistle-blowers.

The second workshop was conducted while the AAMC and AAU were developing their guidelines, and much of the workshop was focused on a draft of those guidelines. Thus, the guidelines and volume 2 are companion pieces that offer a means to address allegations of misconduct, together with useful thinking on the problems that may be encountered when the system is challenged by an actual case. The volume is a critical examination of the variety of ways universities have responded to misconduct and a consideration of how policies have changed, or ought to change, as experience accumulates. Congressional interest has played a decided role in focusing the attention of the academic community on misconduct, and that role is also discussed in the volume, as is a further consideration of whistle-blowers and the need to guarantee them adequate protection from reprisal.

Volume 3 looks at the relation of law and science—perhaps the most unsettled of issues related to scientific misconduct. It compares the legal culture to the scientific culture, speculating on those parts of legal culture, such as due process, that should have a place in misconduct proceedings. But it also considers the losses that the culture of science might have to bear, including loss of the trust that is basic to scientific communication. Problems related to evidence are also dealt with, including such fundamental questions as who owns, and thus should have access to, the research data in a misconduct investigation. Regardless of how hard university authorities try to make misconduct investigations a version of peer review rather than a court proceeding, the law may enter the picture because the stakes are so high: the reputations and livelihoods of both accused and accuser may be at stake, not to mention the honor of the institution at which the alleged misconduct occurred and is being investigated. With good reason, the volume examines how the law might come into play as a result of university proceedings and how journals that publish, and later consider retracting, fraudulent work might be affected by defamation suits. Collectively, these volumes form a primer for university and other authorities on what to expect when an allegation of misconduct arises and on the variety of options to consider at most of the critical points in a misconduct proceeding.

The practical utility of this AAAS project accrues mainly to those authorities in universities, in government, and on editorial boards of journals who might be faced with acting on an allegation of misconduct. At least two other scientific associations, Sigma Xi and the National Academy of Sciences, have crafted documents aimed at serving scientists themselves. Unlike the AAAS workshop documents, these do not contain new insights on heretofore lightly examined topics. Instead, they attempt to package information that every scientist should know in a convenient, widely accessible format. They spell out for scientists and graduate students what is expected of them in the way of ethical conduct.

The two documents cover much of the same territory but in very different styles of presentation. The National Academy's offering, *On Being a Scientist* (Committee on the Conduct of Science, 1989), is written like a heart-to-heart conversation with an everyday person burdened by the pressures, temptations, and uncertainties of modern life. It says, in effect, that there is much uncertainty and discouragement in life. Sometimes a person needs a little help to tell right from wrong—and here is that help. The person to whom Sigma Xi's *Honor in Science* (1986) speaks is a person who may already have been tempted to take some shortcuts. Its chapters have titles like "Everybody Does It" and "Things Are Very Different in My Field." It explains how, despite appearances, certain standards of conduct apply across all of science.

Both documents explain that honesty is necessary to preserve both science and science's utility to society. The ways a person can be dishonest in the design of research and in the collection, interpretation, and reporting of data are explored. Not only do the two documents give guidance as to proper personal conduct; they also explain why a scientist is obligated to report the misconduct of others. And they give the reader some idea how, when, and to whom such a report should be made. Every graduate student in science should carry one or both of these documents through graduate school and into professional life.

SCIENTIFIC SOCIETIES PROMOTE ANALYSIS AND SCHOLARLY DISCUSSION OF MISCONDUCT

Academic and scientific associations have educated the community through their publications. They have given guidance to universities and the federal government regarding ways to prevent misconduct and to handle allegations when these arise. They have warned of possible pitfalls ahead and of issues yet to be addressed adequately. Just as important, they have succinctly summarized the elements of ethical behavior that should characterize a scientist's conduct and have distributed that information in a convenient form. Most of these publications, however, are snapshots of one moment in a dynamic process. One need only compare the AAMC's 1982 guidelines to those it issued in 1990 to know that understanding of misconduct and of how to handle it is changing with time. Because treatment of misconduct is far from a settled matter, the discussion of how to address it must not be limited to those times when congressional interest is piqued. The discussion needs to be ongoing. The federal government has aided this ongoing discussion through a variety of workshops and symposia as well as through requests for public comment on proposed regulatory changes and through the creation of regulations that are reviewed and modified from time to time. (For representative examples, see 42 C. F. R., Chapter I, Subchapter A, Part 2a, and Subchapters D and E, 1995, and 45 C. F. R., Chapter VI, Sections 602, 604, 620, 680–690, 1995, as well as Commission on Research Integrity, 1996; Office of Scientific Integrity Review, 1990; U.S. Department of Health and Human

Services, 1988.) Several scientific societies have also been outstandingly active in promoting the ongoing dialogue over misconduct.

Again, the AAAS is noteworthy. It has used several avenues to maintain discussion. For decades, AAAS's journal *Science* has been a sounding board for views on a broad array of issues related to scientific integrity. As Albert Barber, who was then vice-chancellor of research programs at the University of California at Los Angeles, put it at the 1983 AAAS Symposium on Science, Deviance, and Society, "I find that one of the publications that I read routinely is the AAAS journal *Science*. . . . As a practicing cell biologist I turn first to the Reports section of *Science* to see what new research is being reported, whereas as an administrator, I turn to the News and Comments section first to see what new fraudulent activity is being reported" (Kilbourne & Kilbourne, 1983, p. 91).

Science is a weekly publication, a rarity in science publishing. Its frequency of publication has allowed it to chronicle and comment on the evolution of thinking on misconduct almost as it happens. To be sure, the journal has sometimes been an unabashed apologist for science, as when its then-editor Daniel Koshland (1987) declared that "99.9999 percent of [scientific] reports are accurate and truthful" (p. 141). But it has also been a forum for analysis of many of the important issues with regard to misconduct. Not the least of these has been the question of what constitutes proper behavior for a scientist. As early as 1950 (Pigman & Carmichael, 1950), *Science* gave space to discussion of an ethical code for scientists. It revisited the scientific code and its relationship to ethics in 1977 (Cournand, 1977). In 1981 the journal again devoted space to the issue through a discussion of scientific responsibility (Edsall, 1981). (The AAAS Committee on Scientific Freedom and Responsibility from which this article sprang was established in 1975 to preserve scientific freedom and promote responsible practices in science. That preservation of scientific freedom requires scientists to take responsibility for their actions is an idea that the committee promotes through many means, including occasional *Science* articles.)

In addition to helping define ethical conduct for scientists, *Science* has joined the debate on many thorny issues in misconduct. To name just a few such issues, it has covered assignment of credit in the publication of collaborative research (Cohen, 1995), the merits of open versus closed misconduct hearings (Palca, 1992), and the conduct of universities in the examination of misconduct (Broad, 1982).

It should be noted that, while not reaching as broad a spectrum of scientists, the journals of several other large societies have also kept their members informed of developments in misconduct and have provided analysis. The *Journal of the American Medical Association (JAMA)* fits this pattern and reaches a large audience of medical researchers and practitioners. (See Arkin, 1985a, 1985b, Grouse, 1982, and McBride, 1974, for representative treatments of misconduct in *JAMA.*) For the American Chemical Society, *Chemical and Engineering News* has been the main outlet for news and commentary on misconduct. (See Zurer, 1993, 1994, 1995, for representative articles.) Similarly, for the Institute of Electrical and Electronics Engineers, the journal *Engineering in Medicine and Biology* has filled the news and analysis function. (For representative treatment, see this related series of articles: Fielder, 1992; Richards, 1992; Richards & Walter, 1992; Walter & Richards, 1992.) The informational and analytical roles filled by these publications are essential, the more so because some of them reach a large segment of the scientific community. Thus, they keep relevant issues, together with the range of stances toward those issues, constantly before the eyes of scientists. *Science,* for example, reaches more than 135,000 scientists per week.

But the News and Comment section of *Science,* and the news and analysis approach also found in the other journals cited, is not the best medium for a scholarly treatment of misconduct. Many problems in misconduct deserve examination for their own sakes, not as features of a news-making event. Their importance transcends any single instance of misconduct. They are the questions whose answers provide the deeper understanding of misconduct. They include such things as the cultural and social dynamics of science; the nature and limits of peer review; the structure of the scientific and academic reward systems and the consequences of altering those structures; power relations in science; the strengths and weaknesses of the scientific communication system; and the effects of economic and social stress on scientific productivity. They are questions that demand disciplined study.

Fortunately, there are scientists who study such topics. Many who produce the scholarship that underlies efforts to combat misconduct belong to the Society for Social Studies of Science. The society is eclectic, containing sociologists, psychologists, economists, political scientists, historians, and scientists of other disciplines who make contributions to the general field of science and technology studies. Members publish in their international journal *Science, Technology, and Human Values.* They also publish regularly in the journals *Minerva* and *Science Communication,* which was once called *Knowledge.* In 1995, a new publication outlet became available with the founding of a journal called *Science and Engineering Ethics.* Scholars in this area also publish their findings in books. Support for the work is modest, coming largely from a single source, the Ethics and Values Studies Program in the Social, Behavioral, and Economic Sciences Directorate at NSF.

Because they are the scholars of misconduct, members fulfill a variety of "civic" duties. They testify before Congress. They serve on National Academy of Sciences and Institute of Medicine panels on scientific integrity. They contribute position papers to, and are major participants in, government-sponsored conferences on misconduct: through several venues, they distribute the knowledge that science is using to heal itself. For a small sampling of their work, see Zuckerman (1984) on the clash of norms and deviant behavior in science; LaFollette (1992) on fraud in scientific publishing; Swazey, Anderson, and Lewis (1993) on awareness of misconduct in the scientific community; Woolf (1988) on deception in scientific research; Chubin and Hackett (1990) on peer review; Chalk (1978) on the role of scientific societies in whistle-blowing; Cozzens (1989) on competition and social control in science; and Braxton and Bayer (1996) on levels of formality in actions taken by biochemists who have experienced an incident of misconduct.

Thus far, we have seen with respect to misconduct that scientific societies have played an educational role for scientists, academic administrators, and government officials through symposia, conferences, workshops, and several landmark publications. They have informed scientists of developments in the misconduct area and have provided analyses of key events and issues through scientific journals. And through the discipline of science and technology studies, many of whose members are found in the Society for Social Studies of Science, a knowledge base from which to combat scientific misconduct is being built. These, however, are not the only activities aimed at controlling misconduct with which scientific societies have been involved. Those with primary responsibility for ethics within the societies have been working together to bring some coherence across scientific disciplines to methods for controlling misconduct.

SCIENTIFIC SOCIETIES WORK FOR COMMON STANDARDS OF BEHAVIOR ACROSS SCIENCE

In 1975, AAAS created a Committee on Scientific Freedom and Responsibility to promote the understanding and conviction that scientific freedom cannot be guaranteed unless scientists also accept that they must conduct themselves responsibly. To breach the public trust in science through irresponsible action is to undo the public support that makes scientific freedom possible. The next year, AAAS created an Office of Scientific Freedom and Responsibility to staff the committee. Although its name (it is now called the Scientific Freedom, Responsibility and Law Program) and duties have evolved, the office still exists to promote ethical conduct among scientists. The previously discussed AAAS-ABA National Conference of Lawyers and Scientists, for example, is staffed by the program.

Early in its existence, the program took stock of available guidance on ethical scientific conduct by surveying the country's scientific societies to determine what specific codes of conduct they had created for their members. The findings were published in 1981 (Chalk, Frankel, & Chafer, 1981), but the program has continued to collect and archive society and university ethics codes. These files are now a valuable resource to those wishing to create codes of ethics. Program staff will assist society officers charged with developing such codes.

AAAS also wanted to link those in societies and universities with interests or responsibilities in ethics. It wanted these people to have a network for exchange of knowledge and experiences. So, in the early 1980s, the Professional Society Ethics Group (PSEG) was created. Today PSEG includes ethics officers of universities as well as officers of scientific, engineering, and medical associations with responsibilities in ethics. Members with offices near AAAS headquarters in Washington, D.C., meet several times per year to receive updates on federal regulatory or legislative initiatives that could have an impact on how scientists might need to account for their behavior. They also discuss approaches to ethical questions such as avoidance of conflict of interest by scientists who work as advisors or consultants to government, or fair allocation of patents and rights to develop products based on scientific discoveries achieved through federal or university support.

Of course, not every person concerned with science ethics lives in or near Washington. By 1987, PSEG members saw a need to bring more participants into the ethics discussion. So the group, together with the AAAS Committee on Scientific Freedom and Responsibility and the Scientific Freedom, Responsibility, and Law Program, began to publish a newsletter called *Professional Ethics Report*. The quarterly is a cooperative venture. Members write most articles, but submissions from nongroup members are welcome. It is a means for those concerned with science ethics to inform each other. Ethics activities of scientific societies and universities are chronicled here. Legislation regarding ethics or conflict of interest is explained, new publications in science ethics are reviewed, problems in ethics are discussed, and new research is reported. The newsletter and PSEG are catalysts for achieving a degree of common understanding among ethics officers.

Until recently, teachers of science ethics had no similar device to promote thinking and dialogue. One impediment is that scientists have been unsure of the place of ethics teachers: there has been debate over whether ethics courses produce ethical scientists. Some have argued that ethical behavior is instilled by one's graduate advisor along with skill in experimental methodology and data analysis. Federal authorities have not been entirely sympathetic with this view. In recent years, NIH has required that any application by a university for training funds include provisions for teaching ethics to those who will benefit from the training assistance. Consequently, ethics teachers are playing an increasingly prominent role in the effort to maintain integrity in science.

In 1995, realizing the growing ease with which anyone with a computer and modem can communicate through the Internet, AAAS created a listserv for ethics teachers. It was known as Perspectives on Ethical Issues in Science and Technology (PEIST). Participation was not restricted to ethics teachers, but it was clear from the topics of passionate discussion raised there that PEIST had become a resource for them. Participants not only discuss their approaches to teaching particular aspects of ethics but also carried on spirited discussions about points of ethics. Typically, a participant would raise an issue, offer his or her thinking on it, and sit back as a host of other participants interested in the same topic offered their views, which were, in turn, commented on until everyone who so desired had a say.

The Internet comes as close as any medium we have today to making sharing of thinking on science ethics a "real-time" activity. As a problem or issue arises, this medium makes it possible to gauge the thinking of experts around the country immediately. For example, one discussion that occurred on PEIST in 1995 had to do with whether university departments should put preprints of articles by their faculty on their departmental home pages so that they could be read by anyone on the World Wide Web. On the positive side, this practice would give others in the field immediate access to the latest research. On the negative side, there are questions about whether articles not yet submitted to peer review should be "published," even electronically. There is also the question of whether such prepublication actually constitutes publication and thus could result in a charge of self-plagiarism if the article were submitted for publication to a conventional journal. Finally, there are questions of whether such prepublications could be cited by others; whether they might be listed in a curriculum vitae as publications if publication in a journal did not occur; and, if they were so listed, whether they could be considered legitimate publications in promotion and tenure considerations.

As departments do begin to put the work of faculty members on departmental web pages, journal editors and the scientific community will have to determine how to behave ethically with regard to this particular means of instant communication of research. But submitting the question about such publication to PEIST made it instantly clear what ethical questions would need to be addressed and how at least some of the questions might be resolved.

In creating this listserv, AAAS made available a potentially powerful tool for ethics teachers and for developing thinking on knotty ethical problems. Unfortunately, PEIST was discontinued by AAAS in 1997 when the listserv host, a university that offered listserv space to nonprofit organizations, changed its policy.

It may have been the earliest foray into ordered discussion of science ethics using the Web, but it is unlikely to be the last. The Internet is a relatively new medium, of course. Experimentation is needed to find ways to use it most effectively. For example, although the medium enables rapid exchange of ideas, it is not yet conducive to reaching resolution on the issues raised.

But the scientific community may be able to adapt to this new medium its experience with more conventional means of idea exchange. For example, a consensus conference plays host to the kind of interchange that was seen on PEIST, but with a major difference. The consensus conference has a product, a document that spells out the consensus with respect to the issue at hand. So far, the Internet is mainly process. Will the medium be used to reach consensus on such things as what constitutes ethical behavior in areas like electronic publication or prepublication that were not even options a few years ago? Current experimentation with electronic conferences suggests it may indeed be feasible someday.

SCIENTIFIC SOCIETIES LOOK INWARD AT THEIR OWN ETHICS ACTIVITIES

Thus far, we have examined only outwardly directed activities of scientific and academic societies. We have looked at actions that these societies have taken on behalf of academic administrators, scientists, researchers who study the behavior of scientists, ethics officers, and ethics teachers. But what have societies done to promote the ethical behavior of their own members? The Council of Scientific Society Presidents (CSSP) has spent several years examining just this question and has followed that examination with efforts to bring more societies to adopt codes of ethics and means for eliciting ethical behavior from members.

CSSP, as its name implies, is a society composed of presidents-elect, presidents, and past presidents of the country's major scientific societies. CSSP estimates that the societies whose presidents are members contain more than a million scientists. So CSSP is like AAAS in that its actions can filter quickly to a large number of scientists. Moreover, the deliberations of CSSP members are important in themselves because when they result in consensus on a stance toward a given issue, the effect can be a unity of purpose across the leadership of the nation's scientific societies.

It is significant in this regard that one of CSSP's standing committees is the Ethics in Science Committee. The committee was formed in the mid-1980s as animal rights groups were attacking the use of animals in research and as legislation to regulate such use was working its way through Congress. A few years later, as discussed earlier in this chapter, Congress was also taking a hard look at general science ethics. Thus, the committee took on a dual purpose: to promote the humane care and use of animals in research and to promote ethical behavior among scientists.

In the latter 1980s, the committee took up a long-term project to encourage scientific societies to develop codes of ethics and, where feasible, mechanisms for enforcing those codes. The committee's first step was, in essence, to update the survey of ethical codes first undertaken by AAAS. The committee issued a call for copies of the codes of those societies that possessed them. The codes were analyzed for content. It was found that they separated into two broad categories: those that were simple, general statements urging members to behave ethically and those that spelled out in detail what was expected of members with respect to particular categories of behavior such as research, treatment of students, and research paper preparation. Further, it was found that societies with journals sometimes had separate ethical mandates with respect to publication in journals. These provisions were likely to be found, not in the ethical code, but in publication manuals or printed in a society's journals.

Two factors seemed to influence the likelihood that a society would have a detailed code of conduct: size and makeup of the membership. Many small societies exist to hold an annual meeting and publish a journal. These societies have become very popular among scientists in recent years because each one focuses on a particular subspecialty of a discipline. There seems to be a trend toward scientists' not joining their major disciplinary society but rather joining the society or societies that fit their subarea of research. These smaller societies tend to take in sufficient dues to cover expenses and little more. They often have no written code or have only a general statement of proper conduct, and fear of insolvency seems to be a motivating factor in avoiding detailed conduct codes.

A society that possesses a detailed code, including enforcement mechanisms, opens itself to lawsuits from two directions. Those who are accused of violating a provision of the code and feel wrongly accused may sue the society for libel or defamation of character. On the other hand, if a society member breaks the code in such a way that others are harmed by the member's actions, and if the society takes no action to punish the member, then those who feel wronged may sue the society for not enforcing its code. Small societies without means to withstand the cost of a lawsuit, even one they might win, have been reluctant to put in place ethical codes that proscribe specific behaviors and carry penalties for violation.

Recognizing this problem, which is one that also applies to journal policies on printing of retractions, the AAAS-ABA National Conference of Lawyers and Scientists has called for legislation to shelter vulnerable entities from lawsuit when they make and enforce policies to stem scientific misconduct (AAAS-ABA, 1989b, p. 32). To date, however, no such legislation has become law, and few societies have produced detailed codes that include specific infractions and sanctions. Only 18 of 62 societies that supplied information for a 1995 update of the CSSP survey had any kind of enforcement mechanism.

The CSSP committee has found that large societies with a particular kind of membership are more likely than other societies to have detailed codes of ethics with mechanisms for enforcement and sanctions for violations. These tend to be societies containing members whose work is likely to have a direct impact on the public, such as those containing both scientists and practitioners or those whose science is very applied. The American Psychological Association (APA), for example, has perhaps the most extensive ethical code. Its membership is composed of researchers and clinicians. The American Academy of Forensic Studies has members whose testimony in court can send a person to prison. The Association for Computing Machinery contains, among other scientists, those who design the programs that make the world's computers function. These are societies that can defend themselves in a court of law, and they have members whose improper actions have had adverse effects on members of the public.

From the information that the committee collected, a profile of characteristics of ethics codes was created. This profile, together with copies of the existing codes of CSSP societies, was sent to scientific societies that did not have ethics codes. The intention was to provide these societies with a template for creating an ethical code and to provide a variety of exemplars as additional guides to those who might be charged with creating an ethical code.

In 1994 and 1995, CSSP updated this effort by taking a more detailed survey and again collecting codes of conduct. The results of the survey and copies of the collected codes were published as *Society Policies on Ethics Issues* (1995). Copies were again distributed to officers of scientific societies to continue encouraging societies without ethics codes to create them. The new survey suggested that previous efforts had been worthwhile. Eight societies of the 62 from which replies to the survey were received indicated they were drawing up codes of ethics or were strengthening their existing code. Nevertheless, as reported in AAAS's *Professional Ethics Report* (Jorgensen, 1995), of the societies replying, only "thirty-six or 58% of these professional societies have some written ethics policies," and "only 8 societies have designated a committee or official to investigate allegations of unethical conduct and have sanctions that can be imposed if a member is found to act unethically. Six additional societies have a committee or official but no sanctions, while 4 more have only some means of imposing sanctions" (p. 1). As Jorgensen added, this means that "less than one-third of the societies have any enforcement dimension in their written ethics policies" (p. 1).

What does it take to have both sanctions and enforcement methods in a code of ethics? One may look to the association with the most complete ethics code (a code that runs to 32 pages, in contrast to most codes' one to two pages in length)—APA (APA, 1992). APA is an organization with 155,000 members. Its ethics activities are managed by its Ethics Office, which contains a staff of 11, including three ethics investigators. The office has responsibility for three major activities: maintenance of ethical conduct by members, education of members in what constitutes ethical conduct, and protection of members of the public with whom psychologists have a professional or scientific relationship. This office forms the support staff for a peer review panel called the Ethics Committee. It is the Ethics Committee that reviews cases and either makes or recommends sanctions. An appeals system is built into this framework. Any recommendation of expulsion or stipulated resignation of a member (the most serious sanctions available to the association) goes automatically to the board of directors of the association for a review, which may result in acceptance, rejection, or modification of the recommendation. The board maintains a Standing Hearing Panel for such reviews.

The typical process works like this. An individual, who need not be a member of the association, makes an informal complaint against another individual. This is termed an inquiry. Ethics Office staff check to see that the inquiry is made with respect to an APA member. If the potential complainee is a member, then the complainant is sent a formal complaint form. That form must be received at the Ethics Office before any further action is taken. If the complainee is not a member, then the complainant is so informed, and suggestions as to an appropriate body to receive the complaint may be offered.

When the Ethics Office receives the complaint form, a formal complaint is deemed to have been filed. To be acceptable, a complaint coming from an APA member must be received by APA within one year of the alleged misconduct or within one year of the time the complainant became aware of the misconduct so long as the misconduct occurred within 10 years of the time the complainant became aware of it. Nonmembers have a five-year time period in which to file the complaint. When the complaint is filed, the complainant must also waive any right to have the information collected by the Ethics Committee subpoenaed for use in some other legal proceeding. This provision prevents complainants from using APA's Ethics Office as a convenient way to gather evidence to use in another legal proceeding. Moreover, making a frivolous complaint is a violation of the ethical code and can result in the Ethics Committee's bringing its own case against the complainant.

The filing triggers a preliminary investigation. Both the complainant and the complainee are informed that the investigation has begun, and the complainee is given a copy of the formal complaint along with the information in support of the complaint. The complainee has 30 days to submit an initial response. If the preliminary investigation indicates that the alleged behavior in question would be a violation of APA's Ethical Principles and Code of Conduct (APA, 1992), then a formal case is opened. A Charge Letter is sent to the complainee detailing the charge and the specific sections of the code alleged to have been violated. The Charge Letter may be updated as new information comes in during the course of the investigation. But the complainee has 30 days in which to file an initial response to the Charge Letter. A complainee may be asked to appear before the Ethics Committee. Although the complainee may hire legal counsel, the complainee is expected to respond personally to requests for information from the committee. Failure to provide such information in the prescribed manner is a violation of the ethical code.

The Ethics Committee meets three times per year to take up cases. If the committee determines that a complaint was not supported by the evidence, then it will close the case. If the evidence supports the complaint, then decisions must be made as to severity of sanction. In order of severity, available sanctions include reprimand, censure, and loss of membership in the association through either expulsion or a stipulated resignation (i.e., a resignation with stipulations attached as to further required actions such as admitting guilt). A reprimand is given when the misconduct is unlikely to have harmed another person or to have substantially harmed the profession. A censure is given if the harm to a person or the profession was not substantial. Expulsion or stipulated resignation is the sanction when the misconduct caused substantial harm to a person or the profession. No member against whom a complaint is brought is permitted to resign from the association while a misconduct investigation is underway.

On its own authority, the committee may reprimand or censure. Upon notice of one of these sanctions, a complainee may request independent adjudication. In this case, an independent adjudication panel is formed from among the membership of the board of directors' Standing Hearing Panel. A slate of six members is offered the complainee, from whom the complainee recommends three individuals to review the case. The complainee's recommendation is honored if at all possible. This panel reviews written information about the case and makes a ruling, which becomes the final adjudication.

The committee may recommend a stipulated resignation. If the complainee agrees to this course of action, then the recommendation is forwarded to the board of directors, together with evidence in support of the recommendation. The complainee must also submit an affidavit of resignation. The board has 180 days to accept the resignation or reject it. If the complainee rejects the offer of resignation, the case goes back to the committee for further action unless the committee has previously determined an alternative sanction in the event of rejection. Board acceptance of the resignation becomes the final action in the case of stipulated resignation.

A recommendation of expulsion results in a formal charge's being brought against the member. A formal charge is a recommendation of expulsion. The formal charge is sent from the committee to the APA board of directors together with information in support of the charge. The complainee has 30 days to respond. Nonresponse during this period is considered acceptance of the expulsion. But within the 30 days, the complainee may request a formal hearing. In such a case, the complainee is provided with a slate of six members of the Standing Hearing Committee, at least one of whom must be a public member. From these, the complainee recommends three individuals to hear the case. The chair of the Ethics Committee argues the case against the complainee but may have legal counsel present. The complainee may, at the complainee's expense, be represented by an attorney at this hearing. All evidence that is relevant and reliable is admissible. In advance, both sides must present lists of intended witnesses, together with documents and rebuttal documents that will be used in the case. The Ethics Committee must show that the charges are supported by a preponderance of the evidence.

The Hearing Committee may accept the charges as recommended by the Ethics Committee. Alternatively, it may recommend a lesser sanction or recommend that the charges be dismissed. Within 30 days of the board's receipt of the Hearing Committee recommendation and supporting and rebuttal information, the complainee may file a written response. If this is filed, then the Ethics Committee has 15 days to respond to the response. These and all previous materials are used by the board to rule on the recommendation. It may adopt the recommendation, or it may not accept the recommendation for any of several reasons: incorrect application of ethical standards, erroneous findings of fact, procedural errors, or excessive sanction or stipulation. Should it not accept the recommendation, the case is remanded to the Ethics Committee, which, at its discretion, may continue its investigation, return the case for rehearing before a new Hearing Committee, or it may readjudicate the matter at the committee level. No case to date has reached this level of readjudication.

Only a few scientific societies are of sufficient size or strength to create and maintain an ethical apparatus as complete as that maintained by APA. The association's cost for these activities was about $950,000 in 1995, an amount that dwarfs the total annual budget of many scientific societies. For our purposes, it must be noted that the preponderance of cases processed through the APA Ethics Office involve violations related to clinical practice. Statistics kept by the association show some fluctuation in caseload from year to year (APA, 1990, 1991, 1992, 1993, 1994, 1995). But it appears that a formal complaint is brought each year against approximately 2 members for every 1,000 members of the association. The absolute number of complaints has risen over the years, but the proportion of formal complaints to the size of the steadily growing membership has changed little. It was 1.8 per 1,000 in 1988, 1.9 per 1,000 in 1993, and 2.3 per 1,000 in 1994. The number of cases that result in some kind of sanction fluctuates each year as well, but it appears that about one-third of cases are dismissed and two-thirds go on to some kind of sanction. In 1994, for example, 26% of cases resulted in censure or reprimand, while 36% resulted in expulsion. Between 1985 and 1994, this most serious sanction was meted out 166 times.

For our purposes, however, a critical question is how often cases of *scientific* misconduct come into what is arguably the best of the scientific society systems for receiving and judging allegations of misconduct. APA's classification scheme for types of complaints includes a category called "inappropriate research, teaching, or administrative practices." It includes the offenses that fall within the definition of scientific misconduct and also such academic misconduct as grading violations and violations of student rights. The scientific misconduct portions of this category account for a very small proportion of total cases seen by the APA Ethics Office each year. Between 1988 and 1994, 12 cases of scientific misconduct were opened. Among the subcategories of such misconduct, there were 7 cases of authorship or assignment of credit disputes, 4 cases of improper research techniques, 1 case of plagiarism, no cases of biasing of data, and no cases of violation of animal research subject welfare.

It should be noted that APA monitors actions taken against its members by other authorities and that when such an action occurs, APA will bring a case against its own member without necessarily having received a formal complaint against the individual in question. This self-policing system is thus very thorough. Nevertheless, it results in the opening of only one to two new cases of scientific misconduct per year.

The low incidence reflected in the APA experience is causing some societies to rethink the purposes and powers of ethical codes. Some are thinking that adoption of mechanisms as comprehensive as those of APA may be unnecessary, especially given the controls that are now in place in academia and government. Clear, informative codes that elicit the commitment of members may suffice. As the Association for Computing Machinery noted in the 1993 revision of its code of ethics,

> ACM and many other societies have had difficulties implementing an ethics review system and came to realize that self-regulation depends mostly on the consensus and commitment of its members to ethical behavior. Now the most important rationale for a code of ethics is an embodiment of a set of commitments of that association's members. Sometimes these commitments are expressed as rules and sometimes as ideals, but the essential social function is to clarify and formally state those ethical requirements that are important to the group as a professional association. (p. 1)

ATTEMPTS TO STANDARDIZE PUBLICATION PRACTICES

Beyond their codes, some societies have taken a second step to diminish misconduct within their memberships. They have attempted to draft journal publication procedures aimed at lessening the likelihood that plagiarized, falsified, or fraudulent research articles will be published. They have also attempted to adopt mechanisms to adequately correct the record when fraudulent material is published. *Attempt* is the operative word here because there remains a good deal of disagreement among journal editors over what controls it is proper to impose. The result is that there are not uniform policies across all science, although some disciplines, most notably biology, have taken significant steps toward standardizing publication practices within a single field.

Editors have brought several arguments against strong, standardized journal policies to minimize publication of fraudulent material: the culture of each discipline is unique, making it impossible and undesirable to have one-size-fits-all publication policies; the publication procedures of journals are not effective in enabling the detection of falsified or fraudulent material absent tip-offs from colleagues or coworkers of a person attempting fraudulent publication (although plagiarism is sometimes discovered through the normal journal peer review process); comprehensive correction of the record when retraction of an article is in order is difficult because indexing and abstracting services may not pick up the retraction and, if they do, may not attach the retraction to the article retracted, rendering the positive effect of retraction questionable; overly burdensome publication requirements rest on the whole research community, even though the problem being addressed is caused by a tiny minority of researchers; publication of controversial material such as a retraction of a paper with multiple authors, only one of which engaged in misconduct, can be grounds for libel suits from those who did not engage in misconduct, and these suits would destroy the journal against which the action was brought; the experience of journal editors who took action against parties who engaged in misconduct is that the cases are complex and have unique features that defy being brought under control by any set of policies.

These and other reservations have played an important role in moving journal editors to proceed cautiously on imposing extensive regulations on those who seek to publish research in their journals. There is not space here to explore each of the reservations that have been raised, but many of these arguments, together with a discussion of the social context in which they arise, are to be found in LaFollette's book *Stealing into Print: Fraud, Plagiarism, and Misconduct in Scientific Publishing* (1992).

The report of a rancorous 1990 workshop on data management in biomedical research, sponsored by the Office of Scientific Integrity Review of the Department of Health and Human Services (U.S. Department of Health and Human Services, 1990), also gives some insight into these reservations. Workshop participants included journal editors and officials from government, universities, scientific societies, and publishing houses. Views on many of these reservations are also raised in the transcript of another lively debate among journal editors on what they should do to help control scientific misconduct. The transcript, though difficult to obtain, is in a report to NSF from the Federation of Behavioral, Psychological, and Cognitive Sciences entitled *Final Report, Grant SBE-9012479: Planning Grant on Preserving Scientific Integrity in the Behavioral Sciences* (Johnson & Null, 1994).

Reservations of editors notwithstanding, there have been at least three attempts to bring a degree of uniformity to misconduct-related policies. One of the earliest came from a coalition of editors who became known as the International Committee of Medical Journal Editors (ICMJE). Before taking this name, the editors met in Vancouver informally in 1978 and drew up a set of guidelines for authors who would submit to their journals. By 1982, the group had taken its current name and had produced a second edition of the uniform requirements for manuscripts submitted to biomedical journals (ICMJE, 1982). The committee supplemented its initial offering with a set of guidelines on authorship (ICMJE, 1985). And in 1988, the committee updated its uniform requirements for the third time, appending to it guidance to editors on retraction of research findings (ICMJE, 1988a).

While the guidelines were of great value in focusing the attention of journal editors on categories of control measures deserving of attention, they were not wholly embraced by the research community or even by biological researchers. Conforming to the guidelines is merely an option available to authors submitting to participating journals. Although editors of more than 300 journals worldwide agreed "to consider for publication manuscripts prepared in accordance with the guidance given in the . . . 'Uniform requirements,'" their agreement to consider such manuscripts "does not imply that they endorse . . . the uniform requirements" (ICMJE, 1988b, p. 404). That caveat reflects the reluctance editors still have to adopt a strict and wide-ranging set of common measures to aid in controlling misconduct. Apparently, some editors felt that the ICMJE guidelines were overly stringent.

Thus, in 1984, the Editorial Policy Committee of the Council of Biology Editors, an association of editors of journals in the life sciences and related areas, decided to make a second attempt at drawing up guidelines. The editors set about finding out what editors themselves would consider reasonable approaches in the major journal policy areas related to misconduct. They first conducted a survey of editors. The several hundred editors who participated were given a series of 19 scenarios based on real cases of misconduct. A number of specific questions were constructed around each scenario. The survey was administered in two parts, with the first 10 scenarios presented in the first round and the last 9 in the second round. The members of the Editorial Policy Committee had expected that journal editors had basically similar views on the issues and that the responses would form a kind of consensus around which guidelines could be built. Not so. A great diversity of views was expressed. It was clear not only that constructing policies that would have universal support would be nearly impossible but that some areas of disagreement cried out for more discussion.

Therefore, in the second part of the project, the committee brought together on three days in October 1988 about 175 editors and others concerned with science ethics. NSF support made the conference possible. It was organized around a number of issue areas where there was wide disagreement as evidenced by editor responses to the survey. Such issues included accountability and authorship, control of research data, handling allegations of fraud, the roles of editors in authorship disputes, use of statistics in research reports, repetitive publication, scientific reporting and legal liability, and uses and limits of peer review.

The result of this long labor by the Council of Biology Editors was a book entitled *Ethics and Policy in Scientific Publication* (Council of Biology Editors, 1990). Rather than the set of consensus guidelines the council first thought it could construct, the book contains recommendations in each of the issue areas that the council explored. But each set of recommendations is preceded by an extensive discussion of the range of views extant on each topic. The first half of the book is built around the original 19 scenarios presented in the council survey. The last half details the conference discussions around each of the issue areas mentioned above. Given the continuing disagreement within the editorial community about how best to approach the misconduct issue, this publication may be as close as editors are going to get to a common approach to the problem.

The efforts of the biology editors were widely covered in the science press and attracted the attention of the Forum on Research Management, a group of midlevel federal managers of science and senior scientists from academia that was formed in the early 1980s as a government-university working group on problems of research management. The group is supported by the Federation of Behavioral, Psychological, and Cognitive Sciences, a coalition of 17 behavioral science societies. The group examined whether the thinking emerging from the Council of Biology Editors could easily be adapted to behavioral and social science journal publication. Forum members had great difficulty finding acceptable ways to make these adaptations. Differences between the publication practices of biology and those of the behavioral and social sciences were too great. But the idea of trying to articulate a uniform set of publication practices across the behavioral and social sciences seemed worth attempting. As a result, the federation sought and received NSF funding to convene a panel of behavioral and social science journal editors, society officials, and individuals familiar with science and the law to explore the feasibility of constructing a uniform set of behavioral and social science publication policies.

The experience of the behavioral and social scientists was remarkably similar to that of the biology editors. After detailed, passionate discussion of each of the major areas where policy decisions to control misconduct might be possible, it was clear that even within the subdisciplines of the behavioral and social sciences, there were differences in research and publication traditions of sufficient magnitude to defy their being brought under a single set of controls.

For example, traditions on availability of raw data for examination on demand showed great variation. (In discussions of how to control misconduct, having raw data available for inspection whenever an allegation is made has often been cited as a deterrent to misconduct.) In areas like political science and sociology, where many researchers rely on the same storehouses of raw data built up through national longitudinal samples preserved and maintained for the use of the whole research community, the sharing of data was hardly a question. In experimental areas like psychology, cognitive science, and neuroscience, however, data might occasionally be shared with colleagues, but preservation of data was the responsibility not of the community as a whole but of the individual or individuals who collected it. Moreover, raw data in these areas could be useless unless accompanied by information to show others how the data were coded and what techniques were used for analysis. Requirements for long-term preservation of such data raised problems as mundane as lack of storage space at universities and lack of financial support for principal investigators to organize and ship raw data to a requestor in a format that would make it accessible.

For physical anthropologists, the problems in this area were completely different. Their raw data might well be rare physical objects such as bones or other artifacts and measurements related to the sites where the objects were collected. While these objects are generally preserved, making them available on demand to editors who might wish to review their authenticity is obviously not an easy task, and field measurements are likely to have to be taken at face value unless examiners are able to visit the sites where the measurements were made. Even then, it might be impossible to verify the authenticity of the measurements.

Such variations of practice were found across many issue areas. The editors determined that uniform guidelines were not the most desirable approach to aid editors in dealing with possible instances of misconduct. Instead, as the editors shared their experience in dealing with actual instances of misconduct, it gradually became their consensus that equipping editors to handle misconduct problems intelligently is more useful than trying to compose rules that only poorly fit the realities of the various subdisciplines.

How might that be accomplished? The editors agreed that when they were new editors they would have appreciated knowing the things they eventually learned through experience. (Several with considerable editorial experience, however, also noted that they had never encountered a problem of alleged misconduct, again making the point that misconduct is a rare phenomenon.) Those who had encountered misconduct agreed that few such cases were simple. Most involve several possible breaches of conduct and are complicated by disagreements among the parties involved as to the facts and their interpretation. There are no "typical" cases of misconduct. The editors decided that providing editors with a handbook of exemplars of real misconduct situations accompanied by accounts of ways the problems were actually solved and, perhaps, of mistakes that should have been avoided is the most effective way to help editors fulfill their responsibilities when allegations of misconduct arise.

The editors themselves did not compose such a handbook, and to date it appears that no book precisely fitting their recommendation is available. The Council of Biology Editors book could be considered a partial response, since the scenarios around which the book is built are adaptations of real cases. At least one other book containing case materials has been written. It is called *Research Ethics: Cases and Materials* (Penslar, 1995). This book, however, is aimed at undergraduate and graduate students in science ethics courses, not at working editors. The cases are hypothetical and lack the multilayered quality that characterizes real misconduct cases. The book is meant to stir discussion, so it also does not contain descriptions of how real problems in the area at issue were actually resolved. It is fair to say that the research community has not completed its discussion of how best to employ journal editors in the control of misconduct.

CONCLUSION

Scientists, and the scientific and academic societies with which they associate themselves, have undertaken a sometimes painful odyssey over the past 15 years to discover how to ensure the integrity of scientists and their practices. This journey began in denial, and reservations about the volume of misconduct requiring control are still voiced regularly. Nevertheless, scientific freedom depends on public support, and public support depends on trust. The need to restore that trust has necessitated addressing the problem, regardless of the possibly low incidence of misconduct. Academic associations were among the first to respond. They provided universities with procedures to receive and process allegations of misconduct. Scientific societies have helped to build the knowledge base that allows the scientific community to respond to misconduct. They have also facilitated an ongoing dialogue about misconduct. The umbrella societies for multiple disciplines and multiple scientific societies have taken measures to see that increased numbers of scientific societies have codes of ethics for members, and that, where appropriate, the societies have means for enforcing provisions of the code. The societies not only have looked outward and aided others in controlling misconduct but also have looked inward at their own misconduct control procedures. A number of societies whose members' work can have direct impact on the public have adopted detailed codes of ethics and have created control mechanisms, including sanctions for those who breach the ethical code. Finally, scientific societies publish many of the country's research journals, and associations representing several disciplines have made attempts at creating uniform policies to control misconduct. Differences among the sciences have so far made it impossible to standardize journal policies. Out of the attempt to construct such policies, however, has come some agreement on the general areas that need to be addressed, and this, in turn, has produced policies for individual journals that go some of the distance toward minimizing publication of fraudulent material. Societies and the scientists they contain have taken many steps on the journey to restore trust in science. They also understand that the journey is not complete.

References

American Association for the Advancement of Science–American Bar Association National Conference of Lawyers and Scientists. (1988). *Project on scientific fraud and misconduct: Report on Workshop Number One.* Washington, DC: American Association for the Advancement of Science.

American Association for the Advancement of Science–American Bar Association National Conference of Lawyers and Scientists. (1989a). *Project on scientific fraud and misconduct: Report on Workshop Number Two.* Washington, DC: American Association for the Advancement of Science.

American Association for the Advancement of Science–American Bar Association National Conference of Lawyers and Scientists. (1989b). *Project on scientific fraud and misconduct: Report on Workshop Number Three.* Washington, DC: American Association for the Advancement of Science.

American Psychological Association. (1990). Report of the Ethics Committee: 1988. *American Psychologist, 45,* 873–874.

American Psychological Association. (1991). Report of the Ethics Committee: 1989 and 1990. *American Psychologist, 46,* 750–757.

American Psychological Association. (1992). Ethical principles of psychologists and code of conduct. *American Psychologist, 47,* 1597–1628.

American Psychological Association. (1993). Report of the Ethics Committee, 1991 and 1992. *American Psychologist, 48,* 811–820.

American Psychological Association. (1994). Report of the Ethics Committee. *American Psychologist, 49,* 659–666.

American Psychological Association. (1995). Report of the Ethics Committee, 1994. *American Psychologist, 50,* 706–713.

Arkin, H. R. (1985a). Academic dismissals: Due process, Part 1. *Journal of the American Medical Association, 254,* 2463–2466.

Arkin, H. R. (1985b). Academic dismissals: Due process, Part 2. *Journal of the American Medical Association, 254,* 2653–2656.

Association for Computing Machinery. (1993). ACM code of ethics and professional conduct: Using the new ACM code of ethics in decision making. *Communications of the ACM, 36*(2), 1–9.
Association of American Medical Colleges. (1982). *The maintenance of high ethical standards in the conduct of research.* Washington, DC: Author.
Association of American Medical Colleges. (1990). *Framework for institutional policies and procedures to deal with misconduct in research.* Washington, DC: Author.
Association of American Universities. (1982). *Report of the Association of American Universities Committee on the Integrity of Research.* Washington, DC: Author.
Association of American Universities. (1989). *Framework for institutional policies and procedures to deal with fraud in research.* Washington, DC: Author.
Braxton, J., & Bayer, A. (1996). Personal experiences of research misconduct and the response of individual academic scientists. *Science, Technology, and Human Values, 21,* 198–213.
Broad, W. J. (1982). Harvard delays in reporting fraud. *Science, 215,* 478–482.
Chalk, R. (1978, January). Scientific society involvement in whistleblowing. *Science, Technology, and Human Values, 3,* pp. 47–51.
Chalk, R., Frankel, M., & Chafer, S. (1981). *Professional ethics activities in science and engineering societies.* Washington, DC: American Association for the Advancement of Science.
Chubin, D. E., & Hackett, E. J. (1990). *Peerless science: Peer review and U.S. science policy.* New York: State University of New York Press.
Cohen, J. (1995). The culture of credit. *Science, 268,* 1706–1711.
Commission on Research Integrity. (1996). *Integrity and misconduct in research.* Washington, DC: U.S. Department of Health and Human Services.
Committee on the Conduct of Science. (1989). *On being a scientist.* Washington, DC: National Academy of Sciences.
Council of Biology Editors. (1990). *Ethics and policy in scientific publication.* Bethesda, MD: Council of Biology Editors.
Council of Scientific Society Presidents. (1995). *Society policies on ethics issues.* Washington, DC: Author.
Cournand, A. (1977). The code of the scientist and its relationship to ethics. *Science, 198,* 699–705.
Cozzens, S. E. (1989). *Social control and multiple discovery in science: The opiate receptor case.* New York: State University of New York Press.
Edsall, J. T. (1981). Two aspects of scientific responsibility. *Science, 212,* 11–14.
Fielder, J. (1992, March). Issues in ethics: Misbehavior in science. *Engineering in Medicine and Biology,* pp. 71, 72.
Fraud in biomedical research: Hearings before the Subcommittee on Investigations and Oversight of the House Committee on Science and Technology, 97th Cong., 1st Sess. (1981).
Fraud in NIH grant programs: Hearings before the Subcommittee on Oversight and Investigations of the House Committee on Energy and Commerce, 101st Cong., 1st Sess. (1989).

Grouse, L. D. (1982). Dealing with alleged fraud in medical research. *Journal of the American Medical Association, 248*, 1637–1638.
International Committee of Medical Journal Editors. (1982). Uniform requirements for manuscripts submitted to biomedical journals. *British Medical Journal, 284*, 1766–1770.
International Committee of Medical Journal Editors. (1985). Guidelines on authorship. *British Medical Journal, 291*, 722.
International Committee of Medical Journal Editors. (1988a). Uniform requirements for manuscripts submitted to biomedical journals. *Annals of Internal Medicine, 108*, 258–265.
International Committee of Medical Journal Editors. (1988b). Uniform requirements for manuscripts submitted to biomedical journals. *British Medical Journal, 296*, 401–405.
Is science for sale? Conflicts of interest vs. the public interest: Hearings before the Subcommittee on Human Resources and Intergovernmental Relations of the House Committee on Governmental Operations, 101st Cong., 1st Sess. (1989).
Johnson, D., & Null, C. (1994). *Final report, Grant SBE-9012479: Planning grant on preserving scientific integrity in the behavioral sciences.* Washington, DC: Federation of Behavioral, Psychological and Cognitive Sciences.
Jorgensen, A. (1995). Survey shows policies on ethical issues still lacking enforcement mechanisms. *Professional Ethics Report, 8*(1), 1, 6.
Kilbourne, B. K., & Kilbourne, M. T. (Eds.). (1983). *The dark side of science.* San Francisco: Pacific Division, American Association for the Advancement of Science.
Koshland, D. E. (1987, January 9). Fraud in science. *Science, 235*, 141.
LaFollette, M. C. (1992). *Stealing into print: Fraud, plagiarism, and other misconduct in scientific publishing.* Berkeley: University of California Press.
Maintaining the integrity of scientific research: Hearings before the Subcommittee on Investigations and Oversight of the House Committee on Science, Space, and Technology, 101st Cong., 1st Sess. (1989).
McBride, G. (1974). The Sloan-Kettering affair: Could it have happened anywhere? *Journal of the American Medical Association, 229*, 1391–1410.
Office of Scientific Integrity Review. (1990). *Data management in biomedical research: Report of a workshop April 1990.* Washington, DC: U.S. Department of Health and Human Services.
Palca, J. (1992). Lead researcher confronts accusers in public hearing. *Science, 256*, 437–438.
Penslar, R. L. (1995). *Research ethics: Cases and materials.* Bloomington: Indiana University Press.
Pigman, W., & Carmichael, E. B. (1950). An ethical code for scientists. *Science,* pp. 643–647.
Richards, E. P., III (1992, March). Scientific misconduct, Part 2: What are your constitutional rights? *Engineering in Medicine and Biology,* pp. 73–75.
Richards, E. P., III, & Walter, C. (1992, June). Scientific misconduct, Part 3: Standards for scientific record keeping. *Engineering in Medicine and Biology,* pp. 88–90.

Scientific fraud: Hearings before the Subcommittee on Oversight and Investigations of the House Committee on Energy and Commerce, 101st Cong., 1st Sess. (1989).

Scientific fraud, Part 2: Hearings before the Subcommittee on Oversight and Investigations of the House Committee on Energy and Commerce, 101st Cong., 2nd Sess. (1990).

Sigma Xi, The Scientific Research Society. (1986). *Honor in science.* New Haven, CT: Author.

Swazey, J. P., Anderson, M. S., & Lewis, K. S. (1993). Ethical problems in academic research. *American Scientist, 81,* 542–553.

U.S. Department of Health and Human Services. (1988, September 19). Public health service announcement of development of regulations protecting against scientific fraud or misconduct; request for comments. *Federal Register, 53*(181), 36344–36350.

U.S. House of Representatives, Committee on Government Operations. (1990). *Are scientific misconduct and conflicts of interest hazardous to our health?* (House Rep. No. 101–688). Washington, DC: Government Printing Office.

Walter, C., & Richards, E. P., III. (1992, September). Scientific misconduct, Part 4: The costs of hubris. *Engineering in Medicine and Biology,* pp. 77–79.

Woolf, P. K. (1988, Fall). Deception in scientific research. *Jurimetrics Journal, 29,* 67–95.

Zuckerman, H. (1984). Norms and deviant behavior in science. *Science, Technology, and Human Values, 9,* 7–13.

Zurer, P. (1993, June 14). Scientific misconduct: Appeals hearing probes AIDS virus case. *Chemical and Engineering News,* p. 6.

Zurer, P. (1994, March 21). Chemistry panel weighs misconduct cases. *Chemical and Engineering News,* p. 18.

Zurer, P. (1995, July 3). Commission on Research Integrity reshaping definition of misconduct. *Chemical and Engineering News,* pp. 14, 15.

CHAPTER THREE

Research Universities and Scientific Misconduct: History, Policies, and the Future

Nicholas H. Steneck

At the 1981 congressional hearings on fraud in biomedical research, then-Representative Albert Gore, Jr., asked Philip Felig, the senior mentor in the Vijay Soman case at Yale, "Is it your opinion that the in place system of checks at Yale worked satisfactory?" Felig responded that it was not: "We didn't know how to react. I didn't know how to react at that point, and obviously, we didn't react properly" (*Fraud in Biomedical Research*, 1981, p. 104). Yale was at the time no better or worse off than other universities. Despite growing evidence of misconduct in science during the 1970s, as the decade of the 1980s began, the nation's research universities had not developed or even thought much about scientific misconduct policies. Today they have. In this chapter I briefly trace the events that have seen the nation's major research universities adopt scientific misconduct policies, describe in general terms the forms these policies have taken, and conclude with recommendations for the future. Overall, the story told is one of slow acceptance of responsibility for scientific misconduct on the part of universities, with the agenda for policy formation being set largely by outside forces and individuals.

A DECADE OF RESPONSE, 1981–1991

In retrospect, it now seems almost self-evident that scientific misconduct policies are not only a good idea but a necessity. As university after university learned in the 1970s and 1980s, cases involving scientific misconduct were not covered by the general rules governing academic conduct. Evidence is hard to collect. Experts are needed for investigations and adjudication.

The standards for judging misconduct vary from field to field. Self-investigations raise conflicts of interest.

Though there is general agreement that the most extreme form of scientific misconduct—fraud in research—cannot be tolerated, detecting, proving, and adjudicating research fraud is a complex and difficult task. Having rules for proceeding and standards for judging in place is, if nothing else, a prudent step. This is not the way most scientists and university policy makers saw this issue in the mid-1970s when William Summerlin's "painted" mice were discovered by the press (Hixson, 1976). That anyone in science would deliberately fake the results of an experiment shocked many researchers, prompting some to question their most cherished beliefs about the way science operates. The biologist Peter Medawar (1976) later admitted that when he first saw corneal grafts that Summerlin claimed to have performed on a rabbit, he did not exercise the skepticism that he should have as a scientist: "I could not believe that this rabbit had received a graft of any kind . . . because the pattern of blood vessels in the ring around the cornea was in no way disturbed. Nevertheless I simply lacked the moral courage to say at the time that I thought we were the victims of a hoax or confidence trick" (p. 60). However, the quick and efficient way in which Summerlin was caught reinforced other cherished beliefs about science, particularly the belief in its ability to police and regulate itself. More than any other factor, the widespread belief that error and fraud could be detected and corrected by the scientific community explains why scientists and the policy makers they advised on university campuses felt and have continued to feel no pressing need to institute policies and procedures for dealing with scientific misconduct.

The belief in self-policing and self-regulation in science was not limited to scientists or university policy makers. In by far the best and most penetrating analysis of scientific misconduct written before the 1980s, sociologist Harriet Zuckerman (1977) carefully reviewed both historical and contemporary evidence for insights into the causes, extent, and consequences of scientific misconduct. She described, in detail that is still useful for policy making today, the complexities of the behaviors of scientists and of the established norms in science. But she also firmly believed that science could police its own conduct and had done so in the past. While others were wondering whether this might not change with the new pressures being put on scientists by competition and commercialization, Zuckerman (1977) speculated that self-policing and self-regulation within science would strengthen with increased competition.

> Our analysis of deviant behavior and social control in science has turned up an interesting hypothesis, . . . that the greater the socially induced pressure

for deviant behavior, the greater the likelihood that it will be detected....
The intense competition for making original scientific contributions—the
"race for priority"—and the peer recognition that comes with it created
pressures for deviant behavior.... But that same intense competition as a
system-property also focuses the attention of scientists on particular problems, intensifies their critical review of others' work in the field, and encourages efforts to check important new truth claims through replication. This
should increase the chances that any deviant behavior which does occur will
be identified. (p. 131)

For those who accepted the belief in professional self-regulation, the need for new policies and procedures, particularly ones imposed by the government, was not at all evident.

Scientists and university policy makers also had other pressing problems to confront in the late 1970s. A decade of concern about the use of humans and animals in research, about the implications of the new recombinant DNA technology, and about the seeming inability of science to solve society's pressing social and environmental problems produced other regulatory concerns for universities and their research programs (Handler, 1980; Wuiff, 1979). Faced with the need to establish IRBs (institutional review boards) for human subjects research, oversight committees for animal research, and recombinant DNA boards, and faced with shifting research priorities, economic dislocations caused by the energy crisis, and other pressing issues, it is understandable that universities did not rush to regulate a system that most thought was already working when the Summerlin case became news. As time has gone on, however, the lack of action has become more and more difficult to understand.

In 1980 two new reports of major scientific misconduct once again challenged the view that universities could effectively detect and adjudicate scientific misconduct. The first, the Elias Alsabati case, cast serious doubt on the efficacy of the peer review system. It was eventually discovered that Alsabati had published over 80 plagiarized or otherwise fraudulent articles before being detected (Broad, 1980a, 1980b, 1980c; Broad & Wade, 1982, pp. 38–59). The second, the Vijay Soman case, raised questions about the way Yale University had handled its investigation and conveyed information to Columbia University, which hired Felig (Soman's senior mentor) away from Yale while the investigation was in process (Broad, 1980a, 1980b; Broad & Wade, 1982, pp. 161–180). The visibility and troubling nature of both the events and charges surrounding these and other cases led to the March 1981 congressional hearings (*Fraud in Biomedical Research*, 1981).

The 1981 hearings unfortunately did not provide clear guidance for universities. Felig, as noted, and others did suggest that university misconduct policies needed to be better defined. However, no one claimed that misconduct was rampant in scientific research. Indeed, from Zuckerman's (1977) article on deviant behavior in science through the 1981 hearings and continuing to the present day, two assumptions are common in most discussions of scientific misconduct: (1) there are no reliable estimates of the frequency of misconduct in science, and (2) whatever the numbers might be, scientific misconduct is rare. Moreover, the few reported cases of misconduct did not shake the implicit faith of most scientists and policy makers in the capacity of science to detect and to deal with misconduct. The president of the National Academy of Sciences, Philip Handler, told Congress, "The system succeeds in policing itself" (*Fraud in Biomedical Research*, 1981, p. 21). In anticipation of a possible congressional mandate for the regulation of research, National Institutes of Health (NIH) director Donald Fredrickson stated, "None is necessary, for the natural sciences contain ultimate correctives for any debasement of the knowledge derived from research" (*Fraud in Biomedical Research*, 1981, p. 39). Sociologist Patricia Woolf, though admitting that her views had changed somewhat as a result of the hearings, nevertheless concluded that "the scientific community has a number of built-in controls—negative sanctions and positive rewards—which are a constant reminder to scientists to adhere to rigorous standards" (*Fraud in Biomedical Research*, 1981, p. 344). Thus, as late as 1981, it was still being argued that misconduct in research was an isolated problem that could be kept in check through scientists' self-regulation.

Over the next few years the belief in the inherent ability of scientists to protect their own integrity began to erode, spurred on by another prominent misconduct case at a major university, the John Darsee case at Harvard (Culliton, 1983; Stewart & Feder, 1987), and the publication of Broad and Wade's controversial book *Betrayers of the Truth* (1982). As it did, attention turned to universities as the institutions best suited to monitor research integrity. At the 1981 hearings, NIH director Fredrickson, in rejecting the notion that government could perform this monitoring function, noted: "The universities have always been primarily responsible for a scientist's access to laboratories and other resources maintained for the scientific community. Control of their staff appointments, tenure, and promotions is the real power of the university for the preservation of scientific ethics. The principal responsibility goes along with the ultimate power" (*Fraud in Biomedical Research*, 1981, p. 37).

The shift in focus from science and scientists as the prime monitors of integrity to a recognition of the responsibilities of universities was picked up in a number of reports over the next few years. The Association of American Universities (AAU) recommended in 1982 that "all institutions prepare policies which state clearly the expectations for high standards of ethical behavior of those involved in research." The same year, the Association of American Medical Colleges (AAMC, 1982) concluded that "despite the self-correcting nature of science ... instances of research fraud have occurred and faculties should explore additional measures to decrease further the likelihood that a researcher will risk the odds and commit fraud" (p. 2). The "faculties" referred to in the AAMC statement were primarily university faculties. The additional measures included adopting definitions of, instituting mechanisms for dealing with, and taking steps to discourage scientific misconduct.

At least three justifications were advanced for more university involvement in monitoring and/or fostering research integrity. First, on a practical level, those who were involved in misconduct investigations, such as Felig, knew that policies and procedures were best defined before, not during, an investigation. Second, as Fredrickson had argued, universities were in the best position to monitor research integrity and could reasonably be said to have a responsibility to do so. Third, if these positive arguments were not compelling enough, by the mid-1980s it was becoming apparent that if universities did not act, the government would. For scientists such as Herman Wigodsky (1984), who believed that "the research community and the institutions must, at all costs, protect the intramural and extramural scientific communities from politicization," there was no doubt that "the scientific community must look to policing itself and must demand and encourage the high standards of personal integrity required to carry out research using the scientific method" (p. 5).

The reports, justifications, and admonitions of the early 1980s had minimum impact on the nation's research universities. The University of Michigan appointed the Task Force on Integrity in Scholarship in late 1983, which drafted guidelines for a code of research ethics and recommended balancing policing with education (Steneck, 1984; University of Michigan, 1984).[1] Stanford president Donald Kennedy sent a brief memo on authorship and research ethics to his faculty in 1985 (Stanford University, 1985). However, when Congress once again addressed the issue of scientific misconduct in October 1985, few universities had adopted explicit scientific misconduct policies, and research ethics was still not a major topic for discussions on campuses (Greene et al., 1985).[2] Congress therefore stepped in and took the lead. The 1985 Health Research Extension Act (Pub. L. No. 99–158) and subsequent legislation relating to the NSF (NSF, 1987) finally required universities to (1) develop mechanisms for dealing with scientific misconduct and (2) report activities relating to scientific misconduct to the federal government.

Over the past 11 years (since 1985), there has been a marked upturn in scholarly and professional discussions of research ethics and in related professional activities. By March 1989, most of the major and about half of the middle-range research universities reportedly had adopted scientific misconduct policies (Kusserow, 1989).[3] A much smaller percentage of universities (no estimates are available at the present time) have undertaken systematic efforts to foster research integrity (AAMC, 1992). Whatever one thinks of these activities, the fact remains that they have been and probably continue to be driven largely by the NSF and Public Health Service requirements, which are themselves the product of congressional action. This is not to say that there is not genuine concern and sincere action at the university level, but the impetus for action has largely been external, due even today to the widespread feeling that "if it ain't broke, don't fix it."

POLICIES AND PROCEDURES

The "if-it-ain't-broke-don't-fix-it" argument was not the only reason that universities were slow to adopt scientific misconduct policies. Many also felt that "if it is broke, it can easily be fixed." When asked about the need for misconduct policies, one survey respondent answered, "My assumption is that were a case of fraud to appear, we would handle it in a sensible and prompt manner." Similar optimism is evident in the comment, "We will decide on a plan of action when a problem exists" (Greene et al., 1985, p. 208). Just as there has been and continues to be great confidence in the ability of science to police itself, so too there has been confidence that universities could easily handle scientific misconduct investigations in a prompt, efficient manner if called upon to do so.[4] Some of the earliest university policies were therefore little more than simple statements that investigations should be undertaken in the event of a report of scientific misconduct. The procedures established in the 1982 Yale University Policy Statement on Collaborative Research required that

1. [Suspicion of misconduct] be reported immediately to the Dean of the School or faculty concerned;
2. the Dean ... investigate the matter sufficiently to conclude whether or not there are reasonable grounds to believe that the allegations may be true;
3. if ... there are no reasonable grounds to believe that the allegations may be true, [the Dean] will terminate the inquiry into the matter;
4. if ... the allegations may be true [but sanctions would not likely be severe], the Dean will pursue the matter in accordance with the disciplinary proceedings applicable to the School;
5. if ... the allegations may be true and ... would warrant ... severe sanctions, the Dean shall ... recommend to the President of the University that the University Tribunal be convoked to assume jurisdiction over the matter; and,
6. if the President decides to convoke the University Tribunal, the matter will be dealt with in accordance with the regular Procedures and Regulations of the University Tribunal. (Yale University, 1982, p. 63)[5]

Notwithstanding their simplicity, the early policies established some important principles—in the case of the Yale policy, (a) that a university officer be assigned responsibility for pursuing allegations of scientific misconduct, (b) that charges or allegations be assessed before instituting a full investigation, and (c) that some formally charged body be given responsibility for carrying out investigations and reaching conclusions (adjudication). The Yale policy also reflected the understandable inclination on the part of universities to integrate new scientific misconduct policies with existing academic misconduct policies (see also Emory University, 1983; Harvard University, 1983). However, the early policies left a great deal of room for error and mishandling, which in turn led quickly to recommendations for more comprehensive policies.[6]

For understandable reasons, universities responded to these and other recommendations as well as the various federal mandates in different ways. Some universities still have remarkably brief policies; others have attempted to spell out in great detail the criteria for judging scientific misconduct and the procedures for its investigation. No one policy can be said to be "right" or "wrong," since correctness depends to large extent on local context. Centralization and strict definitions may make sense on some campuses, whereas decentralization and general guidelines may work well on others. Nonetheless, some basic considerations and fundamental principles cannot be ignored in formulating policies and procedures for dealing with scientific misconduct.

Guiding Principles

In theory, there is nothing particularly complicated or mysterious about scientific misconduct investigations. They usually begin with allegations, which need to be assessed. If the assessment leads to a reasonable suspicion of misconduct, the case must then be investigated and finally adjudicated. Because careers can hang in the balance, fairness, due process, and confidentiality are important. A reasonable misconduct policy is therefore one that makes provisions for (1) an initial assessment (more commonly referred to as an inquiry), followed by (2) an investigation and (3) some form of adjudication. The accused must be provided an opportunity to know and confront the evidence. The accuser, commonly known as the "whistleblower," needs to be protected from unjust retaliation. Policies and procedures that meet these objectives provide the essential ingredients for a scientific misconduct investigation. (For a brief summary of these principles, see Mishkin, 1988.)

University scientific misconduct policies generally do not begin with a compressive or explicit list of guiding principles. More commonly they open with general statements about the rarity of scientific misconduct and the need for high standards of integrity in scientific research. Many also describe in more or less detail the normative responsibilities of researchers (Emory University, 1991; Harvard University, 1988; Indiana University, 1989). Although general normative statements and lofty goals are important for setting an overall tone for thinking about integrity, they do not provide the type of realistic guidance that is needed by individuals or committees when they undertake misconduct investigations. Much more useful are explicit statements such as California Institute of Technology's (1989) notice that "the institute must act swiftly and decisively, while affording maximum possible protection both to the 'whistle blower' (complainant) and the accused (respondent)" (p. 1).

An explicit list of practical guiding principles to supplement general summaries of ideals, such as the ones in the Johns Hopkins University's *Policy on Integrity in Research* (1988), would strengthen most misconduct policies. The Hopkins policy draws attention to three crucial actions for promoting integrity:

1. Clearly define individuals' responsibilities in the performance of research.
2. Inform . . . faculty, students and staff of their responsibility.
3. Develop mechanisms to maintain an atmosphere that encourages integrity in research, [to] include: the open exchange of ideas; the free discussion of the pressures that may threaten integrity in research; an emphasis on the quality rather than the quantity of research; and promoting the realization of the interdependence of faculty, students and staff. (pp. 929–930)

Similarly, the "procedures" that follow also focus intensively on key areas and guiding principles, which are articulated under (1) clear reporting, (2) confidentiality, (3) inquiry versus investigation, (4) notification, (5) the role of general counsel, (6) allegations that cut across units, (7) protecting informants, (8) disciplinary actions, and (9) appeals (Johns Hopkins University, 1988, pp. 930–932). Sketching out in specific terms the thinking and obligations that inform scientific misconduct policies is arguably the most important step in the formulation of a responsible policy.

Definitions

The fairness and success of any misconduct investigation rest on definitions. Researchers must know the standards to which they are held accountable and, if they are accused of misconduct, the grounds for basing charges. They must be forewarned what constitutes "misconduct." Reaching consensus on definitions for misconduct can prove to be the most difficult task for any policy maker. Not unexpectedly, universities have reached very different conclusions about definitions. Some have construed misconduct narrowly, focusing on intent and deception: "Research fraud is the intentional falsification or fabrication of data or results, plagiarism, misconduct in the application of research procedures so as to bias results, or other deceptive research or reporting practices" (Johns Hopkins University, 1988, p. 929). Others have adopted broader definitions, which include the abuse of confidentiality; failure to comply with federal, state, and local regulations; dishonesty in publication; property violations; retaliation against whistleblowers; failure to report unethical research practices; and "other practices that seriously deviate from those that are commonly accepted within the scientific and academic community for proposing, conducting, or reporting research" (Michigan State University, 1988, p. 965; Northwestern University, 1989, p. 2; see also University of California, Los Angeles, 1988, p. 892).

The wording of definitions depends on how much or how little a university is trying to achieve through its misconduct policy. At a minimum, every university that accepts federal funds for research must comply with federal regulations, which means accepting responsibility for the areas covered by both NSF and Public Health Service scientific misconduct policies (NSF, 1987; U.S. Public Health Service, 1989). These policies agree that falsification, fabrication, and plagiarism are misconduct. NSF (1991) adds "other acts which seriously deviate" and "retaliation against whistleblowers" (pp. 27–28). In one way or another, the broader focus of the NSF regulations must be encompassed in a university's policies, although it is not necessary that universities do so exclusively through their misconduct policies.

In addition to complying with the federal misconduct regulations, universities must ensure (1) the fiscal responsibility of all research projects; (2) compliance with federal regulations for the use of animals, human subjects, recombinant DNA technologies, and hazardous chemicals; and (3) fair employment practices. Again, there is no need to include these assurances in scientific misconduct policies if they are covered in other policies or procedures.[7]

Finally, most scientific misconduct policies make distinctions between true "misconduct" on the one hand and "honest error," "genuine scientific disagreement," and "sloppy science" on the other. The point of these distinctions is to reduce the possibility that researchers will be penalized for taking intellectual chances or simply being "human"—that is, making honest errors.

Although the distinction between intentional and unintentional error is important, universities must not lose sight of the fact that they have some responsibility to oversee quality. A researcher who consistently fails to follow simple normative rules for responsible research, such as keeping careful records, supervising personnel adequately, or maintaining a clean laboratory, cannot be immune to sanctions forever. Sloppiness or carelessness may well not be appropriate targets for scientific misconduct policies, narrowly considered, but they must be addressed in some way if universities take seriously their responsibilities as custodians of public funds.

The importance of intention is perhaps the most difficult part of any definition of misconduct. There is widespread agreement that deliberate acts to deceive (faking the results of experiments) are wrong and that "honest errors" (making a mistake in the addition or transcription of data) are not. Less agreement exists on how to draw lines between the extremes. When, for example, does inadequate citation become plagiarism? Photocopies, electronic scanning, and computers make it easy to move words from a published article to a manuscript in preparation. Is the researcher who loses track of the source of some specific number of words guilty of scientific misconduct or, more pointedly, of "research fraud"? It is unlikely that any definition of scientific misconduct, no matter how carefully constructed, will ever fully clarify cases that fall in the debatable areas of scientific integrity.

Inquiries or the Assessment of Allegations

Scientific misconduct can be clear-cut and obvious. Something is wrong if two articles that are substantially the same have been published under two different names. It may not be immediately apparent which of the authors has plagiarized the other or whether some other act of deception is taking place, but it would require no more than a few minutes of informal inquiry or assessment to conclude that a fuller investigation is needed. Moreover, in cases such as this there is no need for a third party, the whistle-blower, to make formal allegations. The evidence itself is the source of the allegations.

In cases in which the evidence is not clear-cut and obvious, universities must make two important decisions: first, who is responsible for the assessment of allegations, and second, how deeply that person or an appointed committee should go into the allegations before making a decision to dismiss them or recommend a formal inquiry. As with definitions, there is no single best way of making these decisions.

The decentralized collegial atmosphere that most universities try to maintain inclines toward decentralized reporting to the person who is directly responsible but one step removed from the actions that are being questioned—that is, not the researcher whose practices are being questioned but that person's supervisor. At Indiana University, "wherever possible, complaints should be addressed to the person directly above the respondent, rather than to officials higher in the university administration" (Indiana University, 1989, p. 12). Department chairs, project directors, and deans are in this position and are named in many policies as the appropriate persons to receive and evaluate allegations, sometimes under their own direction but more often with guidance and advice from a higher administrative authority, such as a vice president/chancellor for research or academic affairs, or the university counsel.

However reporting is handled, care needs to be taken to avoid conflicts of interest. For personal or professional reasons, a department chair could be reluctant to accept allegations of misconduct about a senior colleague and longtime friend brought by a recently hired junior researcher or research assistant. For this reason, many university scientific misconduct policies require some degree of disinterestedness and/or assign the responsibility for misconduct assessments and investigations to a designated officer or committee. At the University of Colorado, "All persons having knowledge of misconduct in research ... are encouraged to submit allegations of research misconduct to the Chair of the Standing Committee [on Research Misconduct]" (University of Colorado, 1990, p. 4; see also University of Chicago, 1986, p. 912). More and more universities are appointing designated "misconduct officers" to fill this role.

Many competing interests come into play during the assessment phase of any misconduct case. Some universities require that allegations be submitted in writing to help avoid frivolous charges. In doing so, they run the risk of compromising the confidentiality (which could means the careers) of informants or of failing to pursue potential problems. It is important that assessments be carried out quickly, particularly if the allegations have not been kept confidential, but not too quickly to permit a fair assessment of the allegations. Sometimes outside experts need to be consulted, again at the risk of compromising confidentiality and sometimes of anticipating activities that are more appropriately undertaken in investigations. As with definitions, no set of rules will ever clarify all situations, making it important once again to focus on guiding principles rather than detailed rules and procedures.

Investigations and Adjudication

An investigation is the formal review of allegations or charges for the purpose of determining the facts that will be used in making decisions about guilt or innocence. Adjudication is the process of weighing the facts to reach conclusions and to decide on appropriate responses. At this stage, law and formal rules take precedence over the less formal processes associated with assessments, although obviously basic rights, due process, privacy, and so on have bearing on all aspects of a scientific misconduct case. A case that may have begun as a brief office conversation slowly grows into an assessment, an investigation, and eventually, if the parties cannot agree on a resolution, a pointed and sometimes bitter adjudication.

Given the seriousness of scientific misconduct investigations and their potential impact on the careers of the persons accused, fairness and due process are obviously important. Common sense suggests that the person being accused of misconduct must be aware of the charges and of the evidence on which they are based and have a reasonable opportunity to respond. In practice, following the dictates of common sense (or law) can be difficult. It takes time to assemble evidence, sometimes making it impossible to provide a definitive list of charges at the beginning of an investigation. Universities have adopted different policies on the role of legal counsels in investigations. Some forbid their presence until decisions have been reached and appeals and/or hearings begin. Others allow them to be present to advise but not question. Others allow full participation.

Impartial and knowledgeable investigation committees need to be charged, and outside experts may have to be consulted or hired. If human subjects or animals are involved, their welfare needs to be reviewed. Consideration may have to be given to impounding data if they are not volunteered. Timely reports must be made to the government if federal funds are involved. Investigations should be careful and efficient, meeting deadlines but allowing reasonable time for responses.

In investigations and adjudication, universities need to be mindful of and responsive to the fact that they have conflicting interests. They have obligations to the person or persons accused of misconduct and to the accusers if both are university employees. They have obligations to government (state and federal) and to the public at large. And perhaps most important, they have obligations to themselves to maintain public reputations, active research programs, and good internal working relationships.

Whether universities can successfully manage their conflicting interests in scientific misconduct investigations has been questioned. The way to do so has been debated at length in many meetings, reports, and publications (American Association for the Advancement of Science [AAAS], 1991; AAAS & AAMC 1992; Goodstein, 1991; Institute of Medicine, 1989; Kusserow, 1989; LaFollette, 1988; Littlejohn & Matthews, 1989; Mishkin, 1988; National Academy of Sciences, 1992; *Scientific Fraud and Misconduct,* 1988). The result has been a marked increase in the sophistication (and perhaps also fairness and efficiency) with which universities handle misconduct investigations. The major research universities today have policies and procedures for handling scientific misconduct; a decade ago they did not. These policies and procedures are not, however, foolproof. They do not and cannot resolve all difficulties that arise in the course of scientific misconduct investigations. And in the final analysis, intangibles such as commitment and understanding may have as much to do with how well a university is able to deal with scientific misconduct as formal policies and procedures—intangibles that are difficult to write into any policy.

FUTURE NEEDS

In her 1977 study of deviant behavior in science quoted above, Zuckerman suggested that social control may be weak in science because "scientists have no clients whose rights require immediate protection" (p. 97). Scientists do not have patients. They do not serve individuals directly, as does the physician or the lawyer. Presumably, therefore, society has felt less need to control science, leaving it to scientists themselves to regulate their own behavior in accordance with the "cognitive and moral norms" of their profession (p. 97).

Although there is certainly some historical truth to this argument, an equally plausible argument could be made that 30 years before Zuckerman's study, Vannevar Bush and his wartime scientific colleagues acquired clients for science when they worked out the government-science-university alliance of *Science: The Endless Frontier* (Bush, 1945). The basis of the new professional-client relationship was and remains today the mutual understanding that "the security and prosperity of the United States depend today, as never before, upon the rapid extension of scientific knowledge" (Steelman, 1947, p. 3; President's Council of Advisors on Science and Technology, 1992). Scientific knowledge in turn rests on the expertise of scientists, particularly basic researchers on university campuses (Smith, 1990, pp. 40–52). In the ideal, and in the minds of many scientists, science may be a detached intellectual endeavor, but as a result of the postwar agreements, it is closely and consciously linked to society. These links have given scientists clients. Their clients are the American people, who pay for and benefit from the expansion of scientific knowledge. If social control is weak in science today, it is not because scientists have no clients but because scientists and their clients have lost sight of the true nature of their professional partnership.

In moments of ideal reflection, science and universities on the one hand and government on the other understand that they are partners joined by mutual needs, expectations, and obligations. Each knows that it has responsibilities for the achievement of common goals. However, in the real world of policy making, budgets, and regulation, a less congenial, more adversarial image dominates. Universities see government as an overly possessive and intrusive patron; government sees universities as ungrateful and sometimes irresponsible recipients of public funding.

The uneasiness that has emerged on the scientific-professional side of the government-university partnership in science is endemic to discussions of science policy today. Even supportive documents, such as the report by the President's Council of Advisors on Science and Technology (1992), express concerns about undue government influence. The report begins by talking about "this *partnership* [italics added] of over one hundred and fifty research-intensive universities and the federal government" (p. ix). In the later sections devoted to "Restoring Confidence in our Universities," the federal government is reduced to "sponsor" and "patron," while universities are cautioned that "excessive efforts to anticipate and eliminate all potential problems can lead to bureaucratic strictures that undermine or stifle scientific creativity" (President's Council of Advisors on Science and Technology,

1992, pp. 21–22). The shared goals that underlie the science-government (professional-client) relationship are replaced by mutual skepticism and distrust. Herman Wigodsky expressed a more common and less benign attitude toward government in 1984 when he prefaced his recommendations to universities with the warning: "Government subsidization of research demonstrates that the camel's nose under the tent leads to the camel's presence in the tent as an uninvited guest" (p. 1). When regulations and integrity are at issue, the images of joint partnerships and client-professional relationships in which both parties have responsibilities can quickly be replaced by the image of unreasonable patron, investor, supporter, or regulator constraining the freedom of the truth-seeking scientific investigator.

Given the past decade or more of increased government regulation of research, universities have ample reason to raise questions about regulation. However, for its part as the representative of the clients, government has raised some important questions about the professional practice of the scientists it funds that have not been answered. These questions were succinctly put by Representative Albert Gore at the opening of the 1981 congressional hearings on scientific misconduct. That Gore was speaking for the clients was made clear at the beginning of the hearings: "The American people's investment in science and technology speaks eloquently of our hopes for the future. As chairman of the subcommittee tasked with investigations and oversight, I intend to see that this hope is not misplaced" (*Fraud in Biomedical Research*, 1981, p. 20). As the clients'/investors' representative, Gore went on to pose a series of questions: "Is science really self-correcting?" "Is the peer review process working adequately?" "Are leading scientists who run large laboratories paying enough attention to the work actually being carried out?" "Has the biomedical research enterprise become too big and too varied to be controlled adequately by research institutions themselves and the informal networks within the professions?" (*Fraud in Biomedical Research*, 1981, p. 2). His goal was not to intrude the camel's presence into the tents of scientists; his goal was simply to ask, as any client would, whether the professionals to whom the client had turned for advice and expert knowledge were acting responsibly.

Although not on their own initiative, research universities have taken one important step to ensure the professional responsibility of their research programs. Universities have instituted policies and procedures for reporting, investigating, and adjudicating allegations of scientific misconduct. Presumably, scientific misconduct will be dealt with fairly and efficiently in the future—as fairly and efficiently as any human institution can be expected to work.

As important as this step may be, it unfortunately still does not address the concerns of the client as expressed by Gore. To date, the administrative, academic, and professional communities that make up universities have been unwilling to undertake a serious assessment of the state of their own integrity. Report after report has observed and even lamented the fact that we do not know the real extent of misconduct in science. Rarely has anyone endeavored to tackle the assessment problem head on. Universities and their scientists do not know whether science is self-correcting, whether peer review works, whether supervision is adequate in large laboratories, or whether academic research has become too large and too complex to be controlled by the informal networks within the professions—to restate Gore's questions.

It is true that the exact quantification of the level of scientific misconduct may be an impossible task, but quantitative approximation and qualitative assessments are not. In the late 1960s, AAAS conducted a broad survey of research ethics and integrity, the results of which were informative but unfortunately never published (Cranberg, 1968). More recently, Drummond Rennie, an associate editor of the *Journal of the American Medical Association,* invited scholars to undertake research projects that would shed light on the integrity of peer review and scientific publishing. In 1989 his invitation bore fruit when 300 scholars from 22 countries came together to share their results, which identified important problems and provided guidance for change (Rennie, 1990; and the other articles in that issue of *JAMA*). Surveys have been taken of the integrity of trainees and young researchers and of the practices they see around them—surveys that do not support the contention that misconduct is rare in science (Kalichman & Friedman, 1992). More studies and surveys such as these would provide valuable information for formulating, implementing, and improving scientific misconduct policies. Such efforts constitute a second step to ensure the professional responsibility of university research programs, one that has yet to be embraced very widely in academic research settings.

Finally, there is a third important step for ensuring and improving the professional responsibility of university research programs that is currently up for grabs—namely, educational reform. The federal government has already indicated its interest in and willingness to regulate in this area (NIH, 1989). A few universities have also taken some initiatives by beginning new courses, establishing centers, appointing committees, hiring faculty, and taking other steps to promote discussions of and knowledge about research integrity (Steneck, 1992). The majority, however, are meeting current requirements and waiting to see what happens.

Whatever universities in general decide to do, there will be costs. Putting more resources into self-assessment and efforts to promote integrity will take funds away from traditional areas of research, teaching, and service at a time when funds are increasingly in short supply. Given the other pressing needs that universities have, the wait-and-see attitude could turn out to be the most cost-effective way to proceed. However, if the public, through Congress, is left to decide how research integrity should be regulated and promoted, the costs could be greater. The requirements for record keeping and reporting can easily be increased. As a check on the way its research dollars are being spent, the government could require standardized formats for data collection; routine data audits; long-term, centralized data retention; and external review boards. Increasingly troublesome data disputes have recently led to a recommendation for more clarification on ownership and sharing (Mishkin, 1995).

As this chapter goes to press, it is still unclear, despite over 15 years of debate and a growing number of commissions, committees, reports, articles, and books, which of the partners will play the greatest role in the future in setting and enforcing the scientific misconduct policies that apply to universities. Significant divisions remain over the definition of scientific misconduct between NSF, which favors a broad definition, and the National Academy of Sciences and the Public Health Service, which favor narrower definitions (Buzzelli, 1993; Dresser, 1993; Rennie & Gunsalus, 1993). The adoption of the Public Health Service's revised policies and procedures were slowed by the appointment of a congressionally mandated Commission on Research Integrity, which replaced the Advisory Committee on Research Integrity that I chaired in the early 1990s (*National Institutes of Health Revitalization Act of 1933*, sec. 163). The report of this commission, now commonly referred to as the Ryan Commission after its chair, Kenneth Ryan, has called for shifting more of the responsibility for education and enforcement from the government to universities and professional societies, reflecting some of the same confidence in self-regulation that existed in the late 1970s and early 1980s (Kalichman & Friedman, 1992, p. 1431). How seriously the views of the commission will be taken is difficult to predict, given the deep divisions that still exist between those who trust professional self-regulation and those who do not.

It is also difficult to predict the impact that the latest tool for sharing information, ideas, and points of view—the Internet or World Wide Web—will have on the scientific misconduct debate. University misconduct policies are slowly becoming available on institutional home pages. Educational materials are now readily available through a growing number of Web sites, such as the AAAS's on-line forum *Science Conduct On-Line* (http://sci.aaas.org/aaas/). Extensive documentation on particular cases is also appearing on home pages posted by individuals (e.g., *Walter W. Stewart's Home Page*, http://nyxlO.cs.du.edu:8001/-wstewart/#other) and government agencies (e.g., U.S. Public Health Service's *Welcome to the Office of Research Integrity*, http://phs.os.dhhs.gov/phs/ori/ori__home.html). Therefore, even if we do return to an era of more institutional self-regulation, that self-regulation will increasingly be undertaken.

Notes

An earlier version of this chapter appeared as "Research Universities and Scientific Misconduct: History, Policies and the Future" in the *Journal of Higher Education*.

1. I have used personal copies of this and other university policies cited here and below. Most universities will supply copies of their policies on request. Policies on research misconduct are generally kept by the executive officer in charge of research. They are updated frequently. Therefore, the copies referred to and quoted in this chapter are not necessarily up to date.

2. In 1982–1984, Greene et al. (1985) sent questionnaires to 747 academic institutions (118 medical schools, 423 teaching hospitals, 183 graduate schools, and 23 schools of public health), seeking information on their misconduct policies. They received responses from 493 institutions, 116 of which reported having misconduct policies. Of this number, only 38 had separate policies that explicitly targeted scientific misconduct. If we assume that about half of the 38 were hospitals (the results are reported in aggregate), the total number of "universities" (i.e., academic institutions other than teaching hospitals) having explicit scientific misconduct policies in October 1985, when the Health Research Extension Act was passed, would be about 19. I know of seven universities that fall into this category: Emory, Harvard, Iowa, Maryland, Michigan, Stanford, and Yale. Of this seven, three adopted policies largely in response to major episodes of misconduct on their campuses.

3. These figures are based on the March 1989 Inspector General survey (Kusserow, 1989), which found that 28 of 30 (93%) major (100 or more Public Health Service grants) and 16 of 31 (52%) middle-range (10 to 100 research Public Health Service grants) research universities had scientific misconduct policies (see also Littlejohn & Matthews, 1989).

4. The evidence has not been collected to support either confidence in or distrust of the way in which universities have handled scientific misconduct investigations. The system is clearly not perfect, and some cases have been badly or irresponsibly handled, but we do not know if the latter represent a small or large percentage of the total cases, which number is also unknown.

5. The policy has three additional clauses, which specify the conditions for dismissal, assign responsibility to collaborators, and outline steps for correcting the public record when misconduct is confirmed.

6. The most influential early scientific misconduct policy recommendations were the ones advanced by the AAMC in 1982 in *The Maintenance of High Ethical Standards in the Conduct of Research*. The "Prototype Procedures for Dealing with Alleged Research Fraud" set out in this report pointed to the need to

> protect [the] rights and reputations for all parties involved including the individual(s) who report perceived misconduct in good faith; . . . exclude [from investigations] those with personal responsibility for the 27 research under investigation; . . . [notify] the sponsoring agency . . . that there is an

investigation underway ... [and] of the findings of the investigation [if the alleged fraud is substantiated]; ... review ... all research with which the individual is involved; ... [withdraw] all pending abstracts and papers emanating from the fraudulent research; [and] ... [notify] institutions and sponsoring agencies with which the individual has been affiliated ... if there is reason to believe that the validity of previous research might be questionable. (pp. 4–6)

The AAMC report also recommended the adoption of appropriate definitions of scientific misconduct and "encouraging faculties to discuss research ethics to heighten awareness and recognition of these issues" (p. 20).

7. Unfair retaliation against whistle-blowers could well be handled under employment guidelines rather than misconduct guidelines, and so on.

REFERENCES

American Association for the Advancement of Science, et al. (1991). *Misconduct in science: Recurring issues, fresh perspectives*. Executive Summary. November 15–16, Cambridge, MA.

American Association for the Advancement of Science, & Association of American Medical Colleges. 1992. "Responding to Allegations of Research Misconduct: A Practicum." San Francisco, CA, December 14.

Association of American Medical Colleges. (1982). *The maintenance of high ethical standards in the conduct of research*. Washington, DC: Author.

Association of American Medical Colleges. (1992). *Beyond the "framework": Institutional considerations in managing allegations of misconduct in research*. Washington, DC: Author.

Association of American Universities. (1982). *Report of the Association of American Universities Committee on the Integrity of Research*. Washington, DC: Author.

Broad, W. I. (1980a). Imbroglio at Yale (I): Emergence of a fraud. *Science, 210*, 38–41.

Broad, W. I. (1980b). Imbroglio at Yale (II): A top job lost. *Science, 210*, 171–173.

Broad, W. I. (1980c). Would-be academician pirates papers. *Science, 208*, 1438–1440.

Broad, W. I., & Wade, N. (1982). *Betrayers of the truth: Fraud and deceit in the halls of science*. New York: Simon & Schuster.

Bush, V. (1945). *Science: The endless frontier*. Washington, DC: National Science Foundation.

Buzzelli, D. E. (1993). The definition of misconduct in science: A view from NSF. *Science, 259*, 584–585, 647–648.

California Institute of Technology. (1989, February 24). *Policy on research fraud*. Unpublished document.

Cranberg, L. (1968, September). Ethics of scientists. *Bulletin of the Atomic Scientists, 24*, 39–40.

Culliton, B. J. (1983). Coping with fraud: The Darsee case. *Science, 220,* 31–35.
Dresser, R. (1993). Defining scientific misconduct: The relevance of mental state. *Journal of the American Medical Association, 269,* 895–897.
Emory University. (1983, March 9). *Principles and procedures for investigation of misconduct in research.* Unpublished document, School of Medicine.
Emory University. (1991, July 11). *Guidelines for the responsible conduct of research and scholarship (Draft).* Unpublished document.
Fraud in biomedical research: Hearing before the Subcommittee on Investigations and Oversight of the House Committee on Science and Technology, 97th Cong., 1st Sess. (1981).
Goodstein, D. (1991). Scientific fraud. *American Scholar, 60,* 505–515.
Greene, P. J., Durch, J. S., Horwitz, W., & Hooper, V. S. (1985). Policies for responding to allegations of fraud in research. *Minerva, 23,* 203–215.
Handler, P. (1980). Public doubts about science. *Science, 208,* 1093.
Harvard University. (1983, January 13). *Principles and procedures for dealing with allegations of faculty misconduct.* Unpublished document, Faculty of Medicine.
Harvard University. (1988, February 16). *Guidelines for investigators in scientific research.* Unpublished document.
Hixson, J. (1976). *The patchwork mouse.* Garden City, NY: Doubleday.
Indiana University. (1989, September). *Research ethics: Policies and procedures.* Unpublished document.
Institute of Medicine. (1989). *The responsible conduct of research in the health sciences.* Washington, DC: National Academy Press.
Johns Hopkins University. (1988, May 6). *Policy on integrity in research.* Unpublished document.
Kaiser, J. (1995). Scientific misconduct: Panel urges new approach to inquiries. *Science, 270,* 1431.
Kalichman, M. W., & Friedman, P. J. (1992). UA pilot study of biomedical trainees' perceptions concerning research ethics. *Academic Medicine, 67,* 769–775.
Kusserow, R. P. (1989, March). *Misconduct in scientific research.* Washington, DC: Office of Inspector General.
LaFollette, M. C. (1988, August). *Ethical misconduct in research publication: An annotated bibliography.* Unpublished report for the National Science Foundation.
Littlejohn, M. J., & Matthews, C. M. (1989). *Scientific misconduct in academia: Efforts to address the issue.* Washington, DC: Library of Congress, Congressional Research Service.
Medawar, P. (1976, April 23). The strange case of the spotted mice. *New York Review of Books,* pp. 6–11.
Michigan State University. (1988, July 27). *Statements and procedures for handling allegations of misconduct in science.* Unpublished document.
Mishkin, B. (1988). Responding to scientific misconduct due process and prevention. *Journal of the American Medical Association, 260,* 1932–1940.
Mishkin, B. (1995). Urgently needed: Policies on access to data by erstwhile collaborators. *Science, 270,* 927–928.

National Academy of Sciences, Panel on Scientific Responsibility and the Conduct of Research, Committee on Science, Engineering and Public Policy. (1992). *Responsible science: Ensuring the integrity of the research process.* Washington, DC: National Academy Press.

National Institutes of Health. (1989, December 22). Requirement for programs on the responsible conduct of research in National Research Service Award institutional training programs. *NIH Guide for Grants and Contracts, 18.*

National Institutes of Health Revitalization Act of 1993. Public Law 103–43. 103d Cong., 1st sess., Jan.

National Science Foundation. (1987). Misconduct in science and engineering research: Final regulations. *Federal Register, 52,* 2446–2447 (codified at 45 C. F. R. 689).

National Science Foundation. (1991). *Office of Inspector General, semiannual report to the Congress* (Rep. No. 5). Washington, DC: The Office.

Northwestern University. (1989, September). *Policy on integrity in research and procedures for reviewing alleged misconduct.* Unpublished document.

President's Council of Advisors on Science and Technology. (1992). *Renewing the promise: Research-intensive universities and the nation.* Washington, DC: Government Printing Office.

Rennie, D. (1990). Editorial peer review in biomedical publications: The First International Congress. *Journal of the American Medical Association, 263,* 1317.

Rennie, D., & Gunsalus, C. K. (1993). Scientific misconduct: New definition, procedures, and office—perhaps a new leaf. *Journal of the American Medical Association, 269,* 915–917.

Scientific fraud and misconduct and the federal response: Hearing before the Subcommittee on Human Resources and Intergovernmental Relations of the House Committee on Governmental Operations, 100th Cong., 1st Sess. (1988).

Smith, B. L. R. (1990). *American science policy since World War II.* Washington, DC: Brookings Institution.

Stanford University. (1985, September). *President Kennedy's statement on academic authorship.* Unpublished document.

Steelman, J. R. (1947). *A program for the nation: Science and public policy. The President's Scientific Research Board* (Vol. 1). Washington, DC: Government Printing Office.

Steneck, N. H. (1984, September). Commentary: The university and research ethics. *Science, Technology, and Human Values, 94,* 6–15.

Steneck, N. H. (1992). Fostering integrity in science and engineering research. In National Academy of Sciences (Ed.), *Responsible science: Ensuring the integrity of the research process* (Vol. 2, pp. 3–25). Washington, DC: National Academy Press.

Stewart, W. W., & Feder, N. (1987). The integrity of the scientific literature. *Nature, 325,* 207–214.

University of California, Los Angeles, School of Medicine. (1988, April 4). *Policy and procedures for review of alleged unethical research practices.* Unpublished document.

University of Chicago. (1986, January 24). *Procedures for investigating academic fraud.* Unpublished document.

University of Colorado. (1990, October 1). *Operating rules and procedures of the Standing Committee on Research Misconduct.* Unpublished document.

University of Michigan. (1984, June). *Maintaining the integrity of scholarship: Report of the University of Michigan Joint Task Force on Integrity of Scholarship.* Unpublished document.

U.S. Public Health Service. (1989). Responsibility of PHS awardee and applicant institutions for dealing with and reporting possible misconduct in science. *Federal Register, 54,* 151 (codified at 42 C. F. R. Part 50, 32446–32451).

Wigodsky, H. S. (1984, March). Fraud and misrepresentation in research: Whose responsibility? *IRB: A Review of Human Subjects Research, 6,* 1–5, 62.

Wuiff, K. M. (Ed.). (1979). *Regulation of scientific inquiry: Societal concerns with research.* Boulder, CO: Westview.

Yale University. (1982, May 23). *Yale University policy statement on collaborative research.* Unpublished document.

Zuckerman, H. (1977). Deviant behavior and social control in science. In E. Sagarin (Ed.), *Deviance and social change* (pp. 87–137). Beverly Hills, CA: Sage.

PART II

Theoretical Perspectives

CHAPTER FOUR

A Social Control Perspective on Scientific Misconduct

Edward J. Hackett

Scientific misconduct has drawn intense press coverage and substantial policy attention in recent years. Various explanations have been advanced to account for scientific misconduct, ranging from the individual deviance of scientists to the collective transformation of contemporary science. While each explanation illuminates a facet of the phenomenon, all seem incomplete in some crucial respect and suffer from a dearth of empirical evidence. This chapter first briefly reviews definitions of misconduct and available evidence about its prevalence and critically examines three sorts of explanations: individual psychopathology, anomie, and alienation. Drawing on recent theories of social control, I then suggest a perspective on scientific misconduct that focuses on the social response to misconduct, not the causes of misconduct itself. I close by outlining some of the implications of this perspective for research and policy.

DEFINITIONS OF SCIENTIFIC MISCONDUCT ARE VAGUE AND UNSETTLED

Before a phenomenon can be measured or explained, it must first be defined, yet definitions of scientific misconduct are vague, changeable, and disputed (Buzzelli, 1992; Friedman, 1992; Knoll, 1992; National Academy of Sciences, 1992). It is difficult to settle on a definition of scientific misconduct because research practices are not well codified or understood, the gradations between proper (even exemplary) technique and misconduct are subtle, and the process of settling on a definition is muddled by considerations of the politics and public image of science (Chubin & Hackett, 1990, chap. 5). Behaviors that scientists may be willing to accept among themselves (concerning, e.g., the selection of data for publication or the proper recording and storage of lab notes) may be judged unacceptable by laypersons.

Even within science, the acceptability of certain behaviors has varied over time, from field to field, and by the state of knowledge within a field (Sapp, 1990).

At present the quandary of definition has taken its most pointed form in a dispute between proponents of a quite limited definition of misconduct (as put forth in a 1992 National Academy of Sciences report) and those who favor a more inclusive definition (as employed by the Public Health Service; see U.S. Department of Health and Human Services, 1989) and the National Science Foundation (NSF) (Buzzelli, 1993a, 1993b). The academy report argued that the definition of misconduct in science should be limited to "fabrication, falsification or plagiarism in proposing, performing, or reporting research" (National Academy of Sciences, 1992, p. 27). Questionable research practices, including failure to retain good records, unwillingness to disclose or share data, improper allocation of credit, and the "misrepresentation of speculations as facts," were relegated to a category of lesser severity because such behaviors "do not directly damage the integrity of the research process" (p. 28). Harassment, misuse of funds, vandalism, gross negligence, and similar misbehaviors were placed by the academy panel in a third category because other remedies exist for these generic forms of misconduct.

For the NSF, in comparison, scientific misconduct included fabrication, falsification, plagiary, and "other serious deviation from accepted practices" (Buzzelli, 1993a, p. 647). This more comprehensive definition was intended to reflect the ethics of the scientific community and to provide a forum for adjudicating a broad range of complaints that actually arise in the research process. For example, of the 124 cases considered by NSF during a three-year period, only 10 had to do with data fabrication or misrepresentation, whereas 70 concerned intellectual property rights ranging from plagiary to "theft of research ideas [and] failure to give credit" (Buzzelli, 1993a, p. 584).

The inclusive definition has the advantages of clarity and simplicity—there is only one type of misconduct, not three. By addressing a greater range of behaviors that palpably harm the research enterprise, the inclusive definition may better serve the scientific community's need to air and resolve most complaints on its own, thus reinforcing the professional autonomy and self-regulation of scientists. By casting a broad net, however, the inclusive definition risks expending much energy, emotion, and legitimacy on cases that may be relatively unimportant to science, scientists, and society, whereas the limited definition may have the virtue of concentrating attention on fewer but arguably more serious sorts of misconduct.

COUNTS AND RATES OF MISCONDUCT ARE PROBABLY INACCURATE

Setting aside ambiguities in the definition of misconduct, what is known about the number of cases and their prevalence in the population of U.S.

scientists? Hyperbolic and unfounded claims for the purity (Koshland, 1987) or pollution (Bell, 1992; Douglas, 1992; St. James-Roberts, 1976a, 1976b) of science had been the norm for years. Recent regulations governing the investigation and reporting of alleged misconduct have brought many cases to light and dispelled some of the confusion. Even so, reporting is neither comparable across agencies nor complete, and it is impossible to know what proportion of all occurrences are reported (see National Academy of Sciences, 1992, chap. 4, for a summary).

There are two sources of data about scientific misconduct: official counts of cases processed by oversight offices and survey-based self-reports of scientists' experiences. The two sources suggest rather different rates.

In the three-year period ending July 1992, NSF resolved 67 allegations of misconduct, finding 3 cases of plagiary and 1 case of fabrication (57 more cases remained open). In roughly two years' time, the Office of Scientific Integrity of the Public Health Service closed 110 alleged cases of misconduct in science, completing full investigations of 21 cases and finding misconduct in 15 of the cases (National Academy of Sciences, 1992, pp. 84–85). Drawing upon various sources, Patricia Woolf (1988) counted 26 instances of misconduct for the 1980–1987 period. Taken together, these amount to 45 cases in a 12-year period, or about 4 cases per year.[1]

In contrast, a survey of universities that belong to the Council of Graduate Schools found that about 40% (118) of the graduate school deans received allegations of possible misconduct during the period 1983–1988 and that institutions receiving external research support in excess of $50 million per year were far more likely than others (69% to 19%) to hear such allegations (Swazey, Louis, & Anderson, 1989). Similarly, a survey of members of the American Association for the Advancement of Science conducted in late 1991 found that 27% of the 469 respondents had "'personally encountered or witnessed scientific research that [they] *suspected* was fabricated, falsified, or plagiarized' during the past ten years" (Teich, 1992, p. 187, italics in original). But as Teich noted, possible nonresponse bias, inconsistent definitions across respondents, and vagueness in the meaning of "personally encountered" make it difficult to evaluate this result (pp. 186–187).

What can we conclude from these various sorts of data? Is it true, as Paul Friedman (1992) suggested, that the "prevalence of such fraudulent acts [as deliberate data fabrication, falsification, or plagiary] is known to within an order of magnitude" (p. 154), or are known instances merely the tip of an iceberg (Douglas, 1992)? I certainly share Friedman's exasperation with misconduct and his judgment that sloppiness and minor ethical infractions may damage science far more than the notorious cases of egregious misconduct, but I doubt that the prevalence of misconduct is known within even *two* orders of magnitude.

Thus, it is difficult to know if there is much or little misconduct in science, if the rate has risen or remained constant, or if variation in the number of reported cases indicates change in behavior, ethical standards, reporting systems, publicity, or any combination in unknown proportion. Even if a rate could be calculated, by what standard could we judge if it was large or small, acceptable or reprehensible? In all, knowledge of the number and prevalence of cases scientific misconduct is poor but improving. Yet against this backdrop of disputed definitions and meager data, several reasonable explanations have been offered to account for misconduct.

THREE EXPLANATIONS OF MISCONDUCT

Following the pattern of Zuckerman's (1977, 1988) reviews, major explanations of scientific misconduct are conveniently considered under three broad headings: individual psychopathology, anomie, and alienation. I will briefly review and evaluate each explanation in turn, then offer a more comprehensive perspective on misconduct that focuses on the exercise of social control, not the event of deviant behavior (Scull, 1988, pp. 685–688).

Individual Psychopathology

Individual psychopathology is the simplest, most intuitive, and least satisfying explanation for scientific misconduct. Social scientists may have little regard for this explanation, but it seems widely held among scientists who comment on misconduct. Proponents of this view tend to believe that misconduct is rare, that its occurrence reflects defects of personality or upbringing (significantly, defects acquired before the miscreant's arrival at *their* institution), and that systemic intervention would be useless or damaging. They would "medicalize" the offense, ostracize the offender from the scientific community, and continue with research as usual. In this view, William Summerlin inked dark patches onto a white mouse (to suggest that skin grafts had taken) not because of performance pressure or faulty supervision but because of a medical condition that warranted a year's leave of absence and appropriate treatment (Hixson, 1976).

Efraim Racker (1989), of Cornell University, offered the most persuasive statement of the individual psychopathology explanation. Racker was the graduate advisor of Mark Spector, a "brilliant young man [who] wrote poetry, painted and was a superb experimenter" but who also seeded autoradiograms with a contaminating isotope to fabricate data in support of his hypothesized "kinase cascade" (p. 91). Drawing upon personal experience with this case and three other instances of fraud, Racker distinguished between "professional" perpetrators of fraud—intelligent, informed, skilled experimenters who know exactly which research problems matter most for their field and then convincingly falsify and fabricate experiments to solve those problems—and "amateurs," whose fabrications are clumsy, perhaps trivial, and easily detected (p. 91). Professional fraud, Racker argued, is the product of "mentally unbalanced . . . emotionally and mentally ill" persons who "subconsciously want to be caught" because they must know that the possibility of successfully falsifying such significant scientific work is very small (p. 91). The fraudulent acts of such persons, arising as they do from illness, could be neither detected nor deterred by increased oversight and regulation.

Individual psychopathology is an inviting explanation for the misconduct of otherwise brilliant persons who have a tragic flaw. Yet for most social scientists it is an unsatisfying explanation. First, the attribution of personality disorder, while convenient, is vague and unmeasured. No one has stated precisely what is wrong in such personalities and then measured those qualities. Second, many of the characteristics that seem to underlie putatively defective scientific personalities also seem to characterize effective, even eminent scientists: imagination, boldness, persistence, self-assurance, single-mindedness, and disregard for orthodoxy, to name a few (Mitroff, 1974). Thus, a useful explanation must indicate which *other* factors determine whether such qualities lead to the best or the worst of science and how such factors operate. Third, many of the same personality traits attributed to those accused of scientific fraud have been applied to other scientists whose actions or ideas are controversial or inconvenient, including whistle-blowers such as Margot O'Toole (whose complaints about irreplaceable data initiated the "Baltimore" case), iconoclastic skeptics such as Peter Duesberg (who remains vocally unconvinced that HIV causes AIDS), and zealous inquirers into the soundness of research such as Walter Stewart (who, along with Ned Feder, has been a fraud-buster without a portfolio at NIH). Innovators and critics are often labeled "disordered personalities" as a tactic of control. Finally, the individualistic explanation is too convenient and too self-serving of the interests of established scientists to be accepted on faith and assertion without evidence. The psychology of scientists remains a promising but underdeveloped topic of research (Friedman, 1992; see Fisch, 1977, for a review), and psychological factors probably play a part in scientific misconduct, but the arguments and evidence linking personality to misconduct in science are too thin and unsystematic to warrant much credence.

Anomie

In its contemporary presentation, anomie is connected to deviance through Robert K. Merton's (1938) theory of anomie and social structure. According to this view, deviance may arise when great cultural value is placed on achieving an end but when the means for its achievement are unavailable to persons in certain positions. Under such circumstances, some may reject the culturally prescribed goals, the socially endorsed means, or both, resulting in various sorts of deviant behavior. The extremely high value placed upon originality in science and the differential access to the intellect, training, assistance, research resources, and good fortune necessary to produce such results constitute just such anomic circumstances (Merton, 1938; Zuckerman, 1977, 1988). In addition to Merton's formulation, two further theories of anomie and deviance may be applied to science.

As originally used by Durkheim (1897/1951), by comparison, the term *anomie* signifies a state of moral deregulation resulting from a period of rapid social change during which social arrangements outstrip principles and mechanisms of social control. There is great potential for anomie of this sort in contemporary U.S. science, caused by specialization, technical innovation and the attendant obsolescence of skills, the changing organizational culture of academic science, new goals and bases for legitimating scientific research, and a changing relationship between performance and reward (Hackett, 1990; Hagstrom, 1964). Under anomic circumstances, behavior is only weakly guided by shared rules, and deviance results.

Anomie may also be seen as an extreme form of sociological ambivalence (Merton, 1976), for when there is great uncertainty about which of two or more values to honor in a particular social situation, the resulting behavior may be unpredictable, if not chaotic. The presence of "counternorms" (Mitroff, 1974) and the emergence of new norms of science (Ziman, 1990) and a new entrepreneurial spirit on campus (Etzkowitz, 1983) are precisely the circumstances that might give rise to anomie.

The anomic explanation of misconduct has more sociological appeal than the individualistic explanation, but it is very difficult to substantiate empirically. In Merton's formulation, where anomie results from a gap between cultural goals and structurally determined opportunities and resources, one might predict greater anomie and greater prevalence of misconduct among scientists in positions of lesser prestige and resources. Yet there is no evidence that this is so; on the contrary, a large fraction of known cases involve senior scientists employed by prestigious universities with substantial research programs (Swazey, Louis, & Anderson, 1989; Woolf 1988). But the data are so poor that mere *counts* of incidents are suspect and *rates* are unfathomable, so the proposition remains untested.

The main difficulty with the two more general versions of anomie theory is that anomie is so profound, pervasive, and multifaceted that one would expect almost every scientist to be deviant in some respect. But this pervasive disregard for principle does not seem to plague academic science. According to self-report data, academic scientists claim close adherence to the norms of disinterestedness, universalism, and communality, with substantial deviation only from the norm of organized skepticism (Braxton, 1993, table 2, p. 220).

Alienation

Alienation is the separation of a worker from the work, the self, or other workers. Specialized, segmented work roles cause alienation by restricting the application of talent and creativity in the workplace, thus limiting the worker's opportunities for self-expression and engagement with the work. Accompanying the objective circumstance of being alienated from work are subjective feelings of estrangement, malaise, and disengagement.

Science, long regarded as a calling or vocation that evokes profound personal engagement, would seem the antithesis of an alienating career. But in his lecture "Science as a Vocation," Max Weber (1917/1946) observed that the "large institutes of medicine or natural science are 'state capitalist' enterprises" where one encounters "the same condition that is found everywhere capitalist enterprise comes into operation: the separation of the worker from his means of production. The worker, that is, the assistant, is dependent upon the implements that the state puts at his disposal; hence he is just as dependent upon the head of the institute as is the employee in a factory dependent upon management.... Thus, the assistant's position is often as precarious as is that of any quasi-proletarian existence" (p. 131).

Weber, of course, was arguing that the social organization of academic science in Germany alienated junior scientists. This view of German academic science in the early years of the twentieth century is echoed in social organization and culture of contemporary U.S. academic science (Etzkowitz, 1983; Hackett, 1990; Remington, 1988; Slaughter, 1988). Further, there is some survey-based evidence that U.S. scientists (Czujko, Kleppner, & Rice, 1991; Lederman, 1991) and university faculty report feelings of alienation that are expected to accompany the structural condition (Braxton, 1993, table 2, p. 220).

Alienation can contribute to misconduct by eroding the social circumstances necessary for effective social control (Weinstein, 1979). When research becomes so specialized or so strongly mediated by instruments that a scientist cannot appreciate the connection between daily tasks and the larger purposes of the research, then expedience and wishful thinking may supplant the requisite diligence and skepticism. When the products of research become esoteric in character and collective in production, then the scientist can hardly believe, in Weber's (1917/1946) poignant phrase, that "the fate of his soul depends upon whether or not he makes the correct conjecture at this passage of this manuscript" (p. 135). When the interests of research group members diverge because of gross differences in autonomy, financial reward, job security, career prospects, or recognition for performance, then alienation may rise along with the likelihood of personal animosity and scientific misconduct (Hackett, 1990). When the rewards and satisfactions of science are overshadowed by organizational demands, economic calculations, and career strategies, then science is no longer a vocation.

While the proposed process is different, alienation theory shares many of the same difficulties as anomie theory. The structural circumstances that might give rise to alienation are pervasive, but the level of alienation among scientists has not been measured (and is probably lower than that of other occupations). One would need to decide whether the structural *fact* or the subjective *sentiment* of alienation has priority in an explanation; then one would need a sound measure of misconduct to determine whether alienation has had an effect. Available evidence suggests that structural alienation in science may be common and increasing, so misconduct should also be quite common. To explain its *non*occurrence would require a helper theory of contingencies that trigger (or suppress) the behavior or that facilitate detection and investigation. Given the state of knowledge about misconduct and difficulties in studying deviance, especially among the relatively powerful, such explanations may long remain speculative.

I do not wish to be despairing or disparaging of research into the causes of misconduct in science, yet the preceding overview suggests that explanations cannot be developed or tested without a leap in the quality of data, clarity of definitions, and precision of hypotheses. Such research must go on not only because the proposed explanations are plausible but also to produce incremental gains in understanding and to sustain pressure for better data and research resources. But I fear that those approaches are unlikely to yield much new insight in the near term. Indeed, arguably more important features of the rising concern about scientific misconduct may be overlooked if research is too narrowly focused on the causes of scientists' putative misbehavior. For the balance of this chapter, I wish to use recent ideas in the theory of social control to call attention to the societal reaction to scientific misconduct and to develop this new, more comprehensive perspective on the phenomenon.

SCIENTIFIC MISCONDUCT AND THE EXERCISE OF SOCIAL CONTROL

While we do not know much about the prevalence and causes of scientific misconduct, we do know that the amount of public attention and policy concern devoted to scientific misconduct has grown dramatically over the past two decades, spawning federal guidelines (U.S. Department of Health and Human Services, 1989), investigative offices at the Public Health Service and NSF, congressional inquiries, blue-ribbon panels (National Academy of Sciences, 1992), and uncounted scholarly papers, edited volumes, conferences, journalistic articles, and sessions at professional meetings. Not only the volume of interest in scientific misconduct but also the character of that interest has changed. In 1976, Donald Black observed that the system for penalizing misconduct in science was "informal and decentralized, rarely involving litigation or formal action of any kind" (p. 80). Similarly, in her 1977 review essay, Zuckerman proposed that systematic records of scientific misconduct were not kept because "scientists are themselves the primary consumers of one another's products and services [and] typically have 'clients' who are qualified to appraise the products and services they receive" (p. 107). But in recent years the informal, decentralized, and private process these authors described has given way to one that is formal, centralized, and public.

It may be valuable to ask why such changes in the amount and character of concern have occurred and what consequences they may have for understanding the changing relationship between science and society. Let me first develop a perspective for thinking about efforts to increase external control of science and then turn to some of its implications for research and policy.

The level of social concern about any form of deviance reveals much about the society that disapproves of the behavior. On one side of the coin, social standards are formed and deviance is defined in the act of deciding whether certain behaviors are acceptable. On the other side, "Much of the social control apparatus is consciously fashioned through the visible hand of definable organizations, groups, and classes, rather than being 'naturally' produced by the invisible hand of society" (Scull, 1988, p. 686). This means that changes in the exercise of social control may reflect the distribution of power, lines of conflict, and persuasive ideologies of a society.

Thus, we may ask of misconduct in science, as Donald Black has asked about law and social control in general, how and why certain behaviors are defined as misconduct and placed under increased scrutiny and regulation (Black, 1976, 1984; Scull, 1988). That is, why has scientific misconduct recently received so much public attention and opprobrium? Why have there been calls for increased oversight and regulation? To raise such questions does not deny, excuse, or justify scientific misconduct but calls into question the changing exercise of social control rather than accepting it as arising naturally from a trend of increasing misconduct in science.

When one thinks of how prestigious, successful, powerful, and independent U.S. science has been during the past 40 years, it may seem odd to be concerned about increasing external oversight and control. Yet the notion of a relatively autonomous science is new and fragile, grounded in a constellation of philosophical, political, and technical arguments and abetted by the unique economic and social conditions of the postwar era. As historians remind us, "Scientific activity, the scientist's role, and the scientific community have always been dependent: they exist, are valued, and supported insofar as the state or its various agencies see point in them" (Shapin & Schaffer, 1985, p. 339). What is it about contemporary science that may attract the attention of powerful social interests and invite their efforts to assert greater control over the enterprise?

First, science is becoming increasingly expensive and visible as performance expectations rise, budgets swell, mega-projects emerge (such as the superconducting supercollider and the human genome initiative), science journalism gains prominence, and specialists in public relations tout the latest scientific triumphs. In all, science has become a more public enterprise, winning fame and consuming resources while inviting increased accountability and scrutiny through the mere fact of its success.

Second, science is a resource for power, offering the possibility of control over aspects of nature and the attendant ability to alter the world. Atomic physics, information processing, molecular biology, and the development of various antibiotics and vaccines are among the notable accomplishments of twentieth-century science. Such products and processes are hardly neutral but instead serve the interests of various powerful groups in society.

Third, science is a source of intellectual authority, legitimacy, and prestige, capable of justifying actions that might not otherwise win acceptance. Invocations of science in matters of policy or law lend a logical, objective, and definitive tone to the deliberation. But scientific arguments may also be used to disguise political preferences and the exercise of power, so the ability to influence and invoke scientific research conveys the ability to develop or restrict such arguments. Conversely, elites may wish to control science because independent inquiry may threaten to reveal the exercises of preference and power that might otherwise be concealed under the guise of objective necessity.

Fourth, science is held in such high esteem that some accord it the status and purity normally reserved for a religious order. (Hence the enduring image of science as a vocation or calling to religious office.) Others employ the religious metaphor as a rhetorical device to justify or provoke moral outrage. But in either instance, if science is considered a sacred institution, then misconduct will be sacrilege and will evoke moral outrage. Books about scientific misconduct bearing such titles as *Betrayers of the Truth* (Broad & Wade, 1982), *Impure Science* (Bell, 1992), and *False Prophets* (Kohn, 1986) convey this sense of sacrilege in their images of betrayal, purity, and revelation.

Fifth, the knowledge-based elitism of science may provoke leveling urges, and such urges may be especially intense in times of growing social inequality. In his study of deviance among New England Puritans, Erikson (1966) suggested that in those times of increasing social differences, the pursuit of social deviants gave rise to a moral solidarity that bridged the social distance between people (p. 9). Perhaps the recent rising concern about scientific misconduct represents a similar effort to direct hostility toward an intellectual elite and away from political and social elites.

Last and most important, the past decade or so has seen an intensification of the postwar tendency to forge a more speedy and certain connection between scientific research and such putative national purposes as high-technology medicine, innovative weaponry, policy formulation, international prestige, economic competitiveness, and the resolution of legal disputes (Remington, 1988). To this end, "Congress and the executive branch have sought to transform the very nature of science. Setting research agendas, intervening in peer-reviewed grant decisions, micromanaging federal laboratories, and refusing to fund research that is not politically or morally 'correct' are but a few manifestations of the government's effort to gain a greater control over U.S. research. Nowhere, however, is the heavy hand of the government more apparent than in the area of ethics" (Charrow, 1993, p. 76). Less grandly stated, science has acquired increased importance within organizations (such as universities and businesses), requiring scientists to engage in more intense interactions with lawyers, accountants, public relations specialists, and professional administrators.

For example, as university budgets become more dependent upon research funds, commercial contracts, and indirect cost recovery (Geiger, 1986), scientists may experience organizational pressures to become more entrepreneurial, to undertake more funded research, and to perform it according to businesslike practices of accountability, efficiency, secrecy, and the like. In the aggregate, this may increase competition among scientists for research resources, as more scientists are urged to do more research and prepare more proposals. However, this intensified competition threatens to compromise scientists' standards of cooperation, communication, quality, and problem choice (Hackett, 1990). Similarly, if new results are pushed more rapidly to application (Remington, 1988), then the time available for error correction within science, including detection of misconduct, will be reduced, while the consequences of error become more immediate and serious.

In itself, this tighter coupling of science to other social and organizational purposes would be expected to increase scrutiny and the likelihood of intervention. With more riding on the outcome, those who stand to gain through the efforts of scientists will be motivated to ensure that the promised goods are delivered on time and on budget. Also, it is in the very nature of these professions to manage, regulate, and oversee activities; that is what managers, lawyers, and accountants do for a living. But beyond such obvious effects, tight coupling might also affect the social organization of science, scientists' roles and career opportunities, and even the principles that guide scientists' work (Hackett, 1990; Remington, 1988; Slaughter, 1988).

As scientists are brought into more frequent, intense, and consequential contact with other professions, competition for dominance between professions becomes more likely. In this regard, Jasanoff (1992) has asked, "Why has science—historically so robust in contests for power, prestige, and patronage—proven so weak and defenseless when called to account in legal proceedings?" (p. 345). While she may have overstated the case—science has hardly seemed "weak and defenseless"—the very language used to describe the interaction ("science called to account") reveals much about the relative power of these two professions, the nature of their encounter, and the turf on which it takes place. Within the university, scientists' work falls increasingly under the purview of professional managers, accountants, technology transfer agents, public relations specialists, and development officers. Such interactions also occasion tests of strength between professions wishing to impose their standards on common but contested turf.

IMPLICATIONS FOR RESEARCH AND POLICY

For all these reasons, scientific misconduct and science itself have received increased attention during the past decade. Importantly, this increased attention and its secondary consequences for the social organization of science would be expected even if the (unknowable) rate of misconduct did not change at all. (Indeed, evidence that social judgments may have changed more than scientific behaviors can be found in the "epidemic" of misconduct among scientists long dead, including Freud, Galileo, Kekule, Mendel, Newton, and Pasteur.) But what are the implications for research and policy that follow from viewing public concern about misconduct as a change in the science-society relationship?

Some New Research Ideas

The ideas sketched above suggest new avenues of research and emphasize the pertinence of enduring themes in science studies that have to do with external efforts to control science and the changes in social organization that may result. One theme that would merit more attention is the nature of interactions between science and other professions, including law, engineering, and business. In the case of science and law, which has received much recent attention, we need to know more about the standards of argument and evidence that prevail in each domain and how those standards might be reconciled when they disagree (Roberts, 1992).[2] We also should examine interaction between members of the two professions—say, expert witnesses' testimony in court, judges' decisions about the admissibility of scientific evidence, or lawyers' behavior as participants in research or patent applications—to learn more about the interplay of knowledge and power that occurs in such exchanges. At a more macro social level, the demands that each profession might place on the other, and the consequences of such demands for professional autonomy and practice, are worthy topics of research.

A second theme is how the social organization of science changes in response to new organizational conditions, funding contingencies, and career constraints. Does increased contact between science and industry, for example, alter scientists' research agendas, standards of scholarship, research ethics and practices, professional roles, or definitions of research? The newly acquired "scientific" status of such fields as materials research, decision science, and manufacturing suggests that what is termed "science" may change significantly in response to such connections. Does the scientist's role change as well, "hybridizing" to incorporate elements of the entrepreneur or businessperson? What of the scientist's actions and values?

Third, is there evidence that science is now controlled by other professions, and if so, how and with what consequences was this accomplished? Study of regulations governing misconduct and their application in a broad range of cases may reveal new power arrangements. For example, there has been a neutral, technical tone to much that has been written about the procedures followed by universities and government agencies in the investigation of allegations of scientific misconduct. The impression is that these are procedures devised in the best interests of all, with little attention to the professional values served by the process. Yet one may also view these procedures as tests of strength, pitting scientific standards of investigation, evidence, proof, and procedure against those of law or other professions. In that light, the procedures are explicitly seen as value laden, hardly the neutral, technical protocols they might first appear to be.

Finally, cross-national studies of scientific misconduct and the social response it elicits would be valuable occasions for examining the role of the government agencies, economic interests, university organizations, and ideologies on the exercise of social control over science.

A Reexamination of Policies

Using instances of misconduct to reexamine the science-society relationship also raises questions about recently proposed policies for science. Rising concern about scientific misconduct has elicited calls for *tightening* the connection between science and other professions—policies purportedly designed to wring out misconduct, indifference, and shoddy work—and such calls have met with grudging acquiescence from some scientists. For example, an observer closed his remarks on the increasing external control of science with these words: "Such new procedures would also mean still more academic bureaucracy, still more paperwork, still more committees and powerful chairmen, and further erosion of academic freedom and the attractiveness of a career in research. Is this additional oversight necessary or desirable? Probably not. However, the question is, Do we have a choice?" (Friedman, 1988, pp. 1937–1938).

A second observer contended that as preceptors become responsible for increasing numbers of young scientists, the preceptors find themselves overburdened, unable to transmit the norms, values, standards, and practices of good science at the lab bench as they once had done. Into this vacuum, she argued, the universities must inject more formal controls, more oversight and regulation (Mishkin, 1988, pp. 1932–1936).

The perspective on social control sketched above would not accept such policy conclusions at face value but would raise the possibility that the exercise of social control was motivated by reasons other than the misconduct of scientists. It would demand that we ask whose interests were served and whose were set aside by the proposed actions. Further, the social control perspective would suggest, in conjunction with the alienation and anomie explanations of scientific misconduct, that such policies may be counterproductive because more scrutiny may create more interprofessional conflict, weaken and confuse internal standards of conduct, and further alienate scientists from their work and from one another, resulting in more questionable behavior and more demands to control science.

Instead, policies might be devised to renegotiate the relationship between science and society in a way that might alleviate pathogenic pressures. Some specific suggestions include the following.

1. Loosen the connection between science and other social purposes by reinforcing (rather than supplanting) scientific standards of evidence and argument, ensuring that adequate review and replication stand between research and product, and establishing more realistic hopes about which sorts of problems are amenable to scientific solutions.

2. Reduce and redistribute the financial rewards immediately available to scientists, their companies, and their universities by installing a form of "escrow" account to hold profits for a fixed period of time (Friedman, 1990) and by replacing indirect cost allocations with more stable infrastructural support.

3. Lessen the extremes of reward and status that increasingly characterize science, as they do other activities ranging from publishing to sports, thus relieving some of its unhealthy competitive pressure and debilitating inequality of career prospects and working conditions.

4. Do not allow scientists to take on unreasonable responsibilities for graduate and postdoctoral education, but ensure that they take more seriously their duties as role models and exemplars of ethical conduct.

5. Uncouple graduate student and postdoctoral support from research grants, reversing a trend of the late 1970s and 1980s, to allow students the freedom to leave unsuitable arrangements without jeopardizing their careers.

6. Counteract the tendency to hire more adjunct faculty, doctoral research associates, and others whose standing within the university is insecure. By the very nature of their positions, such persons are more susceptible than regular faculty to inappropriate influence by others and are more easily displaced by changes in the resource environment. (Unfortunately, for precisely those reasons, some institutions find them attractive to hire.)

7. Resist the trend to replace intrinsic rewards and controls with extrinsic ones, as such measures will weaken science's capacity for self-regulation. Instead, take steps to restore and fortify the intrinsic satisfactions of science and its internal mechanisms of social control.

8. Improve public understanding of the practice of scientific research, thus developing a public literate in both the substance and the practice of science. Of particular concern are the overly idealized perceptions of scientific knowledge and research practices held by some judges, public officials, and business executives.

If scientific misconduct and efforts to control it are viewed within the framework of a whole society, not treated as an individual pathology or institutional failing, then it may be possible to understand the origins, significance, and potential remedies for such behavior and to invent new patterns of interaction that may reduce misconduct, alleviate its dangers to others, and avoid harmful remedies.

Notes

John Braxton, Daryl Chubin, Paul Friedman, Nils Roll-Hansen, Robert Silverman, Shana Solomon, David Thaler, Ned Woodhouse, and an anonymous referee provided patient and very helpful comments on versions of this chapter. I wrote the chapter while affiliated with the Laboratory of Molecular Genetics and Informatics at Rockefeller University, supported by fellowship funds that Joshua Lederberg received from the Andrew W. Mellon Foundation. Portions of the argument presented in the last half of the chapter appeared in a supplement of *Academic Medicine*, September 1993.

1. In the summer of 1993, NIH published the names of 15 persons found to have committed scientific misconduct in the NIH Guide to Grants and Contracts (June 25 and July 30, 1993).

2. The recent Supreme Court decision in the case of *Daubert v. Merrell-Dow Pharmaceuticals* will demand greater scientific discernment on the part of judges and, by bringing science and law into more intimate contact with one another, will alter the relationship between science and law in ways that are difficult to predict.

References

Bell, R. (1992). *Impure science.* New York: John Wiley.

Black, D. (1976). *The behavior of the law.* New York: Academic Press.

Black, D. (Ed.). (1984). *Toward a general theory of social control.* Orlando, FL: Academic Press.

Braxton, J. (1993). Deviancy from the norms of science: The effects of anomie and alienation in the academic profession. *Research in Higher Education, 34,* 213–228.

Broad, W., & Wade, N. (1982). *Betrayers of the truth.* New York: Simon & Schuster.

Buzzelli, D. (1992). The measurement of misconduct. *Knowledge: Creation, Diffusion, Utilization, 14,* 205–211.

Buzzelli, D. (1993a). The definition of misconduct in science: A view from NSF. *Science, 259,* 584–585, 647–648.

Buzzelli, D. (1993b). Some considerations in defining misconduct in science. In *Ethics, Values, and the Promise of Science: Forum Proceedings, February 25–26, 1993*. Research Triangle Park, NC: Sigma Xi, the Scientific Research Society.

Charrow, R. P. (1993, March). A primer on research ethics: Learning to cope with federal regulation of research. *Journal of NIH Research, 5,* 76.

Chubin, D. E., & Hackett, E. J. (1990). *Peerless science: Peer review and U.S. science policy.* Albany: State University of New York Press.

Czujko, R., Kleppner, D., & Rice, S. (1991, February). Their most productive years: Young physics faculty in 1990. *Physics Today, 44,* 37–42.

Douglas, J. D. (1992, November/December). Betraying scientific truth. *Transaction, 30,* 76–82.

Durkheim, E. (1951). *Suicide.* Glencoe, IL: Free Press. (Original work published 1897)

Erikson, K. (1966). *Wayward Puritans.* New York: John Wiley.

Etzkowitz, H. (1983). Entrepreneurial scientists and entrepreneurial universities in American academic science. *Minerva, 21,* 198–233.

Fisch, R. (1977). Psychology of science. In I. Spiegel-Rosing & D. J. Price (Eds.), *Science, technology, and society: A cross-disciplinary perspective* (pp. 277–318). Beverly Hills, CA: Sage.

Friedman, P. J. (1988). Research ethics, due process, and common sense. *Journal of the American Medical Association, 260,* 1937–1938.

Friedman, P. J. (1990, October 31). We need to find new ways to help scientists avoid ethical problems without overly limiting research. *Chronicle of Higher Education, 37,* A48.

Friedman, P. J. (1992, December). On misunderstanding scientific misconduct. *Knowledge: Creation, Diffusion, Utilization, 14,* 153–156.

Geiger, R. (1986). *To advance knowledge: The growth of American research universities since World War II.* New York: Oxford University Press.

Hackett, E. J. (1990, May-June). Science as a vocation in the 1990s: The changing organizational culture of academic science. *Journal of Higher Education, 61,* 241–279.

Hagstrom, W. O. (1964). Anomy in scientific communities. *Social Problems, 12,* 186–195.

Hixson, J. (1976). *The patchwork mouse.* New York: Doubleday.

Jasanoff, S. (1992). What judges should know about the sociology of science. *Jurimetrics, 32,* 345–359.

Knoll, E. (1992, December). What *is* scientific misconduct? *Knowledge: Creation, Diffusion, Utilization, 14,* 174–180.

Kohn, A. (1986). *False prophets.* New York: Blackwell.

Koshland, D. E. (1987). Fraud in science. *Science, 235,* 141.

Lederman, L. (1991, January). Science: The end of the frontier? Supplement to *Science.*

Merton, R. K. (1938). Social structure and anomie. *American Sociological Review, 3,* 673–682.

Merton, R. K. (1976). *Sociological ambivalence and other essays*. New York: Free Press.

Mishkin, B. (1988). Responding to scientific misconduct: Due process and prevention. *Journal of the American Medical Association, 260*, 1932–1936.

Mitroff, I. I. (1974). Norms and counter-norms in a select group of the Apollo moon scientists: A case study of the ambivalence of scientists. *American Sociological Review, 39*, 579–595.

National Academy of Sciences. (1992). *Responsible science: Ensuring the integrity of the research process*. Washington, DC: National Academy of Sciences Press.

Racker, E. (1989, May 11). A view of misconduct in science. *Nature, 339*, 91–93.

Remington, J. (1988). Beyond big science in America: The binding of inquiry. *Social Studies of Science, 18*, 45–72.

Roberts, L. (1992). Science in court: A culture clash. *Science, 257*, 732–736.

St. James-Roberts, I. (1976a). Are researchers trustworthy? *New Scientist, 72*, 481–483.

St. James-Roberts, I. (1976b). Cheating in science. *New Scientist, 72*, 466–469.

Sapp, J. (1990). *Where the truth lies: Franz Moewus and the origins of molecular biology*. Cambridge, UK: Cambridge University Press.

Scull, A. (1988). Deviance and social control. In N. Smelser (Ed.), *Handbook of sociology* (pp. 667–693). Beverly Hills, CA: Sage.

Shapin, S., & Schaffer, S. (1985). *Leviathan and the air pump: Hobbes, Boyle, and the experimental life*. Princeton, NJ: Princeton University Press.

Slaughter, S. (1988). Academic freedom and the state. *Journal of Higher Education, 59*, 241–262.

Swazey, J. P., Louis, K. S., & Anderson, M. S. (1989, March). University policies and ethical issues in research and graduate education: Highlights of the CGS deans' survey. *CGS Communicator, 22*, 1–3, 7–8.

Teich, A. (1992, December). Integrity in research: The scientific community view. *Knowledge: Creation, Diffusion, Utilization, 14*, 185–192.

U.S. Department of Health and Human Services. (1989, August 8). Responsibilities of PHS awardee and applicant institutions for dealing with and reporting possible misconduct in science: Final rule. *Federal Register, 54*, 32446–32451.

Weber, M. (1946). Science as a vocation. In H. Gerth & C. W. Mills (Eds.), *From Max Weber: Essays in sociology* (pp. 129–156). New York: Oxford University Press.

Weinstein, D. (1979). Fraud in science. *Social Science Quarterly, 59*, 639–652.

Woolf, P. K. (1988, Fall). Deception in scientific research. *Jurimetrics, 29*, 67–95.

Ziman, J. (1990). Research as a career. In S. Cozzens et al. (Eds.), *The research system in transition* (pp. 345–359). Dordrecht, the Netherlands: Kluwer.

Zuckerman, H. (1977). Deviant behavior and social control in science. In E. A. Sagarin (Ed.), *Deviance and social change* (pp. 87–137). Beverly Hills, CA: Sage.

Zuckerman, H. (1988). The sociology of science. In N. Smelser (Ed.), *Handbook of sociology* (pp. 511–574). Beverly Hills, CA: Sage.

CHAPTER FIVE

Universities and the Regulation of Scientific Morals

Stephen Turner

Should universities be held responsible for policing research misconduct in science? Do they have some special capacity or responsibility for doing so? Do they have an interest in doing so? Much of the policy discussion of the problem has taken for granted that the answers to all of these questions is "yes." But it is also widely recognized that universities may not be very good police. In particular, it is commonly held, as the report of the Commission on Research Integrity (1995) put it, that "inherent institutional conflicts of interest" arise when the university polices itself (p. 22). Similarly, Teich and Frankel (1992) noted, in their pamphlet produced for the American Association for the Advancement of Science–American Bar Association National Conference of Lawyers and Scientists, that

> some critics are skeptical about the universities' willingness and ability to detect and investigate allegations of scientific misconduct. Some past investigations have been characterized as inefficient and superficial, by participants in the process, by federal agencies, and by the Congress. . . . A critical question confronting universities is whether they have the will to pursue misconduct cases with the vigor, thoroughness, and impartiality that is required. . . . Their history and tradition are marked by a reluctance to impose centralized rules of conduct or to monitor misconduct. . . . Moreover, like other organizations, universities may be tempted to minimize the exposure of internal misconduct in the belief that sustaining external support for the institution requires that it shield its members and itself from the perception of deviance by outsiders. (pp. 24–25)

Notions like "policing," "interests," and "conflict of interest" are political notions. But the problem of the role of the university in the regulation of scientific misconduct has not usually been discussed in a political way. It is rarely said precisely what the interests in question are or how they might "inherently conflict."

In this chapter I will describe the main conflicts; show, through an organizational analysis, that they are deeply rooted in the present organization of research universities; and characterize the obstacles within the university to the enforcement of ethical standards for research practice. The obstacles are very significant. Organizational analysis takes many forms, of course, but the approach to be taken in what follows uses the language of political theory and may be characterized as follows (see Turner, 1997). In any system of authority, discretionary power—that is, the right to decide certain questions, and limitations on the right to decide—is governed by rules that serve to distribute discretionary power and to constrain its use. Typically, the power that is employed arises through a scheme of delegation, in which the possessors of power are representatives of some collective body from which the power ultimately derives. The issues that arise in connection with policing research fraud and misconduct are problems of conflict of interest, collective responsibility, representation, and the relation between overlapping forms of authority.

THE CONTEMPORARY AMERICAN UNIVERSITY

The strong presidencies of the early part of the century, which were dominated by the politics of relations between boards of trustees and the university (see Veblen, 1957), gradually gave way to other interests and conflicts. The present discussion of fraud is properly understood in terms of these later conflicts. The sheer size and complexity of university finances, the fiscal reality that benefactions from alumni and tuition gradually came to amount to a lower proportion of the academic budget, and the complexities of the relationship to the federal government all changed these relationships fundamentally. It is to this new set of relationships that I now turn.

In the history of the university, the exercise of collective responsibility has varied. Different forms of governance are prone to different problems of corruption. The northern European university of the last century had its scandals over the sale of degrees, a result of a common pecuniary interest that was stronger than any countervailing collective interest. Oxbridge colleges had no effective means of acting on an interest in specialist competencies and thus were prone to being taken in by clever persons without scholarly substance. The same kinds of considerations arose in connection with the contemporary American university. In connection with research misconduct, the issue is straightforward.

Is there a collective interest of some sort in the suppression or punishment of misconduct, embodied in a representative form, such as a senate, that has sufficient expertise to make reasonable judgments about it? The core collective interest of a faculty as a faculty is in the academic reputation of the university. Robert Merton's (1973) famous paper on "the Matthew effect" points to this interest (pp. 439–459). The individual faculty member benefits in a variety of ways from the general academic reputation of the university and has an interest in preserving it. But this interest is one interest among many. Administrators may have short-term interests that conflict with it, and other elements at the university may find it to be of little significance. The peculiar history of the American university has led to the fragmentation of interests and to a reliance on proceduralism, a form of limiting discretionary power by defining procedures that any decision must follow.

Proceduralism protected the faculty against the arbitrary actions of presidents. But whether it fundamentally changed the balance of power between faculty and administration or established the primacy of the faculty is another matter. In general, administrators responded by diffusing power among large numbers of different bodies so that no bodies had powers that enabled them to effectively counter the will of the administration. The result of this tactic is difficult to characterize briefly, but the main effect is that power is largely hidden in American universities. Presidents typically retain a great many formal powers, but in practice they have responsibility without authority. They are greatly constrained by both internal and external forces (Birnbaum, 1989). To get and preserve support for their decisions, especially the decisions that are of particular importance to them, administrations have created large numbers of committees and similar structures with advisory roles to which unpleasant decisions that are not important to administrators may be delegated. Typically, these committees have no genuine decision-making powers but are merely advisory. The existence of an advisory committee is convenient for various reasons. If it gives advice that the administrator approves of, the administrator can act on the basis of the committee's recommendations and diffuse responsibility. If the advice is not what is wanted, it can be ignored or implemented in ways that the administrator prefers. The composition of committees can often be manipulated behind the scenes in ways that protect the interests of administrators or of particular groups. Thus, committees are often useful devices for the legitimation of decisions that serve to misdirect the attention of the community from the interests that the decisions serve and from the administrators who retain power over the actual decision. Where there was a strong consensus on academic priorities, these myriad bodies, linked by procedures that limited discretionary powers, served to check one another's errors in favor of the consensus. Where there was no such consensus, the bodies were too weak to have much effect or to effectively counter the will of administrators.

To speak about the interests of the university and the ability of the university to police research misconduct requires us to identify the various interests that particular bodies or players might have in relation to research misconduct and to ask questions about their ability to perform the task. The administration, heir to the strong university presidents of the late nineteenth and early twentieth centuries, is the single most important player in the American university, and any analysis must take into account the interests and powers of administrators. The real source of discretionary power in universities is, put simply, money. One area where, in most universities, there is still a considerable amount of discretionary power unchecked by procedures or collective bodies is fiscal decision making and entry into contractual relationships between the university and other bodies. To be sure, most of the fiscal decisions of administrators are greatly constrained by the routine and slow-to-change demands of running the university and by the fact that personnel who cannot be fired consume much of the budget. So the key areas in which administrators are able to exercise power are those in which funds exist or can be developed that are not subject to these constraints. The fiscal operations of universities are often secret or obscured from view. Financial and contractual decisions and many deals and arrangements are not public knowledge or require technical knowledge of budgets and procedures that few faculty members, much less outsiders, possess. Thus, administrative secrecy, either de jure or de facto, is a central fact of the life of universities and is especially relevant to science, for reasons that will become clear in the next section.

THE RISE OF OVERHEAD

Administration is to a large extent about finance, and to understand the interests of administrators and the powers of faculty in relation to administrators is in large part to understand the facts of university finance, particularly as they relate to science. The central fact is this. Federal science funding in large part operates through a kind of subsidy. Grants not only pay the "direct costs" of university science but also pay a great deal more in the form of "overhead" or "indirect" costs. To properly clarify the impact of overhead cost accounting on universities would require an elaborate discussion of the peculiarities of university accounting systems.

The accounting system most universities now use was developed at the early part of the century for purposes that had little to do with such questions as the profitability of various parts of the university. One oddity of university accounting systems is that many of the expenses that are a part of the general cost of the university are in fact distributed in a way that is highly sensitive to the content or type of the activities, but this is not reflected in any manner in the accounting scheme. To have a distinguished department of the history of art with a fine collection and an expensive library is in accounting terms a difficult cost to make sense of within an academic budget scheme. Paintings owned by the university art museum may increase or decrease in value. The budget, however, reflects cash expenditures and not value, so these costs and benefits are simply ignored. Books in the library, similarly, may increase in value or depreciate. But the budgeting mechanisms of the library are generally unconnected to the way in which the library appears on the university budget, so it is impossible to allocate library costs to a specific activity, such as art history. Indeed, no attempt is made to do so, even in those instances in which a school or department is being closed; in these cases, usually the decision has been made for other reasons, and it is rare for a serious attempt to be made at estimating costs and returns on those assets. In short, academic budgeting is based on real numbers, but numbers that reflect cash flows rather than meaningful cost estimates. Overhead payments for research grants are also based on real numbers, but they are numbers within yet another system of accounting that has little to do with either the actual costs or the costs on the university budget.[1]

Universities have money of different kinds—that is, money that can be spent for different purposes. Typically, state universities are allocated funds by the legislature that are restricted and can be spent for specific purposes only. Overhead money is entirely different in character. It is a payment based on estimated values of goods that for the most part the university already possesses and that have already been paid for. In other words, universities, unlike businesses, keep two sets of books. One set involves the actual budget; the other is a set of books negotiated with the federal government to estimate the overhead expenses of research in general. They generally do not keep books that reflect the actual assets of the university or cost estimates in relation to these assets. The overhead rate is itself a number that has little managerial significance and is, if not fictional, very far removed from the actual decision making of the university itself.

The consequence of these various peculiarities of accounting is as follows. The overhead funds paid by the federal government appear to administrators as a kind of cost-free increment or profit that can be applied at will. Obviously, some of the funds may need to be used in support of the activities of scientists themselves, for some categories of expenditure are not "directly" funded and remain the responsibility of the university but are not provided for within the ordinary university budget—that is, they are not already paid for in some other way. But in many universities this amount is quite small, and the bulk of the proceeds of overhead is returned to the administrative units of the university as funds to be allocated for the purposes of administrators or is used for collective purposes, such as the general support of research. The existence of this money creates a novel and potentially very significant source of discretionary power for its possessors and a powerful new interest on the part of administrators in doing what the activity of indirect costs–generating research requires.[2]

To a large extent, the effect of these funds on the balance of power in a given university reflects the political purposes and balance of power that already exist. Where academic authority, or, more simply, the political power of deans and chairs and other administrators, rests on the consent of the professors, the ability to do favors to reward one's supporters (or simply to act in accordance with commonly recognized academic goals and values) is greatly helped by the possession of such funds. In the contemporary American university, a dean or chair is much like an old-style ward politician who dispenses favors and uses this power to keep in power and to excite the efforts of his loyal supporters. The old ward boss dispensed positions in the city parks department. Deans dispense administrative positions, promotions, and raises. These favors are of course limited and largely zero sum. Indirect cost returns provide administrators with a new source of funds. But the existence of these funds is balanced by the expectation of receiving the benefits that the existence of the funds creates. So the effect of these funds is complex. One effect is to increase secrecy, for it is in the interest of the dean or administrator to obscure from his or her supporters the realities of the allocation of these funds so as not to excite the expectations of supporters. The situation in which an administrator cannot fulfill expectations is a situation in which an administrator is likely to lose what "democratic" support or legitimacy he or she possesses.

There are many other complex effects of the existence of overhead funds. Administrators of universities and college presidents have to a large extent been freed of their dependence on boards and wealthy donors by the fact of overhead funds. Boards are unlikely to interfere in issues that arise in connection with funded research because they cannot provide analogous sources of funds and because only the largest endowments will produce income comparable to the income generated by indirect costs. Gifts from alumni or philanthropic benefactors, in any event, are almost always highly restricted in their uses, in sharp contrast to the highly fungible character of funds originating as indirect costs. The hand of the administrator who receives indirect costs is therefore strengthened, and not only against boards. The benefits of tuition payments are also diminished in importance, and consequently so are the activities of teaching that generate tuition. The nexus between teaching and students' willingness to pay for services is often not very clear, and efforts to respond to changes in student demand are often riven with uncertainty and practical difficulty. In comparison to almost all of the other kinds of funding that university administrators may come to receive, then, funds from recovery of indirect costs are simple to predict and relatively simple to secure.

This predictability and quantifiability means that the producers of these funds have a special status unlike the status of those who produce indirect or long-term benefits for the university. They can bargain more effectively with administrators, whose career interests are likely to be short term, and administrators can cite their successes in increasing sponsored research as a piece of quantitative evidence of their ability that is more or less incontrovertible and does not need much "interpretation."

Indirect cost payments also change the fundamental relationship between administrators and scientists, and this change takes away much of the power that these funds place in the hands of administrators. The change itself deserves some analysis. The academic senate of the traditional European university senate served to bind two important kinds of interest—the professors' interest in prestige and professional immortality and the university's collective interest in academic quality. The indirect cost accounting system binds the interests of individual scientists and administrators in a different and less subtle way. Administrators benefit financially from the grant-getting activities of the individual scientist. This benefit is direct. It does not arise through the circuitous route of the reflection of glory from the achievements of the individual scholar onto the university and thence onto its administrative officers. The payment of indirect costs goes directly to the administration and gives it the power of money that can be applied discretionarily.

The system of indirect cost payments thus creates powerful new interests on the part of both scientists and administrators. It remains to be seen what effects these interests might have on the university. One effect is simple. Whatever evaluations a president or a dean or a department chair might make of the true quality of a scientist's work must, in the end, weigh slightly indeed against the reality of that scientist's power to generate indirect costs and the closely connected reality that there is a market of administrators looking for faculty who can generate indirect costs. Scientists who can generate indirect costs are obviously very valuable to the university and to the administrators.[3]

Characteristically, faculty members who are highly successful in obtaining grants that generate indirect costs can be hired only by making costly concessions. Such researchers are in a position to bargain for special facilities, staff support, and other concessions. But the peculiarities of the science labor market, particularly the recent oversupply of scientists, enable administrators to impose special arrangements on indirect cost–generating scientists in some specialties. Indeed, such is the competition and overproduction of Ph.D.'s in many scientific areas that have heavily depended on grant funding that administrators are in a position to offer productive researchers part-time positions with the understanding that to have full salary the faculty member must secure funding to provide income for the rest of the year. Given the level of indirect cost recovery under present systems, a faculty member of this sort may be added, from the administrator's point of view, essentially without cost and with little risk. The faculty member will generate more than enough in indirect cost recovery to pay for the salary outlay the university provides in the four months that the person is paid. Needless to say, the spur to perform on the part of such a "faculty" member is correspondingly harsh. Nevertheless, such faculty members may well earn much more than a "normal" faculty member on a nine-month academic appointment. The existence of these partial appointments is only a signal of a fundamental change in the relationship between administrators and scientists from the older relations of faculty members to administrators.

THE NEW BALANCE: SCIENTISTS AS AGENTS

The basic facts about interests in relation to funded research of the sort that generates some sort of net financial benefit for the university are thus simple. Administrators have an intense interest in exploiting the capacity of the scientists in their employ to generate money for them and an intense interest in increasing the take. In this section I will ask whether this interest vastly outweighs any altruistic interest in the ethics of the research that generates the money or whether the main buyer of research has a means of channeling this interest in such a way as to cause universities to deal effectively with misconduct. I will also ask the question of what interests actually do play a role in the response of the university to misconduct. Many interests, such as the faculty's desire to protect the reputation of the university, the desire of administrators to avoid bad publicity, and the machinery of mandated research misconduct committees, might well serve to balance these interests. But each of these interests is subject to limitations, and each needs to be effectively represented. The problem is the one with which I began. Are there interests that are represented by competent bodies, or that can be represented, that can effectively deal with misconduct, and if so, what might these be? The problem takes a particular form as a result of the primary strategy of the federal government in relation to misconduct—namely, the strategy of compelling universities to police themselves. The form is this: universities and university processes operate within a complex ecology of competing interests, with different groups representing these interests. The problem is whether there are balancing interests that might be structured to serve the purpose of controlling misconduct.

If one needed an example of the intensity of the interest in external funding and the ease with which it overwhelms academic processes, the conduct of the administration of the University of Utah during the "cold fusion" affair should be sufficient to illustrate the point. The conduct of administrators at the University of Utah is in many respects exemplary of the new order and of the core problem with the inherent conflicts of interest in the university. The very fact that considerable sums of money could be made for the university or extracted from the state legislature if the claim of the cold fusion researchers were true imposed an obligation on the administration to do its utmost to ensure that the university benefited from the situation. Fulfilling the administration's responsibilities required, in effect, that they lobby and propagandize on behalf of the researchers, who were in a position to make the university the beneficiary of important developments. If the "university" in the end had a red face over the matter, individual administrators could say that they were only doing their job and that they would have been remiss if they had failed to act to protect the university's financial interest in exploiting the results.[4] The cold fusion case involved a very visible appeal for massive research funding—outside normal channels of funding, of course—as well as the prospect of patent claims. But the same interests hold in the more mundane case of universities competing for funding in traditional scientific grant programs. A standard claim of academic administrators seeking new positions is that they have substantially increased funded research in their current position.

A theoretical account of the relationship between the relevant interests in the university that enabled us to compare the present situation with that of past university forms would be useful. In discussing the classical model of the academic senate, I appealed to a very simple model of the binding of individual interests to collective interests. This model assumed that members of the senate, the professors of a university, in some sense benefited from the eminence of the university and thus of the eminence of their colleagues and in this sense had a collective interest in quality. I noted that this collective interest remained in the contemporary American university. But the relationship between the scientist who generates overhead money and the collectivity is obviously not the same as the relationship between members of an academic senate.[5] All of the professors in the traditional European university operated under more or less the same regime of fees and payments. In the contemporary American university, the situation is quite different: some faculty are employed largely to get grants or to generate outside income of some sort for the university. The recipient of grants is in a market relationship determined by the supply of funds and his or her ability to get the funds and is powerful or powerless accordingly. This power is largely individual in character, and there are enormous inequalities with respect to the ability to get such funds, even between persons with the same academic rank. To understand the "collective" interests of these persons requires an understanding of the relationship itself, which is radically different from the collegial models of the senate or the college.

It is illuminating to think of this new relationship as analogous to the relationship between insurance agents and insurers. Agents may be either employed by a company but largely dependent on commission sales for their income or "independent" of the insurance company but paid by commission. The relationship between scientists and academic administrators is one of mutual dependence and in the case of scientists on partial appointment very closely resembles the situation of an insurance agent employed by a company but paid largely through commissions. Such relationships can go wrong, and it is instructive to ask how they operate in nonacademic settings. In fact, agency relations ordinarily operate in such a way as either to employ checks and balances or to involve very substantial self-policing by professional bodies. Stockbrokers, lawyers, and physicians, for example, are employed as agents. To assure the individual purchaser of services that he or she is not being cheated, these professions each have powerful disciplinary bodies that control through licensure or similar means. No such elaborate controls exist in science, of course, in large part because the scientist does not have individual clients but rather is employed—for example, by a university. The relationship is thus more like that of an insurance agent employed by an insurance company. Among the similarities between the two cases are these. An insurance agent wants a company with a good reputation so that a sale can be made. Thus, an agent is to this extent like a scientist who relies to some extent on the reputation of the university that appoints him or her.

In the case of insurance, a clear conflict of interest is inherent in the relationship. Both agent and insurer want to make sales. But the agent, unlike the insurer, is not personally harmed, at least not directly, by bending the rules in the making of sales. Moreover, and this is critical, the collective interests of the insurance agents of a given company as a group are in conflict with the long-term interests of the insurance company. Similarly, the scientist, like the university, wants grants. The university, it is supposed, has a collective interest in its reputation that imputations of misconduct would damage and thus has an interest in policing misconduct, even by successful grant-getting scientists. But how strong is this interest? An agent who bends the rules and sells policies to those who do not strictly qualify winds up, in the long run, costing the insurance company in the form of claims that would not have been made had the rules been followed. In the short run, the company benefits from its increased sales. An incautious management could produce apparently strong results in the short term by allowing or encouraging agents to write risky policies. This conflict is similar to the conflict between the practitioners of research fraud and the university. In the case of the university, the short-run benefits of grants, the recovery of indirect costs, are similarly tangible, financial, and overwhelmingly important. In the case of the insurance agent, however, there exist both a strong interest and representatives of this interest with means to act on their interests: the shareholders and their representatives have a strong interest in protecting themselves from the activities of rogue agents. The price is financial, and bad policies can result in horrendous real losses, as recently with Lloyd's of London.

An interest in the long-term reputation of the university, or some analogous interest, would have to play a role similar to that of the long-term financial interests of the insurer for there to be any practical interest on the part of administrators in providing the appropriate balance. What is less clear is whether the university has the capacity to defend its interests here and, more interesting, whether the university, unlike the insurance company, might have no serious interest in punishing fraud. The risk that the commission of fraud will be detected and damage the reputation of the university, however, is far less tangible than the risks in the insurance case, and it is far from clear who would be held accountable if such damage occurred. No interest has yet been discussed in this chapter that would balance the desire for funded research, however fraudulent, with any *strong* countervailing force within the university's own constitutional structure. But it is still an open question as to whether there are any counterbalancing forces of this sort at all. To be sure, if an administrator can catch a research miscreant who also happens to be a thorn in the side of the administration, it may be in the interest of the administrator to get rid of the researcher in question by allowing proceedings against him or her on grounds of scientific misconduct. But in the case of the researcher who produces overhead money for the university, there is no such incentive. A finding of research misconduct, especially one that was publicized, would represent a double harm to the interests of the administration. Thus, the eagerness of university administrators to deal with simple research misconduct can scarcely be underestimated.

ARTIFICIAL INTERESTS: GOVERNMENT-MANDATED MISCONDUCT COMMITTEES AND THEIR LIMITATIONS

The government, for reasons made clear in other chapters in this volume, no longer relies solely on the natural self-interest of the university in its reputation but employs a strategy of creating an *artificial* interest in controlling misconduct on the part of the university. Ironically, as I have suggested, the subsidization strategy of the government, the system of indirect cost reimbursement, has provided powerful incentives for universities to fail to discipline researchers who generate grants. So the government is, in effect, balancing the negative effects of its own policies. The legal strategy that is employed by the government to ensure that universities will police themselves is based on the threat of suspending research funds. Thus, it assumes that universities have an overwhelming interest in federal research money and in effect assumes that this interest is far greater than the interest of the university in policing itself or ensuring its good reputation or at least that it is necessary to stiffen the resolve of the university. The mandates force the university to create various specific self-policing measures, such as the creation of research misconduct committees and procedures and procedures for the protection of whistle-blowers, as a condition of the receipt of funds. The method of mandating procedures is very familiar both to the federal government and to universities. It is analogous to the mechanisms used to police affirmative action and sexual harassment.

Mandating committees and the protection of whistle-blowers is a procedural solution, and in themselves the existence of committees to which complaints may be made and the institution of protection for complainants and procedural guidelines for the handling of complaints do change the situation in which scientists and administrators work. But their significance cannot be read simply from the guidelines governing the committees or the form of the committee as a representative body. As we have noted above, advisory committees play a particular role in the post-strong president university. The way they work and the ends they serve reflect the interests and politics of the university, especially the interests of the administration. The key fact to be understood about misconduct committees and procedures is that they are used only at a certain stage in a dispute and have a very limited role even at the stage in which they do function. They are very far from being a kind of star chamber for the prosecution of scientific misconduct. Yet they are like criminal courts in one respect: issues are typically resolved by something analogous to plea bargaining before committee action.

Misconduct committees, at present, are bodies with feeble powers that operate under severe procedural limitations. They are unlikely to develop larger and more meaningful powers in the future, for several reasons. One has to do with the legal standards for establishing misconduct. A constant theme of the literature on research misconduct has been that *intentionality* is the standard for findings of misconduct. This creates evidentiary problems. It is a very difficult standard to meet and is far higher than the standard usually employed in the regulation of professionals. Physicians or lawyers who said that their errors were unintentional would still lose their licenses to practice. Much more stringent standards, such as strict liability or due care, might be employed that would make the process of establishing misconduct much simpler and more objective. It may be noted that in the case of sexual harassment something like a due-care standard is used and that intentions are irrelevant. Moreover, if a researcher harmed by misconduct sues in civil court, the legal standards are more favorable to the complainant. Indeed, even if there is a criminal issue, such as theft, the relevant kind of intent may be much easier to establish than the kind of intent required to establish fraud and misconduct before a university committee.

A second point about intentionality as a standard relates to attempts to educate scientists in appropriate conduct. Many of the standards of conduct that are being proposed by scientists and ethicists interested in these issues to reform what are now regarded as "gray areas" simply are unenforceable and hence meaningless if intentionality is a standard. One of the major sources of dispute in misconduct cases is authorship credit, a topic that the Office of Research Integrity initially considered so difficult to deal with effectively that it declined to involve itself in authorship disputes. The Commission on Research Integrity, in contrast, argued that authorship is at the core of the problem of misconduct and that deception about authorship was a form of deception that ought to be punished in science because of the importance of credit. Intentionality, however, is difficult to prove in relation to authorship disputes precisely because the notion of contribution is a subjective one. People may well believe that they did all the work and that they deserve all the credit. A standard of intentionality means that these beliefs, not any set of objective facts, determine whether misconduct has occurred. And this holds for many other kinds of misconduct as well, especially financial misconduct. The main effect of the standard is thus to make it very difficult to assign responsibility except in the simplest cases and to the most flagrant miscreants. In any event, it is difficult or impossible to state clear rules of research conduct that cover the potentially relevant situations. Committees may write guidelines, under the tutelage of a lawyer, and usually with a model at hand. But ordinarily they do not attempt to reform existing practices, such as courtesy citation, or even to define them. Nor do the committees develop a system of case law and feedback of the sort that courts develop. In part this is simply because of the rarity of cases adjudicated by such committees, but it is also because the processes are typically secret and the conclusions not explained to the academic community at large, and because when lawyers settle such cases through negotiation they demand secrecy from the university as a condition of a resolution.

The contrast with affirmative action and sexual harassment points to a more fundamental political reason for the weakness of such committees. As a rule, a genuinely effective committee would need to respond to other collective interests, and these interests would need to have substantial bodies of discussion to support the implementation of standards and the evolution of standards of conduct. This is evident if we compare the regulation of misconduct in science with the regulation of sexual harassment or with racial and sexual discrimination. In the latter cases there are groups in the university with strong interests in the enforcement of rules and means by which to pursue these interests. The relationship between the university and the courts is quite different in these cases: while it is still true that the university is likely to be a defendant in such cases, it can protect its own interests by self-policing and thus avoid court cases. Indeed, in several cases, notably speech codes, universities have had to be restrained by the courts. It may be highly politically expedient for administrators to give in to demands of discriminated-against groups or sexually harassed persons, and administrators may legitimate themselves by respecting these demands. No comparable political payoff exists in the case of research misconduct.

In short, then, research misconduct committees are weak instruments, governed by cumbersome limitations, without powers of enforcement, and without a strong supporting constituency. Typically they are employed for reasons of administrative expedience, reasons to which I now turn.

THE PRACTICAL INTERESTS OF ADMINISTRATORS

Administrators loathe nothing quite so much as intractable, time-consuming disputes between unreasonable people that are likely to result in bad publicity. They thus have strong interests in resolving disputes of this sort by using informal means of coercion. A typical case of research misconduct is a dispute between researchers that can be resolved without appeal to any formal procedures at all. Authorship disputes, disputes over the ownership and control of data, and disputes over financial arrangements or employment often are the root of misconduct cases, and each of these kinds of disputes can be mediated or dealt with by an administrator. Even the firing of a faculty member confronted with a charge of misconduct can be handled by an administrator, who might negotiate a resignation. Committees deal only with those cases that are not soluble in this way, which is to say that committees typically deal with issues that result from administrative ineptitude, partisanship, or the stubbornness of the parties to the dispute. Thus, the practical issues for administrators are quite different from the hypothetical possibilities that are envisioned in the law.

In reality, research misconduct issues present themselves to administrators as a time-waster with no easy solutions and few possible benefits for the administrator or the university. Typically, they involve complex disputes over matters that cannot be understood properly except by specialists in the research area. They characteristically occur in biomedical science and consequently involve the complex administrative structures and relationships that exist between units and authorities of medical schools, in which the "responsible" administrative units are not clearly identified. And, most irritating from the point of view of administrators, the charge of misconduct not infrequently arises from a junior researcher who has been privy to the misdoings of a senior and presumably valuable researcher. The disputes are rarely easy to resolve, and frequently the factually correct resolution indicates some failure on the part of the university administration with respect to scrutiny and supervision of the offender and thus some sort of liability. These are all good reasons to deal with the issues informally—that is, to suppress them. In the vague early stages of a dispute, the temptation to use the means of coercion and threat available to administrators is strong, and the standard discussion of protecting whistle-blowers reflects a recognition of the fact that powers of intimidation and retaliation exist.

Resolutions may cost something. But from the point of view of administrators, resolving such disputes is simply a cost of doing business as a scientific research establishment. Choosing not to pay the price of resolving the dispute and allowing a case to be dealt with by a research misconduct committee is, from the point of view of the administration, a tactical choice. Sometimes it is a tempting choice. Subjecting a disliked faculty member to an embarrassing and punitive procedure may serve the Machiavellian purpose of maintaining fear of the administrator, or it may simply remove an obstacle or critic or force a retirement. But the tactic is not without risk. A finding of misconduct will trigger certain reporting requirements, may inadvertently harm a star producer, and may increase the legal liability of the university to allow an issue to be examined by a committee. But the fact that committees have only advisory roles and cannot implement recommendations means that the outcomes are still largely in the hands of administrators. Even the threat of losing a court case is reducible to a rough cost-benefit calculus, and individual administrators are rarely held responsible for legal outcomes harmful to the university, so uncertain are legal processes generally and so poorly developed is the law with respect to scientific misconduct. In any case, the sheer cost and uncertainty of litigation mean that at the final stages of a serious case, the issues are very likely to be handled by lawyers and settled out of court.

PUBLIC RHETORICS AND THEIR CONSTRAINTS

From the point of view of the public, the problem of misconduct in science is parallel to the problem of welfare fraud and raises similar moral issues. Welfare funds, like most funds for science, are derived from taxation, and taxation is a product of the coercive operations of the state. Because taxes are extracted through coercion, the things for which they are spent have a higher moral significance than funds that are used by individuals to purchase goods or services. The rule of "buyer beware" does not apply: misconduct with these funds is not merely "misconduct" but stealing. This is emphatically not the view of scientists or administrators, and both scientists and administrators have distinctive attitudes toward the problem of research misconduct that are systematically at variance with the rhetoric they ordinarily employ in condemning it.

Like welfare administrators, academic administrators and scientists seek to minimize the problem of fraud, to limit publicity about it, and to showcase examples of the successful prosecution of fraud. They see the key problem as one of the suppression of bad publicity. Publicity is the source of the one of the conflicts of interest that arises in the case of whistle-blowing. The whistle-blower produces, or represents a threat of producing, the precise thing that the university has an interest in suppressing: publicity that shows that the university permits and even encourages research misconduct.

STRANGE BEDFELLOWS? THE COMMON INTERESTS OF RESEARCH MISCREANTS AND ADMINISTRATORS

One of the effects of the evolution of the American university has been to diffuse responsibility and to proceduralize decision processes in such a way that formal responsibility can be evaded. This means that it is easy for administrators to individually excuse themselves from formal responsibility for the misdoings of individual researchers. Several additional developments make it difficult to pin formal responsibility on administrators. The mere fact of the semiprofessionalization of academic administration (i.e., the fact that administrative careers now involve for the most part a career path that separates quite early from the career path of successful researcher), together with the specialization of science, means that it would be unrealistic to expect academic administrators to understand what individual scientists do and consequently that it is absurd to hold them individually responsible. It would be very difficult to establish intentional wrongdoing on the part of administrators, even in those cases in which the administrator behaved especially egregiously (e.g., to punish whistle-blowers or to create an atmosphere of pressure that encouraged researchers to engage in misconduct), because the administrator could almost always claim to have not explicitly ordered wrongdoing or to have failed to understand that wrongdoing was taking place.

To take a prominent case, the administrators and attorneys who were involved in the promotion of the claims of Pons and Fleischmann with respect to "cold fusion" could not be held to have intentionally misrepresented the facts simply because they could not be said to have properly understood the facts in the first place. They relied on the assurances of the researchers. This may have been an error, or imprudent, but it was not intentional wrongdoing. Indeed, the responsibility of an academic administrator in such cases would be to exploit the researcher's work on behalf of the universities. So not only do administrators have no clearly enforceable responsibility to deal with misconduct, but their practical responsibilities push them into the arms of the successful miscreant.

Informal responsibility is another matter. Administrative careers are governed by the perceptions of other administrators, particularly their perceptions of behind-the-scenes competence. Disputes that give rise to charges of misconduct and are not "handled" before they become public issues are marks of administrative incompetence. To be sure, administrators may persuade their peers that the problems are not their fault. But a nasty dispute of any kind can be a career-destroying event for an administrator. In contrast, unethical behavior and charges of unethical behavior by subordinates are not only tolerated but expected. There is a strong sense in which it is accepted, at certain levels of leadership, that subordinates and collaborators will engage in unethical behavior and that this is simply the price of getting things done.

Scientists who get caught up in attacks by whistle-blowers are themselves often regarded as, in effect, victims of the possession of power and the enmity and risks that go along with possessing power. Boards of trustees and scientific administrators alike seem to be capable of a great deal of forbearance in these cases. Indeed, in several cases, notably the Baltimore case, it appears that the central figures were able to persuade higher-ups and boards of trustees that their accusers were cranks. Scientists themselves, it seems, are somewhat less generous. David Baltimore, for example, found that he was shunned in such a way that his work as president of Rockefeller University was made impossible.

Informally, then, the calculations of administrators are quite different. "Handling" matters, suppressing problems, and isolating troublemakers: these are the basic skills that keep a career alive. Suffice it to say that whistle-blowers are troublemakers from the point of view of administrators and that there is a de facto community of interest between the miscreant and the administrator, each of whom wants the problem to go away. Protecting whistle-blowers is a major concern of the authors of mandates for self-policing, and their concern is well justified by this odd community of interest.

Another interest, perhaps even stronger, binds the successful researcher engaged in misconduct to administrators. At the moment, a series of court cases in which researchers have sued to protect their legal rights from research miscreants has created a strong pattern: the university and the research miscreant are codefendants. In this situation, the university research misconduct committee represents, in effect, the first line of defense for the university in what will potentially become a civil action against the university, in large part because such committees typically operate under standards of evidence that make it more difficult to establish wrongdoing than it is to establish harm in a civil court.

THE INTERESTS OF SCIENTISTS

Scientists, for their own reasons, have very little interest in the punishment of research misconduct through formal procedures. As I have suggested, there is a vast difference between misconduct and the appearance of misconduct. Actual misconduct is often difficult to detect. The scientific result that no one uses or that is buried in a mass of other contrary scientific results has little impact aside from a minor nuisance or noise effect in the scientific communication system. A major claim, such as the claim made in the cold fusion case, is consequential and does waste the time of a large number of scientists; thus, it wastes the money of the agencies and universities who are paying for science. But the misconduct is detected and once detected has no further consequences.

Established scientists generally take the view that they are in a position to protect themselves against research miscreants and often consider themselves able to judge the scientific integrity and quality of researchers in their own area. In biomedical science, where standards of conduct for physicians are somewhat modified by virtue of the intrusion of medical notions of utility, which sometimes lead in directions that conflict with notions of scientific disinterestedness, many researchers are involved with drug companies and medical manufacturers in ways that other researchers regard as ethically dubious, and there is a certain amount of shunning that takes place as a result of these judgments. However, researchers typically regard these means of dealing with misconduct as sufficient and typically do not see themselves as harmed by research misconduct on the part of others.

Scientist-administrators may feel a personal responsibility for ridding the university of a research miscreant, and scientists competing directly for resources may have an interest in getting rid of an unscrupulous colleague. But more often they would say that they are inconvenienced by poor-quality research and that misconduct itself rarely has any effect on their own research work. Moreover, scientists have a strong interest in avoiding the creation of new regimes of accountability and scrutiny that would be distractions from their own scientific work. Most scientists feel that they devote far too much time already on problems of paperwork in acquiring supplies for laboratories and dealing with bureaucratic demands. Any sort of formal procedure that would increase these demands for bureaucratic intrusion into the laboratory would be definitely against the interests of the individual scientist and would be strongly resisted. Scientists obviously cannot *say* very explicitly that they feel that a great deal of research misconduct is in fact tolerable and that they would prefer that the issue be ignored. Nevertheless, this is what they would prefer.

CONCLUSION: THE CASH NEXUS AND MORALITY

The implications of what I have said here should be clear. Universities lack the political will to deal with research misconduct and indeed have no genuine interest in dealing with the problem of research misconduct. There is only the flimsiest sort of collective interest in the reputation of the university that can be an anchor for an effort to deal effectively with research misconduct. The "faculty" have no effective power, and the manner in which scientists have come to be funded destroys the notion of the faculty as a meaningful collective body. The interests of the administration are squarely with the successful researcher—that is, one who brings in grant money and especially overhead. The history of research misconduct episodes generally bears out the overwhelming importance of the power to generate money. When the research miscreants have been powerful senior scientists, little or nothing has been done to curtail their activities, and universities have been reluctant to move against them.

The primary incentive governing universities in their decisions involving science, I have argued, is overhead money. If the funding system was changed in such a way that there was in effect no benefit for universities to employ research scientists or if the benefits were entirely neutral, there would be no reason for universities to tolerate research misconduct except where the scientist procured for the university some other valued good, such as reputation. The present problem of research misconduct seems to derive almost entirely from the peculiar constellation of interests produced by the system of research overhead costs. It is thus especially striking that none of the reports on research misconduct deals with this issue, much less suggests changes in the system. The reasons for this are quite simple. The system, as I have shown, greatly increases the power of both scientists and administrators.

Research misconduct committees, I have suggested, have many weaknesses. They depend, in the end, on one tangible force: the sense of honor that is part of the identity of scientists. The present "balance of forces" bearing on the regulation of scientific misconduct thus relies very heavily on something that this system has almost certainly served to erode. By making science profitable, and thus making scientists, as individuals, powerful, the system has provided incentives for misconduct of a kind hitherto unknown in the history of science.

Inventing a moral sense of responsibility where none existed previously is a difficult trick. But there is a base for it in scientists' general sense of honor. It could be done through some relatively simple institutional innovations. If funding agencies insisted on, and paid for, scientists to serve as scientific auditors and held them coresponsible on matters of research conduct (perhaps in a system in which overhead was paid for this function), direct, above-salary payments made to scientists who served as "auditors," or "peer auditors," of the grants of another scientist would create an ethics buddy system, create the conditions for discussion of research misconduct matters, provide a role for "wisdom," and produce "shaming" effects simply by virtue of the fact that someone who agreed to be a "buddy" for the purposes of the certification of the conduct of a research project could not be held to be nonresponsible by virtue of ignorance of the science. Responsibility for being informed about the conduct of the research would be a matter of working for pay, of doing one's job.

Notes

1. The political origins of the system of indirect costs are in appeals made by universities that already had a great deal of funding and wished to defray unreimbursed costs. There was never an intention to create the present system of de facto subsidy (see Harvard, 1961/1972).

2. In my own university, for example, some of the overhead is returned as a kind of kickback to the principal investigator, some to the dean of the college, and some to the department chair. Only the principal investigator may take this as a salary or cash benefit. In other cases the funds are applicable toward expenses.

3. The value of other kinds of valued faculty members may nevertheless also rise as an indirect consequence of the fact that a faculty member who generates a large amount of overhead is in a position to demand, often quite reasonably, an enormous amount of support and consideration on perfectly reasonably competitive grounds. In making these demands, the eminent grant-getting scientist makes the salary demands or demands of support of other kinds of eminent faculty cheap by comparison, and also more affordable, if the administrator can support these other faculty out of indirect costs or at least defray their costs in part through money mobilized by indirect cost system. But faculty members who do not generate indirect costs are to a great extent ornamental.

4. In fact, they went very far beyond merely protecting their interests. But in the end, the dispute split the administration, partly as a result of threatening letters sent by attorneys for Pons and Fleischmann to a university scientist who questioned the research after being officially asked to do so by the administration. Top university administrators informed the scientist that the university would not legally indemnify him, thereby seriously compromising basic principles of academic freedom. Huizenga (1993), in a history of the affair, called this act "serious, serious mishandling" (p. 170), but it was clearly an act that reflected administrators' willingness to sacrifice truth, decency, and academic freedom in support of their goals. The conduct of the administration, and especially of the president, Chase N. Peterson, was usefully examined in Huizenga (1993).

5. I leave aside the issue of the structure of American medical schools, which originates in the organization of hospitals rather than anything like the senatorial tradition. In a word, the organization of medical schools is baronial. This structure has significant implications for the problem of misconduct, especially misconduct on the part of prominent department chairs.

References

Birnbaum, R. (1989). Responsibility without authority: The impossible job of the college president. In J. C. Smart (Ed.), *Higher education: Handbook of theory and research* (Vol. 5, pp. 31–57). New York: Agathon.

Bryce, J. (1908). *The American commonwealth* (Vol. 1, 2nd ed., rev.). New York: Commonwealth. (Revised eds. published 1916–1917, 1931–1933, New York: Macmillan)

Commission on Research Integrity. (1995). *Integrity and misconduct in research.* Washington, DC: U.S. Department of Health and Human Services.

Complainant wins *qui tam* suit on theft of intellectual property. (1995, September). *R. I. Newsletter [Office of Research Integrity, U.S. Public Health Service], 3*(4), 1–2.

Harvard and the federal government: A report to the faculties and governing boards of Harvard University. (1972). In J. Penick, C. Pursell, M. Sherwood, & D. Swain (Eds.), *The politics of American science, 1939 to the present* (rev. ed.). Cambridge, MA: MIT Press. (Original work published 1961)

Huizenga, J. (1993). *Cold fusion: The scientific fiasco of the century.* New York: Oxford University Press.

Merton, R. K. (1973). *The sociology of science, theoretical and empirical investigations.* Chicago: University of Chicago Press.

Teich, A., & Frankel, M. (1992). *Good science and responsible scientists: Meeting the challenge of fraud and misconduct in science.* Washington, DC: American Association for the Advancement of Science.

Turner, S. (1997). Tenure and the constitution of the university. *PS: Political Science and Politics, 30,* 17–20.

Veblen, T. (1957). *Higher learning in America: A memorandum on the conduct of universities by business men.* New York: Sagamore.

PART III

Policy and Law Perspectives

CHAPTER SIX

Toward a Guiding Framework for Self-Regulation in the Community of the Academic Profession

John M. Braxton

Individual scientists, laboratories, universities, scientific societies and journals, private foundations, and governmental agencies share responsibility for deterring, detecting, and sanctioning scholarship misconduct (Chubin, 1983). These loci of responsibility constitute a trans-scientific community in which the roles that members play in addressing misconduct depend on the issues and interests at stake (Fox & Braxton, 1994).

Although private foundations and governmental agencies hold some responsibility for addressing misconduct, the primary obligation for deterring, detecting, and sanctioning scientific improprieties rests with "the community of the academic profession."[1] This community is organized around the various academic disciplines of the natural sciences, social sciences, and humanities,[2] and it has several levels: individual scientists, laboratories, universities, scientific societies, and academic and professional journals.

The primacy of the obligation of the community of the academic profession for exercising responsibility for misconduct stems from three factors. First, the lay public maintains strong expectations for the "community of the academic profession" to regulate itself by enforcing standards and ethical principles for research conduct (Anderson & Louis, 1991; Goode, 1969). The failure to self-regulate results in the loss of the lay public's trust (Goode, 1969). Second, this community exerts more social control over the research conduct of individual academic professionals than do either private foundations or governmental granting agencies. Such social control manifests itself in the graduate school socialization, colleague assessment of professional performance for promotion, tenure and salary increases, and the allocation of rewards and recognition for scholarly accomplishments (Anderson & Louis, 1991). Third, members of the academic profession assert that responsibility for addressing issues of misconduct rests within this community (American Association for the Advancement of Science [AAAS], 1991; Teich, 1992).

Although the primary obligation for exercising self-regulation for scholarly malfeasance resides in the community of the academic profession, several factors mitigate efficacious self-regulation in this community. First, members of the community of the academic profession view misconduct in science as a rare event (Bell, 1992; Douglas, 1992; St. James-Roberts, 1976; Zuckerman, 1977). Second, the academic community has not institutionalized the surveillance of misconduct (Weinstein, 1979; Zuckerman, 1977). Third, the sanctioning of misconduct is best described as decentralized and informal (Black, 1976; Zuckerman, 1977, 1988). Fourth, universities have been sluggish in their development of policies and procedures to handle allegations of misconduct (Steneck, 1994).

These four factors strongly suggest that self-regulation is not a naturally occurring process in the community of the academic profession. Consequently, the academic profession needs a guiding framework for the self-regulation of scholarly misconduct. Without such a guiding framework, self-regulation is likely to remain haphazard and subject to the preferences of the lay public.[3]

Scholars of misconduct offer answers to such questions as why misconduct occurs (Zuckerman, 1977, 1988) and what can be done to control misconduct (Chubin, 1983). Scholars also advance definitions of misconduct associated with the four stages of the research process: production, reporting, dissemination, and evaluation (Chubin, 1985). However, such a guiding framework has not been posited by scholars of misconduct. Consequently, the purpose of this chapter is to posit such a framework.

This framework allocates responsibility to the various levels of the community of the academic profession—individual scientists, laboratories, universities, scientific societies, and academic and professional journals—for deterring, detecting, and sanctioning misconduct associated with each of the four stages of the research process. Chubin's definitions of misconduct associated with each of the four stages of the research process are consistent with the definitions of scientific misconduct promulgated by the Commission on Research Integrity (1995) and the Public Health Service (Price, 1994).

Such a framework can be used by the community of the academic profession to guide its self-regulatory process. Moreover, scholars of misconduct and public policy makers can use this framework to appraise the efficacy of self-regulation by this community.

However, the effectiveness of such a framework depends on its institutionalization by the various levels of the community of the academic profession. For such institutionalization to occur, the community must view self-regulation as serving its own interest. The lay public has exercised social control because of various incidents of misconduct during the past two decades (Hackett, 1994). Such control has manifested itself in congressional action, which established the Office of the Inspector General (National Science Foundation) and the Office of Research Integrity (Public Health Service and National Institutes of Health). The creation of these offices has led to the development of policies and procedures by universities to address allegations of misconduct (Steneck, 1994). Consequently, self-regulation by the academic profession has been largely in response to such social control. Thus, I first provide a set of theoretical formulations for why professional interests are served by self-regulation.

SELF-REGULATION AND PROFESSIONAL SELF-INTEREST

Goode (1969) contended that mastery and control of a basic body of abstract knowledge and the ideal of service are the core generating traits that differentiate an occupation from a profession. These two core generating traits justify a profession's claim for autonomy.

The ideal of service, or what Parsons (1939) called the "collectivity orientation," is the obligation of professionals to make their choices on the basis of the needs and welfare of their clients (Goode, 1969). Thus, professions provide disinterested service to clients (Goode, 1957; Parsons, 1951). Barber (1978) contended that professions both acknowledge and embrace this special obligation. Moreover, professions garner high social status from the ideal of service because this service ideal makes a profession a social necessity (Abbott, 1983). High social status also emanates from the purity of professional motives indexed in the ideal of disinterested service to clients (Abbott, 1983).

Formal and informal codes of conduct provide guides for professional behavior consistent with the ideal of service (Bucher & Strauss, 1961; Goode, 1957; Greenwood, 1957). These formal and informal codes provide the basis for self-regulation by the community of the profession. Such codes are inculcated through the graduate school socialization process (Goode, 1957).

Moreover, the community of the profession allocates the highest rewards of prestige to individuals who conform to such formal and informal codes, and it sanctions individuals who deviate from such codes. The sanctioning of offenders is necessary to preserve the prestige, reputation, and autonomy of the community of the profession (Goode, 1957).

The failure to sanction offenders violates the lay public's trust in the community of the profession to provide disinterested service to clients. Violation of the public's trust also erodes its belief in both the social necessity of the profession and the purity of its motives. As a consequence, the social status and reputation of the community of the profession are lowered. Professional autonomy is also constrained. Thus, the sanctioning of offenders serves to maintain the public's trust in the profession's faithfulness to the ideal of service.

These formulations can be extended to the community of the academic profession. Although teaching and research form an integrated core of activities for the academic profession (Braxton & Toombs, 1982; Parsons & Platt, 1973), research or scholarly role performance is of particular interest here. Because the goal of scholarly role performance is the creation of knowledge (Merton, 1942, 1973), the knowledge base of an academic discipline is the client of scholarly role performance. Standards and ethical principles for research conduct safeguard the welfare of the knowledge base of an academic discipline (Anderson & Louis, 1991) and serve as a guide to the choices made by scholars in conducting their research and scholarship. Violations of these standards and ethical principles constitute scholarly misconduct because these violations detrimentally affect the knowledge base of an academic discipline, the client of scholarly role performance.

Thus, the deterrence, detection, and sanctioning of scholarly wrongdoing are abiding concerns of the community of the academic profession. They enable this professional community to maintain its reputation among the lay public for disinterested service in the pursuit of knowledge and to retain professional autonomy by preserving the public's trust in the ability of the community of the academic profession to self-regulate.

Deterrence, detection, and sanctioning of misconduct also safeguard the welfare of the knowledge base of academic disciplines. Misconduct hampers the advancement of knowledge and misleads scholars by creating blind alleys of research and scholarship (Braxton, 1993; Chubin, 1983). Moreover, the value pattern of cognitive rationality dictates attentiveness to the well-being of this knowledge base. Parsons and Platt (1973) asserted that cognitive rationality is the integrative value of the academic profession. Platt, Parsons, and Kirshstein (1976) defined it as the value placed on the comprehension and solution of intellectual problems in rational terms. Consequently, detection, deterrence, and sanctioning of misconduct is congruent with the high value placed on cognitive rationality.

NECESSARY PROCESSES FOR SELF-REGULATION

For self-regulation of the academic profession to be efficacious, the following social processes are necessary:

1. Doctoral study is regarded as a powerful socialization process (Hagstrom, 1957). Through this socialization process, norms, attitudes, and values are inculcated in aspirants to the academic profession (Braxton, Lambert, & Clark, 1995; Merton, Reader, & Kendall, 1957). For self-regulation to be

effective, this socialization process should emphasize standards and ethical principles for research conduct. Standards and ethical principles germane to the four stages of the research process—production, reporting, dissemination, and evaluation—identified by Chubin (1985) should be instilled through this process. Consequently, the doctoral socialization process serves as an important mechanism of deterrence and detection of wrongdoing (Zuckerman, 1977, 1988) associated with each of the four stages of the research process.

Because individual scientists are agents of socialization through formal course work (Toombs, 1977) and interpersonal interactions with students (Cole & Cole, 1973), individual academic professionals shoulder a major responsibility for the prevention and observation of scholarly misconduct connected with each of the four stages of the research process. Academic departments also jointly share this obligation with individuals. Individuals and academic departments discharge this responsibility by ensuring that standards and ethical principles pertinent to each of the four stages of the research process are inculcated through departmental graduate training programs.

2. Zuckerman (1988) contended that doctoral socialization does not fully ensure the prevention and identification of research malfeasance. Consequently, mechanisms of surveillance are needed to bolster doctoral socialization. A necessary requirement for such mechanisms is that they enable individual scientists, graduate students, or other research personnel to directly observe possible occurrences of misconduct. Because such mechanisms enable misconduct to be observed, prevention of misconduct also occurs. Scientists are less likely to engage in misconduct if their acts are observable by others. Surveillance mechanisms designed to detect and deter misconduct associated with each of the four stages of the research process are needed.

Although other levels of the community of the academic profession assume some responsibility for the development and use of such mechanisms, ultimate responsibility rests with individual scientists to prevent and detect wrongdoing across the four stages of the research process. Because scientists are more likely to deviate from ethical principles when they perceive that their colleagues are violating these principles (Braxton, 1990), individual scientists bear major responsibility for deterring wrongdoing by conforming to standards and ethical principles connected with the four stages of the research process. The detection of scientific malfeasance also ultimately depends on the watchfulness of individual scientists (Chubin, 1983).

3. Effective self-regulation also requires a system of positive rewards and negative sanctions (Merton, 1973; Zuckerman, 1977). Such a system requires the punishment of individuals found guilty of violating standards and ethical principles associated with the four stages of the research process.

The severity of a sanction depends on several factors: the degree of harm done by an impropriety to the community of the academic profession's reputation with the lay public for its faithfulness to the ideal of service to clients, the extent of harm done to the knowledge base of an academic discipline by an incident of wrongdoing, and the extent of harm done to the career of a scientist's graduate student or other personnel. The allocation of sanctions according to the degree of harm is consistent with consequentialist ethics. This approach to ethical theory asserts that misconduct has occurred if harm occurs from the focal action (Peach, 1995).

The harshest sanctions should be apportioned for wrongdoing that adversely affects either the knowledge base of an academic discipline or the reputation of the academic profession with the lay public. However, the most harm to reputation, the knowledge base, or individual careers occurs when research begotten through an impropriety is published in an academic journal or book. Great harm results because publication in a refereed academic journal signifies that peer gatekeepers certify the research conducted and its knowledge claims.

The locus of responsibility for sanctioning wrongdoing depends on the level of the academic profession possessing the type of sanction befitting the impropriety. The locus of responsibility also depends on the site of the offense: the laboratory, the academic department, the academic journal review process, or the scientific society.

This system of rewards and sanctions ultimately relies on individuals who personally experience misconduct to report suspected incidents of misconduct. Individuals who did not personally experience misconduct but who receive reports of it also need to take appropriate action. Appropriate action includes talking directly to the offending individual, professionally boycotting the offending individual, and reporting the incident to a university research integrity committee (Braxton & Bayer, 1996). Reporting the occurrence to the editor of an academic journal or to a scientific society is an additional action. Such a system requires procedures to handle allegations of wrongdoing.

RESEARCH STAGES AND RESPONSIBILITIES

In addition to the ultimate responsibilities of individual scientists for self-regulation through engagement in the three social processes discussed above, other levels of the community of the academic profession—laboratories, academic departments, universities, academic journals, and scientific societies—have specific obligations for deterring, detecting, and sanctioning misconduct associated with each stage of the research process. The capability of universities to carry out their specific responsibilities may be greatly restricted by their "lack of political will" to address scholarly misconduct. In chapter 5 of this volume, Turner argues that such a lack of political will stems from the overhead revenues obtained through the research grants of individual scientists. However, the responsibilities outlined here for universities are promulgated to promote further analysis and discussion of the responsibilities of universities. Moreover, the lack of political will at the level of the university to sanction scholarly misconduct in general and misconduct associated with the production stage of the research process in particular does not restrict laboratories and academic departments from assuming their obligations. Furthermore, academic journals and scientific societies are unaffected by the obstacles within universities that Turner delineates as limiting their enforcement of ethical standards.

Table 6.1 exhibits the responsibilities for deterring and detecting scholarship misconduct that might be assumed by various levels of the community of the academic profession, whereas table 6.2 displays the types of sanctions that might be meted out by these levels of the community of the academic profession. These specific responsibilities are described below.

Production

This stage entails the development of ideas for research projects, the collection of data, record keeping, and analysis of data, including bench procedures and coding (Chubin, 1985). Plagiarism, appropriation of ideas from others, fabrication, and data trimming represent types of misconduct occurring in this stage of the research process (Chubin, 1985).

Deterrence and Detection

Laboratories and academic departments bear a major responsibility for deterring and detecting misconduct associated with this stage of the research process. This obligation is discharged through the development and enforcement of policies and procedures for research conduct in the laboratory or an academic department. Chubin (1983) suggested such policies and procedures. He recommended that data logs and data books be kept open in the laboratory and that all individuals be able to have access to them. Computer printouts and other raw data could also be kept in an open place and available to all. Another policy suggested by Chubin is the development of explicit rules for laboratory conduct that would be displayed in the laboratory or academic department.

Academic departments assume an additional responsibility for deterring and detecting wrongdoing by rewarding replications of research done by others through reappointment, tenure, promotion, and salary increments. Zuckerman (1977, 1988) asserted that replication of research represents an important mechanism for the deterrence and detection of fabrication and data trimming. Replication serves as a deterrent because scholars fear that their improprieties, especially fraud and fabrication, will

Table 6.1: Suggested Responsibilities for Deterring and Detecting Misconduct, by Stage of the Research Process

Levels of the Community of the Academic Profession

Research Stage	Labs	Departments	Universities	Associations	Journals
Production (e.g., plagiarism, appropriation of ideas from others, data fabrication and trimming)	Open data logs, data books, raw data, and computer printouts, and establish lab conduct rules	Reward replications in faculty personnel decisions	Reward replications in faculty personnel decisions	Give imprimatur on lab and department policies and procedures	Encourage replication and conduct random data audits
Reporting (e.g., cooking of data, suppression of data, failure to cite, and exaggerated knowledge claims)	Dry run seminars, internal manuscript review	Dry run seminars, internal manuscript review			Peer reviewer detection, random data audits
Dissemination					
Authorship credit	Dry run seminars, internal manuscript review	Dry run seminars, internal manuscript review			
Multiple journal submissions					Policy of certifying singular submission
Pirating of research findings					Peer reviewer code of conduct
Citation fabrication	Dry run seminars, internal manuscript review	Dry run seminars, internal manuscript review			
Foot dragging on supplying raw data					Random raw data audits
Failures of acknowledgment	Dry run seminars, internal manuscript review	Dry run seminars, internal manuscript review			Policy of requiring acknowledging anonymous peer review comments

Table 6.1 continued

Levels of the Community of the Academic Profession

Research Stage	Labs	Departments	Universities	Associations	Journals
Evaluation					
Unavailability of raw data from author	Open access to raw data, data books, lab books, and computer printouts	Open access to raw data, data books, lab books, and computer printouts			
Peer silence	Conduct rules proscribing peer silence	Conduct rules proscribing peer silence		Code of conduct proscribing peer silence	
Negligence in application of research	Client satisfaction surveys	Client satisfaction surveys		Code of conduct principle	
Negligence in incorporating research in the curriculum		Colleague classroom observations		Code of conduct principle	

be detected by their colleagues through the failure to replicate their findings (Zuckerman, 1977, 1988).

Universities and academic journals also should encourage replications. Like academic departments, universities should give some weight to replications of research in the tenure and promotion of faculty (Braxton, 1993; Fox & Braxton, 1994). Academic journals bear responsibility for replications by encouraging the submission and acceptance of manuscripts reporting replications of previous research.

In addition to editorial policies supportive of replication, academic journals exercise responsibility for production-stage improprieties by conducting random audits of raw data for manuscripts under peer review (Rennie, 1989; Shapiro & Charrow, 1989).

Scholarly societies and associations play an important role in deterring and detecting wrongdoing by putting the imprimatur of the association on the above preventative policies and procedures. See table 6.1 for a summary of these suggested responsibilities.

Sanctions

Universities bear the chief responsibility for the sanctioning of plagiarism, data trimming, and fabrication. If not corrected before public presentation, such misconduct detrimentally affects both the reputation of the academic profession among the lay public and the welfare of the knowledge base of an academic discipline. Consequently, strong sanctions are necessary. Universities have an array of strong sanctions for such offenses (Fox & Braxton, 1994) given that universities have the authority to terminate both untenured and tenured professors for cause. However, as Turner notes in chapter 5 of this book, universities exhibit great reluctance to mete such sanctions. Such reluctance needs to be overcome for professional self-regulation to be effective.

Academic journals also have stringent sanctions at their disposal. Academic journals can sanction offenders by refusing to publish research begotten through misconduct. Printing retractions of tainted research represents another sanction available to academic journals (Fox, 1994).

Academic associations and societies can dispense strong sanctions for plagiarism, data trimming, and fabrication in that they can deny membership to individuals found guilty of such offenses by university research integrity committees. Scientific societies can also take responsibility for the punishment of such offenders by assuming the role of a third party in cases where wrongdoing occurring in one university is detected by an individual at another university. As a third party, a committee of the scientific society can recommend sanctions to be meted out by the university of the offending individual. Table 6.2 provides a summary of these suggested sanctions.

Table 6.2: Suggested Responsibilities for Sanctioning Misconduct, by Stage of the Research Process

Levels of the Community of the Academic Profession

Research Stage	Labs	Departments	Universities	Associations	Journals
Production (e.g., plagiarism, appropriation of ideas from others, data fabrication and trimming)			Major responsibility to mete out strong sanctions such as termination	Responsibility to mete out strong sanctions such as denial of membership, third-party role in university integrity committees	Responsibility to mete out strong sanctions such as refusal to publish manuscript, printing of retraction of tainted research
Reporting (e.g., cooking of data, suppression of data, failure to cite, and exaggerated knowledge claims)	One-time offenders, responsibility for verbal reprimand or professional boycotting of offending individual, correction before journal submission	One-time offenders, responsibility for verbal reprimand or professional boycotting of offending individual, correction before journal submission	Major responsibility for repeat offenders, less severe sanction than termination	Responsibility for some sanctions such as debarment from holding office or associational meetings	If detected by review, then responsibility to reject or require substantial revision of the focal manuscript
Dissemination					
Authorship credit	Responsibility for appropriate credit attribution before manuscript submission to a journal	Responsibility for appropriate credit attribution before manuscript submission to a journal			If identified by review, then editors either reject manuscript or make manuscript acceptance contingent on appropriate author credit
Multiple journal submissions					Enforcement of singular manuscript submission policy

continued

Table 6.2 continued

Levels of the Community of the Academic Profession

Research Stage	Labs	Departments	Universities	Associations	Journals
Pirating of research findings					Removal of peer reviewers from panel of reviewers by editor
Citation fabrication	Correction of citations before manuscript submission to a journal	Correction of citations before manuscript submission to a journal			Rejection of manuscripts by authors who fail to provide requested raw data
Foot dragging on supplying raw data					Manuscript acceptance contingent on acknowledgments
Failures of acknowledgment	Correction of acknowledgments before manuscript submission to a journal	Correction of acknowledgments before manuscript submission to a journal			
Evaluation					
Unavailability of raw data from author	Force provision of requested raw data	Force provision of requested raw data	Major responsibility for meting out such harsh sanctions as promotion delay or salary freeze		
Peer silence	If minimal damage to knowledge/reputation, then lab director should verbally reprimand offender	If minimal damage to knowledge/reputation, then chairperson should verbally reprimand offender	If damage to knowledge/reputation is extensive, reprimand by research integrity committee		

Table 6.2 continued

	Levels of the Community of the Academic Profession				
Research Stage	Labs	Departments	Universities	Associations	Journals
Negligence in application of research	If harm minimal, restriction of consulting activities of offender	If harm minimal, restriction of consulting activities of offender	If harm extensive, then sanctions range from verbal reprimand to delaying promotion or freezing salary of offender		
Negligence in incorporating research in the curriculum	If harm minimal, frequent colleague classroom observations conducted	If harm minimal, frequent colleague classroom observations conducted	If harm extensive, sanctions range from reprimand to delaying promotion or freezing salary of offender		

Reporting

Chubin (1985) described this stage of the research process as the selection and presentation of research findings. Presentations take the form of practice seminars in academic departments and laboratories or formal presentations to colleagues (Chubin, 1985). Reporting findings to the news media and holding press conferences are additional presentation forms. Improprieties in reporting include misrepresentation of findings and various forms of nonpresentation such as "cooking" or suppressing data, failing to cite the pertinent work of others, and making exaggerated claims for the findings of research (Chubin, 1985).

Deterrence and Detection

Laboratories and academic departments hold key responsibilities for discouraging and discerning improprieties associated with the reporting stage of the research process. Their enforcement of policies and procedures stipulating open and available log books, data books, raw data, and computer printouts serves to deter data suppression. Laboratories and departments also assume this obligation by enforcing policies requiring "dry run" seminars for laboratory and department colleagues. Internal manuscript review by laboratory and department colleagues before public presentation or submission to a journal could discourage data cooking, exaggerated claims for the findings of research, and the failure to cite relevant research literature.

Academic journals play a key role in both the deterrence and the detection of the "cooking" of data, the failure to cite appropriate literature, and the making of overstated knowledge claims. The failure to cite relevant research can be deterred and detected by peer reviewers familiar with the research literature of a focal topic, who can identify pertinent literature that should be cited. Because peer reviewers evaluate the knowledge claims made by authors, the making of overstated knowledge claims can also be prevented and identified. Finally, suppressed and "cooked data" can be prevented and detected through the use of random audits of raw data and supporting research records by academic journals. A summary of these suggested responsibilities is given in table 6.1.

Sanctions

The locus of responsibility for sanctioning depends on both the type of infraction and whether a manuscript containing such improprieties has been submitted to an academic journal. If published, manuscripts that misrepresent the data, make exaggerated knowledge claims, or "cook" or suppress data not only can tarnish the reputation of the community of the academic profession but can detrimentally affect the knowledge base of an academic discipline. However, less harm occurs to both than that caused by plagiarism, fabrication, or data trimming. Termination of employment is too stringent for such misbehavior unless the offender has repeatedly engaged in such behavior. In such cases, universities should assume the primary responsibility for sanctioning. However, the assumption of such responsibility by universities may be problematic given Turner's formulations advanced in chapter 5.

Responsibility for sanctioning the authors of published manuscripts containing the focal improprieties also resides with academic societies. Sanctions for individuals found guilty of such wrongdoing might include not being able to hold association positions such as president, secretary, or board member. Another sanction might be preventing the offending individual from participating in societal activities for a specified period of time.

In other cases, such as one-time occurrences or unsubmitted manuscripts, verbal reprimands or professional boycotting may be sanctions of suitable severity. Laboratories and academic departments are responsible for meting out such actions. If a manuscript has not been submitted for publication, then laboratories and academic departments also assume responsibility for ensuring that the detected improprieties are corrected before a manuscript is submitted to a journal.

If these offenses are detected through the journal manuscript review process, then academic journals assume responsibility for meting out sanctions. These sanctions include the outright rejection of a manuscript or substantial revision to rectify the identified problem. Table 6.2 summarizes the various sanctions suggested for allocation by the levels of the community of the academic profession.

Dissemination

Four substages make up this stage of the research process (Chubin, 1985). In the substage of *prepublication distribution of the findings* of research beyond the local laboratory or department, research findings are dispersed through preprints, correspondence with colleagues, telephone conversations, and invited colloquia. The second substage is the *submission of a manuscript* for publication; the third is scholar activity in the *processing of the manuscript by an academic journal*; and the fourth is the *revision and publication* of the manuscript reporting research findings.

Improprieties associated with the prepublication distribution of research findings involve the allocation of authorship credit for the reported research. Such wrongdoing takes two principal forms: the failure to acknowledge the contribution of collaborators and the attribution of authorship credit when it is not due (Chubin, 1985).

Two types of misconduct occur in the substage of manuscript submission, one committed by authors and the other by peer reviewers. Authors engage in wrongdoing when they simultaneously submit a manuscript to more than one journal (Chubin, 1985). Journal peer reviewers engage in wrongdoing when they pirate data from a manuscript under their review (Chubin, 1985).

The fabrication of citations and "foot dragging" in providing journal editors with requested raw data represent forms of misconduct associated with the substage of processing of manuscripts (Chubin, 1985).

Wrongdoing connected with the publication substage of the dissemination stage involves the failure to acknowledge reviewers of preprints, data sources, anonymous peer reviewer comments, and the financial support of granting agencies (Chubin, 1985).

Deterrence and Detection

The primary locus of responsibility for deterring and detecting wrongdoing associated with the dissemination stage depends on the type of misconduct to be discouraged or identified. The chief responsibility for deterring misattribution of authorship and failure to acknowledge collaborators rests with laboratories and academic departments. Their enforcement of policies designed to deter reporting-stage misconduct also serves to hinder misbehavior related to preprint distribution. Policies stipulating "dry run" seminars and internal manuscript review serve to deter both the failure to acknowledge research collaborators and the tendency to assign authorship credit when it is not due. Individuals attending "dry runs" and participating in internal reviews of manuscripts can detect such improprieties due to the enforcement of these policies.

Academic journals bear major responsibility for deterring and detecting both the simultaneous multiple submission of manuscripts to journals and the pirating of research data by peer reviewers for submitted manuscripts. Such responsibility can be discharged through the enforcement of policies created to deter such misbehavior. Authors submitting a manuscript for publication consideration should be required to certify that the focal manuscript has not been simultaneously submitted to another journal. The pirating of research findings can be deterred through the promulgation and enforcement of a code of conduct for journal peer reviewers. Proscriptions regarding the pirating of research findings should be one tenet of such a code of conduct. Through the execution of these policies, journal editors detect the focal acts of malfeasance.

The primary obligation for preventing wrongdoing associated with manuscript processing depends on the infraction. Laboratories and academic departments shoulder principal responsibility for discouraging the fabrication of citations in manuscripts submitted to academic journals, whereas academic journals bear the primary obligation for preventing "foot dragging" in supplying editors with raw data. Policies requiring the internal review of manuscripts and "dry run" seminars also serve to deter the fabrication of citations. Thus, laboratories and academic departments discharge this obligation through their enforcement of such policies. Individuals attending such seminars and participating in internal reviews of manuscripts can detect such wrongdoing because of the administration of such policies.

Editors of academic journals deter and detect author reluctance to supply raw data for submitted manuscripts through the enforcement of journal policies stipulating audits of raw data.

The locus of the principal responsibility for discouraging wrongdoing connected with the revision of manuscripts and their publication also depends on the act of malfeasance. The failure to acknowledge anonymous peer review comments can be deterred through the creation and implementation of a policy requiring that the author of a manuscript acknowledge the comments made by anonymous peer reviewers that the author uses in making revisions to the manuscript. Journal editors bear the sole responsibility for the prevention and identification of such misbehavior through their enforcement of such a policy.

However, laboratories and academic departments shoulder the principal obligation for the prevention of failures by authors to acknowledge, in manuscripts accepted for publication, preprint readers, data sources, and funding agencies. Such responsibility is discharged through the enforcement of policies requiring "dry run" research seminars and internal review of manuscripts. By policy, authors participating in "dry run" seminars would be required to list such acknowledgments. Such acknowledgments would also be required in manuscripts submitted for publication consideration by academic journals. Because of the execution of such a policy, individuals attending "dry run" seminars or participating in the internal review of manuscripts could identify failures to make acknowledgments. A summary of these responsibilities for deterring and detecting misconduct of the dissemination stage is displayed in table 6.1.

Sanctions

Sanctions for misconduct associated with the dissemination stage should be less stringent than for either the production or the reporting stages because the knowledge base of an academic discipline is not usually harmed by such incidents of wrongdoing. Moreover, such wrongdoing is unlikely to taint the lay public's opinion of the academic profession. Nevertheless, wrongdoing associated with the dissemination stage should not go unpunished because of its detrimental consequences to the careers of graduate students and colleagues.

Laboratories and academic departments are accountable for sanctioning individual organizational members by requiring that appropriate acknowledgments be made before the focal manuscript is submitted to a journal. Journal editors who identify through the manuscript review process that authors have failed to give appropriate acknowledgments have the obligation to sanction this failure by either rejecting the focal manuscript or making its acceptance contingent on appropriate acknowledgments.

Academic journals have the principal responsibility for sanctioning authors who fail to provide requested raw data by rejecting the focal manuscript for publication. Academic journals should also take responsibility for reproving peer reviewers who pirate research findings from the manuscripts they review by removing them from the journal's panel of reviewers and, possibly, by reporting this impropriety to the research integrity committee of the offending individual's university for harsher punishment. Table 6.2 shows a summary of the suggested sanctions for infractions associated with the dissemination stage of the research process.

Evaluation

Once research findings have been published, the scientific community appraises such findings. Such appraisal takes the form of attempts to replicate the focal study or to refute its methodology or interpretation of its findings (Chubin, 1985). The evaluation stage also entails the application of the focal findings to practical problems as well as their incorporation into graduate and undergraduate college curriculums (Chubin, 1985).

Misconduct occurs with replication and refutation if the author maintains that the raw data for the focal study are unavailable or if peers are silent even though they have doubts about the reported method or the interpretation of findings (Chubin, 1985). Wrongdoing associated with the application of research findings to practical problems or with their incorporation into the curriculum occurs when such findings are used in a negligent manner or are misrepresented (Chubin, 1985).

Deterrence and Detection

The locus of responsibility for deterring and detecting these forms of misconduct varies. Laboratories and academic departments are accountable for both the discouragement and the observation of author claims of raw data unavailability. Such accountability is exercised through the enforcement of policies requiring open access to raw data.

Laboratories and academic departments also are accountable for peers who remain silent despite their suspicions concerning reported methods and interpretations. The incorporation of proscriptions regarding silence into the rules for laboratory and departmental conduct would serve to deter and detect this impropriety.

Academic societies have an obligation to prevent and identify peer silence. The promulgation of a code of ethics proscribing such behavior is one way academic societies can assume such an obligation.

The key responsibility for the deterrence and detection of negligence and misrepresentation of research in application and in the curriculum rests with laboratories and academic departments. Laboratories can execute this responsibility by developing and administering surveys that assess satisfaction with the applications based on research findings. Business and industry officials could complete such surveys. Academic departments can exercise their obligation to deter and detect negligence and misrepresentation in the curriculum through the implementation of a policy of periodic colleague evaluations of classroom instruction. One focus of such evaluations would be accuracy in the presentation of course content.

Academic societies can play a role by including these improprieties as prohibited behaviors in associational codes of ethics. In particular, such codes of ethics should provide guidelines for the inclusion of research in textbooks. Table 6.1 contains a summary of the responsibilities suggested for different levels of the community of the academic profession.

Sanctions

The level of the community of the academic profession accountable for the punishment of wrongdoing associated with the evaluation of research varies by the transgression. Universities bear the principal obligation for sanctioning an author's claims of the unavailability of raw data needed for replication when harsh sanctions are needed. If the focal research involves public health or societal well-being, then harsh punishment should be considered, both because it would help maintain the lay public's trust in the academic profession and because the knowledge base of an academic discipline could be harmed if replication was hindered. In such cases, universities might reprove such individuals by delaying promotion in academic rank and freezing salaries. If the individual is untenured, then dismissal for cause might be an appropriate action to take. At a minimum, laboratories, academic departments, and universities should force the recalcitrant individual to provide the requested raw data.

The locus of responsibility for sanctioning peer silence depends on the extent of injury inflicted on either the knowledge base of a discipline or the reputation of the community of the academic profession. If extensive damage is done to either the knowledge base or the profession's reputation, strong action should be taken. In such cases, universities are accountable. At a minimum, such individuals should be reprimanded by research integrity committees or by academic affairs officers.

For situations in which the harm done to either knowledge or reputation is minimal, responsibility for action rests with laboratories and academic departments. Laboratory directors and department chairs can exercise such responsibility by reprimanding the offending individual.

Responsibility for the sanctioning of negligence and misrepresentation of research also depends on the extent of harm done to the reputation of the academic profession, the knowledge base of an academic discipline, students as clients of teaching role performance, or business and industry as clients of research applications. If harm is done to any of the above entities, then universities bear the chief responsibility of meting out sanctions for negligence or misrepresentation of research. At a minimum, such sanctions should be a reprimand by an academic affairs officer. Maximum punishments might be freezing the offending individual's salary or delaying his or her promotion in academic rank. However, universities may be reluctant to apply such sanctions given their lack of political will to redress scientific wrongdoing (as Turner argues in chapter 5 of this book).

If the harm is minimal, then laboratories and academic departments shoulder this responsibility. If the offense occurred in the application of research, the consulting activities of the offending individual could be either restricted or curtailed. If the offense involved teaching or the curriculum, colleague classroom observations of the offending individual's courses could be conducted on a routine basis. A summary of possible sanctions for wrongdoing associated with the evaluation stage of the research process is shown in table 6.2.

ISSUES NEEDING RESOLUTION

For this normative model for professional self-regulation to be implemented, the following two issues need resolution.

1. Trust, respect, and protection of colleagues are fundamental characteristics of a profession (Freidson, 1975). These characteristics clash with mechanisms of surveillance, for such mechanisms imply mistrust of colleagues to conduct ethical research. Thus, the issue is: How can the community of the academic profession maintain trust, respect, and protection of colleagues while institutionalizing mechanisms of surveillance?

One approach for creating balance between these conflicting forces requires that scientific societies assume leadership in the promulgation of the various mechanisms of surveillance discussed here. Agreement among members of such societies on the need for such mechanisms would foster their institutionalization. Such mechanisms would serve to maintain the autonomy of the scientific community by preserving the lay public's trust in its ability to self-regulate.

2. Zuckerman (1988) contended that ambiguity surrounds the appropriate match between the act of wrongdoing and its sanction. The notion of harm to the reputation of the academic profession, the knowledge base of an academic discipline, and the careers of individuals provides a vocabulary for reducing such ambiguity and a basis for apportioning sanctions for wrongdoing. Nevertheless, the following issues need some resolution for this notion to be useful: How can harm be assessed? Can the magnitude of

harm be objectively assessed? If harm can be ascertained, what types of sanctions are appropriate?

Although discussion of these issues should take place on all levels of the community of the academic profession, scientific societies should assume leadership for developing guidelines for the resolution of these issues. Peer agreement on the assessment of harm and suitable sanctions has the most meaning when it is forged in the interuniversity setting of a scientific society.

CONCLUSION

Teich (1992) reported that most members of the AAAS believe that the community of the academic profession should regulate itself. This chapter offers a framework to guide such self-regulation. Moreover, the underlying premise of this framework is that two professional interests are best served by effective self-regulation: the preservation of autonomy and adherence to the ideal of service to clients. If the various levels of the community of the academic profession—individual scientists, laboratories, academic departments, universities, academic journals, and scientific societies—embrace this premise, then effective self-regulation will ensue and professional self-interests will be served.

Notes

1. The notion of community of the academic profession is derived from Goode (1957).
2. Light (1974) and Ruscio (1987) questioned the unitary structure of the academic profession. Becher (1987), however, asserted that the academic profession is composed of various segments, or disciplines, that are loosely assembled under an umbrella academic profession. The notion of segments within a broader profession is derived from the formulations of Bucher and Strauss (1961).
3. This notion extends Durkheim's (1951) view that nonconformity is the natural state of human behavior. Without control mechanisms in place, individuals are free to behave according to their own preferences.

References

Abbott, A. (1983). Professional ethics. *American Journal of Sociology, 88*, 855–885.
American Association for the Advancement of Science. (1991). *Professional Ethics Report, 5*(1), 2–3.
Anderson, M. S., & Louis, K. S. (1991). The changing locus of control over faculty research: From self-regulation to dispersed influence. In J. C. Smart (Ed.), *Higher education: Handbook of theory and research* (Vol. 7, pp. 57–101). New York: Agathon.

Barber, B. (1978). Control and responsibility in the powerful professions. *Political Science Quarterly, 93*, 599–615.
Becher, T. (1987). The disciplinary shaping of the academic profession. In B. R. Clark (Ed.), *The academic profession: National, disciplinary and institutional settings* (pp. 271–303). Berkeley: University of California Press.
Bell, R. (1992). *Impure science.* New York: John Wiley.
Black, D. (1976). *The behavior of law.* New York: Academic Press.
Braxton, J. M. (1990). Deviancy from the norms of science: A test of control theory. *Research in Higher Education, 31*, 461- 476.
Braxton, J. M. (1993). Review essay: Priority disputes and peer review: Academic self-regulation. *Review of Higher Education, 17*, 95–104.
Braxton, J. M., & Bayer, A. E. (1996). Personal experiences of research misconduct and the response of individual academic scientists. *Science, Technology, and Human Values, 21*, 198–213.
Braxton, J. M., Lambert, L. M., & Clark, S. C. (1995). Anticipatory socialization of undergraduate college teaching norms by entering graduate teaching assistants. *Research in Higher Education, 36*, 671–686.
Braxton, J. M., & Toombs, W. (1982). Faculty uses of doctoral training: Consideration of a technique for the differentiation of scholarly effort from research activity. *Research in Higher Education, 16*, 265–282.
Bucher, R., & Strauss, A. (1961). Professions in process. *American Journal of Sociology, 66*, 325–334.
Chubin, D. E. (1983). Misconduct in research: An issue of science policy and practice. *Minerva, 23*, 175–202.
Chubin, D. E. (1985). Research malpractice. *Bioscience, 35*, 80- 89.
Cole, J. R., & Cole, S. (1973). *Social stratification in science.* Chicago: University of Chicago Press.
Commission on Research Integrity. (1995). *Integrity and misconduct in research: Report of the Commission on Research Integrity.* Washington, DC: U.S. Department of Health and Human Services, Public Health Service.
Douglas, J. D. (1992). Betraying scientific truth. *Transaction, 30*, 86–82.
Durkheim, E. (1951). *Suicide.* Glencoe, IL: Free Press.
Fox, M. F. (1994). Scientific misconduct and editorial and peer review processes. *Journal of Higher Education, 65*, 298–309.
Fox, M. F., & Braxton, J. M. (1994). Misconduct and social control in science: Issues, problems and solutions. *Journal of Higher Education, 65*, 373–383.
Freidson, E. (1975). *Doctoring together: A study of professional social control.* New York: Elsevier.
Goode, W. J. (1957). Community within a community. *American Sociological Review, 22*, 194–200.
Goode, W. J. (1969). The theoretical limits of professionalization. In A. Etzioni (Ed.), *The semi- professions and their organization* (pp. 266–313). New York: Free Press.
Greenwood, E. (1957). Attributes of a profession. *Social Work, 2*, 44–55.
Hackett, E. J. (1994). A social control perspective on scientific misconduct. *Journal of Higher Education, 65*, 242–260.

Hagstrom, W. O. (1957). *The scientific community.* New York: Basic Books.
Light, D. (1974). Introduction: The structure of the academic profession. *Sociology of Education, 47,* 2–28.
Merton, R. K. (1942). Science and technology in a democratic order. *Journal of Legal and Political Sociology, 1,* 115–126.
Merton, R. K. (1973). *The sociology of science: Theoretical and empirical investigations.* Chicago: University of Chicago Press.
Merton, R. K., Reader, G. G., & Kendall, P. L. (1957). *The student-physician.* Cambridge, MA: Harvard University Press.
Parsons, T. (1939). The professions and social structure. *Social Forces, 17,* 457–467.
Parsons, T. (1951). *The social system.* New York: Free Press.
Parsons, T., & Platt, G. M. (1973). *The American university.* Cambridge, MA: Harvard University Press.
Peach, L. (1995). An introduction to ethical theory. In R. L. Penslar (Ed.), *Research ethics: Cases and materials* (pp. 13–26). Bloomington: Indiana University Press.
Platt, G. M., Parsons, T., & Kirshstein, R. (1976). Faculty teaching goals, 1968–1973. *Social Problems, 24,* 298–307.
Price, A. R. (1994). Definitions and boundaries of research misconduct: Perspectives from a federal government viewpoint. *Journal of Higher Education, 65,* 286–297.
Rennie, D. (1989, January 6). How much fraud? Let's do an experimental audit. *AAAS Observer,* p. 4.
Ruscio, K. P. (1987). Many sectors, many professions. In B. R. Clark (Ed.), *The academic profession* (pp. 331–368). Los Angeles: University of California Press.
St. James-Roberts, I. (1976). Are researchers trustworthy? *New Scientist, 72,* 481–483.
Shapiro, M., & Charrow, R. (1989). The role of data audits in detecting scientific misconduct. *Journal of the American Medical Association, 261,* 2505–2511.
Steneck, N. H. (1994). Research universities and scientific misconduct: History, policies and the future. *Journal of Higher Education, 65,* 310–330.
Teich, A. H. (1992). Integrity in research: The scientific community view. *Knowledge: Creation, Diffusion and Utilization, 14,* 185–192.
Toombs, W. (1977). Awareness and use of academic research. *Research in Higher Education, 7,* 743–765.
Weinstein, D. (1979). Fraud in science. *Social Science Quarterly, 59,* 639–652.
Zuckerman, H. E. (1977). Deviant behavior and social control in science. In E. Sagarin (Ed.), *Deviance and social change* (pp. 87–138). Beverly Hills, CA: Sage.
Zuckerman, H. E. (1988). The sociology of science. In N. J. Smelser (Ed.), *Handbook of sociology* (pp. 511–574). Newbury Park, CA: Sage.

CHAPTER SEVEN

Scientific Misconduct and Editorial and Peer Review Processes

Mary Frank Fox

In recent decades, hardly a year has gone by without the surfacing and unraveling of a notorious case of misconduct in science: Soman's fabrication of data and his retraction in 1979 of 12 papers, the majority published in collaboration with the holder of an endowed chair at Yale University Medical School; the biologist Alsabati's rash of plagiarized papers, which came to light in 1980; Spector's unreplicable explanations of virus as a unified cause of cancer, aired in 1981; the unfolding in the same year of Darsee's fabrication of data, which resulted in the publication of over 100 papers while he was at Emory and at Harvard; the 1986 announcement by a University of California–San Diego committee that nearly half of the 147 articles (137 published) of a rising radiologist, Slutsky, had been found to be "fraudulent" or "questionable"; the cases of Glueck's misrepresentation of data on cholesterol and heart disease and Breuning's articles based upon nonexistent experiments of psychotropic drugs to control behavior of the mentally retarded within institutions, both of which came to light in 1987; and the 1992 finding of the federal Office of Research Integrity (ORI) that Gallo, codiscoverer of the cause of AIDS, had falsely reported a critical fact in his 1984 scientific paper to gain credit for himself, followed in 1993 by its dropping charges because of the more stringent standards for assessing misconduct in the U.S. Department of Health and Human Services under which ORI operates.[1]

Yet despite the surfacing of these cases and the volley of responses and counter-responses between the principals, the federal government, and the scientific community at large, few new mechanisms are in place to identify and correct scientific misconduct. To a large extent, scientists continue to rely upon "routine processes of self-correction" in science (Chubin &

Hackett, 1990, p. 134). Chief among these are the editorial and peer review of journals.

If peer and editorial processes are relied upon as "the linchpin of science" (Ziman, 1968, p. 148), then it is critical to analyze the roles of editors and peer reviewers in detecting and sanctioning misconduct, the structural problems inherent in review, and the best means of enabling peer and editorial roles as corrective processes in scientific misconduct. These are the concerns of this chapter. In addressing them, I argue that the editorial and peer review process can play a part in responding to misconduct but that it is a limited corrective role.

EDITORS, PEER REVIEWERS, AND THEIR ROLES IN DETECTING/SANCTIONING MISCONDUCT

At the onset, it is important to recognize the roots of scientific publishing. Before the middle of the seventeenth century, scientists communicated through correspondence, exchange of findings, and private printing of results. The communication was informal, haphazard, and without editorial intervention or authority. In 1665, the first scientific journals, the *Journal des Scavans* and *Philosophical Transactions of the Royal Society*, appeared. Journals provided wider access to new scientific work, helped verify findings, laid claim to priority and credit for discoveries and advancements, and provided permanence (archiving) of contributions (Zuckerman & Merton, 1973). In this way, the "mere printing of scientific work" was transformed to "publication" (Zuckerman & Merton, 1973, p. 462). These original functions of publication have retained and provide a basis for publication as the central social process of science (Fox, 1983).

Because journal publication is central to the *normative conduct* of science, it is understandable that it might be regarded as a means for addressing *misconduct* as well. It is here that editorial and peer review practices come into play. Since the time that the first journals were published by scientific societies, articles have carried some authority of the scientific community.[2] Consequently, from the beginning, editors and reviewers performed a role in published work, and this was the origin of the "organizational machinery" of peer review (Zuckerman & Merton, 1973, p. 469). What are the problems and prospects of this reviewing machinery in confronting and correcting misconduct?

PROBLEMS

Fundamental to the problems are the loose definitions of *review* and *misconduct*, both conceptually and operationally. Although experts were used to scrutinize manuscripts even at the time of the first scientific journals, the practice of sending manuscripts out for review did not actually become widespread until recently, in the 1950s (Burnham, 1990). Earlier, in the prewar decades, review proceeded with reading by the editor or a small in-house staff. James McKeen Cattell, who edited *Science* for 50 years (1894–1945), depended upon his son to review papers. It was only after Cattell's death that the American Association for the Advancement of Science took control of the journal and adopted outside peer review (Sun, 1989).

When the convention of peer review spread, it often proceeded with the services of an editorial board, a group usually known and chosen by the editor. Some have argued that peer review functioned well under these circumstances, more prevalent earlier, because submissions were fewer and the editor was acquainted with the qualifications and backgrounds of the referees (Glenn, 1979). Because the reviewers had "official status" as members of the editorial board and a relationship with the editor, a certain accountability ensued. Further, because submissions were limited, the editor could read each paper, critique it, and assess the reviews as well as the paper in question (Glenn, 1979).

However, with a high volume of submissions, turnover of editors, and dependence upon ad hoc reviewers and often a part-time (nonprofessional) managing editor, circumstances are different. Referees may be chosen with few grounds for assessing their competence as reviewers and with no mechanism for monitoring their performance (Glenn, 1979). Beyond issues of competence are considerations of reviewers' engagement with a manuscript and their affective and aesthetic responses, as noted in Silverman's (1988) sensitive analysis of peer judgment. As Silverman said, reviewers do not simply address a manuscript rationally; they respond from "experiences, biases, knowledge, expectations, interests, and hopes" (p. 364), which are, in turn, a basis for judgments rendered.

Such conditions of peer review as well as quality of manuscripts received and the maturity of manuscripts upon submission vary for journals (Silverman, 1988). Where circumstances of slack selection and monitoring of reviewers do exist, however, some question the very meaning of *peer* and *review* (Chubin & Hackett, 1990). The meaning of *fraud* or *misconduct* is even more ambiguous. Because of this ambiguity, it is not necessarily certain to either editors or reviewers what constitutes misconduct and thus what they should or should not respond to as illegitimate.

Basic to fraud is the issue of deception—actions intended to deceive, "to make a thing appear to be what it is not" (LaFollette, 1992, p. 36). Clearly fraudulent, then, are the forging or altering of data or materials, the false representation of authorship or originality of data, and misrepresentation intended to "advance one's own career or position [or] harm another's career or position" (LaFollette, 1992, p. 41). If such behavior occurs and is detected by editors or reviewers, they are likely to define it as fraudulent—whether or not they take sanctioning action.

Yet deception ranges, and some forms are more pernicious than others. For example, fragmentation of publication, the dividing of one integral set of findings into numbers of units published simultaneously in different journals or sequentially in the same journal, is deceptive because it is usually associated with deliberate overinterpretation of a fragmented piece to give the appearance of its self-containment (Angell, 1983, p. 4). Fragmentation has been deplored but is widely practiced and is regarded as more benign than the forging, cooking, and trimming—fabrication and falsification—of data. Along the continuum of deception, but also more ambiguous than fabrication and falsification, is "prematurity" of publication, the reporting of findings before conclusive completion and verification of work. The peril here lies in stopping the experiment, investigation, or inquiry when one "likes the findings," rather than spending time looking for systematic error (Branscomb, 1985, p. 422).

Also deceptive, yet more ambiguous than fabrication and falsification, is nominal or honorary authorship, a practice whereby persons not wholly accountable for the work have their names affixed to publications with motives to increase the bibliographies of a number of persons and sometimes to create the impression of a luminary (though nominal) contributor to the publication (Angell, 1983; LaFollette, 1992). The question becomes "Whose work is it?" and the answer is probably more consequential in the case of fraudulent work from which parties may subsequently try to disassociate themselves than it is for work for which multiple parties are trying to take credit. But in either case—claims to disassociation or to credit—fictional authorship is deceptive.

Because these latter practices, fictional authorship as well as fragmentation and premature publication, are less clearly fraudulent than the forging or altering of data and materials, they have not been given close attention by editors. But as we shall see, practices such as nominal coauthorship have been part and parcel of patterns damaging to the integrity of science. They should come under the mantle of surveillance or at least official policies of unacceptable behavior for authors.

Flagrant cases of scientific fraud (e.g., the work of Darsee and of Slutsky) have resulted in streams of published articles, often in prestigious journals. The articles had passed through review. How effective, then, is review as a means of detecting fraud? Where do problems lie with the process? As the University of California–San Diego committee investigating charges of fraud in the articles of Slutsky put it, "Plausible, internally consistent fabrications like those in the work of Darsee and of Slutsky, cannot be detected by the peer review system" (Engler, Covell, Friedman, Kitcher, & Peters, 1987,

p. 1385). Reviewers are accustomed to responding to honest error rather than fraud.

First, reviewers lack the information to detect or assess fraud in articles. Replication has often been offered as an antidote to fraud, but reviewers certainly cannot replicate the work sent to them. In an age of big science, neither can others. Replication is costly. Funding is not often available for studies that are duplicative. And scientific credit accrues to new, rather than redundant, findings (Engler et al., 1987). When replication does take place, it is likely to occur in highly competitive, intensely active research areas where the potential might exist for modification of others' findings (Fox, 1990).[3]

Beyond this, reviewers have normative disinclination to acknowledge fraud. The editorial relationships (editor, author, reviewer) rest upon trust, such that levels of skepticism are low and belief in the scientific ethos of truth seeking is high. Scientists have tended to perceive themselves as "defenders of objectivity in an irrational world" (LaFollette, 1992, p. 3). Attentiveness to deceptive practices means confronting conflict in the operations of science—greed and aggrandizement as well as desire to understand how nature works. Because there are stakes in certain pretense, especially a strong stake in continued public support and funding for higher education, scientists (and scholars) have been loath to face (much less to resolve) the inherent contradictions in their work and within their employing institutions (see, e.g., Fox's 1992b analysis of the unacknowledged strain between research and teaching as it reflects the ambivalence of institutional functions in academia).

Even when reviewers do detect suspicious findings, they have been reluctant to alert editors to the offense (Banner, 1988). One of the most insidious features of science and academia, more broadly, is that the players show a preference for talking about, rather than taking action on, offense and offenders. Gossip about, rather than action on, fraud allows people to vent indignation or dissatisfaction yet avoid the due process and accountability of investigation.

A chilling chronicle of such inaction of disciplinary authorities (though not of certain valiant, independent persons) is the case of Jayme Sokolow within the profession of history, as recorded by Mallon in *Stolen Words* (1989). According to this account, in 1980 Sokolow submitted to the *Journal of the Early Republic* an article that was allegedly a nearly verbatim appropriation of a portion of the 1968 doctoral dissertation of a fellow historian, Stephen Nissenbaum. Sokolow followed this with a string of submissions to publishers of a manuscript that allegedly appropriated the phrases, sentences, and interpretations of Nissenbaum's 1980 book, based upon his dissertation. Sokolow's manuscript was ultimately published in 1983 by Fairleigh Dickinson Press. Despite pleas of Nissenbaum to the American

Historical Association (AHA) to adjudicate the case by at least recording the matter in one of the AHA publications, the case never saw the full light of revelation, much less redress. In 1986, Sokolow was accused again of allegedly plagiarizing another doctoral dissertation (Mallon, 1989; Nissenbaum, 1990).

The Sokolow case has been told and retold through scholarly circles but not subjected to action. The AHA issued no reprimand. As Nissenbaum (1990) put it, "Every institution, publisher, and professional association that has dealt with the Sokolow case has tried to employ only informal procedures—discreet, understated, and off the record" (p. A52). When official bodies withhold action, such cases continue to fester, with no effective outcome and with much potential damage to all involved, including the larger scientific or scholarly community.

This points to the ambiguity of policies and procedures in responding to allegations of fraud, especially as they relate to variations that exist by discipline. Illegitimate—fraudulent—as well as legitimate activity in science (and scholarship) takes place within disciplines or fields. Thus, types (and rates) of misconduct vary by disciplines (and subfields), depending upon their levels of research activity, intellectual fragmentation, locus of creativity in publication, coauthorship, and replicability of work (Fox, 1990). For example, because of this intellectual fragmentation, social science fields, in particular, lend themselves to variably incomplete and inaccurate reporting of others' research in construction of an argument. Thus, in one examination of 17 social psychology books, very few authors were found to have given an accurate report of a given published experiment; rather, they reported portions of the experiment as it supported the theme of their respective books (Ben-Yehuda, 1985). To take another example, the social sciences, more than the natural sciences, represent a disciplinary context prone to plagiarism specifically. This is because in the social sciences, and to a greater extent in the humanities, the publication is a creative work, susceptible to pirating and appropriation of language, text, and form. In the natural sciences, in contrast, the research is the creative work and the publication a mere snapshot of the process (Fox, 1990, p. 69). Coauthorship, on the other hand, is more characteristic of the natural sciences, and thus offenses of "loose authorship," and the diffusion of responsibility entailed, are more characteristic of these fields (Fox, 1990, p. 69). Such disciplinary variations can further muddle the already ambiguous issue of what constitutes a legitimate allegation of fraud and how one should respond to it.

If an allegation of misconduct is brought to the attention of the editor, another set of problems arises because it is unclear to whom an editor is accountable in the case of misconduct. Is the editor responsible for informing the offender's institution and the funding agency sponsoring the work, or is primary accountability to the subscribers who have paid for sound articles and to the publisher who has a stake in valid content? As LaFollette (1992) said, "These interests should converge" (p. 88). If they do not, it may be because the norms of research can diverge from concerns of publishing. For example, the publishers' concerns with "success and survival" may mean that financial gain or loss looms largely in editorial decisions and actions. Responding to fraud in an article published in a journal incurs "costs in time, money, and resources" (LaFollette, 1992, p. 69). This can undermine journals, which often operate on a marginal financial basis.

Thus, the editorial process is fraught with ambiguity in the meaning of review and misconduct, lack of information for detecting or assessing fraud in articles, normative disinclination to acknowledge and respond to fraud, variations in the type of misconduct by disciplinary area, and unclarity about those to whom an editor is accountable in the case of misconduct. Given these problems with review as a check on scientific misconduct, what are the solutions? Is there an improved role for editorial and peer review in detecting and sanctioning misconduct?

PROSPECTS AND SOLUTIONS

First, reviewers can be alerted to attend to warning signals in the possibility of fraudulent work. Such signals include data that fall into place too well, variables with little variance, or a burst of contribution from an author who has had no involvement in a research area (the latter dependent, of course, upon anonymity or nonanonymity of authors in the review process). These signals are not proof of fraudulent work, but they may point to greater possibility of wrongdoing (Angell, 1983).

A body of work notable for its warning signals was that of Cyril Burt, the psychologist who won the 1971 Thorndike Prize of the American Psychological Association. Burt's work on inheritability of intelligence, based upon studies of separated twins over a 50-year period (1913–1966), reported correlations that were not just similar but identical, despite the increasing number of subjects in the sample. It was only after his death that parties examining the whole of his work brought the fraud to light (Hearnshaw, 1979; Kamin, 1974). How did the fraud evade earlier detection? On a piece-by-piece basis, Burt presented plausible explanations, and when asked to share his data, he constructed it from published correlations. But inescapable also is that his conclusions about IQ and inheritance enjoyed a hospitable political audience, eager to embrace the findings about inheritability.

Second, journals can hold coauthors responsible for work offered as collaborative. In the infamous case of Darsee's articles based upon fabricated findings, his coauthors claimed that they had no direct contact with the work, that they were not aware of the experiments reported under their names, or even that they did not know their names were on an abstract until after it was published (Relman, 1983). The same is true in the case of Slutsky and his 93 coauthors (Engler et al., 1987; University of California–San Diego Medical School, 1987). At the peak of his publication, Slutsky was producing one paper every 10 days. In response to the University of California–San Diego investigating committee, Slutsky's coauthors claimed that they had no involvement in communication with the journals and that they had not seen written comments of the reviewers.

Whether such disclaimers of coauthors are ex post facto or not, journals can help avoid such diffusion and denials of responsibility by requiring the signature of each coauthor and a statement that the coauthor is confident about the content and willing to defend the paper. This may not prevent concerted fraud, but it makes clear the authors' responsibility.

Third, journals can ask that tables of data for figures routinely be submitted so that reviewers may ascertain whether a figure is a fair representation of the data (Engler et al., 1987). In addition, journals can establish policies whereby reviewers may ordinarily request, without fanfare, supplementary data for consideration. This introduces grounds for routinized scrutiny and a procedural climate for surveillance.

To determine the extent of fraudulent work in scientific journals, one proposal has been that of a "data audit" (Rennie, 1989; Shapiro & Charrow, 1989). Under this proposal, a group of editors of journals would notify prospective authors of the possibility of an audit when their papers were accepted. For a set of papers across journals, auditors would compare original data as requested with the data actually published in the article. Such audits might demonstrate the extent of fraud and, in doing so, reveal what needs to be corrected and where. The proposal, however, is not free of problems. Participation in such an audit has a coercive element for an author, and it affects editorial relationships. Further, it is unclear how the rights of parties participating might be protected. And except for establishing the extent of fraud—a measurement issue—the proposal does not indicate how cases of fraud so detected might be treated (LaFollette, 1992, pp. 197–198).

Fourth, when deception is established, journals should print a retraction, at the very least. While some journals have good records in this regard, others are lax. Uniform procedures of retraction are not in place at journals, and cases tend to be handled on an ad hoc basis, sometimes formally but often informally, and even silently without retraction (Angell, 1983; LaFollette, 1992).

The depth of this problem is indicated in the response and nonresponse of journals following the disclosures of fraud in Slutsky's work by the UC–San Diego investigating committee. The committee notified the editors of the 30 journals in which Slutsky's articles had been published. Half of the editors did not respond to the committee's letter. The character of responses received is revealed in this statement of the committee's chair:

> At least one expressed outrage at the poor quality of the research supervision at UCSD ... that would have allowed such extensive fraud to exist and go undetected for so long. Some expressed complete willingness to publish the statements we furnished.... Others edited out the statement that we believed the author's previous withdrawal of certain papers implied an acknowledgment of fraud, whether or not the committee had classified the paper as fraudulent or questionable. Some thought it necessary to publish a statement about valid papers. (LaFollette, 1992, p. 183)

Eighteen months after the committee sent its letters, only some of the journals had published a retraction or statement about Slutsky's work.

Journals can respond to misconduct, but they are not the basic instruments for preventing it. Preventing fraud means identifying the forces that permit or promote it. It hurts, rather than helps, the cause of conduct to respond to fraud by wringing one's hands and proclaiming individuals gone mad. To do this is to reduce the behavior to an individual aberration and to avoid institutional analysis—and correction.

Science exists in organizational settings. The work is done within organizational policies and procedures; it relies upon the cooperation of others; it requires human and material resources (Fox, 1992a, p. 105). When misconduct occurs, it may be part of an organizational climate permitting it through "vague and inconsistent rules [and] weak mechanisms of oversight and correction" (Chubin & Hackett, 1990, p. 137). Particular associations of climate and fraud are not known, however, and have yet to be investigated.

One organizational factor purported to promote fraud is "pressure to publish." The impression that publication pressures encourage misconduct is probably tied to the observation that some of the most notorious cases of fraud occurred in laboratories with prodigious publication levels. For example, in the five years preceding the surfacing of the fabricated work of Darsee and of Soman, Braunwald (Darsee's chief at Harvard) published 171 papers, and Felig (Soman's chief at Yale) published 191 (Woolf, 1986). Yet pressure to publish—show findings, obtain funding—may be more likely to account for dull literature than fabricated research articles (Maddox, 1983, p. 361). And in social sciences, particularly, research productivity is so low[4] that "pressure to publish is a hollow refrain in these fields" (Fox, 1990, p. 69).

Factors that may be more revealing in accounting for misconduct are conflicts in the values of science—for example, entrepreneurship as well as basic discovery (LaFollette, 1992). The economic stakes of science have heightened. Matters of profit and financial gain are nontrivial concerns. Thus, the charge of misconduct against Gallo for falsely reporting a critical fact in his 1984 paper on AIDS to gain credit for himself is probably tied to issues of economic stakes. The royalties from the blood test for AIDS earn Gallo and his French counterpart, Dr. Luc Montagnier of the Pasteur Institute, $100,000 a year, and the returns to the U.S. government totaled $50 million between 1985 and 1992 (Hilts, 1992). The dispute between Gallo and Montagnier was actually adjudicated by the presidents of the United States and France, who agreed to a 50–50 split of patent royalties from the blood test for AIDS. This, however, did not end the controversy, and lawyers for the Pasteur Institute maintained that the United States should give up its patent claims because of Gallo's alleged misappropriation of the virus linked to AIDS from the French institute (Hilts, 1993).

Likewise, the 1987 controversy surrounding Paul Chu's alleged misrepresentation of two papers on superconductivity had a connection to profitable commercial applications. In this case, Chu submitted two papers to *Physical Review Letters* with the symbol *Yb* (ytterbium) substituted for *Y* (yttrium). Chu said that this was a "typographical error." Others maintained that it was a deliberate effort to throw off competitors (reviewers of the papers). After submitting the papers, Chu and his colleagues applied for a patent. Chu also held a press conference to announce his findings—without giving the composition of the superconductivity material. Chu says he was not aware of the error in the papers until he received the proofs, just before the press conference. The last day before corrections could be made, he returned the proofs with the correction (Kolata, 1987).

SUMMARY AND CONCLUSION

Editorial and peer review have a part in detecting and sanctioning scientific misconduct, but it is a limited role. The definitions of both *review* and *misconduct* are loose and ambiguous, contributing to the difficulty of journals' addressing fraud. In addition, reviewers lack information to detect fraud and are disinclined to acknowledge it. Policies and practices of journals in responding to fraud are unclear and tied to disciplinary variations in misconduct. Further, the responsibilities and accountability of journal editors are unclear. Some solutions are available: reviewers can be alerted to warning signals of fraud; coauthors can be held responsible for work; journals can introduce routinized means of scrutinizing data; and retraction of deceptive articles can be expected. Yet although journals can improve means of responding to fraud, they are not basic instruments in preventing it.

николай Notes

For their reading of and comments on an earlier version of this chapter, I thank John M. Braxton and Robert J. Silverman.

1. Not to go unmentioned is the seemingly endless (1986–1996) affair of the disputed paper in *Cell* by Imanishi-Kari, with Nobel laureate David Baltimore as one of five other coauthors. This case, which split the scientific community,

ended in a June 1996 resolution by the appeals panel of the U.S. Department of Health and Human Services, which determined that the preponderance of evidence cleared Imanishi-Kari of charges of misconduct (see the "Conclusion" of this book).

2. The degree of gatekeeping varies. Some journals (often with high acceptance rates) largely put forth ideas for consideration in the articles published, while others (often with low acceptance rates) publish articles validated with review.

3. Social sciences do not fit these conditions. Further, the greater the reliance of the field upon "interpretation," the lower the prospects for replication of work. In the case of some types of research (e.g., fieldwork), observations may be "unique" (Fox, 1990).

4. A third of social scientists publish nothing over the course of their careers (Fox, 1989; Ladd & Lipset, 1977a and b; Porter, Chubin, Rossini, Boeckmann, & Connolly, 1982).

REFERENCES

Angell, M. (1983). Editors and fraud. *CBE Views, 6*, 3–8.

Banner, J. (1988). Preserving the integrity of peer review. *Scholarly Publishing, 19*, 109-115.

Ben-Yehuda, N. (1985). *Deviance and moral boundaries.* Chicago: University of Chicago Press.

Branscomb, L. (1985). Integrity in science. *American Scientist, 73*, 421–423.

Burnham, J. (1990). The evolution of peer review. *Journal of American Medical Association, 263*, 1323–1329.

Chubin, D., & Hackett, E. (1990). *Peerless science: Peer review and U.S. science policy.* Albany: State University of New York Press.

Engler, R., Covell, J., Friedman, P., Kitcher, P., & Peters, R. (1987). Misrepresentation and responsibility in medical research. *New England Journal of Medicine, 317*, 1383–1388.

Fox, M. F. (1983). Publication productivity among scientists. *Social Studies of Science, 13*, 285–305.

Fox, M. F. (1989, Summer). Disciplinary fragmentation, peer review, and the publication process. *American Sociologist, 20*, 188–191.

Fox, M. F. (1990, Spring). Fraud, ethics, and the disciplinary contexts of science and scholarship. *American Sociologist, 21*, 67–71.

Fox, M. F. (1992a). Research productivity and the environmental context. In T. Whiston & R. Geiger (Eds.), *Research and higher education* (pp. 103–111). Buckingham, UK: Society for Research into Higher Education/Open University Press.

Fox, M. F. (1992b). Research, teaching, and publication productivity: Mutuality versus competition in academia. *Sociology of Education, 65*, 293–305.

Glenn, N. (1979). Accountability and the journal article review process. *Contemporary Sociology, 8*, 785–786.

Hearnshaw, L. (1979). *Cyril Burt, psychologist.* London: Hodder & Stoughton.
Hilts, P. (1992, December 31). Federal inquiry finds misconduct by a discoverer of the AIDS virus. *New York Times,* pp. 1, 20.
Hilts, P. (1993, November 13). Misconduct charges dropped against AIDS virus scientist. *New York Times,* pp. 1, 9.
Kamin, L. (1974). *The science and politics of IQ.* Potomac, MD: Lawrence Erlbaum.
Kolata, G. (1987, May 8). Yb or not Yb? That is the question. *Science, 236,* 663–664.
Ladd, E., & Lipset, S. M. (1977a, November 21). Survey of 4,400 faculty members at 161 colleges and universities. *Chronicle of Higher Education,* p. 12.
Ladd, E., & Lipset, S. M. (1977b, November 28). Survey of 4,400 faculty members at 161 colleges and universities (continued). *Chronicle of Higher Education,* p. 2.
LaFollette, M. (1992). *Stealing into print.* Berkeley: University of California Press.
Maddox, J. (1983). Is science really a pack of lies? *Nature, 303,* 361–362.
Mallon, T. (1989). *Stolen words.* New York: Ticknor & Fields.
Nissenbaum, S. (1990, March 28). The plagiarists in academe must face formal sanctions. *Chronicle of Higher Education,* p. A52.
Porter, A., Chubin, D., Rossini, F., Boeckmann, M. E., & Connolly, T. (1982). The role of the dissertation in scientific careers. *American Scientist, 70,* 475–481.
Relman, A. (1983). Lessons from the Darsee affair. *New England Journal of Medicine, 308,* 1415–1417.
Rennie, D. (1989, January 6). How much fraud? Let's do an experimental audit. *AAAS Observer,* p. 4.
Shapiro, M., & Charrow, R. (1989). The role of data audits in detecting scientific misconduct. *Journal of the American Medical Association, 261,* 2505–2511.
Silverman, R. (1988). Peer judgment: An ideal typification. *Knowledge: Creation, Diffusion, Utilization, 9,* 362–382.
Sun, M. (1989, May 26). Following the Royal Society's lead. *Science, 244,* 910.
University of California–San Diego Medical School. (1987). The morality of scientists, II. *Minerva, 25,* 504–512.
Woolf, P. (1986). Pressure to publish and fraud in science. *Annals of Internal Medicine, 104,* 254–256.
Ziman, J. (1968). *Public knowledge.* Cambridge, MA: Cambridge University Press.
Zuckerman, H., & Merton, R. (1973). Institutionalized patterns of evaluation in science. In R. Merton (Ed.), *The sociology of science* (pp. 460–496). Chicago: University of Chicago Press.

CHAPTER EIGHT

Including Ethics in Graduate Education in Scientific Research

Stephanie J. Bird

Although science educators and researchers have generally believed that their educational responsibilities were limited to teaching scientific concepts and principles and laboratory techniques, preparation for a career in science goes beyond a solid grounding in science. A number of additional skills are required, including how to present scientific studies in both an oral and a written form, how to evaluate data (one's own and those of other investigators), and how to obtain funding. In addition to, and in many respects as a part of, the professional skills that one is expected to learn are the ethical values and the professional standards and expectations of one's peers in the discipline. Thus, colleagues expect coworkers to know how to credit properly the contributions of others and to take seriously the responsibilities of authorship. In addition, the general public, which usually provides the funds and resources for scientific research and in whose name research is carried out, expects that the ethical values of society will be upheld. Thus, for example, it is presumed that researchers will treat research subjects humanely, whether they are human volunteers or nonhuman animals.

Professional standards and ethical values may vary from field to field or within a discipline. Indeed, even within the same field, standards, expectations, and ethical values seem to be evolving. Nonetheless, understanding professional values and standards is critical to success in any profession, including science.

However important this aspect of professional education is, it has been largely neglected, generally relegated to informal, impromptu conversations. The assumption remains that, for the most part, students and junior colleagues will pick up necessary information regarding acceptable practices by observing good examples and by reading between the lines. With some reflection, it is apparent that this approach is inadequate. There is growing recognition within, as well as beyond, the scientific community that there is a need to explicitly communicate both the range and limits of acceptable practices to junior investigators. Moreover, the National Institutes of Health (NIH, 1989, 1990, 1992) has imposed a requirement that pre- and postdoctoral trainees receive formal education in the proper conduct and reporting of research. We can expect that in the process of reflecting on professional standards of practice and their underlying assumptions and ramifications, more senior researchers will reaffirm and clarify the expectations and standards of the community for themselves and their colleagues. The academic and scientific communities have developed various materials, techniques, and strategies to respond to the growing awareness of the need to address this issue.

WHY THE ATTENTION TO ETHICS IN SCIENCE?

Well-publicized examples of egregious misconduct have shaken public and governmental confidence in the scientific community's ability, and interest, in regulating and policing itself (Braxton & Bayer, 1996). At the same time, society, students, and members of the scientific community itself expect that junior researchers will learn the ethical standards and values of the profession. A survey of 2,000 faculty at major research universities across the country found that essentially all faculty believe that, to a greater or lesser extent, the academic and research community has a collective responsibility for the ethical professional conduct of graduate students (Swazey, 1993). This is not surprising, since graduate students, like postdoctoral trainees, will be colleagues in a relatively short period of time. Their professional behavior will reflect favorably or unfavorably upon the institutions where they train and upon the individuals who train them. Equally important is the fact that the behavior of science professionals reflects upon the scientific and, depending upon their workplace, academic communities. The lack of public trust resulting from a perceived lack of integrity has significant ramifications for public funding of scientific research and higher education and for the use of research in the development of public policy decisions associated with the applications and implications of science and technology.

THE ROLE OF THE RESEARCH COMMUNITY IN TEACHING THE RESPONSIBLE CONDUCT OF RESEARCH

Yet it is not simply because of the potential implications of omission that it is essential to convey professional values and ethical standards. It can be seen as a professional responsibility, an obligation conferred by the role of educator, to agree to prepare individuals for the profession that is before them (Bird, 1994; Gorovitz, 1998). An awareness and understanding of the professional values and ethical standards inherent in the practice of science are part of the array of "survival skills" required to succeed as a professional (Bird, 1994; Rittenhouse, 1996).

Both faculty and students believe that the most effective ways to provide information on professional standards and values are through interactions with faculty in the course of research and informal discussions when ethical issues or problems occur (Swazey, 1993). Unfortunately, this does not generally take place. Only a small percentage of graduate students indicate that they get much input on the details of good research practice from even the most supportive faculty member.

The mismatch between what faculty believe is their responsibility and the activities in which they actually invest time and resources is not surprising. Certainly, there are very real practical constraints. In general, faculty have experienced a significant reduction in the time they can devote to training graduate students due to increasing professional demands, including efforts to obtain the ever more elusive research funding. Teaching students "the niceties" of responsible research conduct takes a back seat to the primary and considerable effort of ensuring that there are funds to carry out research in the first place. In addition, faculty tend to have increasing numbers of graduate students and postdoctoral trainees in the laboratory, thereby decreasing the amount of time available for one-to-one interactions. Moreover, the scientific community has been reluctant to seriously and formally take on the training of graduate students and trainees in responsible research conduct because, paradoxically, they have not seen it as their responsibility. There is a widely held perception that young adults enter graduate school with their moral compasses fully formed and that if training in the responsible conduct of research were important in graduate science education, it would already be part of that education.

Furthermore, the vast majority of senior researchers themselves received no formal, organized, explicit training in the proper conduct and reporting of research. As a result, they generally have no clear idea of how or where to begin. Their discomfort in teaching their students and trainees about the standards and values of their profession is exacerbated by the fact that scientists are not always aware of, or even open to, the notion that ethical issues are inherent to science. Science is often described as a search for the truth, and thus it is commonly believed that "scientific knowledge is value-free and in itself carries no ethical implications" (Wolpert, 1996). As one of my colleagues once told me, "There are no ethical issues in science. If one ever did arise, I would sit down and figure out the right thing to do, and then do it." There is the seeming expectation that the occasional ethical problem will have a single, obvious solution. Most practicing scientists are not prepared for the ethical issues in science to be complex and multifaceted and to have multiple solutions. Moreover, the "best" solution, like beauty, is likely to be in the eye of the beholder, since different participants in the problem are likely to experience different advantages or disadvantages, benefits and burdens, depending on its resolution and will therefore have differing views regarding which is a better, or even acceptable, solution. It is not surprising that the culture of science, the lack of preparation of members of the community to discuss these issues clearly and openly with trainees, and the complexity of the issues subtly woven through the system of scientific practice all combine to make the community reluctant to discuss the responsible conduct of research.

Nevertheless, the community is changing. It is responding to both internal and external pressures, some of which are discussed elsewhere in this volume. Prompted by Congress, NIH and the Public Health Service now require that pre- and postdoctoral trainees to whom they provide financial support receive instruction in the proper conduct and reporting of research (NIH, 1989, 1990, 1992). The National Academy of Sciences produced and has recently revised *On Being a Scientist* (Olson, 1995), a booklet designed to identify, clarify, and encourage discussion of various aspects of research ethics. It points out that "research ethics is not a complete and finalized body of knowledge ... and all researchers have a responsibility to move the discussion forward." The Councils of the National Academies of Sciences and Engineering and the Institute of Medicine have encouraged all members of the scientific community, researchers, universities, and professional organizations to be involved. This was echoed by Bruce Alberts, president of the National Academy of Sciences, and Kenneth Shine, president of the Institute of Medicine, when they emphasized the important role of individual researchers in identifying and clarifying the ethical standards and values of responsible research practice and in instructing trainees in research ethics (Alberts & Shine, 1994).

However reluctant they may be, it is critical that individual researchers be involved in the discussion of research ethics. Practicing researchers are essential to the process because they are the experts on the professional standards and ethical values of their discipline and on their own expectations with regard to the behavior of their colleagues. The members of the scientific community set the standards that determine which behaviors are acceptable and which are unacceptable. Because they are the experts and therefore, rightly, provide credibility to discussions of research ethics, research practitioners must be not only sought but encouraged, solicited, prodded, persuaded, recruited and, if necessary, drafted into the development and implementation of activities aimed at teaching the responsible conduct and reporting of research.

CAN RESEARCH ETHICS BE TAUGHT?

Given the widely held view that graduate students arrive at educational institutions with their ethical views set, it is critical to examine the question of whether in fact research ethics can be taught to any effect. The answers to this question lie both in the nature of moral development and in the purpose of these types of programs. Extensive work by James Rest (1986, 1988) and others (Bebeau, 1991; Piper, Gentile, & Parks, 1993; Thoma, 1994; Trow, 1976) has shown that moral development—that is, development in the way individuals approach and resolve ethical issues—continues at least throughout formal education. Young adults in their 20s and 30s are capable of changing their strategies for addressing moral problems as they modify the assumptions and perspective that influence their assessment of what is right or wrong in the light of new knowledge. Such modification seems to be linked to the individual's fundamental reconceptualization of society and his or her role in it. Moral development continues at least during the time that individuals are in college or professional schools. Formal education with regard to moral reasoning can influence individuals' awareness of relevant factors and their reasoning about moral problems. In addition, it has been shown that an individual's behavior reflects his or her moral perception and judgment.

Given that today's graduate students and postdoctoral associates come from all parts of the globe as well as the nation, it is essential that educators and senior researchers attend to the diversity of perspectives that these trainees represent. Later moral development is most certainly built on the foundation laid down early in life. Thus, differences in culture and background can affect attitudes, beliefs, and values regarding ethically "acceptable" standards and practices. As much as possible, in discussions of research practices it is important to make underlying assumptions and values explicit rather than expecting that everyone holds the same basic assumptions and thus brings the same understanding of a situation to the discussion.

The external pressures that have resulted in programs designed to teach research ethics lead to the expectation that teaching the responsible conduct of research will eliminate instances of misconduct in science. But this expectation may be more appropriately identified as a pedagogical hope than as an instructional objective (Elliott & Stern, 1996). A more reasonable and realistic purpose for programs designed to teach research ethics to students is in fact to teach the elements of the responsible conduct of research. This consists of four goals (Vivian Weil, personal communication, April 1993).

The first goal is to increase awareness and knowledge of professional standards, conventions, and ethical values. This includes identifying and clarifying the range of acceptable and unacceptable practices, identifying and examining the assumptions that underlie acceptable practices, and exploring the immediate and long-term implications of different research practices.

A second goal is to increase awareness of the ethical dimensions of the practice and application of science. To a significant degree, ethical issues will become apparent in the process of addressing the first goal.

A third goal is to provide students with experience in making and defending decisions regarding ethical issues. All too often, when individuals are confronted with ethically problematic circumstances, a quick response is required, and there is not sufficient time to adequately analyze the situation. Yet time is required to decide if any ambiguities in the situation need to be clarified—that is, what, if any, additional information is needed; to assess the role of the various actors, their rights and responsibilities; to determine the range of possible choices of action; and to consider the short and long-term ramifications of these choices. Practice will enable students to develop some skill in sorting out the issues and forming a reasonable plan of action to address the problem.

Thus, a fourth goal is to teach students how to determine what additional information they need to reach a decision and how to obtain it.

Given the research on moral development, it is expected that meeting these goals will influence attitudes and behavior. Furthermore, faculty, postdoctoral trainees, and staff at all levels will benefit from an open discussion that encourages participants to think explicitly about their own standards and values, their expectations regarding the behavior of colleagues, and their awareness of conventions.

FORMATS FOR TEACHING RESPONSIBLE RESEARCH CONDUCT

Although NIH (1989, 1990, 1992) requires pre- and postdoctoral trainees to receive some formal education in the proper conduct and reporting of research, it does not specify the exact nature of that education with regard to structure, format, or topics. Yet in the course of reviewing programs that have been developed at various institutions in response to that requirement, NIH has identified key elements of effective programs (Glowinski, 1993). Program elements that seem to promote successful training include:
- Program sessions that are interactive
- Program sessions that are required
- Programs that start early in year one of graduate school and continue in subsequent years
- Programs that have broad-based participation by faculty and administration

In addition, outside speakers and activities outside the program, such as faculty seminars, laboratory work, and other courses, should reinforce the messages of the required program.

These observations have implications for the types of programs developed by research and educational institutions and professional societies.

Strategies for teaching the responsible conduct of research include formal courses; departmental or intrainstitutional seminars; modules within established courses that integrate discussion and analysis of ethical issues into regular course material; and mentoring programs and informal, mentoring relationships. Each approach has advantages and disadvantages (Bird, 1993).

Courses

A formal course in responsible research conduct emphasizes the importance of discussing research ethics by a grade and highlights the complexity of the topic. In a course, it is possible to cover more subjects systematically than in an occasional lecture or seminar, and each subject can be covered more thoroughly. For example, it is possible to have a succession of class meetings discussing the scientific method in theory and practice; sources of bias and their impact on hypothesis development and on the collection, selection, analysis, and interpretation of data; issues associated with the reporting of research results to the scientific and nonscientific communities; publication practices; the peer review process; the impact of funding on the direction of research; and examples of the use and misuse of research findings in the development of public policy.

However, there are potential disadvantages to a course on the responsible conduct of research. It may be marginalized if it is an elective taught by faculty from outside the department with little connection to the field and to the opinion leaders and leading faculty within the department. In addition, a course on research ethics may seem to absolve the rest of the faculty from the need to address ethical issues in their own courses or with their research groups. Moreover, a course highlights, and can limit the understanding of acceptable practices to, the opinions of the faculty who participate in the course. Without explicit attention, the rationale, justification for, and even existence of alternative practices that may be widely accepted in other venues will be lacking.

Disadvantages can be avoided or overcome in a variety of ways. If there is substantial involvement of several leading faculty who are well thought of and highly placed (e.g., the chair of the department), the value of a course can be enhanced. In addition, if the course is required or is a limited elective highly recommended by faculty advisors, it will be more effective and more highly respected by students and trainees alike. Furthermore, to the extent that its messages and topics are reflected and reinforced in other courses, seminars, and laboratory discussions and by example (e.g., by explicit acknowledgment of the contributions of collaborators in an oral presentation), the influence of a course will be increased.

Seminars

Departmental seminars, unlike undergraduate or even graduate courses, stress the importance of these issues for, and to, the whole community and provide an opportunity for many more faculty to be involved, to share their views, and to clarify the expectations of professional colleagues and the standards of the profession. This ensures that a wider perspective will be presented, highlighting, when appropriate, the range of acceptable practices and areas of consensus regarding unacceptable practices. This can be informative for postdocs and other faculty as well as students. In addition, departmental seminars allow a broader range of individuals (e.g., research, technical, clerical, and other support staff as well as faculty, postdoctoral associates, and students) to participate in and learn from the discussion. This is particularly valuable because support staff are often left out of the discussion, and their ethical concerns are generally not taken into consideration. For example, authorship may be important to technical, nonacademic staff even when it does not affect promotions and other aspects of career advancement.

In a one- to two-hour seminar or workshop on credit and responsibility in science, it is possible to examine the ways in which contributions to a research project are attributed; the various functions that authorship plays not only in distributing credit for contribution but in hiring, career advancement, and funding decisions; the criteria for, and differing expectations about, authorship; differing conventions regarding the order of authors and their potential implications; and various perspectives on the responsibilities associated with authorship. These aspects of the topic can be presented with reference to the literature on the subject in a relatively brief way, followed by interactive discussion of one or two scenarios or cases that exemplify variations on the theme.

However, seminars can have disadvantages as well. It is likely that fewer topics will be covered in a seminar format. More importantly, if most faculty do not attend or participate in departmental or intrainstitutional seminars that focus on the responsible conduct of research, they effectively and powerfully convey the message that these are not really important issues. Even with significant, unambiguous faculty support, seminars can imply that ethical issues are at the margin of science because they are appropriate only as an occasional topic of interest.

At the same time, a regular seminar series focusing on various aspects of the responsible conduct of research, and in which many faculty are actively involved, conveys to students the importance of discussing professional values. They may begin to see how professional standards evolve, as well as the central, if subtle, role of professional standards and values in professional development.

Integration into All Courses

Integrating ethical concerns into courses, especially core courses, underlines the fact that ethical issues are inherent rather than tangential to the discipline and to the profession. However, if the material is not a part of the course grade, it can send the opposite message. Moreover, some important topics (e.g., authorship, safety, discrimination in the workplace) may not be covered because they do not fall obviously within the purview of a particular subject. This latter problem is resolved if issues of responsible research conduct are integrated into courses that also focus on the skills necessary for successful professional advancement (e.g., oral and written presentations, laboratory management, teaching).

Mentoring Programs

Programs of all types should be supplemented with the example of faculty. However, good examples are essential but not sufficient. The rationale, policy, and philosophy that underlie even the most exemplary behavior may well be inscrutable without explanation. Furthermore, differences in cultural background and experience, as discussed above, mean that an explicit discussion of the philosophy or rationale upon which policy decisions are based may be required.

Not all faculty can correctly be considered mentors. By the broad definition of Hall and Sandler (1983), mentors share their experience and expertise. In addition, they take an active interest in the professional development of those they mentor.[1] This definition often leads to the assumption that a thesis advisor (or research supervisor for postdoctoral associates) will be a mentor. This is an obvious mentoring pair, but the responsibilities of the thesis advisor are to ensure that the student fulfills the departmental and institutional requirements for the degree. These responsibilities are not necessarily congruent with those of a mentor. Indeed, in surveys of graduate students, the individual identified as the most supportive faculty member was not necessarily the thesis advisor.[2]

Nevertheless, a thesis advisor should be one of several mentors to graduate students because, as mentioned above, so much more must be learned, beyond scientific concepts and laboratory techniques, for students and trainees to become successful science professionals, whatever their discipline. In an academic setting, these skills include writing and reviewing papers and grant proposals; data collection, selection, analysis, interpretation, and presentation; and balancing the demands of research, lab management, teaching, training of graduate students, and other institutional, organizational, and additional professional activities. Integral to each of these components are ethical considerations that are associated with professional standards and ethical values. Because no single individual is likely to be proficient in every aspect of the profession, and because with time students and their former advisors often become separated geographically, trainees need to be able to turn to a number of different individuals for advice regarding various professional skills.

The responsibilities of research supervisors of postdoctoral trainees are even less clearly defined. Yet it is even more important that they be mentors and make explicit the information that is generally implicit but critical for a successful transition to an independent research career. Because this period is, by definition, a time of transition and because few institutional supports are available to them, postdoctoral associates are especially in need of supportive, senior, well-connected colleagues. Parenthetically, it is clear that, for the same reasons, junior faculty also need mentors.

Much of what is most important to learn for professional success can be learned to some degree from courses, seminars, and books, but most faculty and students believe that mentors are best, especially for some topics such as peer review. However essential mentoring is, few individuals are naturally good mentors, though most can usually be trained. Unfortunately, there are few programs for training mentors, especially in an academic setting. Given the fact that current graduate students and postdoctoral associates will soon be in a position to train students and postdocs of their own, training individuals to become mentors is an appropriate component of teaching the responsible conduct of research.

An in-depth discussion of mentoring, including what it is and is not, what qualities are important, and the responsibilities of mentors and their "mentees," is beyond the scope of this chapter (see Bird, in press; National Academy of Science, 1997). However, it is important to note that programs and activities that facilitate and encourage mentoring, as well as programs that train mentors, are a key component of teaching the responsible conduct of research.

An ideal approach to teaching the responsible conduct and reporting of research would include all of the above activities: specific courses, departmental seminars, interdepartmental workshops, discussion of aspects of research ethics in courses and in laboratories as appropriate, and one-on-one mentoring. Each element would complement and supplement the others, with all components reinforced by role models who practiced what they preached. However, substantial resources are not generally made available to implement a broad range of programs and activities focusing on the responsible conduct of research. This reflects the scientific community's reluctance to incorporate this topic into graduate education. As indicated above, not only the support but the wholehearted involvement of research faculty at all levels is critical to the success of such activities. Thus, establishing an effective program will require initial efforts that appropriately recognize and utilize financial resources and personnel. You can start only where you are, not where you would like to be.

APPROACHES AND MATERIALS

There is a growing body of materials designed to facilitate the teaching of research ethics. These include books, videotapes, collections of cases, special issues of journals, and the "Educational Forum" section of *Science and Engi-*

neering Ethics. Most of the best include or incorporate case studies or scenarios, using them to highlight both the reality and the complexity of the ethical issues. They demonstrate the ways in which ethical issues are interwoven into the practice of science, often arising out of confusion and misunderstanding about conventions and/or responsibilities or out of individuals' different expectations, values, or needs. Differences and misunderstandings are exacerbated by lack of communication. When used appropriately, these specific examples can serve as excellent teaching tools, catalyzing discussion and facilitating an examination of underlying assumptions, sources of misunderstanding and miscommunication, and broader implications of various choices and decisions. (See, e.g., Bird & Housman, 1994, 1995, 1997; Swazey & Bird, 1995, 1997; Weil & Arzbaecher, 1995, 1997.)

Although some prefer cases that involve incidents culled from news articles, examples that involve "real" people can introduce extraneous discussions based on rumors or other versions of the events described and may also bring concerns regarding legal liability. In addition, such cases invite judgments regarding who made what mistakes and inevitably summarize a lengthy chain of events rather than highlighting the particular instances in which individual choices about specific actions were made. This can be counterproductive if a goal of programs designed to teach the responsible conduct of research is to prepare students to assess the source and focus of the problem and give them practice in designing solutions and in identifying what additional resources they need. More narrowly focused narrative cases or scenarios encourage and facilitate consideration of the range of possible solutions to the problem. They highlight the possibility of more than one acceptable solution as well as specific consideration of unacceptable solutions. It is important to recognize that what seems like the "best" solution can depend upon point of view: different individuals may have different advantages, disadvantages, benefits, or losses depending on who makes what choice. Thus, a graduate student, a postdoc seeking a job, and the head of the lab may each see a discussion of authorship differently. In addition, as mentioned above, differences in culture, experience, and background can substantially affect perception of the relevant aspects of a given situation. Therefore, in examining a case, it may be helpful to have each member of a discussion group restate the situation or identify the problematic circumstances that he or she sees in order to uncover differences in perceptions and assumptions. It would not be surprising if a student from New York City and a student from Omaha, Nebraska, or a female graduate student from Taiwan and a male postdoc from Tel Aviv, perceived different issues and had differing concerns.

There is considerable discussion regarding the inclusion of ethical theory in programs on responsible research conduct. It has the advantage of introducing a body of literature that often helps to clarify the issues and of providing a common base of understanding and language with which to examine the topic. It also helps to prevent the discussion of cases from becoming a litany of "old war stories" that can imply that there is no organized way of thinking through ethical problems. However, too much emphasis on ethical theory can make the subject seem abstract, remote, and inaccessible. For occasional, relatively brief events of one to two hours, one approach is to incorporate a didactic component into the program that identifies the key issues, relevant literature, regulations, and conventions and that provides a foundation and framework for the discussion of a particular set of topics.

TOPICS

A number of topics are appropriate to consider depending on the discipline, the context of the presentation, and the audience. The many aspects of the practice and application of research raise a wide range of issues, concerns, and implications worthy of examination. Discussion of several different topics emphasizes the many ethical dimensions of the practice and application of science. The issues may include those related to a specific workplace, methodology, or discipline or to features systemic to the practice of science. Topics specific to the work environment range from issues of safety to the selection, analysis, and presentation of data, to the use of animals or humans as research subjects, to the relationship between those who work together in a setting in which sexual harassment or the expression of prejudice can occur. The nature of science and the scientific community encourages discussion of various topics, including peer review, mechanisms for attributing credit and the responsibilities of authorship, the impact of funding on the direction of research, potential for conflict of interest, and openness and secrecy in science.

Beyond the practice of science, in a world where science and technology increasingly affect or form the basis of public policy in such diverse areas as health, the environment, military weaponry, and industry, the applications of science and technology, risk assessment and management, and the use of expert scientific testimony in the courtroom are only a sample of the many thought-provoking topics that would complement discussions of research practice in a program exploring the responsible conduct and reporting of research.

EVALUATION

Strategies for assessing the efficacy of programs in responsible research conduct are only beginning to be developed. However, it would be naive to assume that any program or discussion of the responsible conduct of research, no matter how carefully thought out, could be sufficient, in and of itself, to determine attitudes and behavior. To the extent that students and trainees perceive or believe that other, less desirable but more expedient behavior is ever occasionally or generally accepted, or even encouraged or rewarded (e.g., including as an author one whose contribution would not normally merit inclusion), it seems likely that junior researchers will act accordingly (Eastwood, Derish, Leash, & Ordway, 1996). Exemplary behavior on the part of senior researchers is necessary, though not sufficient, as a component of teaching responsible research conduct. By explicitly discussing the range of ethical issues, common conventions, and professional values and standards, the scientific community acknowledges the complexity of the issues and the need to work through them. Specifically discussing these topics also reaffirms the responsibility of the research community, individually and collectively, to provide this information to its new members.

Notes

1. Note that this definition of a mentor is in contrast to the ideal Mentor of Greek mythology, the teacher of Ulysses' son Telemachus, who was omniscient, sensitive, wise, and powerful. The perception that an actual mentor will match this ideal is a widely held, though unconscious, expectation that is rarely fulfilled.

2. The most supportive faculty member as identified by the student most frequently expressed continuing interest in the student's progress, provided letters of recommendation, and helped students obtain financial support (Swazey, 1993).

References

Alberts, B., & Shine, K. (1994). Scientists and the integrity of research. *Science, 266,* 1660–1661.

Bebeau, M. J. (1991). Can ethics be taught? A look at the evidence. *Journal of the American College of Dentists, 58,* 5, 10–15.

Bird, S. J. (1993). Teaching ethics in the sciences: Why, how and what. In *Ethics, Values, and the Promise of Science: Forum Proceedings, February 25–26, 1993* (pp. 228–232). Research Triangle Park, NC: Sigma Xi, the Scientific Research Society.

Bird, S. J. (1994). Overlooked aspects in the education of science professionals: Mentoring, ethics, and professional responsibility. *Journal of Science Education and Technology, 3,* 49–55.

Bird, S. J. (In press). Mentors, advisors and supervisors. In G. C. Roberts & R. L. Sprague (Eds.), *The role of mentoring in teaching research ethics.* Champaign: University of Illinois Press.

Bird, S. J., & Housman, D. E. (1994). Trust and the collection, selection, analysis and interpretation of data: A scientist's view. *Science and Engineering Ethics, 1,* 371–382.

Bird, S. J., & Housman, D. E. (1995). Conducting and reporting research. *Professional Ethics, 4,* 127–154.

Bird, S. J., & Housman, D. E. (1997). Conducting, reporting and funding research. In D. Elliott & J. E. Stern (Eds.), *Research ethics: A reader* (pp. 98–112, 120–138). Hanover, NH: University Press of New England.

Braxton, J. M., & Bayer, A. E. (1996). Personal experiences of research misconduct and the response of individual academic scientists. *Science, Technology, and Human Values, 21,* 198–213.

Eastwood, S., Derish, P., Leash, E., & Ordway, S. (1996). Ethical issues in biomedical research: Perceptions and practices of postdoctoral research fellows responding to a survey. *Science and Engineering Ethics, 2,* 89–114.

Elliott, D., & Stern, J. (1996). Evaluating teaching and students' learning of academic research ethics. *Science and Engineering Ethics, 2,* 345–366.

Glowinski, I. (1993, April). *How do you measure success? Benchmarks to guide evaluation of curriculum and instruction.* Paper presented at "Educating for the Responsible Conduct of Research: NIH Policy and Other Mandates," a conference organized by Public Responsibility in Medicine and Research (PRIM&R), Boston.

Gorovitz, S. (1998). Ethical issues in graduate education. *Science and Engineering Ethics, 4,* 225–240.

Hall, R. M., & Sandler, B. R. (1983). *Academic mentoring for women students and faculty: A new look at an old way to get ahead.* Washington, DC: Association of American Colleges.

National Academy of Sciences. (1992–1993). *Responsible science: Ensuring the integrity of the research process* (2 vols.). Washington, DC: National Academy Press.

National Academy of Sciences. (1997). *Advisor, teacher, role model, friend: On being a mentor to students in science and engineering.* Washington, DC: National Academy Press.

National Institutes of Health. (1989, December 22). Reminder and update: Requirement for programs on the responsible conduct of research in National Research Service Award institutional training programs. *NIH Guide for Grants and Contracts, 18.*

National Institutes of Health. (1990, August 17). Reminder and update: Requirement for programs on the responsible conduct of research in National Research Service Award institutional training programs. *NIH Guide for Grants and Contracts, 19,* 9.

National Institutes of Health. (1992, November 27). Reminder and update: Requirement for programs on the responsible conduct of research in National Research Service Award institutional training programs. *NIH Guide for Grants and Contracts, 21,* 2–3.

Olson, S. (1995). *On being a scientist: Responsible conduct in research* (2nd ed.). Washington, DC: National Academy Press.

Piper, T. R., Gentile, M. C., & Parks, S. D. (1993). *Can ethics be taught?* Boston: Harvard Business School Publishing Division.

Rest, J. R. (1986). Moral development in young adults. In R. A. Mines & K. S. Kitchener (Eds.), *Adult cognitive development: Methods and models* (pp. 92–111). New York: Praeger.

Rest, J. R. (1988, Winter). Can ethics be taught in professional schools? The psychological research. *Easier Said Than Done*, pp. 22–26.

Rittenhouse, C. D. (1996). Survival skills and ethics training for graduate students: A graduate student perspective. *Science and Engineering Ethics, 2,* 367–380.

Swazey, J. P. (1993). Teaching ethics: Needs, opportunities, and obstacles. In *Ethics, Values, and the Promise of Science: Forum Proceedings, Feburary 25–26, 1993* (pp. 233–242). Research Triangle Park, NC: Sigma Xi, the Scientific Research Society.

Swazey, J. P., & Bird, S. J. (1995). Teaching and learning research ethics. *Professional Ethics, 4,* 155–178.

Swazey, J. P., & Bird, S. J. (1997). Teaching and learning research ethics. In D. Elliott & J. E. Stern (Eds.), *Research ethics: A reader* (pp. 1–19). Hanover, NH: University Press of New England.

Thoma, S. J. (1994). Moral judgments and moral action. In J. R. Rest & D. Narvaez (Eds.), *Moral development in the professions: Psychology and applied ethics* (pp. 199–211). Hillsdale, NJ: Lawrence Erlbaum.

Trow, M. (1976). Higher education and moral development. *AAUP Bulletin, 61,*(4), 20–27.

Weil, V., & Arzbaecher, R. (1995). Ethics and relationships in laboratories and research communities. *Professional Ethics, 4,* 155–178.

Weil, V., & Arzbaecher, R. (1997). Relationships in laboratories and research communities. In D. Elliott & J. E. Stern (Eds.), *Research ethics: A reader* (pp. 69–92). Hanover, NH: University Press of New England.

Wolpert, L. (1996, March 24). The dangerous defiance of science. *London Sunday Times,* Sec. 3, p. 6.

CHAPTER NINE

Legal Aspects of Scholarship Misconduct

Barbara A. Lee

Misconduct in scholarship covers a wide range of behaviors, and an equally diverse group of legal doctrines is related to this misconduct. For researchers who receive grants from public agencies, federal and state laws regulate how the funds are spent and provide penalties for fraudulent or unethical conduct in using the funds or in reporting the research results. But even if a scholar does not receive funding from public sources, scholarship misconduct may have legal consequences for the scholar or for the college or university that employs the scholar. And those individuals who report alleged scholarship misconduct may be protected by the legal system under certain circumstances or may face liability under other legal doctrines.

The problem of scholarship misconduct and the response of the public and the U.S. Congress have been discussed in earlier chapters. Although the federal regulations that articulate the responsibilities of the institution to investigate possible fraud in federally funded research impose potentially severe sanctions on both the institution and the accused researcher, other sources of law also can impose liability on the institution, the accused individual, the accuser, or all three if misconduct in scholarship is alleged or proven. This chapter examines those sources of law, analyzes how they apply in situations of allegations of scholarship misconduct, and discusses how institutions and the individuals involved may use these laws either to seek to rectify alleged misconduct or to protect themselves from unjust or frivolous allegations.

FEDERAL LAWS PROTECTING RESEARCH INTEGRITY

There are three categories of federal laws related to scientific misconduct: laws that regulate the conduct of the recipient of a federal grant or contract, laws that protect creators or inventors of intellectual property from its appropriation by others, and laws that provide for prosecution of individuals who defraud the federal government, including those that provide incentives for "whistle-blowers" to bring actions against individuals or institutions suspected of misconduct in the use of federal funds. This section of the chapter will discuss each category of laws briefly.

Regulation of Federally Funded Research

Federal and state agencies[1] that award research grants or contracts have developed a plethora of regulations regarding the use of the funds, the filing of reports, and the grantee's[2] response to allegations of research misconduct. The federal agencies providing the majority of research funds to institutions are the Public Health Service (PHS) and its subunit, the National Institutes of Health, and the National Science Foundation (NSF). Both agencies have promulgated definitions of "misconduct" in science; these definitions are similar but not identical and have been criticized as overly broad.

PHS defines misconduct in science as "fabrication, falsification, plagiarism, or other practices that seriously deviate from those that are commonly accepted within the scientific community for proposing, conducting, or reporting research. It does not include honest error or honest differences in interpretations or judgments of data" (42 C. F. R. 50.102). The inclusion in the definition of "other practices that seriously deviate from those that are commonly accepted" has been criticized as sweeping too broadly and potentially including scientific practices that are not fraudulent or improper but that merely differ from the "accepted" scientific approach (National Academy of Sciences, 1992). Nevertheless, many colleges and universities have adopted the PHS definition, although it does not include improper actions such as sabotage or refusal to cooperate with an investigation into alleged scientific misconduct (Parrish, 1994, p. 520). Although there have been several attempts to revise the PHS definition in the past several years, none of these attempts have been successful to date (Commission on Research Integrity, 1995, p. 2).[3] It has been difficult to strike a balance between clarity in the definition and development of a definition that covers all potential instances of behavior that could constitute scientific misconduct.

The NSF defines science misconduct as
1. Fabrication, falsification, plagiarism, or other serious deviation from accepted practices in proposing, carrying out, or reporting results from activities funded by NSF; or
2. Retaliation of any kind against a person who reported or provided information about suspected or alleged misconduct and who has not acted in bad faith. (45 C. F. R. 689.1(a))

Although most of the highly publicized cases of scholarship misconduct have involved the fabrication of scientific data,[4] many accusations involve plagiarism or intellectual theft. According to Parrish (1994), approximately 30% of the cases involve investigations by the Office of Research Integrity (ORI), which investigates PHS grantees, and approximately 50% of the NSF cases involve allegations of plagiarism (p. 521). ORI defines plagiarism as "the act of appropriating the literary composition of another, or parts of passages of the writings, or the ideas (intellectual theft) or language of the same, and representing them as one's own thoughts. Although intellectual theft is traditionally used to indicate the stealing of ideas, as opposed to the theft of written material (plagiarism), by definition, it is a subset of plagiarism" (*OIG Newsletter,* cited in Parrish, 1994, p. 522). NSF does not have a definition of plagiarism because it determines whether the conduct constitutes a "serious deviation" from accepted scientific practice; copying of a set of words or phrases to describe a common procedure, although technically plagiarism, is not scientific misconduct under either NSF or PHS policy (Parrish, 1994, p. 522).

When the recipient of the grant or contract receives information that suggests that research misconduct may have occurred, both federal agencies require the institution to conduct an initial inquiry to determine whether an investigation is warranted. If the individual or individuals conducting the inquiry believe that an investigation should be done, the recipient institution must notify either PHS or NSF (depending on the source of the funding) that an investigation will be conducted to determine whether misconduct has occurred. Regulations of both agencies require the recipient to advise the funding agency of the results of the investigation. Both agencies also spell out time lines for the investigation, the type of information that is to be transmitted to PHS or NSF, and due-process and confidentiality guarantees. The agencies may accept the findings of the award recipient; they may also modify or reject the findings without an investigation, or they may launch their own investigations. If either the recipient or the agency finds that misconduct has occurred, the agency may impose one or more penalties on the recipient, including debarment from future grants or contracts. Despite the severity of the penalties for institutions that do not comply with these requirements, a review of institutional recipients of federal research grants conducted by ORI concluded that over 80% of these institutions did not fully comply with federal regulations (Walker, 1996, p. A29).

ORI is responsible for monitoring and investigating complaints of alleged misconduct in research lodged against recipients of research funding from PHS.[5] ORI is an independent entity within the U.S. Department of Health and Human Services; its director reports directly to the Secretary of Health and Human Services, although day-to-day oversight of its activities is the responsibility of the Assistant Secretary for Health. ORI replaced two offices that had previously investigated alleged misconduct—the Office of Scientific Integrity (OSI), which had been located within the National Institutes of Health, and the Office of Scientific Integrity Review (OSIR), located in the office of the Assistant Secretary of Health (Parrish, 1994, p. 518).

Within NSF, the Office of the Inspector General receives institutional reports of investigations and conducts investigations of alleged misconduct on behalf of NSF. For both agencies, the office investigating the allegation is separate from, and is not subordinate to, the office that awarded the funds and monitors the progress of the research. If the investigation discloses that potential criminal acts have occurred, the agencies may refer the case to the Department of Justice or the Federal Bureau of Investigation. If the institution determines that an individual has engaged in misconduct, and if the agency accepts that finding, the individual has the right to appeal that finding in an administrative hearing that, for ORI investigations, is conducted by the U.S. Department of Health and Human Services' Departmental Appeals Board (Howard, 1995). Individuals found to have engaged in misconduct under NSF regulations also have the right to appeal within NSF (Howard, 1995, p. 335).

Penalties for funding recipients may include immediate suspension or termination of the funding for the project. They may also include debarment from future federal contracts or awards from that agency for a specified period of years. Individuals found to have engaged in misconduct may be barred from serving on peer review panels, from receiving future federal funding from the agency, or from participating in research projects with other recipients of research funds. Lesser penalties include letters of reprimand or a requirement of prior approval for certain grant-funded activities.

Although both agencies rely on the recipient to conduct the initial inquiry and the investigation, only ORI requires the institution to have written policies and procedures for "reviewing, investigating, and reporting allegations of misconduct in science" to the agency. In April 1995, ORI issued "Model Policies and Procedures for Investigations of Scientific Misconduct," which, although they are not legally binding on institutions, are clearly intended to influence the way that institutions develop their policies and procedures for responding to allegations of scientific misconduct. Although several scholarly and professional organizations had published studies of institutional policies and practices before the 1995 model policies, a review of these policies found that there was no consistency in how institutions handled investigations of alleged misconduct (Howard, 1995, p. 334). Given the potentially serious implications of an allegation of scientific misconduct, from staining a reputation to ending a career, institutions need to develop policies and procedures that guarantee due process to the accused and to the accuser. Failure to do so can result in challenges by either the accused or accuser—for public institutions, under the U.S. Constitution's Fourteenth Amendment (due-process clause), and for private institutions, under contract theories.

Federal Laws Protecting Intellectual Property

Copyright Law

Under federal copyright law (17 U.S.C. sec. 101 et seq.), authors and artists have the exclusive right to their writings and creations, subject to limitations specified in the law and court decisions interpreting those laws. The law covers a wide range of "creations," including architectural designs, computer software, videotapes, audio tapes, standardized tests, and visual art, as well as written works.

Federal copyright law specifies the circumstances under which copyrighted material may be used by others. Under the "fair use doctrine," copyrighted work may be used "for purposes such as criticism, news reporting, teaching (including multiple copies for classroom use), scholarship, or research" (17 U.S.C. sec. 107). The law lists four factors that must be considered in order to determine whether use of copyrighted material without prior permission falls within the protections of the fair use doctrine:

1. the purpose and character of the use, including whether such use is of a commercial nature or is for nonprofit educational purposes;
2. the nature of the copyrighted work;
3. the amount and substantiality of the portion used in relation to the copyrighted work as a whole; and
4. the effect of the use upon the potential market for or value of the copyrighted work.

The use of the material must satisfy all four criteria in order to be a "fair use" under the copyright law. The fair use doctrine has been interpreted as requiring authors who wish to quote directly a long passage from a written work, or to include exact copies of drawings or designs in an article or book, to obtain permission from the holder of the copyright to reproduce the material. Authors who have not retained the copyright to their own published work must seek permission from the copyright holder (e.g., a journal or book publisher) before they can reproduce their own material.

A copyright holder who believes that the copyright has been infringed may file a lawsuit in federal court for damages. Damages may be calculated on the basis of the loss of revenue to the copyright holder (e.g., if a faculty member photocopies portions of a work instead of requiring students to purchase the work) or the loss in value occasioned by the infringement (e.g., if an author quotes unpublished material that is copyrighted).

As noted above, the fair use doctrine applies to unpublished as well as published material. If an individual plagiarizes material that is protected by copyright, damages could include both the diminution in value of the material and any potential decrease in value of the material occasioned by the plagiarizer's claiming authorship rather than attributing it to its real source.

Authorship disputes may involve copyright issues. For example, in *Weis-*

mann v. Freeman (1989), a medical school professor was sued by his former research assistant. The professor and research assistant had coauthored several works; the professor added some new material to a work written solely by the research assistant (although based in part upon their coauthored work) and published it as his own. The former research assistant, now a professor herself, sued. The court, ruling for the former research assistant, stated that each "derivative work" of an earlier coauthored work was a new work and thus that the professor's attribution of the work to himself violated the fair use doctrine. The case is significant because it recognized that the failure to acknowledge the work of another—even a former coauthor—is a potential violation of federal copyright law.

From the perspective of scholarship misconduct, the most likely application of copyright law would be to plagiarism in a written document or work of art. The copyright holder, in addition to obtaining damages under this law, could also sue the infringer using fraud, theft, or other civil tort theories.

Patent Law

Federal law also provides protections for discoverers or inventors. Multiple issues may arise when a discovery is made that has potential commercial value. Who owns the patent rights? What can be patented? What constraints can be placed by the patent holder on the replication of a discovery? Faculty, institutions, and funding sources all have strong interests in the answers to these questions.

Under federal law (35 U.S.C. sec. 101 et seq.), the holder of a patent has the exclusive right to the invention for 17 years if the holder registers the patent with the U.S. Patent and Trademark Office and describes the invention or discovery in sufficient detail. The invention or discovery must meet certain criteria, such as "novelty" and "nonobviousness," to be accepted for registration by the U.S. Patent and Trademark Office.

If an unauthorized use of the patented item or process occurs, the patent holder may bring infringement proceedings in federal court. Damages may include lost profits or a reasonable royalty for the use of the item or process; triple damages if willful infringement is found; and, in some cases, reasonable attorney's fees.

Considerable scholarly and legal debate has surrounded the issue of patenting genetically altered living things (Lyon & Gorner, 1995). The U.S. Patent and Trademark Office has issued patents for such "discoveries," and this, in turn, has increased the cost of doing research on these animals and plants. Furthermore, colleges and universities, faced with the huge potential profits from these substances, have placed restrictions on how they are to be used. The ability to patent these research materials raises difficult ethical and legal questions because the patent holder may insist upon a royalty or may require a researcher to purchase the patented research material rather than producing it in his or her own laboratory. Although commentators have suggested that there should be a "research exemption" so that researchers can replicate living or nonliving substances that are patented in order to extend scientific knowledge, no such exemption has been created. Thus, scientists who cannot or choose not to pay royalties or other fees for using patented research material may find themselves facing patent infringement proceedings if their research replicates the patented "invention" of another scientist. Because patent law does not require that an infringement be intentional, a scientist who unwittingly replicates a patented invention of another could be liable for patent infringement.

Colleges and universities should have clear written policies about patent ownership and should ensure that faculty and research staff understand and agree to abide by these policies before it is necessary to determine who owns a patent. For discoveries resulting from federally funded research, the patent law provides that colleges and universities may retain title to those inventions except in certain limited exceptions related to national security. But if the discovery is made by an employee and there is no specific language that specifies patent ownership, state property law will typically govern, and the employee will usually be the patent owner.

Criminal and Civil Prosecutorial Laws

A third category of federal law enables either the government or an individual "whistle-blower" to seek remedies for the misuse of federal funds. Fines of several thousands of dollars and even imprisonment are permitted by the criminal laws; civil laws have larger monetary penalties but do not involve imprisonment for those found to have defrauded the federal government.

Criminal Laws

Two criminal statutes are drafted broadly enough to permit prosecution of recipients of federal funds or individuals who work in projects financed by those funds. The first statute, the false statements statute, provides:

> Whoever, in any manner within the jurisdiction of any department or agency of the United States knowingly and willfully falsifies, conceals or covers up by any trick, scheme, or device a material fact, or makes any false, fictitious or fraudulent statements or representations, or makes or uses any false writing or document knowing the same to contain any false, fictitious or fraudulent statement or entry, shall be fined under this title or imprisoned not more than five years, or both. (18 U.S.C. sec. 1001)

This statute has been interpreted to apply to false statements made in either grant applications or grant reports (i.e., fraud), as well as to the appropriation of another individual's words in applications or reports (i.e., plagiarism) (Edgar, cited in Sise, 1991, p. 418). The government establishes the "knowing" element of the act by proving that the applicant or report author was aware that the data were false or had been fabricated or that some publication upon which the application or section of the grant report was based had been fabricated or falsified. An illustrative case using this law is *United States v. Breuning* (1988), in which Dr. Stephen Breuning pleaded guilty to violating the false statements law by submitting false data to support a grant proposal (Sise, 1991, pp. 401, 420). He was sentenced to two years' imprisonment for each of the two counts in the indictment (all but 60 days of which was suspended), was ordered to pay restitution and engage in community service, and was barred from working as a research psychologist for five years (Kuzma, 1992, p. 403, citing the unpublished judgment in *United States v. Breuning*, 1988).

A second federal law, the criminal false claims statute (not to be confused with the civil false claims statute, to be discussed next), also provides for criminal penalties for those who defraud the government. This statute provides: "Whoever makes or presents to any person or officer in the civil, military, or naval service of the United States, or to any department or agency thereof, any claim upon or against the United States, or any department or agency thereof, knowing such claim to be false, fictitious, or fraudulent, shall be imprisoned not more than five years and shall be subject to a fine in the amount provided in this title" (18 U.S.C. sec. 287). Although this statute is often used to prosecute doctors who submit false claims for Medicare reimbursement, it can also be used against scientists who make some representation or claim in a grant proposal that they know is false with the intent of receiving funding from the federal government (Sise, 1991, p. 422).

Criminal actions are possible under other federal statutes, including laws against mail fraud or wire fraud (Kuzma, 1992, p. 401). And it is possible that scholars accused of fraudulent conduct could be prosecuted under state criminal laws as well, particularly those prohibiting theft or misappropriation of property (p. 400).

Civil Actions

Because the standard of proof for criminal laws is substantially higher than for civil claims, it is more likely that a recipient of federal funds who is accused of scholarship fraud will face a civil than a criminal charge. The civil statute, the Federal False Claims Act, is also called the *qui tam* statute. As is not the case with claims under federal criminal law, a private individual with knowledge of the fraudulent behavior may bring a claim under the False Claims Act (and is called a "*qui tam* plaintiff").

The law imposes liability upon any person who knowingly does any of the following: "Makes a false or fraudulent claim for payment or approval; conspires to defraud the government by getting a false claim paid; provides false information regarding compliance with terms of a federal contract; or provides a false record or statement to the federal government" (31 U.S.C. sec. 3729).

If the plaintiff proves a violation of the act, the plaintiff may receive between 25% and 30% of the damages assessed against the defendant. Because the statute provides for civil penalties of not less than $5,000 or more than $10,000, plus three times the amount of damages actually sustained by the federal government, the financial incentives for *qui tam* plaintiffs are obvious. If the U.S. Department of Justice decides to join the litigation, the amount that can be recovered by the plaintiff drops to 15% to 25%, but the government bears most of the cost of the litigation. A successful *qui tam* plaintiff receives reasonable attorney's fees as well as the recovery described above. Although the plaintiff may receive less than the statutory amount if the case is settled rather than litigated to its conclusion, a sizable recovery is still possible. Furthermore, the law forbids retaliation against the plaintiff by the plaintiff's employer. This provision is particularly important for postdoctoral students or junior researchers who provide information about scholarship fraud by their supervisors or senior colleagues because many have lost their jobs or seen their careers stalled or ended after they have made these accusations (Sise, 1991, p. 410). Penalties that an institution could face for retaliation against whistle-blowers are discussed in the section of this chapter on tort law and whistle-blower claims.

The False Claims Act was originally passed in 1863 to respond to claims of fraud by federal contractors during the Civil War. Congress increased the amounts that private plaintiffs could recover to their current rate in 1986 because of mounting concern about fraud by federal defense contractors (Perzan, 1992, p. 655). Plaintiffs receive these amounts even if the defendant settles the case before or during trial (31 U.S.C. sec. 3730 (d)(2)).

To state a lawful claim, the *qui tam* plaintiff must demonstrate that he or she is the "original source" of the information; a lawsuit based upon information available to the public would not be cognizable under this statute. The plaintiff must also demonstrate that the information was offered to the government before the plaintiff initiated the litigation. If the Justice Department decides to enter the case, it may convince the court to dismiss the plaintiff as a party, particularly if there is evidence that the plaintiff has filed the lawsuit in order to harass or retaliate against the defendant (Perzan, 1992, p. 657).

Institutions as well as researchers face potential liability under *qui tam* lawsuits. The law was used to recover funds from the University of Utah and the University of California at San Diego for the alleged fraud of Dr. John L. Ninnemann, who was accused of falsifying research results concerning the body's immune reaction when the skin is burned (Hilts, 1994, p. 9). The universities settled the case for $1.6 million, and the former colleague of Ninnemann who brought the lawsuit received 15% of the settlement amount. The universities had maintained that Ninnemann was guilty not of fraud but of "sloppiness" and had decided not to pursue charges against the researcher (Hilts, 1994, p. 9).

More recently, the University of Alabama and four of its researchers were found guilty under this law by a federal jury in Baltimore, who awarded $1.9 million to the National Institutes of Health and the *qui tam* plaintiff. This award was overturned on appeal, but the case is instructive as an example of the use of the *qui tam* law (*United States ex rel. Berge v. Board of Trustees of the University of Alabama*, 1997). In this case, the plaintiff, a former colleague of the accused researchers, asserted that she had collected and analyzed the data that the researchers had published as their own without crediting the contribution of the plaintiff. The data were also used by these researchers to obtain additional grants. Because the university had made brief inquiries in response to the plaintiff's claim but had decided not to pursue the investigation, it was joined as a defendant and shared in the jury's finding of liability. Before reversal by the appellate court, the university had been ordered to pay $1.66 million, $498,000 of which would have gone to the plaintiff. The four researchers had been ordered to pay a total of $50,000 to the plaintiff and $215,000 in punitive damages.

The university appealed the jury's verdict on a variety of issues, including the fact that the judge had refused to permit the jury to be told that the *qui tam* plaintiff would receive a financial recovery if the jury found in her favor. The appellate court ruled that the plaintiff had not demonstrated any violation of the False Claims Act and that the jury's verdict was against the weight of the evidence (*United States ex rel. Berge v. Board of Trustees*, 1997, p. 1462).

Another judge in the same federal district dismissed a *qui tam* lawsuit brought by a former postdoctoral fellow at the Brain Tumor Research Center of the University of California at San Francisco. The plaintiff had sued the university and several researchers that it employed, asserting that she had been unable to replicate results that the researchers published a decade earlier. The trial judge characterized the case as a scientific dispute rather than fraud (*United States ex rel. Milam v. Regents of the University of California*, 1995) and suggested that the *qui tam* law was inappropriate to resolve such disputes.

PROTECTIONS FOR THE ACCUSED SCHOLAR: CONSTITUTIONAL AND CONTRACT CLAIMS

Federal regulations may interact with, complement, or conflict with the institution's own regulations and procedures for dealing with faculty and staff misconduct. It is very important for the institution's faculty and administrators to think carefully, *before* a case of alleged misconduct arises, about how the institution can best respond to such a charge. First, does the institution have clear policies prohibiting scholarship misconduct? Are the faculty and staff aware of these policies? Are the policies incorporated into handbooks and/or contracts so that the institution can demonstrate that its faculty and staff were aware of the policies?

An authority on scientific misconduct and due process has recommended that institutions, at a minimum, include the following types of misconduct in their definition:

1. knowing misrepresentation of data, research procedures, or data analysis;
2. plagiarism and other improprieties of authorship (such as improper inclusion or exclusion of authors;
3. violation of federal, state, or institutional rules on research involving human subjects, animals, DNA, new drugs and devices, and radioactive materials. (Mishkin, 1988, p. 1933)

The institution's policy not only should define scholarship misconduct but should state clearly what the sanctions will be for those who violate the policy. If the institution intends to impose discipline or termination sanctions or to report the misconduct to funding agencies, scholarly journals, licensing boards, or other entities, the policy should say so.

The process for responding to alleged misconduct by federally funded researchers has been outlined above. The two-part process may serve as a model for institutions to use even if the accused individual or individuals are not involved with a federal or state grant. If a bifurcated process, such as that described above, is used, the institution must determine who will conduct the inquiry and whether outside experts in the accused researcher's specialty will be brought in to conduct the investigation. The institution also needs to decide whether it will use a panel of faculty, outside experts, or a combination of both to consider the evidence and render a ruling on whether misconduct has occurred.

Until a final determination is made, the institution must protect the rights of all parties to the investigation—the accuser, the accused, and any other individuals who may have been involved in the research or who have information about the allegations. Due-process requirements, discussed below, require that the accused individual have the right to confront the accuser and to be informed of the evidence underlying the accusation.[6] This information is required at the formal hearing stage; during the initial inquiry, the institution may wish to protect the confidentiality of the accuser if that is possible. The institution will also need to monitor the actions of the accused individual or individuals to ensure that retaliation against the accuser does not occur. If the complaint is made anonymously, this presents a difficult problem for the institution in that it must respond but may not be able to provide the accused individual with full due-process protections because the identity of the accuser is unknown. Even if an allegation is made anonymously, however, the institution must evaluate its credibility and look into the allegation.

Once it has been determined that scholarship misconduct sufficient to violate the institution's policy (or state or federal law) has occurred, the institution must make more decisions. If it is decided to institute disciplinary or discharge proceedings, the institution's policies and any applicable state law must be followed. Procedures for preserving data (lab notebooks, samples of specimens, original copies of documents) should be developed and followed carefully.

Given the strong constitutional and state law protections for employees with an expectation of continued employment, faculty and administrators need to consider carefully how the institution's procedures for responding to scholarship misconduct interact with its disciplinary and dismissal policies and procedures. One source of guidance on appropriate procedures for dismissal of tenured faculty is found in the American Association of University Professors (AAUP)'s "Recommended Institutional Regulations on Academic Freedom and Tenure" (AAUP, 1995, pp. 21–30). Even those institutions that have not adopted the AAUP policy statements should consider following their guidance, particularly for cases in which the researcher's job and/or reputation is at risk. Institutions may face liability under a variety of legal theories if the dismissed researcher claims that the investigation was unfair or biased or that due process was not observed (*Angelides v. Baylor College of Medicine,* 1997; Walker, 1997).

Under the Fourteenth Amendment, public employees may not be deprived of "life, liberty, or property without due process of law." Numerous decisions by the U.S. Supreme Court have established that public employees who have a legitimate expectation of continued employment have a property interest in their jobs (*Perry v. Sindermann,* 1972). Tenured faculty fall into this category, as do faculty or staff who are protected by an employment contract that has not yet expired. Therefore, individuals in these categories have a property right in continued employment, of which they cannot be divested without due process.

Liberty interests involve one's right to take advantage of other employment opportunities and are closely related to the protection of one's professional reputation. If a public institution stigmatizes an individual in such a way that the individual's reputation is impugned, a liberty interest may be at stake. Individuals with a property or liberty interest are entitled to due process in the determination of whether they engaged in misconduct.

Due-process protections require the institution to provide the accused with the following:

1. Notice of the charges
2. The names of witnesses and the information they have provided or will provide
3. A meaningful opportunity to be heard
4. A hearing held within a reasonable time
5. A hearing conducted before an impartial panel with appropriate expertise
6. A decision made on the basis of the evidence presented at the hearing, and made by an impartial decision maker (Kaplin & Lee, 1995, p. 289)

Although due-process protections do not require an adversary, trial-type proceeding with all the trappings of litigation, institutions that believe a researcher has engaged in scholarship misconduct and use that finding to discipline or discharge a researcher with a property or liberty interest as defined above will need to provide a hearing and, very likely, the presence of counsel to advise the accused.

PRIVATE INSTITUTIONS ARE BOUND BY STATE CONTRACT LAW

Although colleges and universities are free to develop their own policies and procedures, most have created a form of tenure or an expectation of continued employment for faculty that can only be removed for serious misconduct or other sufficient cause. Employment of staff and untenured faculty is subject to any contract or policy documents with contractual status under state law.[7] Although the Constitution's due-process requirements do not bind private institutions, affording the same type of hearing and access to counsel will help ensure that the decision to discipline or discharge is made on the basis of sufficient evidence and that the accused researcher has had an opportunity to rebut the evidence produced by the institution.

Although scholarship misconduct is not a new problem, it is not a frequent problem at most institutions, and it is unlikely that most faculty or administrators have ever been required to participate in an inquiry, investigation, or hearing. Particularly if the accused individual has a strong record of external funding or a high profile, it may be tempting for institutional administrators or the accused individual's colleagues to conduct a superficial inquiry and exculpate the individual. Hasty or inadequate investigations may result in the funding agency's deciding to take over the investigation, while overly aggressive investigations and inattention to due process or contractual protections may result in legal liability for the institution. Striking the appropriate balance and ensuring that the rights and interests of all parties to the misconduct investigation are protected is easier to advocate than it is to implement.

STATE LAW TORT AND WHISTLE-BLOWER CLAIMS

The college or university is not the only potential defendant when an accusation of scholarship misconduct is made. The scholar accused of unethical or unlawful behavior may sue the accuser, college administrators, faculty involved in the inquiry or investigation, or others for defamation. And if the job or reputation of the individual making the accusation is in jeopardy, he or she may also may sue the institution, the accused individual, or both, for defamation. He or she also may seek protection under state whistle-blower laws.

Defamation

In a defamation claim, the plaintiff asserts that a communication to a third party, either in writing (libel) or orally (slander), harmed the individual's reputation or damaged the plaintiff's career or employment opportunities. In accusations of scholarship misconduct, the accused, the accuser, or both may claim that their reputation has been harmed. If the university employs both the accused and the accuser, it may find itself a defendant in defamation litigation by *both* the accused and the accuser.

To make a successful claim of defamation, a plaintiff must establish all of the following elements:
1. A false and defamatory statement was made about that individual.
2. The information was communicated to a third party.
3. The individual who communicated the information was at least negligent about ascertaining its truth, or the individual knew that the information was false.
4. The statement caused harm to the plaintiff. (Restatement Second of Torts, sec. 558, cited in Willborn, Schwab, & Burton, 1993, p. 223)

Truth is an absolute defense to a defamation claim. However, given the complexities of establishing the existence of scholarship misconduct and proving that the misconduct was intentional, it may be difficult for an institutional or individual defendant to establish that the accusation was "true" rather than "very likely." Therefore, institutional or individual defendants are more likely to successfully avoid defamation liability if they can demonstrate that they are protected by a "qualified privilege."

In essence, a "privilege" allows an individual or entity to defame an individual if this is done for an appropriate purpose. To establish the qualified privilege, the defendant has to demonstrate that the statement
1. was made with a good faith belief that it was true;
2. served a business interest or had a business purpose [as in the case of a statement made during an inquiry or investigation of alleged research fraud];

3. was limited to the business interest or purpose to be served;
4. was made on a proper occasion; and
5. was communicated to appropriate parties only (Green & Reibstein, 1992, p. 64)

Although the five criteria might appear to be reasonably simple to establish if the investigation was done in a professional manner, misusing information, communicating information to individuals without a "business" need to know the information, or failing to carefully verify the facts before communicating them as "facts" can result in the loss of the privilege. It is not necessary that the plaintiff prove that the defendant acted with malice or improper intent. Simply acting in a careless, negligent manner will suffice for defamation liability if the plaintiff can prove that harm ensued.

A dispute between two faculty members who had collaborated on scientific research projects resulted in defamation liability for one of the faculty members. In 1989, Professors Arroyo and Rosen, who were on the faculty of the University of Maryland at Baltimore, drafted a paper summarizing the results of their joint research. They submitted the paper to a journal, which returned the paper to them with suggestions for revisions. Professor Arroyo, without consulting Professor Rosen, made the revisions and resubmitted the paper, which was accepted for publication. When Professor Arroyo told Professor Rosen, several months later, that the paper had been accepted, Rosen disagreed with the new conclusions of the revision and asked Arroyo to withdraw the paper. Arroyo appealed to the dean, who asked several external experts to review the paper. The experts agreed that the paper should be withdrawn. Arroyo then filed a complaint against Rosen with the OSI (the precursor of the ORI). The university conducted an investigation that ultimately exonerated Rosen. Arroyo then provided the local newspaper with an internal university document criticizing some of Rosen's actions. Rosen sued Arroyo for defamation and invasion of privacy and was awarded $75,000 in damages. The verdict was upheld on appeal (*Arroyo v. Rosen*, 1994).

The implications of defamation law for institutions and individuals involved in scholarship misconduct allegations are clear. Inquiries and investigations must be conducted by individuals who understand the operation of the qualified privilege. All charges against the accused individual (or against the accuser if the charge is found to be without merit) must be supported by facts that can be documented. To the extent possible, confidentiality as to the identity of the accused, the accuser, and other individuals potentially involved in the alleged misconduct should be maintained. Careful adherence to the requirements of the privilege should not unreasonably constrain the investigation but should provide potential defendants with a measure of protection if defamation litigation ensues.

Although defamation is the most likely claim that the accuser or institutional representatives may encounter, the accused individual may include other tort claims in the litigation. Potential claims include intentional or negligent infliction of emotional distress, invasion of privacy, and intentional or negligent interference with contract. This latter claim would involve an allegation that the accuser or institutional representatives (administrators or faculty) attempted to cause the termination of the accused individual's employment by bringing allegedly false charges against him or her. As with defamation claims, remedies involve both compensatory and punitive damages.

Whistle-Blower Laws

Individuals who have knowledge about misconduct in scholarship understandably are often reluctant to report this information because they fear retaliation from the accuser or from the institution. Particularly when the accuser is a student or a staff member, or a faculty member who is junior to the accused researcher, the possibility of retaliation is very real.[8] But whistle-blowers who are employees may be protected by laws designed to discourage such retaliation. Approximately half of the states have enacted "whistle-blower laws" that protect employees from discipline or discharge or from other forms of retaliation for reporting alleged wrongdoing by the employer or one of its employees. Although some of these state laws protect only public employees, a growing number of states are providing this protection to employees of private organizations as well. Federal employees are protected by the Whistleblower Protection Act of 1989 (Pub. L. No. 101–12). The federal law requires the employee making the accusation to first report the problem to the Office of Special Counsel, while state whistle-blower laws typically require the employee to notify a representative of management before disclosing the information externally.[9]

Most state whistle-blower laws protect only those employees who report a violation of law or a public safety or health hazard to a public agency. For example, New Jersey's Conscientious Employee Protection Act would not protect an employee who "blew the whistle" to a newspaper but would protect the employee who reported the violation to a state or federal agency, including the police and the state legislature (N.J.S. A. sec. 34:19–4).

Under these laws, any negative employment action against a whistle-blower that could be traced directly to the reporting of scholarship misconduct could be overturned by a state court if the misconduct violated state or federal law or if it posed a threat to the public health or safety. Most whistle-blower laws provide at least for equitable remedies, including reinstatement and back pay. Some laws allow punitive damages and/or civil penalties to be assessed against the employer.

Whistle-blowers who expose violations of institutional policy without a strong link to a statutory violation or safety hazard could have difficulty prevailing under state whistle-blower laws. For example, an individual who exposed plagiarism by a researcher whose misconduct violated institutional policies but did not violate the law or have health or safety implications might have difficulty challenging a retaliatory discipline or discharge decision by the institution. Tort claims or breach of contract claims would probably be more successful for this type of whistle-blower.

For whistle-blowers in states without antiretaliation laws, one additional source of protection is possible. Under the common law of some states, an employee who is disciplined or discharged in retaliation for an act that benefits the public may be protected under the "public policy" exception to the employment-at-will doctrine. Under this legal theory, the employer who discharges an employee for disclosing wrongdoing by the employer, if that wrongdoing either violated a law or threatened the public safety or health, can be found liable for the "tort of wrongful discharge" and can be required to pay compensatory and/or punitive damages (although the employee does not have the right to be reinstated under this theory). Although employees in those states with statutory protection for whistle-blowers have a more certain source of protection against retaliation, the public policy doctrine has been used successfully by employees who were discharged for refusing to violate the law on behalf of their employers or to participate in a cover-up (*Gantt v. Sentry Ins.*, 1992).

Institutional representatives who receive the allegations of scientific misconduct must document the institution's response to the whistle-blower and must be able to demonstrate the steps that were taken to protect the whistle-blower from retaliation. Should it be determined that the allegations are false, the institution may still need to exercise caution in dealing with the whistle-blower. Many state laws provide that whistle-blowers who are honestly mistaken about the "problem" they have reported are *still* protected by these laws; only a knowingly or maliciously false report would remove the laws' protections.

The protections afforded to whistle-blowers by state statutory and common law make it clear that institutions—their administrators and faculty—need to respond to allegations of scholarship misconduct appropriately and to document that they have investigated the charges and have protected the whistle-blower from retaliation (unless and until a finding is made that the allegations were knowingly false or frivolous). Given these protections plus the protections available to whistle-blowers under federal law that were discussed earlier in the chapter, institutions that reject allegations without an investigation or that assume that the claims are unfounded without a thorough inquiry may face financial liability and public humiliation.

SUMMARY

As this chapter suggests, a plethora of legal theories comes into play when an allegation of scientific misconduct is made. The law imposes certain requirements on each party—the accused, the accuser, and the employing institution—and it also provides a number of protections for each.

The Accused

When an individual who receives federal funds is accused of scientific fraud, the regulations of the funding agency, as well as the policies of the institution, control the investigation process. The regulations require that the accused be afforded a form of due process, although the institution may attempt to protect the identity of the accuser, at least during the initial stages of the inquiry and investigation process. Failure to cooperate with an investigation or destruction or altering of laboratory notebooks or other evidence could be grounds for discipline or discharge.

Other legal theories, such as copyright or patent law, require that the plaintiff (in these cases, the accuser) prove the violation by the preponderance of the evidence. And if the accused sues the accuser (or the institution) for defamation, the accused is entitled to demonstrate that his or her reputation was tarnished through malicious or negligent acts of the accuser or the institution.

Under the False Claims Act, a criminal law, the accused is presumed innocent until proven guilty by the government. Accused individuals (and their codefendant institutions) risk liability for enormous sums, for the damages awarded include return of the federal funds, which, presumably, would already have been spent.

For the accused, the advice of counsel who is thoroughly familiar with federal intellectual property law and Constitutional law is critical. Given the seriousness of these charges and the potential consequences for the individual's career and personal finances, the selection of counsel is a critical decision.

The Accuser

The personal, financial, and career implications of making an accusation of scholarship misconduct are as serious for the accuser as for the accused. The accuser may face retaliation by the accused (often a supervisor, mentor, or advisor), the employing institution, and the discipline of which the accuser is a member. Although the institution may attempt to protect the identity of the accuser, at some point his or her identity may be disclosed, particularly if a formal hearing with due-process protections is held. The accuser is vulnerable to litigation by the accused, alleging defamation, invasion of privacy, intentional or negligent infliction of emotional distress, or other tort claims.

The institution may chose to believe the accused and may discipline or discharge the accuser.

Accusers have some protection under state whistle-blower laws (in those states in which such laws exist) and may be able to defend defamation lawsuits if they can demonstrate that they acted in good faith and without malice (or if they can prove that the fraud actually occurred). And, of course, if the accuser is the "original source" of the information concerning the misuse of federal funds, he or she may file a *qui tam* action in federal court and stands to gain a measure of the damages if the recipient of the funds is judged guilty of their misuse.

The Institution

The heaviest responsibility, and the largest potential for financial loss, is borne by the institution. If the allegation involves federal or state funds, the institution must follow the agency's regulations regarding the conduct of an inquiry and/or investigation and the reporting of the results. The institution may be required to repay the funds, which can be a serious problem if part or all of the funds have already been spent. The institution may also be debarred from receiving funding in the future.

The institution risks legal liability if it disciplines or discharges the accused individual, even if the accusation has been established as true. For public institutions, Constitutional protections for the accused require that due-process guidelines be followed carefully. Contract law requires that all institutional policies and procedures be adhered to. Tort law poses potential liability if confidentiality is breached or if the accused can demonstrate that one or more institutional officials were overzealous in their attempt to "punish" the accused. And, of course, the *qui tam* laws present potential financial liability for those institutions who are unsuccessful defendants in such lawsuits.

Given the seriousness of the potential legal claims and the size of the potential financial penalties that each of these parties may face, it is incumbent upon every institution—even those that consider themselves primarily teaching institutions—to familiarize themselves with the issues; to train faculty, students, and administrators about the parameters of ethical scholarship; and to develop procedures so that the institution can respond appropriately and promptly if a problem arises. The next section suggests the approach that institutions might wish to take.

CONCLUSION

Despite the amount of literature on scholarship misconduct, many institutions have yet to encounter their first case of scholarship misconduct. This is not to say that the problem is insignificant—a 1990 study estimated that

20% of U.S. scientists had directly experienced fraud (NSF, 1990, cited in Braxton, 1994, p. 239). This estimate does not include the experiences of scholars in nonscience fields who may have had their work plagiarized, who may not have received authorship credit for work in which they participated, or who may have seen their ideas appropriated without attribution. Even institutions whose mission is primarily teaching rather than research can encounter alleged or actual scholarship misconduct, and it is important that institutional policies be in place so that the institution can respond quickly and appropriately if such allegations are made.

If the institution has no policies, it might consider establishing a joint faculty-administration committee to develop them, referring to the model policies discussed earlier in the chapter. Experienced administrators or legal counsel at other institutions could also be consulted for assistance. And, of course, the institution's own counsel should review the final draft of the policy to ensure that it protects whatever Constitutional or contractual rights employees are afforded and that it complies with any applicable federal or state laws. Consideration should also be given to how investigations will be conducted to maximize confidentiality and minimize the potential for defamation or other tort claims. Procedures to protect accusers and other individuals related to the case from retaliation should also be developed before they are needed.

Scholarship misconduct is a serious problem and requires serious consideration by the institution's leadership, both in the administration and in the faculty. Given the narrow line that the institution walks between its obligations to the grantor, to the accused scholar, to the accuser, and to the general public, the institution needs to be prepared to respond carefully, comprehensively, and with sensitivity to the rights and concerns of all affected parties.

Notes

I acknowledge with thanks the assistance of Debra Parrish, Esq., who reviewed an initial draft of this chapter, and the research assistance of Debra Casey, Esq.

1. This discussion will focus on the requirements of federal funding agencies; although many state agencies have their own regulations and requirements for grantees, discussion of state agency requirements is beyond the scope of this chapter.
2. Although some federal research grants are made to individuals, most are awarded to colleges or universities rather than to individuals. For purposes of this chapter, the discussion will focus on institutions as the recipients of federal funds; federal regulations covering the responsibilities of the grant recipient would, of course, also apply to any individual who was a direct recipient of a federal research grant or contract.

3. In late 1995, the Commission on Research Integrity, a group of scientists, lawyers, and university administrators, released a report entitled *Integrity and Misconduct in Research*. The report recommended a revised definition of research misconduct and also recommended that research institutions develop specific guidelines for good scientific practices, which would be disseminated to faculty and students. The report can be downloaded from the Office of Research Integrity's home page at http://ori.dhhs.gov/other/material.html.

4. See, e.g., cases described in Kuzma (1992).

5. Research funded and regulated by the Food and Drug Administration (FDA) is excluded from the mandate of ORI; the FDA retains the authority to investigate alleged misconduct in the research that it funds and regulates (59 Fed. Reg. 2856, January 19, 1994).

6. In contrast, individuals may make anonymous complaints to ORI or NSF, and their identity may never be revealed. Under the agencies' regulations, the investigation may go forward and sanctions may be imposed without the accused individual(s) being informed of the identity of the accuser.

7. For a discussion of legal theories affording contractual status to faculty and staff handbooks, see Kaplin and Lee (1995, pp. 150–157).

8. Retaliation against senior faculty also occurs; for an account of retaliation against a department chairperson, see Poon (1995).

9. The ORI also has jurisdiction over retaliation claims by whistle-blowers. The definition of misconduct in science includes retaliation as a form of misconduct (45 C. F. R. 689.1(a) and (b)).

References

American Association of University Professors. (1995). *Policy documents and reports*. Washington, DC: Author.
Angelides v. Baylor College of Medicine, 117 F.3d 833 (5th Cir. 1997).
Arroyo v. Rosen, 648 A.2d 1074 (Md. App. 1994).
Braxton, J. (1994). Introduction. *Journal of Higher Education, 65*, 239–241.
Commission on Research Integrity. (1995). *Integrity and misconduct in research*. Washington, DC: U.S. Department of Health and Human Services.
Gantt v. Sentry Ins., 824 P.2d 680 (Cal. 1992).
Green, R. M., & Reibstein, R. J. (1992). *Employer's guide to workplace torts*. Washington, DC: Bureau of National Affairs.
Hilts, P. J. (1994, July 23). Two universities to pay U.S. $1.6 million in research fraud case. *New York Times*, p. 9.
Hilts, P. J. (1995, May 19). A university and 4 scientists must pay for pilfered work. *New York Times*, p. A20.
Howard, E. (1995). Science misconduct and due process: A case of process due. *Hastings Law Journal, 45*, 309–358.
Kaplin, W. A., & Lee, B. A. (1995). *The law of higher education* (3rd ed.). San Francisco: Jossey-Bass.
Kuzma, S. M. (1992). Criminal liability for misconduct in scientific research. *University of Michigan Journal of Law Reform, 25*, 357–421.

Lyon, J., & Gorner, P. (1995). *Altered fates.* New York: Norton.

Mishkin, B. (1988). Responding to scientific misconduct: Due process and prevention. *Journal of the American Medical Association, 260,* 1932–1936.

National Academy of Sciences. (1992). *Responsible science: Ensuring the integrity of the research process. Executive Summary.* Washington, DC: Author.

Parrish, D. (1994). Scientific misconduct and the plagiarism cases. *Journal of College and University Law, 21,* 517–554.

Perry v. Sindermann, 408 U.S. 593 (1972).

Perzan, C. P. (1992). Research and relators: The False Claims Act and scientific misconduct. *Washington University Law Quarterly, 70,* 639–664.

Poon, P. (1995). Legal protections for the scientific misconduct whistleblower. *Journal of Law, Medicine and Ethics, 23,* 88–95.

Sise, C. B. (1991). Scientific misconduct in academia: A survey and analysis of applicable law. *San Diego Law Review, 28,* 401–428.

United States ex rel. Berge v. Board of Trustees of the University of Alabama, 104 F.3d 1453 (4th Cir. 1997).

United States ex rel. Milam v. Regents of the University of California, 912 F. Supp. 868 (D. Md. 1995).

United States v. Breuning, Criminal No. K-88–0135 (D. Md. Nov. 10, 1988).

Walker, P. V. (1996, July 19). Many universities fail at policing misconduct. *Chronicle of Higher Education,* p. A29.

Walker, P. V. (1997, June 6). Two lawsuits may change handling of research-misconduct charges. *Chronicle of Higher Education,* pp. A27-A28.

Weissman v. Freeman, 868 F.2d 1313 (2d Cir. 1989), cert. denied, 110 S. Ct. 219 (1989).

Willborn, S. L., Schwab, S. J., & Burton, J. F. (1993). *Employment law.* Charlottesville, VA: Michie.

PART IV

Empirical Treatments

CHAPTER TEN

Disciplinary and Departmental Effects on Observations of Faculty and Graduate Student Misconduct

Melissa S. Anderson, Karen Seashore Louis, and Jason Earle

Socialization of graduate students to the life of academic research occurs primarily in the context of a department in a university. It is here that students learn, both formally and informally, what behaviors are expected and rewarded in academic research and what constitutes unacceptable deviation from shared norms of conduct. In particular, this socialization is critical to the deterrence of academic misconduct (Zuckerman, 1988). Unfortunately, as recent, highly publicized cases of research fraud illustrate, graduate students sometimes witness misconduct by faculty or peers in their own programs. While many in the academic community dismiss these cases as the work of inexplicable deviance on the part of individuals, discussions within the academy and in the popular press suggest that contextual factors may be involved. As Victor and Cullen (1988) pointed out, there is growing recognition that social context is critical to understanding moral and ethical behavior.

In this chapter, we examine the effects of departmental and disciplinary contexts on graduate students' exposure to misconduct. Specifically, we analyze the influences of departmental structure, departmental climate, and discipline on graduate students' observations of three forms of misconduct: research, employment, and personal.

BACKGROUND

Academic Disciplines

Academic disciplines (or fields of study) play an important role in graduate students' acquisition of values and beliefs during their socialization. For many graduate students the primary motivation for entering the academic profession is the lure of working in a particular discipline (Ruscio, 1987). In addition to their particular knowledge bases and requisite skills, academic disciplines have distinct cultures with different beliefs, norms, values, patterns of work, and interpersonal interaction (Becher, 1984, 1987).

Graduate students' socialization experiences vary depending on the culture of the discipline as well as the nature of the research (Becher, 1987). For example, graduate students in fields like chemistry are apt to work cooperatively in teams with an advisor, other graduate students, and a laboratory supervisor. In laboratory work, they will also be more likely to work "at the bench," in an area already established by the advisor. In contrast, graduate students in disciplines such as sociology generally work in a much more independent fashion: "They are treated like self-employed persons or individuals of independent means" (Becher, 1987, p. 282). These students are usually allowed to determine their own lines of research, and they generally meet less often, even sporadically, with their advisors (Kleinman, 1983).

Academic Departments

The academic department, the primary unit of the university, is the local incarnation of the discipline or field of study (Becher, 1987). Becher and Kogan (1992) claimed that the department is "especially important in the determination of professional values" (p. 87). In particular, departmental structure and climate have been shown to affect the professional values that graduate students acquire during socialization (Anderson & Louis, 1994).

Department Structure

Van Maanen and Schein (1979) described six different structural dimensions of organizational subunits that affect the values and beliefs of "recruits" during the socialization process. Of these, four dimensions are particularly important to the present analysis. The first is collective versus individual socialization. Some departments move large cohorts of students together through a common set of courses and research experiences, whereas other departments work with students "singly and in isolation from one another through a more or less unique set of experiences" (Van Maanen & Schein, 1979, p. 233). A second dimension is formal versus informal socialization. Formal socialization involves sending graduate students through officially prescribed processes that are designed especially for the neophyte and that clearly set the neophyte apart from "full-fledged" members of the department. In informal socialization there is less distinction between newcomers and the more experienced, and recruits learn through an apprenticeshiplike process or trial and error. A third dimension is fixed versus variable socialization.

Fixed socialization offers students "precise knowledge of the time it will take to complete" a portion or all of a graduate program (Van Maanen & Schein, 1979, p. 244), whereas variable socialization not only makes the timing of a student's progress through a program indefinite but also causes considerable variation in timing across students. Finally, the investiture versus divestiture dimension in socialization affects the self-image or personal identity that a student brings to a department. Investiture affirms and supports the student's self-concept upon entry, but divestiture changes or suppresses it.

Department Climate

Another aspect of academic departments that can influence the socialization of graduate students is climate. *Climate* refers to the perceptions of the psychologically important aspects of a work environment, as shared among organizational participants over time (Ashforth, 1985). The climate of a department or organization affects the activities and attitudes of department members (Ashforth, 1985). Victor and Cullen (1988) suggested that an organization's climate can have ethical dimensions as well. They identified the ethical work climate as an institutionalized normative system that guides the ethical behavior of employees. From an analysis of survey responses from nonacademic employees, they derived five dimensions of ethical climate. The first dimension, *caring*, represents primarily a benevolent orientation, emphasizing the good of all. Second, the *law and code* dimension reflects a "cosmopolitan" perspective in referring to a social system broader than the immediate context. Third, the *rules* aspect of climate focuses on local regulations and procedures. Fourth, the *instrumental* dimension represents egoism as a criterion for ethical behavior. Finally, *independence* reflects the influence of personal morality.

METHODS

Data Collection

To investigate the effects of discipline, department structure, and department climate on graduate student observations of misconduct, we employ data from a survey of 2,000 doctoral students in research universities, conducted as part of the Acadia Institute's Project on Professional Values and Ethical Issues in the Graduate Education of Scientists and Engineers.[1] Our sampling procedure involved three levels of selection: disciplinary fields, academic departments, and individual doctoral students.

Our choice of academic disciplines reflects three considerations. First, the overall project's focus on research and graduate education in the sciences (including the social sciences) and engineering led us to select fields from these areas. Second, we made use of Biglan's (1973a, 1973b) typology of academic fields to select disciplines representing different orientations to academic work (not explored in this study). Third, we chose disciplines in which substantial numbers of doctoral degrees are currently being awarded so as to afford us an adequate sample size. These considerations led us to select four disciplines: chemistry, microbiology, engineering, and sociology.

Within these disciplines, we selected academic departments on the basis of the number of doctoral degrees granted in recent years. This consideration reflects our desire to focus on those departments that are currently producing the greatest numbers of future academic researchers. We also wanted enough responses from individual departments to permit analyses of the effects of specific department characteristics on graduate students.

Our selection of departments was based on data for the period July 1985 to June 1988 from the *Directory of Graduate Programs: 1990 and 1991* (Educational Testing Service, 1989), produced by the Graduate Record Examinations Board and the Council of Graduate Schools in the United States. Given the large size of many chemistry departments, we chose only those that awarded 50 or more Ph.D.'s during this period. For the other disciplines, we selected departments that awarded at least 20 Ph.D.'s during this period. This procedure yielded 100 departments: 30 in chemistry, 25 in civil engineering, 21 in microbiology, and 24 in sociology.

To select students within these departments, we asked the chairs of these departments to provide the names and addresses of doctoral students who were currently enrolled full time in their departments. As the survey was to be sent out during the fall term, we requested that first-year doctoral students be removed from the lists, on the assumption that these students would not yet be familiar enough with graduate study to provide informed responses. All but two of the department chairs (one in microbiology and one in sociology) complied with the request. From the student lists we randomly selected 500 from each of the four disciplines for a total stratified sample size of 2,000. We pretested the questionnaire by administering it to groups of students in related disciplines and then discussing with them issues of clarity, interpretation, and relevance. Special effort was made to include foreign graduate students in the pretests to ensure that the questionnaire was easily understood and appropriately interpreted by non-native English speakers. Wording on the questionnaires was adjusted by field where appropriate: chemists and microbiologists received questionnaires referring to "scientists," whereas civil engineers and sociologists received questionnaires referring to "engineers" and "social scientists," respectively.

We mailed the questionnaires in November 1990. They were coded by discipline and by institution but not by individual respondent. The sensitive nature of some of the items on the survey made it imperative to ensure respondents' confidentiality; consequently, each questionnaire packet contained a separate postcard by which the student could notify us that he or she had returned the questionnaire without having that information linked in any way to the student's questionnaire. With appropriate follow-up procedures, we obtained an adjusted response rate (omitting master's candidates, first-year doctoral students, and others who did not meet the sample criteria) of 72%.

The analyses presented here are based on data from 73 departments, each having at least 9 respondents, producing a subsample size of 1,261. This provision is necessary for the appropriate application of hierarchical linear modeling, as discussed below. On average, each department has 17.27 respondents.

Definition of Variables

The dependent variable for this analysis is academic misconduct. Here we include not only misconduct specific to the academic enterprise but also misconduct related to nonspecific employment and interpersonal interactions. We asked students to report their own experiences with a broad array of misconduct behaviors on the part of graduate peers and faculty in their departments. The survey question was, "In this program, have you *observed* or had other *direct evidence* of any of the following types of misconduct? Please indicate the number of graduate students and faculty members whose misconduct you have observed/experienced."

Thirteen items followed, representing a range of misconduct behaviors (see Appendix A). Responses were coded as *none* (0), *1–2* (1), *3–5* (2), and *more than 5* (3). Because one form of misconduct (cheating in course work) was not appropriate for faculty, there were 12 faculty items and 13 student items, with coded responses ranging from 0 to 3. We then added the 25 scores for observed misconduct by faculty and students to create a composite variable, *overall misconduct,* with a potential range from 0 to 75.

We created three other composite variables by adding misconduct scores for items within specific categories of misconduct. *Research misconduct* refers to behaviors that violate the norms and standards specific to the academic enterprise. *Employment misconduct* includes conduct that would be deemed inappropriate or illegal in most organizations. *Personal misconduct* refers to inappropriate or illegal behaviors among individuals, again with reference to the broader social context. The specific items assigned to these three misconduct types are listed in Appendix A. The potential ranges for these variables depend on the number of items included: research (0 to 33), employment (0 to 24), and personal (0 to 18).

To test the effects of departmental structure, departmental climate, and academic discipline on students' experiences with misconduct, we included related independent variables at the department level. We derived structure and climate scales from a factor analysis of relevant items.[2] The components of the scales used in the hierarchical analysis, as well as all associated reliabilities, are presented in Appendix B (see Anderson & Louis, 1994, for a complete listing of the structure and climate scales). The structure and climate scales were aggregated to the department level, with each department assigned its mean for each variable. Academic discipline was represented by dummy variables, where the chemistry variable took on the value of 1 for chemistry departments and so on for the other disciplines. Where appropriate, we used sociology as the discipline for comparison by omitting the associated dummy variable from the analysis.

We included three control variables at the individual level (gender, citizenship status, and years in the graduate program), on the assumption that they may affect the extent to which graduate students report direct knowledge of misconduct. For example, female scholars may have different socialization experiences than their male colleagues (Clark & Corcoran, 1986), including different opportunities to work closely on research with colleagues. Also, our research (Anderson & Louis, 1994) has found significant differences in the professional normative orientations of U.S. and international students, which may affect the extent to which these two groups identify misconduct by faculty and student peers. Gender and citizenship status are included as dummy variables, with a value of 1 for female and international students, respectively. The third control variable is the number of years that the student has been in his or her current graduate program. The sampling procedure ensured that each respondent had been in his or her department for at least one year.

Table 10.1 presents basic descriptive statistics for the variables used in this analysis. Overall, just over one-third (34.3%) of the respondents are international graduate students. There are, however, significant differences across disciplines in the proportions of international students. In civil engineering, about 60% are non-U.S. citizens, whereas in chemistry and microbiology, approximately half that proportion are international students. Fewer than one-quarter of the sociology students are internationals. There are also significant differences in the proportions of women in the fields considered. Overall, 36.9% of the respondents are women, with the highest proportions being in sociology (55.1%) and in microbiology (45.4%). Civil engineering has the lowest proportion of women (13.9%).[3] The students represented in this analysis have been in their present graduate programs for an average of 2.94 years, with disciplinary averages ranging from 2.63 years for civil engineering to 3.48 years for sociology.

Overall, employment and personal misconduct vary significantly across disciplines, but research misconduct does not. All of the misconduct scores have rather high standard deviations. Overall reported misconduct is highest in chemistry and sociology and lowest in civil engineering. Employment misconduct is equally high in chemistry and microbiology and equally low in the other fields, while personal misconduct is highest in sociology and lowest in civil engineering.

Table 10.1: Descriptive Statistics, by Discipline

	All	Chemistry	Civil Engineering	Microbiology	Sociology	Test Statistic Disciplines for Differences across Disciplines
Number:						
Respondents for this analysis	1,261	327	256	352	326	
Departments	73	22	15	17	19	
Proportion:						
International	34.3	29.4	59.8	30.1	23.8	$\chi^2 = 94.104***$
Female	36.9	27.3	13.9	45.4	55.1	$\chi^2 = 126.759***$
Mean (Standard Deviation):						
Years in department	2.94	2.82	2.63	2.79	3.48	$F = 13.097***$
	(1.85)	(1.50)	(1.55)	(1.52)	(2.51)	
Overall misconduct	6.64	7.28	5.03	6.73	7.17	$F = 5.5370***$
(potential range 0 to 75)	(7.36)	(8.27)	(5.90)	(7.14)	(7.49)	
Research misconduct	2.26	2.52	1.89	2.36	2.18	$F = 2.2204$
(potential range 0 to 33)	(3.04)	(3.30)	(2.57)	(3.04)	(3.12)	
Employment misconduct	2.19	2.51	1.79	2.54	1.82	$F = 6.617***$
(potential range 0 to 24)	(2.88)	(3.37)	(2.40)	(2.94)	(2.55)	
Personal misconduct	2.19	2.25	1.35	1.83	3.17	$F = 25.9026***$
(potential range 0 to 18)	(2.73)	(3.05)	(1.88)	(2.28)	(3.07)	

***$p < .001$.

Analytic Approach

Our investigation focuses on departmental and disciplinary effects on reported levels of misconduct. There are, however, individual-level variables (gender, citizenship status, number of years spent in the department) that, as noted above, may influence the level of misconduct that a student observes. A hierarchical linear model (Bryk & Raudenbush, 1992; Bryk, Raudenbush, Seltzer, & Congdon, 1989) permits us to analyze department-level effects while controlling appropriately and simultaneously for the individual characteristics.[4]

When ordinary least-squares regression models are used to investigate cross-level effects, they are susceptible to error. Such models either estimate parameters at the individual level by associating a particular group's characteristics with individuals or estimate parameters at the group level by aggregating individual scores. In either case, variance cannot be correctly assigned to the level at which it actually exists (Bryk & Raudenbush, 1992, p. xiv).

Hierarchical linear modeling (HLM) provides a way to estimate cross-level effects while avoiding errors due to aggregation at the department level and errors due to imputation at the individual level (Raudenbush & Bryk, 1986). It does so by estimating parameters at both levels simultaneously through an iterative procedure, assigning variance to the individual or department level as appropriate. Accurate estimates of parameter variance are necessary for testing hypotheses about the significance of the parameter estimates (Bryk & Raudenbush, 1992).

RESULTS

Table 10.2 presents parameter estimates for four versions of the hierarchical linear model, one for each measure of reported misconduct. Bivariate correlations of the variables that appear in the models are presented in Appendix C.

Overall Misconduct

Departmental climate is the strongest predictor of overall misconduct. Competition has a positive effect on mean levels of overall reported misconduct as well as a positive effect on the relationship between years in program and misconduct. The latter effect means that being in a competitive department increases the likelihood that a student will observe misconduct over time. Two other climate variables affect overall misconduct through years in program. Departments that value individual over collaborative research have a positive effect on the relationship between time in program and misconduct. Like competition, individualism appears to increase a student's chances of witnessing misconduct the longer he or she stays in the graduate program. Also, departments in which students feel that their assistantship obligations are delaying their progress show a negative effect, meaning that in these departments, students who have been around longer do not report more misconduct than the more recent entrants. Onerous assistantship obligations may effectively buffer students from exposure to contexts in which other students tend to observe misconduct. The very obligations that keep them from progressing may also keep them from knowing either appropriate standards or how their peers and professors deal with their work.

As for the other variables in the overall misconduct model, no structure variable has any significant effect. With respect to disciplinary effects, only civil engineering departments have, on average, significantly lower levels of reported misconduct than the reference departments of sociology. The independent effects of the control variables appear in the "Base" column of table 10.2. Only one of the control variables proves to have an important influence on reported misconduct, apart from departmental effects: international students report significantly fewer observations of misconduct in their programs. Perhaps they do not witness as much misconduct, or if they do, they either may not consider the behavior inappropriate or may be ambivalent as to the degree of impropriety involved.

Research Misconduct

Of the specific forms of misconduct, research misconduct proves the most difficult to predict using our departmental and disciplinary variables. Only one structure variable, the extent to which the student feels that his or her advisor and others provide useful feedback and evaluation, affects levels of observed misconduct in research.

The effect is negative, through years in program, meaning that departments that provide this kind of structured feedback are places where students are less likely to witness research misconduct over the duration of their graduate years. The control variable, time in program, has a separate, positive effect on research misconduct: that is, in general, the longer one is in a program, the more likely one is to observe research misconduct.

Employment Misconduct

Climate effects prove important in the employment misconduct model. Higher levels of competition and student-faculty collaboration on publications are associated with more reports of employment misconduct, with direct effects on average levels of reported misconduct as well as effects through years in program. That is, in competitive and collaborative departments, students report more employment misconduct, and the longer students stay in the program, the more likely they are to witness misconduct. When students have to compete for scarce resources and faculty attention or

Table 10.2: Hierarchical Linear Model of Overall, Research, Employment, and Personal Misconduct

	Base	Structure		Climate		Discipline	
Overall Misconduct							
Intercept (B0)	3.704*			.565*	Competition	−1.669*	Civil Engineering
Years (B1)	−2.102	−.217	Structured Feedback	.433*	Competition		
		.227	Group Size	−.819*	Obligations		
				.893	Publications		
				1.203*	Individualism		
International (B2)	−1.311**	—		—		—	
Research Misconduct							
Intercept (B0)	2.380***						
Years (B1)	1.875*	−.148*	Structured Feedback				
		.068	Group Size				
International (B2)	−.326						
Employment Misconduct							
Intercept (B0)	2.136	−.356***	Structured Feedback	.287*	Competition	.334	Chemistry
				1.053***	Publications	0.626*	Microbiology
Years (B1)	−2.136*	.112	Group Size	.227**	Competition		
				−.385*	Obligations		
				.402*	Publications		
				.421	Individualism		
International (B2)	−0.807***	—		—		—	

Table 10.2 *continued*

	Base	Structure		Climate		Discipline	
Personal Misconduct							
Intercept (B0)	−3.058	.178*	Divestiture	.394**	Competition	−.343	Chemistry
		.063	Collaboration	.354	Solidarity	−.804	Civil Engineering
						−.836	Microbiology
Years (B1)	.164			.135*	Competition		
				−.337*	Obligations		
International (B2)	1.747			−1.173*	Individualism	.499	Microbiology
Female (B3)	.618**	—		—		—	

*$p < .05$. **$p < .01$. ***$p < .001$.

when they work collaboratively with faculty, they appear more likely to be aware of instances of employment misconduct on the part of their student peers or faculty. As in the overall misconduct model, heavy obligations of graduate assistantships are associated with lower levels of reported employment misconduct over time. When such obligations interfere with students' academic progress, those who stay around longer are not as apt to see misconduct of this kind.

Of the structure variables, only one, structured feedback, proves significant in the employment misconduct model. It has a negative effect on average level of reported employment misconduct, indicating that a good working relationship with one's advisor and evaluation that is constructive, prompt, and detailed significantly decreases student reports of misconduct. This finding suggests that in departments in which students get adequate attention they also see their professors and peers handling research ethics and financial affairs in appropriate ways. An alternative explanation, that in departments that pay adequate attention to students the students do not have as many opportunities to observe misconduct in this area, appears unlikely.

Microbiology is the only field that shows significantly more reported employment misconduct than the reference discipline, sociology. Compared to the other fields, microbiology has more new opportunities for funding and consulting because of new applications and product development in industries related to the field. Until arrangements with external organizations become better established, they may be more complicated and problematic, leading to more instances of questionable behavior.

Two of the control variables proved to have independent effects. Unexpectedly, years in program has a negative effect on employment misconduct. It may be that students who observe a great deal of misconduct in this area, which encompasses forms of misconduct that would be inappropriate in any work context, do not continue in the program. Also, international students report lower levels of misconduct than their U.S. peers. Since the items in the employment scale refer to research policies and use of funds, it may be that international students are simply less aware of formal standards for the conduct of research in the United States and regulations governing the appropriate expenditure of institutional and research dollars.

Personal Misconduct

Climate again dominates the department effects on reported personal misconduct, with competition and graduate assistant obligations playing the same roles as in overall and employment misconduct. Individualism again proves significant, but this time its effect is through the control variable for international citizen status. The coefficient is negative, meaning that the more a department values individual over collaborative research, the less likely international students are to observe personal misconduct, presumably because they have less interaction with others in their work.

The effects of structure show up only for the divestiture variable. Divestiture, the student's experience of losing part of his or her previous sense of self, has a positive effect on personal misconduct. Departments that divest students by changing them in ways they do not like, by not reinforcing their prior values, self-image, and way of thinking about the world, by expecting their academic responsibilities to come before all else, or by giving them humiliating evaluations or inconsistent advice are places where students report seeing higher levels of personal misconduct. There are no significant disciplinary differences in the personal misconduct model.

The control variable for gender has a significant, positive effect on mean reported personal misconduct. Female students are more likely to witness sexual harassment, discrimination, and exploitation than their male peers. (As explained above, the reference group here is U.S. males who have been in their departments an average length of time.)

DISCUSSION

In this chapter we have examined the way in which the contexts of discipline and department affect the extent to which graduate students witness or come to have direct knowledge of violations of the norms and standards of academic research. The mean misconduct scores in table 10.1 can be interpreted as meaning that in any of our three misconduct categories, the average graduate student in this study has been exposed to misconduct by two to five graduate students or faculty members. Clearly, the behaviors represented in our misconduct scales vary greatly in terms of gravity and potential impact for both the student witness and the academic enterprise. Still, there is no doubt that many students are in contact with misconduct in their graduate programs. Also, students are unlikely to report these instances to institutional authorities: 53% of our respondents say they probably or definitely could not report cases of suspected misconduct by faculty without expecting retaliation (29% in the case of misconduct by a fellow student). Furthermore, 77% of the respondents report that their departments are not very, or not at all, active in preparing graduate students to recognize and deal with ethical issues in their fields.

Although students report observation of as much research misconduct as other forms, there is little evidence of departmental structure or climate effects on research misconduct. In other words, our data support arguments that fraud, plagiarism, and related forms of misconduct are the results of individual predilections or failures of judgment that might be controlled through institutional oversight and peer review but that cannot easily be prevented by restructuring or reorienting departments.

Our findings suggest a different story for employment and personal misconduct. Faculty tend to assume that working closely with professors and other graduate students exposes graduate trainees to the values that will support them throughout their careers. Yet students who work in collaborative settings are more likely to encounter conflict of commitment and downright white-collar crime. Highly competitive environments also tend to increase students' chances of observing misconduct. Where resources and faculty time are at a premium and where favoritism is a fact of department life, students are more likely to report experiences with infractions of employment regulations and violations of interpersonal norms.

At the descriptive level there are important differences between disciplines. Chemistry students are most likely to be exposed to research misconduct, chemistry and microbiology students are most likely to observe employment misconduct, and sociology students are most likely to be exposed to personal misconduct. These disciplinary differences largely disappear in the cases of research and personal misconduct in our hierarchical analysis when we control for the characteristics of departments.

These findings are clearly preliminary in the sense that we have sampled only four disciplines and have not collected the kind of qualitative data that would permit us to examine the socialization process in a detailed way. In addition, in this chapter we have examined the context of graduate education and experiences with misconduct only from the perspective of students. Nevertheless, the study has a number of possible implications for the design of graduate programs.

First, it suggests that between exposure to misconduct and the absence of opportunities to discuss these issues openly, future researchers are being socialized in an environment that may create ambivalence about basic values of the academy—namely, the obligation of the scholarly community to uphold the highest standards of research behavior and to enforce the values of the broader society regarding the behavior of professional employees. Misconduct cannot, in all likelihood, be prevented, but recent calls for increased opportunities for students and faculty to talk about scientific values (culminating in the requirement by the National Institutes of Health that all institutions receiving training money provide such an experience) seem a minimal response.

Second, our data suggest a disturbing conclusion: that students who have the best opportunities to learn the skills needed to conduct research (by having close, collaborative relationships with faculty and peers) are also those who are most likely to be exposed to forms of behavior that are either contrary to university policy or illegal. The finding that professionals in training exhibit increasing levels of cynicism and "hardening" is not new (Becker & Greer, 1958). However, it does point to a clear dilemma in the structuring of socialization settings. Many universities are currently revising policies concerning faculty integrity with an eye toward, at minimum, raising the level of awareness of what constitutes appropriate behavior by an employee of the university. Our data suggest that efforts to develop and disseminate policies should pay more attention to the role of the graduate student.

Third, the finding that there are no disciplinary differences in the rates of observed research misconduct and personal misconduct when we control for department characteristics is important because recent discussions of misconduct in the press have tended to focus almost exclusively on the life or health sciences. Our findings suggest that all disciplines, as well as institutions, must attend to the variety of ways in which graduate students may be exposed to problematic behavior. In particular, because certain forms of research misconduct may be discipline specific, professional associations should play a role in designing programs or other mechanisms to sensitize graduate students to issues that they may face in their education and beyond.

Fourth, the results suggest that departmental climate and structure critically affect the graduate student's experience of employment and personal misconduct. We speculate that large research projects that have many graduate and postdoctoral students associated with one or two professors may breed the competitive environments that are associated with employment and personal misconduct. The problematic nature of a competitive environment may also be associated with extreme individualism—faculty and students "out for themselves" rather than considering the implications of their immediate actions for the institution, discipline, or colleagues.

The fact that climate (a relatively modifiable variable) is more important than structure (more difficult to change in the short run) suggests that there are things that departments can do to affect the context for graduate education in a relatively short period of time. Departments whose faculty give supportive attention and constructive, prompt, and detailed feedback tend to be places where ethical problems in research and employment are much less common. Departments and universities may then be able to make long-term changes to address more openly the ambiguities in the conditions for ethical socialization that have been illuminated in this chapter.

APPENDIX A: SURVEY ITEMS COMPOSING MISCONDUCT SCALES

MISCONDUCT

In this program, have you *observed* or had other *direct evidence* of any of the following types of misconduct? Please indicate the number of graduate students and faculty members whose misconduct you have observed/experienced.

Number of Students: *none* (0), *1–2* (1), *3–5* (2), *more than 5* (3)
Number of Faculty: *none* (0), *1–2* (1), *3–5* (2), *more than 5* (3)

Research Misconduct = Sum of Student and Faculty Scores for the Following:
   Plagiarizing
   Falsifying or "cooking" research data
   Inappropriately assigning authorship credit
   Overlooking others' use of flawed research data or the questionable interpretation of data
   Failing to present data that contradict one's previous research
   Cheating in course work (students only)

Employment Misconduct = Sum of Student and Faculty Scores for the Following:
   Ignoring research policies (e.g., animal care, human subjects, biosafety)
   Trying to get by on the work of others
   Using university resources for outside consulting work or other inappropriate personal purposes
   Misusing research funds

Personal Misconduct = Sum of Student and Faculty Scores for the Following:
   Sexually harassing another person
   Discriminating against others on the basis of race, ethnicity, gender, etc.
   Using one's position to exploit or manipulate others

All Misconduct = Research + Employment − Personal Misconduct

Appendix B: Survey Items Composing Structure and Climate Scales

Structure

Structured Feedback (alpha = .74)
   Is there at least one faculty member (including your advisor, if appropriate) in your department who is particularly supportive of you and your work?
   When your work is evaluated, how often do you find the evaluation constructive?
   When your work is evaluated, how often do you find the evaluation promptly provided?
   When your work is evaluated, how often do you find the evaluation detailed?
   I am satisfied with the amount and quality of time spent with my advisor.

Divestiture (alpha = .64)
   When your work is evaluated, how often do you find the evaluation humiliating?
   The advice and information I receive from faculty is inconsistent.
   Faculty expect my responsibilities as a student to come before all other responsibilities.
   Graduate school has positively reinforced my prior values, self-image, and way of thinking about the world. (reverse-coded)
   Graduate school is changing me in ways I do not like.

Collaboration
    Most students do their dissertation research as part of a larger, collaborative project.

Group Size
    In a typical week, with how many faculty members, research associates, post-doctoral fellows, and graduate students do you work on research projects?

CLIMATE

Competition (alpha = .68)
    People have to compete for departmental resources.
    A few students get most of the attention and resources.
    Faculty are willing to bend the rules for some students but not others.
    Students have to compete for faculty time and attention.

Solidarity
    There is a sense of solidarity among the students who enter the program at the same time.

Obligations
    My graduate assistant obligations are delaying my progress.

Publications
    Students and faculty collaborate on publications.

Individualism
    This department values individual research over collaborative research.

Appendix C: Correlation Coefficients (N = 1261)

	Overall Misconduct	Research Misconduct	Employee Misconduct	Personal Misconduct	Years	International	Female	Chemistry	Civil Eng.	Microbiology	Sociology
Overall Miscon.	1.00										
Res. Miscon.	.88**	1.00									
Empl. Miscon.	.87**	.66**	1.00								
Person. Miscon.	.81**	.55**	.54**	1.00							
Years	.14**	.10**	.12**	.15**	1.00						
International	−.12**	−.06*	−.15**	−.10**	−.08**	1.00					
Female	.07*	.01	.01	.17**	.07*	−.17**	1.00				
Chemistry	.05	.05	.06*	.01	−.04	−.06*	−.12*	1.00			
Civil Eng.	−.11*	−.06*	−.07*	−.16*	−.09**	.27**	−.24**	−.30**	1.00		
Microbiology	.01	.02	.08**	−.08**	−.05	−.06	.11**	−.37**	−.31**	1.00	
Sociology	.04	−.02	−.08**	.21**	.17**	−.13**	.22**	−.35**	−.30**	−.37**	1.00
Str. Feedback	−.33**	−.24**	−.29**	−.32**	−.11**	−.03	−.01	−.02	−.03	.07*	−.02
Divestiture	.37**	.28**	.31**	.37**	.09**	−.11**	.12**	.05	−.14**	.03	.04
Collaboration	−.04	−.00	.01	−.12**	−.16**	.02	−.10**	.09**	.08**	.18**	−.35**
Group Size	−.05	−.04	−.03	−.07**	−.08**	.05	−.08**	.19**	−.10**	.11**	−.20**
Competition	.36**	.24**	.25**	.43**	.12**	−.03	.09**	−.12**	.02	−.17**	.28**
Solidarity	−.04	−.02	−.03	−.04	−.00	−.22**	.06*	.08**	−.10**	−.01	.02
Obligations	.08**	.05	.04	.11**	.05	−.03	.04	−.02	−.08**	−.03	.12**
Publications	−.16**	−.11**	−.05	−.25**	−.21**	−.04	−.12**	.24**	.03	.24**	−.51**
Individualism	.13**	.08**	.08**	.17**	.10**	.01	.04	−.10**	.00	−.08**	.17**

Appendix C *continued*

	Str. Feedback	Divestiture	Collaboration	Group Size	Competition	Solidarity	Obligations	Publications	Individualism
Str. Feedback	1.00								
Divestiture	−.46**	1.00							
Collaboration	.09**	−.08**	1.00						
Group Size	.08**	−.02	.16**	1.00					
Competition	−.36**	.37**	−.16**	−.11**	1.00				
Solidarity	.17**	−.09**	.02	.02	−.11**	1.00			
Obligations	−.11**	.20**	−.06*	−.12**	.20**	−.00	1.00		
Publications	.31**	−.24**	.28**	.20**	−.35**	.15**	−.17**	1.00	
Individualism	−.15**	.19**	−.25**	−.09**	.30**	−.04	.12**	−.25**	1.00

* $p < .05$. ** $p < .01$.

Notes

This study is part of the Acadia Institute's Project on Professional Values and Ethical Issues in the Graduate Education of Scientists and Engineers, supported by Grant No. SBE-8913159 from the National Science Foundation (NSF). We wish to thank the following NSF components for the funding they have provided to the Ethics and Values Studies Program for support of the project: the Directorate for Behavioral, Social, and Economic Sciences; the Directorate for Biological Sciences; the Directorate for Engineering; the Directorate for Mathematical and Physical Sciences; and the Office of the Inspector General. Any opinions, findings, conclusions, or recommendations are our own and do not necessarily reflect the views of the NSF. We also wish to thank John Braxton, Robert J. Silverman, Judith P. Swazey, and two anonymous reviewers for their helpful comments.

1. The Acadia Institute, Bar Harbor, Maine, is a nonprofit organization devoted to the study of policy and ethical issues in higher education and medicine.

2. For example, in the climate case, a principal-components factor analysis with varimax rotation was used with the climate-related items. The analysis produced eight factors. For two factors that loaded highly on several variables (humane and competitive environments), scales were computed as a sum, with unit weights of the set of variables identified as loading heavily on a given factor. The remaining factors consisted of two or three variables that were not highly correlated; in these cases a single indicator variable with a nonskewed distribution was selected. The structure variables were constructed in the same way.

3. Recent data from the Department of Education ("Earned Degrees," 1993) indicate that approximately 25% of the Ph.D.'s awarded by U.S. institutions in 1990–91 went to "nonresident aliens," whereas about one-third of our respondents are international students. The difference is probably due to our focus on science and engineering fields. The same source indicates that the proportion of women in our sample is virtually identical to the proportion of women receiving Ph.D.'s nationwide in 1990–91. Even by discipline, our sample is quite close to national percentages. The national proportions of women (with our sample proportions in parentheses) are physical sciences, 20 (chemistry, 27); engineering, 9 (civil engineering, 14); life sciences, 37 (microbiology, 45); and social sciences, 35 (sociology, 55).

4. The HLM model is based on two equation types. The first type expresses the individual-level, dependent variable as a function of the individual-level control variables. In our analysis, this equation takes the form: Misconduct = $B_0 + B_1$(Years in Program) + B_2(International) + B_3(Female) + R, where "misconduct" represents any one of our misconduct variables (overall, research, employment, or personal) and the error term, R, represents variation at the individual level. We use deviations from the mean for the "Years" variable because this makes interpretation of the parameter estimates easier. Because this equation is at the level of individual respondents, there is one such equation for each person in the sample (1,261, except the few cases that have missing data on relevant variables).

The other equation type appearing in an HLM model expresses a relationship between the group-level variables and the B coefficients of the first equation. These coefficients are not, of course, measurable variables but are estimated in an iterative way in an HLM analysis. The model has one equation of this type for each B coefficient in the first equation. In our case, the equations are:

$$B0 = C00 + C01(\text{Department Variable 1}) + \ldots + C0k(\text{Department Variable } k) + U0$$
$$B1 = C10 + C11(\text{Department Variable 1}) + \ldots + C1k(\text{Department Variable } k) + U1$$
$$B2 = C20 + C21(\text{Department Variable 1}) + \ldots + C2k(\text{Department Variable } k) + U2$$
$$B3 = C30 + C31(\text{Department Variable 1}) + \ldots + C3k(\text{Department Variable } k) + U3$$

where the department variables are the department means for the structure and climate scales, as well as the discipline dummy variables (with sociology omitted, as the comparison group). The U error terms represent department-level random error. There is one such set of equations for each department under consideration (73 departments).

Together, the individual- and group-level equations make up the HLM model. We use this model to investigate two kinds of effects of the department variables (structure, climate, and discipline). The first is the effect of these variables on the mean level of observed misconduct in a department. This effect is represented by the C parameters in the first (B0) department-level equation. In each model, the mean referred to here is the mean of the observed misconduct scores for a given department, adjusted for the control variables included in the model. For example, when the standardized "years" variable and the dummy "international" variable are included as controls, the mean is computed for the (theoretical) reference group: U.S. citizens who have been in their programs an average length of time.

The second effect we investigate is the influence of the department-level variables on the relationships between observed misconduct and the control variables. All combinations of these effects are represented by the C parameters in the other (B1, B2, and B3) department-level equations. For example, B1 represents the effect of the control variable "years in program" on the dependent variable "misconduct." Then, C11 represents the effect of the first department variable (say, "structured feedback") on B1, that is, on the relationship between "years in program" and "misconduct."

Preliminary analyses of reduced-form models, having no predictor variables (Bryk & Raudenbush, 1992, pp. 61–64), verified that each misconduct scale varies significantly across departments. To select the best set of individual-level control variables for each misconduct type, we did preliminary analyses on reduced models that included only the controls (years in program, international status, and gender) and the dependent variables (Bryk & Raudenbush, 1992, pp. 66–70; Raudenbush & Bryk, 1986). For each form of misconduct, we found that the years-in-program variable had a significant effect that varied across departments. This variable thus appears in each model with a coefficient, B1, that is a function of the department-level variables. The dummy variable for international student status has a significant effect on overall and employment misconduct, but because the effect does not vary significantly across departments, it appears in these models with a fixed-effect parameter B2. International status has only a marginal effect ($p < .08$) on research and personal misconduct, but we chose to include this variable in these cases as well, particularly because the effect varies across departments, marginally for research misconduct and significantly for personal misconduct. In these models, the parameter B2 thus appears as a function of the department variables. Finally, the dummy variable for female students shows a significant effect (without significant variation across departments) only in the case of personal misconduct. The related parameter, B3, appears only in this model, with a fixed effect.

We also used reduced-form models to inform our selection of department-level variables. It was not possible to include all of the eight structure scales, the eight climate scales, and the three discipline dummy variables simultaneously due to limitations in the size of the database and the capacity of the HLM program (Scientific Software, 1991). In searching for a parsimonious set of department variables for each model, we performed preliminary analyses with only the eight structure scales. Rather high correlations among the scales (see Appendix C) indicated a potential problem with multicollinearity in the HLM model. We therefore did a separate analysis for every individual structure scale. These analyses produced the same pattern of effects as for the eight combined, indicating no substantial problems with multicollinearity. We followed a similar procedure, with the same results, for the climate scales. We then included in the full model only the structure variables that had significant effects. These variables appear, moreover, only in the parameter equations where the preliminary analysis showed significant effects. To illustrate, in the overall misconduct model, the structure variable "structured feedback" had a significant effect on the years-in-program parameter B1 but not on the base parameter B0. It therefore appears in the full model's B1 equation only. We followed the same procedure for selecting climate scales and disciplinary dummy variables to be included in the full model.

REFERENCES

Anderson, M., & Louis, K. (1994). The graduate student experience and subscription to the norms of science. *Research in Higher Education, 35,* 273–299.

Ashforth, B. (1985). Climate formation: Issues and extensions. *Academy of Management Review, 19,* 837–847.

Becher, T. (1984). The cultural view. In B. Clark (Ed.), *Perspectives on higher education: Eight disciplinary and comparative views* (pp. 165–194). Berkeley: University of California Press.

Becher, T. (1987). The disciplinary shaping of the profession. In B. Clark (Ed.), *The academic profession* (pp. 271–303). Berkeley: University of California Press.

Becher, T., & Kogan, M. (1992). *Process and structure in higher education.* London: Routledge.

Becker, H. S., & Greer, B. (1958). The fate of idealism in medical school. *American Sociological Review, 23,* 50–56.

Biglan, A. (1973a). The characteristics of subject matter in different academic areas. *Journal of Applied Psychology, 57,* 195–203.

Biglan, A. (1973b). Relationships between subject matter characteristics and the structure and output of university departments. *Journal of Applied Psychology, 57,* 204–213.

Bryk, A., & Raudenbush, S. (1992). *Hierarchical linear models.* Newbury Park, CA: Sage.

Bryk, A., Raudenbush, S., Seltzer, M., & Congdon, R. (1989). *An introduction to HLM: Computer program and user's guide.* Chicago: Scientific Software, Inc.

Clark, S., & Corcoran, M. (1986). Perspectives on the professional socialization of women faculty: A case of accumulative disadvantage? *Journal of Higher Education, 57,* 20–43.

Earned degrees conferred by U.S. institutions, 1990–91. (1993, June 2). *Chronicle of Higher Education,* p. A25.

Educational Testing Service. (1989). *Directory of graduate programs: 1990 and 1991* (Vols. A, C, & D). Princeton, NJ: Author.

Kleinman, S. (1983). Collective matters as individual concerns: Peer culture among graduate students. *Urban Life, 12,* 203–225.

Raudenbush, S., & Bryk, A. (1986). A hierarchical model for studying school effects. *Sociology of Education, 59,* 1–17.

Ruscio, K. (1987). Many sectors, many professions. In B. Clark (Ed.), *The academic profession* (pp. 331–368). Berkeley: University of California Press.

Scientific Software. (1991). *HLM distribution package, version 2.20.* Chicago: Author.

Van Maanen, J., & Schein, E. (1979). Toward a theory of organizational socialization. In B. Straw (Ed.), *Research in organizational behavior* (Vol. 1, pp. 209–264). Greenwich, CT: JAI.

Victor, B., & Cullen, J. (1988). The organizational basis of ethical work climates. *Administrative Science Quarterly, 33,* 101–125.

Zuckerman, H. (1988). The sociology of science. In N. Smelser (Ed.), *Handbook of sociology* (pp. 511–574). Newbury Park, CA: Sage.

CHAPTER ELEVEN

Perceptions of Research Misconduct and an Analysis of Their Correlates

John M. Braxton and Alan E. Bayer

The lay public presumes that professions are self-regulating. In exchange for self-regulation, professions are granted autonomy over the conduct of their professional roles (Goode, 1969). In the academic profession, self-regulation encompasses the full spectrum of scholarly activities, including the enforcement of both standards and ethical principles for the conduct of research (Anderson & Louis, 1991). However, the effectiveness of self-regulation in the academic profession is currently being challenged.

To elaborate, misconduct in science is perceived by the public as growing in recent years, if not pervasive throughout science. In a recent survey of a sample of members of the American Association for the Advancement of Science (AAAS), the nation's largest umbrella organization for the scientific community, three-fourths of those responding believed that media coverage had exaggerated the problem (AAAS, 1992). Nevertheless, 37% of those polled did believe that instances of fraud and misconduct have increased over the last decade. Moreover, a separate assessment by the National Science Foundation (Office of the Inspector General, 1990) concluded that "about 20 percent of scientists say that they have directly encountered fraud, and about 20 percent of graduate deans have dealt with verified cases of misconduct in the past five years" (p. 1). This conclusion is derived from a review of six survey studies that measured the extent of misconduct in science and engineering.

These perceptions and experiences have fostered a broad range of actions by the scientific community. These include
- A call to graduate programs in science to integrate course work on ethics into the curriculum
- Numerous sessions and panel discussions scheduled at a variety of professional association meetings

- Editorials in a variety of professional journals
- Changed editorial policies of some journals, which now require each author of a paper to acknowledge his or her contribution and responsibility for the content of the articles
- A regular quarterly newsletter, *Professional Ethics Report*, published by AAAS as a means to inform the general community of scientists on evolving issues and actions
- Congressional committee hearings on misconduct in medical and scientific research
- Revised or new codes of ethics that address fraud and misconduct by a large number of scientific professional organizations and associations
- Mandatory requirements to establish institutional panels to oversee issues related to research ethics and allegations of scientific misconduct at research universities receiving federal research funds
- Establishment of new offices in a variety of federal agencies supporting scientific research that are expressly charged with establishing policies and procedures regarding allegations of misconduct, addressing charges of misconduct, overseeing investigations, and recommending or meting out sanctions

This range of actions represents the exercise of some degree of responsibility for deterring, detecting, and sanctioning research misconduct by the various loci of responsibility for addressing misconduct identified by Chubin (1983): the laboratory, the institution of employment, scientific societies and journals, governmental agencies, and private foundations. Utmost, however, is the responsibility of professional peers for detecting and deterring research wrongdoing (Chubin, 1983). Thus, professional peers are of critical importance to the efficacy of the variety of actions, listed above, that have been taken by the scientific community. If individual academics do not detect and address misconduct, then such wrongdoing is unlikely to be sanctioned. Despite the importance of the actions of individual academics to the process of self-regulation, Chubin (1983) pointed to the "silent suspicions of peers regarding violations of ethical principles and norms which are left undocumented" and asked why they do not speak out (p. 187). Moreover, when science faculty do take action, it is generally informal and decentralized (Black, 1976; Zuckerman, 1977, 1988). What accounts for these "social facts"?

ATTITUDES AND BELIEFS

Various attitudes and beliefs regarding professional regulation in general and scientific misconduct in particular have been offered to account for these "social facts." They can be assorted into the nine categories described below.

Ambiguity in Determining Misconduct

Cournand and Meyer (1976) contended that the ambiguity of ethical principles in science makes it difficult to determine if misconduct has occurred. Further ambiguity is rooted in the nature of research specialization, which makes it difficult for scholars outside a given area of specialization to judge research malfeasance (Weinstein, 1979).

Career Effects

Individuals aware of misconduct are concerned that if they raise questions regarding the conduct of their colleagues, their own reputations will be tarnished and their chances for resources for their research and career advancement will be harmed (Tangney, 1987).

Functional Criteria for Sanctions

Freidson (1975), in his work on professional regulation in medicine, observed that whether a particular sanction will prevent future occurrences of misconduct is a basis for the selection of a particular sanction. Such actions as making appeals to a colleague's conscience fit such a criterion. Sanctions for the sole purpose of punishing the offending individual are to be avoided, according to this criterion.

Governmental Debarment

The fear of government debarment of research grant monies may be a deterrent to individual academic scientists' taking some action for personally known incidents of scientific impropriety (Broad, 1981).

Locus of Responsibility

The laboratory, the university of employment, professional societies, scholarly journals, governmental agencies, and private foundations are organizations responsible for detecting and deterring scientific wrongdoing (Chubin, 1983). Individual academic scientists may believe that these organizations bear the major responsibility for detecting and taking action for wrongdoing rather than themselves.

Professional Etiquette

Freidson (1975) has identified several prescriptions that govern the relationship among colleagues when a professional impropriety has taken place: a colleague should not be criticized either publicly or in private, the career and reputation of one's colleagues should not be damaged, and tact should be used when confronting an offending colleague. An additional tenet of professional etiquette is that no individual scientist has the right to assume a policing role for the scientific community (Culliton, 1974).

Reputational Effects

Taking action when a colleague is suspected of misconduct can have adverse effects on the reputation of the university, department, or laboratory in which the impropriety took place (Culliton, 1974). In addition, the reputation of the department chair or laboratory director of the offending individual may be harmed (Culliton, 1974).

Rationalization

Broad (1981) suggested that some scholars believe that advancement of knowledge is all that matters and not whether misconduct is addressed.

Symbolic Criteria for Sanctions

Freidson (1975) held that symbolic criteria for the selection of sanctions for professional wrongdoing entail judgment of whether a sanction will be embarrassing to the offending individual. Thus, formal sanctions and the public disclosure of actions taken are to be avoided. Appropriate sanctions are those that are informal and confidential. Moreover, economic sanctions are regarded as being demeaning to a person of professional status.

Such an array of attitudes and values raises a question as to whether more general and parsimonious patterns of interrelationship among these categories might be discerned. Given that little or no systematic research has been conducted on this rudimentary question (Braxton, 1986), the first stage of this research entails the identification of a more general and more parsimonious underlying structure for the nine a priori categories of possible attitudes and beliefs of academic scientists described above.

SHAPING INFLUENCES

If such a structure of attitudes and beliefs is identified, then what factors—individual, departmental, institutional, and professional—contribute to the shaping of such attitudes and beliefs? The intraprofessional status of an individual academic scientist, the cohesion of the academic department, institutional pressures for external grant support, and professional solidarity are factors that can shape attitudes and beliefs toward misconduct in general and taking action for such wrongdoing in particular. A general hypothesis is advanced for each of these possible shaping influences. These hypotheses are as follows.

1. Intraprofessional Status: Abbott (1983) defined intraprofessional status as an individual's stature in his or her professional community. The higher the intraprofessional status of an individual academic scientist, the more favorable are attitudes toward taking action for scientific misconduct. This hypothesis springs from research indicating that intraprofessional

status is positively related to both a belief in and compliance with ethical principles (Abbott, 1983; Carlin, 1966; Handler, 1967).

2. Departmental Cohesion: The greater the level of social cohesion in an academic department, the less favorable are the attitudes toward taking action for scientific misconduct held by individual academics. Social cohesion of an academic department is marked by sharing of common norms, values, and patterns of interaction. Such properties of social cohesion are consistent with Merton's (1968) concept of culturally induced social cohesion. Such social cohesion is threatened by action toward a colleague who has violated a scientific norm or ethical principle of research (Ellison, Keenan, Lockhart, & Van Schaick, 1985).

3. Institutional Pressure for Grants: The greater the institutional pressure for academic scientists to receive external grant support, the less favorable are the attitudes toward taking action for scientific misconduct held by individual academics. Pressure for external grants has been cited as a reason for fraud as well as a reason for little or no individual action against scientific wrongdoing (Holton, 1986; Remington, 1988; Tangney, 1987).

4. Professional Solidarity: Less favorable attitudes toward taking action against scientific wrongdoing are held by individual academics who have a strong belief in professional solidarity. Freidson (1975) contended that the function of professional solidarity is to protect the profession from lay interference, as well as to allow each individual professional a maximum degree of autonomy. Thus, professional solidarity constrains taking action against scientific impropriety.

Because these hypotheses have not been the focus of empirical research on academic scientists (Braxton, 1986), the testing of these four hypotheses was the focus of the second stage of this study. Although the formulations undergirding each of these four hypotheses are not necessarily in opposition to one another, each hypothesis does address a different locus of possible influence. To gain what Platt (1964) called "strong inference," these hypotheses will be simultaneously tested. The findings of this study will contribute not only to our knowledge and understanding of self-regulation in the community of academic scientists but also to our understanding of why individual academics who experience misconduct are often silent, as Chubin (1983) contended.

METHODS

Data Collection

The population of inference for this inquiry is biochemists holding tenure-track appointments in U.S. universities. A systematic sample (every *n*th listing, or the next listed individual meeting the selection criteria) of 802 biochemists was drawn from the Biochemistry section of the American Chemical Society's *Directory of Graduate Programs* (1991). Only senior-level (associate professor and professor) tenure-track faculty in U.S. universities with chemistry or biochemistry Ph.D. programs were eligible for selection. These criteria to select only more senior academic research scholars were employed to target a group who were maximally likely to have considered and crystallized issues of misconduct and ethics in scientific work.

During the winter of 1992, the National Scientific Conduct Assessment survey instrument was designed by the authors and mailed to the sample drawn. This instrument was designed and constructed for this piece of research. It contains items that operationalize the various variables required to answer this study's research questions and test the four general hypotheses advanced.

A total of 334 surveys were received, for a response rate of 41.6%. However, data analyses were conducted using a sample of 311 biochemists because the sample was restricted to tenured, full-time faculty. This difference between the number responding and the number selected reflects cases where the faculty member held a more senior rank but had not yet received tenure, had changed status since compilation of the *Directory,* or reported that he or she was not on full-time status.

Mailing-wave analyses were executed to determine whether the obtained sample was representative of the population of tenured academic biochemists. These tests indicated that no bias existed on any of this study's independent or dependent variables. Thus, the obtained sample is representative of the population of inference.[1]

Research Design

To test the four general hypotheses, a research design composed of six independent variables, two control variables, and a set of dependent variables that correspond to each of the patterns of attitudes and beliefs to be subsequently described was used. Three of the six independent variables measured different facets of intraprofessional status; the other three were departmental cohesion, institutional pressure for external grants, and professional solidarity. Because being a department chair and professional age might influence attitudes and beliefs regarding misconduct and action for it, these two variables were introduced as controls in this research design.

Control Variables

Being or having been a department chair was controlled in this study because handling unsatisfactory faculty performance and unethical behavior is among the responsibilities of the department chair (Tucker, 1981). Because chairs possess formal authority, their attitudes and beliefs regarding misconduct and taking action for incidents of scientific wrongdoing are likely to differ from those of other faculty.

Professional age also may influence attitudes and beliefs concerning scientific impropriety and was controlled in this study. Academic scientists of advancing professional age may have had more opportunities to personally experience misconduct during their careers than their less advanced colleagues. Such opportunities may serve to shape their attitudes and beliefs regarding misconduct and its sanctioning in ways that are different from those of individuals who have had fewer personal experiences with scientific wrongdoing.

Intraprofessional Status Variables

Such individual professional characteristics as research publication record, success in getting external grant support, and the prestige of one's current academic department are indices of intraprofessional status. Put differently, these characteristics are indicators of an individual's stature in his or her professional community. Thus, these three facets of intraprofessional status were included in this study.

Publication productivity is an indicator of intraprofessional status because prolific scientists are more likely to receive colleague recognition than are their less productive counterparts (Cole & Cole, 1967, 1973; O'Rand, 1977). Success in receiving external grant support is likewise an index of intraprofessional status because it is a form of colleague recognition (Hackett, 1990). Moreover, the competition for grants from both private foundations and federal agencies is keen (Chubin & Hackett, 1990). The prestige of one's current academic department is also an indicator of intraprofessional status, as it represents a form of colleague recognition or stature in an academic discipline (Cole, 1978; Cole & Cole, 1967; Lightfield, 1971).

Other Variables

The operational definitions of the preceding control and independent variables as well as departmental cohesion, institutional pressure for external grants, and the composite measure of professional solidarity are exhibited in table 11.1. Each of these variables was derived from items contained in the National Science Conduct Assessment. The dependent variables are subsequently described and are shown in table 11.2.

DATA ANALYSIS

Principal-components analysis and multiple regression were the two statistical procedures used. Given that there is no theory to guide the development of a more general and parsimonious set of attitudes and behaviors other than the nine a priori categories previously described, principal-components analysis was used (Kim & Mueller, 1978) in this inquiry's first stage. The scree test was used to determine the number of factors to be retained, and varimax was the method employed to rotate the initial principal-components analysis.

The second stage entails the testing of the four general hypotheses. For this task, multiple regression was used. Separate regression equations were estimated for each of the patterns of attitudes and beliefs identified. Since these hypotheses were simultaneously tested, the following independent and control variables were included in each of these equations: being or having been a chair, professional age, publication productivity, current external grant support, prestige of current academic department, departmental cohesion, institutional pressure for external grants, and professional solidarity. The .05 level of statistical significance was used to identify both statistical reliable equations and nonchance, net effects of the independent and control variables.

FINDINGS

Table 11.2 displays the results of the principal-components analysis. Means and standard deviations for all variables are shown in table 11.3, and zero-order intercorrelations for this study's variables are shown in table 11.4. Summary statistics for each of the multiple-regression equations solved are reported in table 11.5.

Patterns of Attitudes and Beliefs

Five patterns of attitudes and beliefs concerning professional self-regulation and scientific misconduct were identified through the principal-components method of factor analysis employed. The scree test suggested that a five-factor solution was appropriate. These five patterns were derived from the varimax rotation of the initial principal-components analysis. This rotated factor structure accounted for 54.03% of the variation. Table 11.2 shows the percentage of variance explained by each factor, the factor loadings of each of the specific variables (survey items) for each of the five factors discerned, and the Cronbach alpha estimates of internal consistency reliability for each factor.

Reputational Harm is the first pattern of attitudes and beliefs discerned. The specific attitudes and beliefs composing this factor are consistent with Culliton's (1974) assertion that individuals may be reluctant to take action because of the adverse effect such action may have on the reputation of a university, a laboratory, or the laboratory director or department chair.

The second factor identified was named *Sanction Criteria* because the specific attitudes and beliefs composing this factor pertain to criteria that

Table 11.1: Definitions of Control and Independent Variables

Variable	Definition
Control Variables	
1. Department Chairperson	Survey item: "Are you, or have you ever been, a department head/chair or a dean?" (no = 0, yes, but not now = 0, and yes, and am currently = 1)
2. Professional Age	Survey item: "Year highest degree received" (1992 minus year indicated).
Independent Variables	
1. Intraprofessional Status: External Grants	Survey item: "In the past three years, how many grants or contracts have you been awarded that were in excess of $10,000 and for which you were the principal or co-principal investigator?" (log of number of grants indicated).
2. Intraprofessional Status: Prestige of Employing Graduate Department	Ratings of graduate departments in biochemistry or chemistry conducted by Jones, Lindzey, and Coggeshall (1982). (standard scale, mean = 50, SD = 10)
3. Intraprofessional Status: Publication Productivity	Survey item: "In the past three years, how many professional journal articles have you published?" (log of number of articles indicated)
4. Departmental Cohesion	Composite of eight survey items: 1. "Having a good working relationship with my departmental colleagues is important to me." 2. "My academic department works best when there is a minimum of controversy among its members." 3. "Personal relationships among faculty in my department are good." 4. "Faculty in my department are in agreement about the fundamental nature of the discipline." 5. "Faculty in my department share similar values and beliefs about how research in the discipline should be conducted." 6. "Faculty in my department routinely discuss their research with one another." 7. "Faculty in my department routinely give advice on research to one another." 8. "Faculty in my department routinely discuss with one another the problems they are having with their research." (1 = strongly agree, 2 = agree somewhat, 3 = disagree somewhat, 4 = strongly disagree). Cronbach alpha = .84

continued

Table 11.1 *continued*

Variable	Definition
5. Institutional Pressure for Grants	Composite of three survey items: 1. "In my university it is very difficult for a person in my field to achieve tenure if he or she does not receive any externally funded grants for research." 2. "In my university it is very difficult for a person in my field to get promoted if he or she does not receive any externally funded grants for research." 3. "In my university, salary increments are largely determined by a scientist's ability to secure externally funded grants for his or her research." (1 = strongly agree, 2 = agree somewhat, 3 = disagree somewhat, 4 = strongly disagree). Cronbach alpha = .74
6. Professional Solidarity	Composite of six survey items: 1. "Scientists should trust one another in their research pursuits." 2. "Scientists should display respect for one another." 3. "Scientists owe one another protection from public interference in determining science policy." 4. "Scientists should be free to conduct their research without interference from other scientists." 5. "Scientists are accountable only to themselves for their research practices." 6. "An individual scientist does not have the right to monitor the research activities of other scientists." (1 = strongly agree, 2 = agree somewhat, 3 = disagree somewhat, 4 = strongly disagree). Cronbach alpha = .61

may be used to select the type of action to be meted out for misconduct (Freidson, 1975). This pattern contains a mixture of both the functional and symbolic criteria delineated by Freidson (1975). Such criteria suggest that only informal and lenient sanctions should be used.

Whistle-Blower Stigmatization was the label given to the third factor extracted. The specific attitudes and beliefs composing this factor indicate that individuals are wary of taking action for wrongdoing because they fear that their own scientific careers will be adversely affected by such action. This factor is consistent with Ellison et al.'s (1985) contention that individuals taking action against a colleague are labeled or stigmatized by their own organizations and that such labeling results in a decrease in their organizational status.

Table 11.2: The Five Patterns of Attitudes and Beliefs (Dependent Variables), with Survey Items and Loading

I. Reputational Harm

Action against a colleague who is guilty of scientific misconduct must avoid harming

—the reputation of my university	.91
—the reputation of my academic department	.91
—the reputation of my department chairperson or laboratory director	.88
—the reputation of my academic discipline	.85

Action against a colleague who is guilty of scientific misconduct must avoid institutional

—debarment from federal research grant monies	.66

% variance explained = .2023
Cronbach alpha = .89

II. Sanction Criteria

Actions for the sole purpose of punishing an individual who is guilty of scientific misconduct should be avoided.	.74
Only actions which appeal to the conscience of an individual who is guilty of scientific misconduct should be taken.	.73
Actions which are likely to adversely affect the financial well-being of an individual who is guilty of scientific misconduct should be avoided.	.69
Any action taken should be kept in strict confidence so as not to publicly embarrass an individual who is guilty of scientific misconduct.	.66
Only actions which may prevent future occurrences of scientific misconduct by an offending individual scientist should be implemented.	.63

% variance explained = .1071
Cronbach alpha = .76

III. Whistle-Blower Stigmatization

Taking action against a colleague suspected of scientific misconduct can harm one's own chances of obtaining research grant monies.	.85
Taking action against a colleague suspected of scientific misconduct can damage one's own academic career.	.85
Accusing a colleague of misconduct would lead to departmental conflict.	.76

% variance explained = .1007
Cronbach alpha = .79

continued

Table 11.2 *continued*

IV. Professional Etiquette

One needs to be very tactful when speaking in private with a colleague suspected of scientific impropriety.	.74
A colleague suspected of scientific misconduct should not be publicly confronted before other colleagues.	.71
Damage to the career of a scientist who is thought to have engaged in scientific impropriety should be avoided.	.68

% variance explained = .0738
Cronbach alpha = .58

V. Ideological Desensitization

It is difficult for a scientist to judge whether misconduct has occurred in a research specialty different from one's own.	.67
Only individuals who have scientific credentials pertinent to a case of alleged misconduct should be involved in any deliberations on such a case.	.66
Some scientific misconduct can be tolerated as long as it does not hinder the advancement of knowledge in my discipline.	.57
Responsibility for acting on cases of scientific misconduct should rest with the administration of a university.	.41
Responsibility for acting on cases of scientific misconduct should rest with professional associations.	.40

% variance explained = .0564
Cronbach alpha = .43

Note: Response code: 1 = strongly agree, 2 = agree somewhat, 3 = disagree somewhat, 4 = strongly disagree.

Professional Etiquette was the name given the fourth extracted factor. The specific attitudes and beliefs of this factor are fully congruent with Freidson's (1975) rules of professional etiquette.

The fifth factor was named *Ideological Desensitization* because the specific attitudes and beliefs of this factor suggest dissociation from the social significance and ethicality of one's work. Put differently, this pattern of attitudes and beliefs speaks to the absolvement of the individual for taking responsibility for addressing colleague wrongdoing. This pattern is consistent with what Derber (1982) has termed a dissociated "ideological desensitization" because the individual denies responsibility for dealing with either the ethical issues of professional work or its social significance and instead shifts such responsibility to the employing organization or an outside agency.

Given such a structure of five attitudes and beliefs toward taking action for scientific wrongdoing, what influence do such factors as intraprofessional status, departmental cohesion, institutional pressure for grants, and professional solidarity have on these attitudes and beliefs? Before this ques-

Table 11.3: Means and Standard Deviations for Variables

Variables	Mean	SD
Control Variables		
Chair	0.12	0.329
Profage	26.17	7.789
Independent Variables		
Grants	1.03	0.565
Prestige	52.19	8.501
Publications	2.14	0.822
Cohesion	1.78	0.559
Pressure	1.53	0.575
Solidarity	2.27	0.469
Dependent Variables		
Harm	2.74	0.889
Criteria	3.18	0.552
Stigma	2.24	0.700
Etiquette	1.88	0.674
Ideological	2.76	0.496

tion can be addressed, composite variables representing each of these five patterns of attitudes and beliefs need to be developed. These five composite variables composed the dependent variables of this study's research design. They are factor-based scores (Kim & Mueller, 1978) because only those specific attitudes and beliefs that had a loading of .400 or higher on the target factor were included in the construction of each composite variable. Each of these composite measures was calculated by summing the values of individual responses to each specific attitude or belief and then by taking the mean value of these summations.

Shaping Influences

With these composite variables in place, it is now possible to determine the effects of the four shaping influences on each of the five patterns of attitudes and beliefs. Put differently, this study's four general hypotheses were ready for testing. Because the four hypotheses were tested simultaneously, the findings are organized around the five patterns of attitudes and beliefs rather than by hypothesis. The summary statistics for each of the five multiple-regression equations solved are reported in table 11.5.

Reputational Harm

Both departmental cohesion (beta = .143, $p < .05$) and professional solidarity (beta = .257, $p < .0001$) exert the predicted influences on reputational harm. Thus, support is provided for both hypothesis 2 and hypothesis 4.

Table 11.4: Zero-Order Correlations among Variables

Variables	1	2	3	4	5	6	7	8	9	10	11	12	13
Control
1. Chair	—												
2. Profage	.00	—											
Independent
3. Grants	.09	-.27	—										
4. Prestige	-.03	.08	.07	—									
5. Publ	.11	-.28	.60	.20	—								
6. Cohesion	-.14	-.04	-.05	-.00	-.04	—							
7. Pressure	.06	-.08	.09	-.08	.15	-.02	—						
8. Solidarity	.01	-.05	.05	.15	.05	.12	-.02	—					
Dependent
9. Harm	-.05	.09	-.07	.10	-.07	.15	-.09	.26	—				
10. Criteria	.16	-.08	.01	.08	.06	-.09	-.10	.25	.29	—			
11. Stigma	-.05	.18	.03	.20	.17	-.23	.14	-.08	-.01	-.04	—		
12. Etiquette	-.02	.01	-.01	.03	.05	.02	.05	.17	.17	.14	.03	—	
13. Ideol	-.01	-.06	.02	.09	.06	-.04	.02	.36	.17	.28	.01	.08	—

Table 11.5: Summary Statistics for the Multiple-Regression Equations Solved

	\multicolumn{5}{c}{Dependent Variables}
	Harm	Criteria	Stigma	Etiquette	Ideological
Control Variables					
Chair	−.034	.178**	−.046	−.049	−.030
	(−.093)	(.299)	(−.097)	(−.105)	(−.049)
Profage	.134*	−.092	.255**	.059	−.026
	(.015)	(−.006)	(.021)	(.005)	(−.002)
Independent Variables					
Grants	.002	−.093	−.201*	−.150	.017
	(.003)	(−.089)	(−.243)	(−.185)	(.015)
Prestige	.071	.018	.139*	−.065	.019
	(.008)	(.001)	(.011)	(−.006)	(.001)
Publications	−.077	.021	.324**	.135	−.018
	(−.084)	(.014)	(.271)	(.113)	(−.011)
Cohesion	.143*	−.089	−.163*	.014	−.124*
	(.228)	(−.086)	(−.198)	(.017)	(−.114)
Pressure	−.029	−.074	.160*	.087	−.006
	(−.046)	(−.071)	(.197)	(.108)	(−.006)
Solidarity	.257***	.230**	−.085	.182	.402***
	(.488)	(.265)	(−.122)	(.267)	(.441)
Intercept	0.688	2.972***	1.109**	1.247	1.968***
Variance explained	.130***	.106**	.219***	.061	.170***

Note: Metric coefficients are enclosed in parentheses.
*p < .05. **p < .01. ***p < .0001.

However, hypothesis 4 is afforded greater support than hypothesis 2 because the strength of the effect of professional solidarity is greater than that of departmental cohesion.

None of the three indices of intraprofessional status have a statistically reliable influence on reputational harm. Moreover, institutional pressure for external grant support does not have a statistically significant effect on reputational harm. Consequently, neither hypothesis 1 nor hypothesis 3 is supported.

However, professional age exerts an influence on reputational harm. As professional age increases, an individual's concern over harm to the university's and colleagues' reputations created by taking action for scientific wrongdoing decreases (beta = .134, $p < .05$). The percentage of variance explained by this equation is 13.0%.

Sanction Criteria

Of the independent variables, only professional solidarity has an effect on sanction criteria. As a belief in the prescriptions of professional solidarity (beta = .230, p < .01) increases, the tendency of an individual to endorse the use of informal and lenient sanctions for scientific improprieties also increases. Therefore, support is provided only for hypothesis 2.

In addition to professional solidarity, being a department chair influences this pattern of attitudes and beliefs. More specifically, department chairs (beta = .178, p < .01) are less likely to endorse the use of informal and lenient sanctions than are academics who are not department chairs. The equation estimated explains 10.6% of the variance.

Whistle-Blower Stigmatization

Of the four possible sources of influence, only professional solidarity does not have a statistically reliable effect on whistle-blower stigmatization. All three indices of intraprofessional status exert an influence. Publication productivity (beta = .324, p < .01) and prestige of one's academic department (beta = .139, p < .05) both have the expected influence. However, recent receipt of external grant support has an effect contrary to what was anticipated (beta = -.201, p < .05). Therefore, partial support for the first hypothesis is given.

Institutional pressure for external grant support also has the expected influence on whistle-blower stigmatization. The greater the perceived institutional pressure for receiving external grant monies (beta = .160, p < .05), the more likely individuals are to be inclined toward avoiding action that would stigmatize themselves as whistle-blowers. Hence, support for third hypothesis is provided.

However, the influence of departmental cohesion on whistle-blower stigmatization is contrary to the prediction of hypothesis three. As departmental cohesion decreases (beta = -.163, p < .05), the belief that taking action for colleague misconduct can be stigmatizing increases. Put differently, cohesive departments buffer individuals from fear of being labeled a whistle-blower. Likewise, professional age also shields an individual from fear of being stigmatized as a whistle-blower because as professional age increases (beta = .255, p < .01), the individual is less likely to endorse the attitudes and beliefs surrounding whistle-blower stigmatization. The percentage of the variance explained by this equation is 21.9%.

Professional Etiquette

Because the regression equation estimated for this pattern of attitudes and values is statistically nonsignificant, none of the four hypotheses are provided empirical backing.

Ideological Desensitization

This pattern of attitudes and beliefs is influenced only by departmental cohesion and professional solidarity. The influence of departmental cohesion is contrary to its predicted effect, given that as departmental cohesion increases (beta = -.124, $p < .05$), the tendency of biochemists to dissociate themselves from responsibility for addressing misconduct decreases. However, professional solidarity exerts the expected influence on this pattern of attitudes and beliefs. As a belief in professional solidarity increases (beta = .402, $p < .0001$), the tendency of individuals to distance themselves from colleague misconduct also increases. Thus, support for the fourth hypothesis is given.

Given that none of the measures of intraprofessional status have a statistically significant influence on ideological desensitization, support for the first hypothesis is not rendered. Support for the second and third hypotheses is also not provided because neither departmental cohesion nor institutional pressure for external grants has a statistically reliable effect on ideological desensitization. Moreover, neither of the two control variables has a nonchance influence on this pattern of attitudes and beliefs. The percentage of variance accounted for by this estimated equation is 17.0%.

DISCUSSION

Because of highly visible incidents of scientific fraud and growing perceptions of improprieties in science, the scientific community has taken a number of remedial steps, as described and itemized at the beginning of this chapter. Moreover, there has been a concomitant increase in books and journal articles on the subject. Yet even the more research-based of these works have tended to be descriptive, and others are more qualitative reports, including case studies and anecdotal accounts.

In contrast, this present research is more empirical and analytical than most prior research. First, nine categories of attitudes and beliefs regarding scientific misconduct and professional regulation were derived from the extant literature. Hypotheses were then advanced for each of four factors—individual, departmental, institutional, and professional—that might generally contribute to each of these attitudes and beliefs. A survey instrument was designed to assess these variables, and results were analyzed on the basis of the responses of 311 senior-level university scientists selected from Ph.D. programs around the United States.

From the array of attitudes and beliefs included in the survey instrument, factor analysis yielded a five-factor solution. These patterns were identified as (1) reputational harm, (2) sanction criteria, (3) whistle-blower stigmatization, (4) professional etiquette, and (5) ideological desensitization. For each of these dependent variables, multiple-regression procedures were employed to identify the principle correlates. None of the four hypotheses was supported as regards biochemists' attitudes on professional etiquette in dealing with scientific impropriety. For each of the other dependent variables, some support for each of the hypotheses was found, and the amount of explained variance in the multiple-regression equations was statistically significant.

However, this study is limited in several ways. The conclusion advanced and the implications of the findings of this study are tempered to some extent by these limitations. First, the sample consisted of tenured faculty only. Both the pattern of attitudes and beliefs identified and the extent of support for the four hypotheses might have been different if untenured faculty had been included in this study. Future research should include both untenured and tenured faculty.

Second, this study was restricted to one academic discipline. Thus, it needs to be replicated using academic disciplines other than biochemistry because a different pattern of results might be obtained with different disciplines.

A third limitation is that the measures of departmental cohesion, institutional pressure for grants, and professional solidarity represent the perceptions of the survey respondents. The effects of these three structural variables on the five patterns of attitudes and beliefs might have been different if "objective" or independently derived measures of these constructs had been used in this study. For example, future research might measure institutional pressure for grants by using the dollar amount of external research grant monies awarded faculty during a particular period of time. This variable could also be measured by asking academic deans and vice presidents for academic affairs to indicate the level of importance attached to external grant awards in determining tenure, promotion, and salary for faculty in their college and university. Departmental cohesion and professional solidarity could be measured by using the aggregated responses of the members of the focal individual's academic department. Put differently, these two structural factors could be assessed at the level of the department rather than at the level of the individual.

A fourth limitation is that some of the individual survey items that make up the Professional Solidarity scale are somewhat similar in content to some of the individual survey items composing the five patterns of attitudes and beliefs in general and the Ideological Desensitization scale in particular. Thus, it is possible that the magnitude of the statistically reliable influence (beta weights) of professional solidarity on reputational harm, sanction criteria, and ideological desensitization may be inflated to some extent.

CONCLUSION

From this study's pattern of findings, it is concluded that individual achievement characteristics (professional career age and administrative experience as a department head) and individual status within the scientific community (publication productivity and prestige of current academic department) sometimes influence patterns of attitudes and beliefs regarding scientific misconduct. However, whereas these factors may induce individuals to endorse attitudes supportive of taking action regarding misconduct, such inclinations are counterbalanced by the structure of the scientific community (professional solidarity), the degree of institutional pressure for external grants, and the structure of academic departments (departmental cohesion). Given such countervailing forces, individual scientists may experience ambivalence among these countervailing forces. Such possible ambivalence may, in turn, help account for the decentralized and informal character of sanctions taken for research wrongdoing and ethical violations. This hypothesis should be the focus of future research. Such research should also attend to the effects of the five patterns of attitudes and beliefs on the actions taken by individuals who have personally experienced scientific wrongdoing.

The attitudes and beliefs identified concerning scientific misconduct also have implications for future research on the process of self-regulation in the academic profession. Beyond an individual's personal response, these attitudes and beliefs may play a role in situations surrounding an alleged impropriety. Such situations include an individual's reaction to graduate students' suspicions of misconduct, discussions among colleagues concerning the reporting of an incident of misconduct to university officials, and the deliberations of university research misconduct committees.

Individual scientists may communicate these attitudes and beliefs to graduate students who suspect either a faculty member or another graduate student of research wrongdoing. In conversations with such graduate students, an individual may make, in particular, statements expressive of ideological desensitization, whistle-blower stigmatization, and professional etiquette. Because the graduate school socialization process is held to be a deterrent to scientific misconduct (Zuckerman, 1977, 1988) as well as a locus of the inculcation of attitudes, values, and beliefs regarding professional self-regulation (Braxton, 1991), the extent to which the five attitudes and beliefs are transmitted to graduate students is worthy of future research.

Also deserving of future research is the content of discussions among colleagues concerning whether a suspicion of misconduct should be reported to university officials responsible for handling allegations of misconduct. In such discussions, individuals may express such attitudes and beliefs as reputational harm, ideological desensitization, and professional etiquette. These attitudes and beliefs may, in turn, affect the way allegations of wrongdoing are handled by colleague groups.

The deliberations of university scientific misconduct committees may also be influenced by the attitudes and beliefs concerning scientific misconduct discerned in this study. In particular, decisions on the type of sanction to be meted out to culpable individuals may be shaped by sanction criteria and reputational harm. The contents of such deliberations should also be the focus of future research.

In addition to the above research directions, future research should include other sources of possible influence on the five patterns of attitudes and beliefs. Lack of endorsement of scientific normative and ethical principles (Braxton, 1991; Zuckerman, 1977, 1988), pressure to publish (Ben-Yehuda, 1986; Chalk, 1985; Goldman, 1987), and faculty entrepreneurship, or conducting research because of its commercial potential (Peters & Etzkowitz, 1990), are some factors that have been advanced to account for scientific misconduct (Louis, Anderson, & Rosenberg, 1993). By extension, these factors may also influence one or more of the five patterns of attitudes and beliefs toward taking action for scientific wrongdoing identified here. A different pattern of findings regarding the effects of the various sources of influence on the attitudes and beliefs might have obtained if these additional factors had been included in this inquiry. Thus, future research should include such possible sources of influence.

Because the patterns of attitudes and beliefs identified are not viewed as being exhaustive of attitudes and beliefs toward taking action for scientific wrongdoing, the identification of additional attitudes and beliefs should be the target of further research. For example, Shaw (1989) offered some possible explanations for the failure of the literary community to take action in cases of alleged plagiarism. Some possibly pertinent attitudes and beliefs that can be gleaned from Shaw's discussion are the tendency of individuals experiencing misconduct to deny its occurrence or offer extenuating circumstances for its occurrence, the tendency to view the incident as an exception rather than as characteristic of the offending individual's work, and the tendency to make an accusation of misconduct only when the act represents a pattern of impropriety. Such possible attitudes and beliefs should be included in future research.[2]

The above research directions, as well as research addressing the limitations of this study, may provide added insight into the decentralized and unsystematic nature of addressing scientific misconduct observed by Black (1976) and Zuckerman (1977, 1988). Such research not only will increase our understanding of the process of self-regulation in the academic profession but may also have implications for the development of institutional and public policy directed toward the establishment of a more universalistic standard and response to scientific wrongdoing by the academic profession.

Notes

The research of this chapter was partially supported by funds from the vice president for research at Syracuse University. We are grateful for this support. We also wish to express appreciation to Robert J. Silverman, editor of the *Journal of Higher Education (JHE)*, Mary Frank Fox, and two anonymous *JHE* reviewers of this chapter for their helpful comments for the improvement of this work.

1. This method of determining a sample's representativeness is consistent with procedures suggested by Goode and Hatt (1952) and Leslie (1972). Analyses of variance were conducted for all variables except that of department chairship. The chi-square test of independence was used for this variable given its dichotomous scoring (*chair* = 1, *not a chair* = 0). Three mailing waves composed the groups used for these comparisons: responses to the initial mailing, responses following a postcard reminder, and responses after a second survey mailing.

2. We would like to express appreciation to an anonymous reviewer of this manuscript for suggesting Shaw's work to us.

REFERENCES

Abbott, A. (1983). Professional ethics. *American Journal of Sociology, 88,* 855–885.

American Association for the Advancement of Science. (1988). *Professional Ethics Report, 1*(4).

American Association for the Advancement of Science. (1992). *Scientific ethics and responsibility: AAAS opinion poll summary report.* Washington, DC: Author.

American Chemical Society. (1991). *Directory of graduate programs.* Washington, DC: Author.

Anderson, M. S., & Louis, K. S. (1991). The changing locus of control over faculty research: From self-regulation to dispersed influence. In J. C. Smart (Ed.), *Higher education: Handbook of theory and research* (Vol. 7, pp. 57–101). New York: Agathon.

Ben-Yehuda, N. (1986). Deviance in science. *British Journal of Criminology, 26,* 1–27.

Black, D. (1976). *The behavior of law.* New York: Academic Press.

Braxton, J. M. (1986). The normative structure of science: Social control in the academic profession. In J. C. Smart (Ed.), *Higher education: Handbook of theory and research* (Vol. 2, pp. 309–357). New York: Agathon.

Braxton, J. M. (1991). The influence of graduate department quality on the sanctioning of scientific misconduct. *Journal of Higher Education, 62,* 87–108.

Broad, W. J. (1981). Fraud and the structure of science. *Science, 212,* 137–141.

Carlin, J. (1966). *Lawyers' ethics.* New York: Sage.

Chalk, R. (1985). Overview: AAAS Project on Secrecy and Openness in Science and Technology. *Science, Technology, and Human Values, 10,* 28–35.

Chubin, D. E. (1983). Misconduct in research: An issue of science policy and practice. *Minerva, 23,* 175–202.

Chubin, D. E., & Hackett, E. J. (1990). *Peerless science: Peer review and U.S. science policy.* Albany: State University of New York Press.

Cole, S. (1978). Scientific reward systems: A comparative analysis. In R. A. Jones

(Ed.), *Research in sociology of knowledge, science and art: An annual compilation of research* (pp. 167–190). Greenwich, CT: JAI.
Cole, S., & Cole, J. R. (1967). Scientific output and recognition: A study in the operation of the reward system in science. *American Sociological Review, 32*, 377–390.
Cole, J. R., & Cole, S. (1973). *Social stratification in science.* Chicago: University of Chicago Press.
Cournand, A., & Meyer, M. (1976). The scientist's code. *Minerva, 14*, 79–96.
Culliton, B. (1974). The Sloan-Kettering affair: A story without a hero. *Science, 184*, 644–650.
Derber, C. (1982). Managing professionals: Ideological proletarianization and mental labor. In C. Derber (Ed.), *Professionals as workers: Mental labor in advanced capitalism* (pp. 167–190). Boston: G. K. Hall.
Ellison, F., Keenan, J., Lockhart, P., & Van Schaick, J. (1985). *Whistleblowing research: Methodological and moral issues.* New York: Praeger.
Freidson, E. (1975). *Doctoring together: A study of professional social control.* New York: Elsevier.
Goldman, A. H. (1987). Ethical issues in proprietary restrictions on research results. *Science, Technology and Human Values, 12*, 22–30.
Goode, W. J. (1969). The theoretical limits of professionalization. In A. Etzioni (Ed.), *The semi-professions and their organization* (pp. 266–313). New York: Free Press.
Goode, W. J., & Hatt, P. K. (1952). *Methods in social research.* New York: McGraw-Hill.
Hackett, E. J. (1990). Science as a vocation in the 1990s: The changing organizational culture of academic science. *Journal of Higher Education, 61*, 241–279.
Handler, J. F. (1967). *The lawyer and his community.* Madison: University of Wisconsin Press.
Holton, G. J. (1986). Niels Bohr and the integrity of science. *American Scientist, 74*, 273–343.
Jones, L. V., Lindzey, V. E., & Coggeshall, P. E. (1982). *An assessment of research doctorate programs in the United States.* Washington, DC: National Academy Press.
Kim, J. O., & Mueller, C. W. (1978). *Factor analysis: Statistical methods and practical issues.* Beverly Hills, CA: Sage.
Leslie, L. L. (1972). Are response rates essential to valid surveys. *Social Science Research, 1*, 323–334.
Lightfield, E. T. (1971). Output and recognition of sociologists. *American Sociologist, 6*, 128–133.
Louis, K. S., Anderson, M. S., & Rosenberg, L. (1993, April). *Academic misconduct and academic values: An exploration of the contributing roles of productivity, entrepreneurship and department climate.* Paper presented at the annual meeting of the American Educational Research Association, Atlanta, GA.
Merton, R. K. (1968). *Social theory and social structure.* New York: Free Press.

Office of the Inspector General. (1990). *Survey data on the extent of misconduct in science and engineering.* Washington, DC: National Science Foundation.

O'Rand, A. M. (1977). Professional standing and peer consultation status among biological scientists at a summer research laboratory. *Social Forces, 55,* 921–937.

Peters, L. S., & Etzkowitz, H. (1990). University-industry connections and academic values. *Technology in Society, 12,* 427–440.

Platt, J. R. (1964). Strong inference. *Science, 146,* 347–353.

Remington, J. A. (1988). Beyond big science in America: The binding of inquiry. *Social Studies of Science, 18,* 45–72.

Shaw, P. (1989). *The war against the intellect: Episodes in the decline of discourse.* Iowa City: University of Iowa Press.

Tangney, J. P. (1987). Fraud will out—or will it? *New Scientist, 115,* 62–63.

Tucker, A. (1981). *Chairing the academic department.* Washington, DC: American Council on Education.

Weinstein, D. (1979). Fraud in science. *Social Science Quarterly, 59,* 639–652.

Zuckerman, H. E. (1977). Deviant behavior and social control in science. In E. Sagarin (Ed.), *Deviance and social change* (pp. 87–138). Beverly Hills, CA: Sage.

Zuckerman, H. E. (1988). The sociology of science. In N. J. Smelser (Ed.), *Handbook of sociology* (pp. 511–574). Newbury Park, CA: Sage.

CHAPTER TWELVE

Understanding the Potential for Misconduct in University-Industry Relationships: An Empirical View

Teresa Isabelle Daza Campbell and
Sheila Slaughter

As numbers of university-industry relationships have increased over the past 15 years, the instances of scientific misconduct also appear to have increased (Blumenthal, Causino, & Louis, 1996; Louis, Anderson, & Rosenberg, 1995).[1] Generally, scholars have tried to explain the apparent rise in misconduct by studying norms and counternorms of scientists and engineers to see if groups of individual scientists are developing values that encourage misconduct (Barber, 1952; Merton, 1957; Merton & Barber, 1963; Mitroff, 1974; Storer, 1966). However, these studies on individual scientists' misconduct do not look closely at external and organizational influences and do not examine the dynamics of the intricate partnerships formed between university and industry representatives to see how these relationships might shape academic conduct.

We used DiMaggio and Powell's (1983) theory of institutional isomorphism to examine the views of representatives from industry and academe toward specific statements that addressed issues related to potential conflict and misconduct, broadly defined. We analyzed approximately 575 survey responses from members of the university and business communities, using factor analysis and analysis of variance,[2] in search of increased congruence in the perspectives and norms of members of these communities who interact frequently with each other. By identifying areas of consensus among collaborative[3] agents, we gained insight into the specific areas in which academics and industry representatives are shaping the notions of acceptability within the scientific community, and we investigated whether they may be constructing new norms that fit the needs of both environments. When the academic community begins to hold a supportive view toward statements describing activity that moves away from widely held notions of acceptable academic conduct, then the opportunities for inappropriate behavior and potential for misconduct become heightened.

As university and industry representatives begin to work together more closely and frequently, they pursue professional avenues and approaches that are mutually agreeable. The literature outlines a number of areas where university-industry activity introduces issues and incentives that may be antithetical to traditional academic norms. These academic traditions, values, and beliefs draw primarily upon academic freedom (Slaughter, 1988), Mertonian-type norms (Barber, 1952; Braxton, 1986; Merton, 1957; Merton & Barber, 1963; Storer, 1966; Webster, 1991) and notions of equity and public service (Campbell, 1995) that have become woven into the fabric of academe (Slaughter & Rhoades, 1990). In compromising to meet each others' needs, university and industry representatives involved with the opposite sector are likely to be developing new norms within the academic system that accommodate interaction between the academic and for-profit sectors. As these new approaches become more frequent, they gain increased acceptance by the scientific community. The more a particular behavior is sanctioned by the scientific community, the more likely it is that increasing numbers of scientists will choose to engage in that behavior. When shifts in perspective occur concerning issues of misconduct, broadly defined, there is a high potential for misconduct, and inappropriate behavior is likely to be fostered.

As Buzzelli (1996) succinctly stated, "One of the major issues in defining misconduct in science is whether scientists can continue to be judged according to the scientific community's own standards of practice" (p. 937). When representatives of industry and academe begin to share more positive views toward specific topics that deviate from traditional academic norms, opportunities for inappropriate actions are likely to increase. Thus, positive views toward statements in this study point to the scholarly community's acceptance of certain activities as appropriate, and thus an increased likelihood that researchers will engage in these activities. By capturing acceptance of conduct that deviates from academic tradition, this study highlights areas in which misconduct might occur. Similarly, negative views toward statements that reflect nontraditional values or norms indicate that the scientific community censures that activity, thus diminishing the likelihood that the conduct will occur. To illustrate, consider the survey statement "An academic influences research results to ensure continued sales for a company." The majority of the respondents in this study viewed the statement in a negative light, suggesting that they view fabrication of research results as inappropriate. Since most academics do not support the alteration of research data to assist a firm in sustaining its sales, it is *not* likely that misconduct will occur in this area.

In contrast, imagine a hypothetical scenario in which the respondents held the opposite view. If the participants had viewed the statement more positively, their responses would have suggested a research climate that supported the altering of results for the purpose of sustaining the sales of a sponsoring company, indicating an climate in which the likelihood of this type of misconduct was increased.

Decision makers in universities, firms, and the federal government are eager to focus their diverse efforts on minimizing inappropriate behavior, and this study seeks to illuminate key areas that may become problematic. We categorized these areas as potential conflict of interest (e.g., revenue-generating activities), potential conflict of commitment (e.g., distribution of time and energy among the various academic duties), and potential conflict over internal equity (e.g., ability to garner rewards within the organization). By identifying any emerging shifts in researchers' views of appropriate and inappropriate activities related to these topics, we illuminated the areas in which decision makers can intervene effectively to shape future activity in a manner that is beneficial to both organizational sectors. Our survey did *not* capture particular instances of misconduct, nor did it seek to identify all of the possible forms of misconduct; rather, it measured the perspectives of representatives in academe and industry toward specific activities in order to discover whether close interaction between academe and industry creates a climate that multiplies the opportunities for misconduct.

THEORY

Institutional isomorphism (DiMaggio & Powell, 1983) deals with the question of why so many organizations are alike, rather than different, and suggests that organizations, and the actors within them, become more similar as a result of three simultaneously occurring forces: the requirements of external or regulatory agencies (coercive isomorphism), the cues from other organizations in their environment about how to respond to problems and uncertainty (mimetic isomorphism), and the influences of peers or professional groups across organizations (normative isomorphism).[4] DiMaggio and Powell addressed enterprises that operate in the same environment or field; they did not look at organizations in different fields, since they assumed that environment, or shared fields, would play a major part in explaining the sameness of organizations. In contrast, we theorized that academics involved with industry and businesspersons involved with the academy might share an environment, given that they confront similar fiscal constraints and governmental regulations, look to each other for cues about organizational mechanisms to deal with the changing environment, and share their emerging values as they increasingly interact in professional situations. We hypothesized that the views of members of the academy and industry who were involved in partnerships toward statements related to potential conflicts and misconduct would differ from the views of individuals who were not involved in collaborative relationships.

CONCEPTUALIZATION OF MISCONDUCT

For this study, we follow Louis et al.'s (1995) definition of misconduct, in which any actions that violate the standards of a given community are viewed as potential misconduct. This is consistent with the U.S. Public Health Service's (1995) intent to "protect the integrity of science, the federal interest in funded research, and the interest of institutions in which research is conducted" (p. 3). The fundamental concern is that the integrity of research and the objective, rational, legitimate practice of scholarly activity be upheld. Today, as officials in the federal government and in universities have recognized that a wide range of actions might have a negative impact on the conduct of research, misconduct is no longer limited solely to fabrication, falsification, and plagiarism. Now, "Misconduct is based on the premise that research misconduct is a serious violation of the fundamental principle that scientists be truthful and fair in the conduct of research and the dissemination of research results" (U.S. Public Health Service, 1995, p. 13).

We use this broad definition of misconduct to embrace the broad spectrum of areas in which difficulties might arise. Our purpose is to point out some of the more controversial areas in which opportunities for misconduct might exist. Primarily, our topics of investigation fall under the rubric of potential conflicts. This is an area that remains largely unexplored but is a likely breeding ground for misconduct.

DESIGN AND METHOD

Targeted Survey Population

To identify and investigate values in higher education as a whole, we surveyed institutions across the Carnegie spectrum, rather than looking solely at research institutions. Similarly, we included a wide array of businesses across a broad spectrum of commercial pursuits, not limiting our study to large-sized businesses in high-technology fields. The survey instrument was mailed to the 12 largest public[5] institutions in all of the Carnegie classifications (Carnegie Foundation for the Advancement of Teaching, 1987), ranging from Research I universities to liberal arts colleges. The largest 60 companies, ranked by stock market value and listed in *Business Week*'s (1993) "R&D Scoreboard," were included. Input from representatives of medium- and smaller-sized firms across a number of product and service groups was solicited by mailing surveys to individuals in the highest and lowest ranked firms within each of the "R&D Scoreboard" industrial sector categories and in the top 45 small companies listed in *Inc. Magazine* (Mangelsdorf, 1992) among the 500 fastest growing independent, private companies in the United States. This yielded a total of 86[6] colleges/universities and 165 firms. This survey population, selected in a manner that facilitated representation from a diverse group of academic institutions, was compatible with our goal of building a broad-based understanding of these topics.[7]

Because we wanted to see if members of the academy and company representatives involved in university-industry partnerships were developing an organizational field distinct from academics and businesspersons *not* participating in university-industry relations, we surveyed faculty involved in business partnerships and faculty not involved, as well as businesspersons who participated in university partnerships and those who did not. Given that we think faculty in many fields are cultivating entrepreneurial opportunities (Slaughter & Leslie, 1997), we looked not only at scientists and engineers but at faculty in the social sciences, fine arts, and business as well. By including faculty from a variety of disciplines, we could establish a baseline understanding of how the topics addressed in each statement were perceived. Given the nature of the questions, we believe that any disciplinary differences that may exist are not profound.[8] However, combining the views of academics from different disciplines may be a limitation of this study, and this is an area worthy of further investigation in future studies.

Survey Sample

Responses were received from over 96 university administrators and 275 faculty members representing science and engineering (120), business (85), and social science and fine arts (70). Similarly, responses were received from industrial sector employees involved in research (135) as well as those not involved in research (70). Calculation of the survey response rate proved to be a challenge, since targeted respondents were asked to distribute questionnaires to individuals within their department; it was impossible to determine whether these unknown potential respondents actually received a survey instrument. Although it is conceivable that many of these anonymous respondents never had an opportunity to participate, particularly in cases where the known and targeted respondent chose not to reply in a deliberate effort to follow the most discreet course, it was assumed that the additional surveys were distributed. On this conservative assumption, the minimum response rate for eligible survey participants was 34%. These respondents represented 76% of the targeted organizations.[9]

To analyze the data, we grouped respondents on the basis of their involvement with the private sector (see note 3). This resulted in two sets of respondents, one primarily from the hard sciences (collaborative faculty) and the other primarily from the soft sciences (noncollaborative faculty). These distinctions are not absolute; if representatives from the soft sciences indicated that they were involved with firms (which some did), they were included in the collaborative group. Likewise, some members of the hard sciences did not work with firms and were thus grouped with those not involved with industry.

Questionnaire

Unlike other studies that use distinct survey instruments for academe and industry, our study used a questionnaire that contained the same statements for both of these audiences; the two surveys were different only with regard to demographic data, which requested information relevant to the particular sector.[10] We drew heavily on the literature in formulating the survey questions. We presumed that after a decade or more of participating in university-industry partnerships, we would be able to see areas of compromise and agreement among the two sectors. We asked survey questions that were designed to tap complex areas of value convergence, rather than assuming separate and dichotomous norms for universities and industries, and to address issues frequently raised as areas in which inappropriate conduct might occur. (For a sample of our survey questions, see tables 12.1, 12.2, and 12.3, below.)

This approach provided us with a unique opportunity to probe possible social relationships by analyzing respondents' views toward the same statements. When analyzing academics, we did not separate administrators from faculty. When analyzing businesspersons, we did not separate CEOs from lower level management or management from industrial scientists. We made this decision for technical and substantive reasons. Four categories ("university involved," "university not involved," "industry involved," and "industry not involved") were easier to manage than eight and yielded more powerful statistical results, particularly considering that this was the first study to explore these specific issues empirically. We wanted to focus on similarities and differences between academe and industry as a whole to establish a baseline understanding of these topics. This lack of separation of administrative and faculty responses (and managerial and employee responses) can be viewed as a limitation of the study; we plan to explore possible differences among the views of these two groups in a future study (Campbell & Slaughter, forthcoming).

POTENTIAL CONFLICT AND MISCONDUCT

Through the use of factor analysis, the topics that tap misconduct were grouped into three aspects of potential conflicts: potential conflict of interest, potential conflict of commitment, and potential conflict over internal equity. The factor analysis used an oblique rotation,[11] acknowledging the possibility that the constructs were somewhat related. The correlations were not strong, indicating that distinct concepts had been identified. Scales for each of the three types of conflicts were developed, and the reliabilities of each of these groupings ranged from a standardized alpha of .64 to .75.[12] As discussed previously, because these scales dealt with respondents' views toward potential conflicts created by partnerships between universities and external entities, they have important implications for misconduct, broadly defined.

Results—Potential Conflict of Interest

Summary Scale

Generally, strong isomorphism[13] was found in the responses of collaborative individuals in academe and industry with regard to potential conflict of interest (see figure 12.1). These statements (see table 12.1) portrayed close relationships and illustrated revenue-generating opportunities among universities and firms (Campbell, 1997). Academics involved with industry and businesspersons involved with academe not only demonstrated isomorphism but also responded positively to the scaled measure of potential conflict of interest and, as expected, most of the individual statements composing the summary scale. Academics not involved with firms and businesspersons not involved with academe held views that were distinct from those of their involved colleagues. They were supportive of closer relations with the business community but were not as positive toward increased revenue-generating opportunities as their involved counterparts.

Specifically, survey respondents viewed potential conflict of interest primarily in terms of financial and revenue-generating activities. The responses of those involved were more similar to each other than to the responses of noninvolved individuals, confirming isomorphic influences and suggesting the possible creation of an organizational field that bridges university and business. The following examination of individual statements revealed positive views toward topics that depart from traditional academic norms, suggesting increasing acceptance within the scientific community that might lead to misconduct.

Individual Statements

To identify specific areas that might contribute to a climate of increased potential misconduct, we desegregated the individual statements within the conflict-of-interest scale and examined the respondents' perspectives on each, using analysis of variance. Consistent with findings related to the overall scale, the views of university members involved with industry differed to a statistically significant degree from the views of their noninvolved university colleagues on 9 of 13 items. In the main, the involved academics were

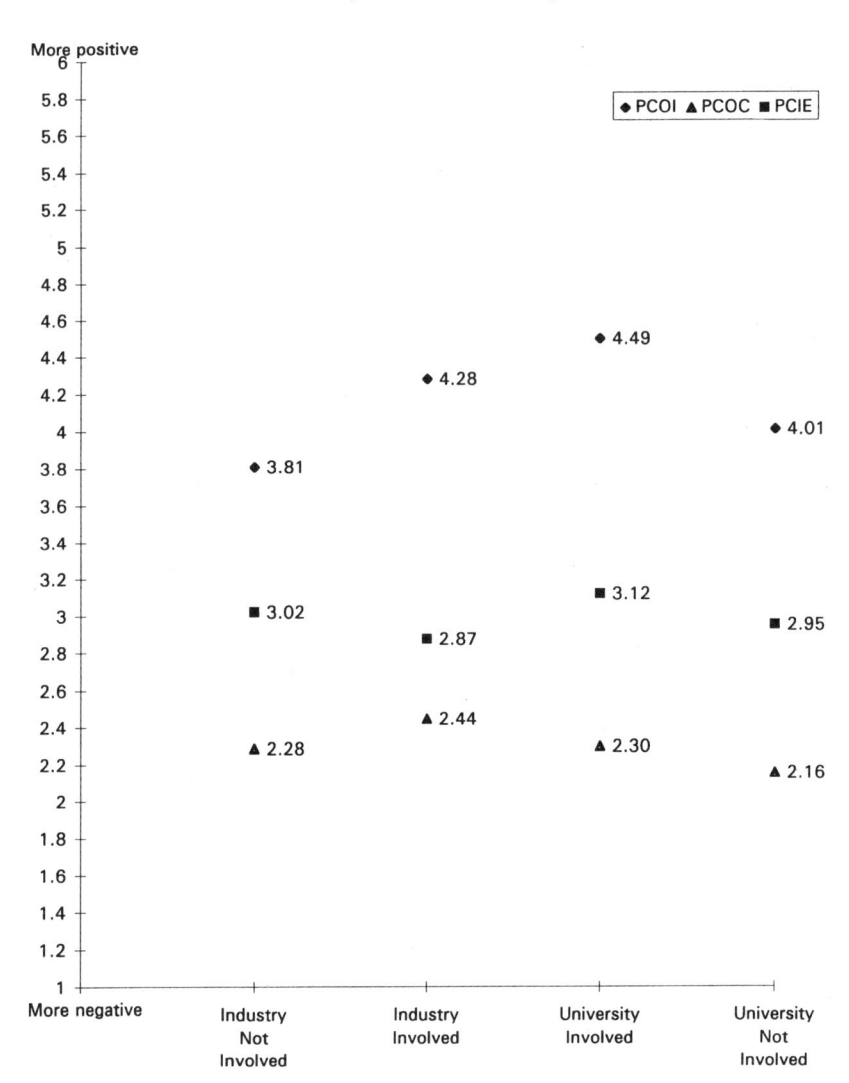

Figure 12.1 Comparison of Responses Based on Involvement

more supportive than the noninvolved academics, to a statistically significant degree, of propositions that presented university-industry relationships as financially beneficial to the organization (items 1, 2, 3, and 11) and more supportive of individual involvement in profit making (items 5, 6, and 7). However, on other items that supported financial interaction between universities, isomorphism between involved academics and involved industry representatives was not found. Since no statistically significant differences were found, all academics were like-minded (items 4, 8, 9, and 10), suggesting a consensus among academics that universities should have the right to retain profits from inventions made by faculty.

These results suggest that the current climate is one in which revenue-generating activity is condoned and patents and licenses are viewed as opportunities for financial gain. Individual profit through royalties and copyrights is viewed more favorably by those involved in collaborative relationships with firms, suggesting increased acceptance of the notion that academics should gain financially from their academic pursuits. If the quest for revenue becomes so resolute that it supersedes adherence to academic norms such as impartiality, replicatability, and objectivity, opportunities for misconduct may increase.

The supportive responses to items 12 and 13 were anticipated on the basis of discussions in the literature. Academics involved with industry were likely to prefer to define their work as part of their service responsibilities; we surmise that this reflects efforts to keep their tripartite role manageable.

Results—Potential Conflict of Commitment

Summary Scale

The statements grouped under potential conflict of commitment (see table 12.2) suggested that respondents think of these topics in terms of academics' commitment to their academic duties vis-à-vis their loyalty to a research sponsor (Campbell, 1997). Statements in this group related to allocation of time, inappropriate influence, and failure on the part of academics to disclose commercial information to the university. Generally, those involved did not demonstrate a uniquely isomorphic response to these items that was distinct from the views of noninvolved participants. Further, all groups tended to be relatively unsupportive of academics who prioritize their loyalty to a sponsor, or commercial concerns, above university duties. The overall nonsupportive response to these items suggests that the potential for misconduct in these areas is relatively low; however, a closer look at perspectives toward individual statements highlights specific areas that might raise questions in the future.

Individual Statements

Involved and noninvolved academics held views that were significantly different toward item 8, suggesting that those involved in partnerships were willing to reduce teaching and other university responsibilities in order to give more attention to industry-sponsored research. This points to a potential for undesirable conduct that is extremely difficult to detect and prove: an academic might pursue grant-seeking and/or other activities that advanced his or her personal financial gain instead of selecting activities that

Table 12.1: Potential Conflict of Interest: Percentage of Respondents Indicating a More Positive View of Statements

Statement	Industry Not Involved (n ≥ 65)	Industry Involved (n ≥ 137)	University Involved (n ≥ 289)	University Not Involved (n ≥ 131)
Industry profit from collaborative research is in the public's interest.	76.7	91.4	85.3‡*	67.4
University income from collaborative research is in the public's interest.	72.5	85.8	93.2†‡	83.7
A university invests the institution's funds to start firms organized by faculty or former students.	12.9	29.7	32.0‡	16.7
A university is involved financially with more than one firm within a specific research area.	58.5	62.8	72.5	63.4
An academic receives more than a third of the royalty from a specific patent while holding a position in the university.	52.9	67.6	79.1‡‡	67.4
An academic receives more than a third of the profits from books s/he authored while holding a position in the university.	72.9	74.4	89.2†*	84.1
Academics should hold patents.	52.9	56.0	80.4‡‡*	78.0
Universities should hold patents.	57.3	69.2	82.1†	75.9
A company retains partial ownership of all research it sponsors, including joint research with universities.	84.3	90.7	65.0†*	61.3
Public institutions should grant exclusive licenses.	33.8	58.8	62.8	56.0

Table 12.1 continued

Statement	Industry Not Involved (n ≥ 65)	Industry Involved (n ≥ 137)	University Involved (n ≥ 289)	University Not Involved (n ≥ 131)
Exclusive licenses should be viewed as promoting mutual interest for both universities and industry to maximize the chance of making the discovery available to the public.	49.3	69.1	77.1‡	67.7
University-industry collaborative activity should be considered part of the public service aspect of academics' responsibilities.	79.1	79.4	82.9‡*	68.1
Academic salaries should be market driven, even if science and engineering professors are paid more than liberal and fine arts professors.	81.2	88.6	83.3‡*	63.1

†Indicates significantly different responses between involved university and involved industry respondents (at the .05 level).
‡Indicates significantly different responses between involved university and noninvolved university respondents (at the .05 level).
*Indicates significantly different responses between noninvolved university and involved industry (at the .05 level).

Table 12.2: Potential Conflict of Commitment: Percentage of Respondents Indicating a More Positive View of Statements

Statement	Industry Not Involved (n ≥ 65)	Industry Involved (n ≥ 137)	University Involved (n ≥ 289)	University Not Involved (n ≥ 131)
An academic engages in outside activities that require more than the usual university allotment of one day per week.	26.1	26.2	24.8	15.9
An academic prioritizes her/his obligations to a for-profit organization above her/his university-related activities.	12.9	12.9	9.4†*	4.3
A company representative prioritizes her/his obligations to a university above her/his company-related activities.	25.7	18.0	17.6	20.9
An academic holds a management position in a company that is related to the academic's area of expertise in the university.	50.0	50.4	50.2	43.5
An academic influences research results to ensure continued sales for a company.	7.1	7.8	4.4	4.3
An academic uses federal money to provide equipment or partial funding to an industry-sponsored activity without the federal agency's approval.	1.4	9.2	5.7	2.9
A company representative knowingly uses the company's support to influence an academic's performance of research.	73.9	35.8	14.0†*	10.4
A company representative influences a cooperative university researcher to give primary attention to the industry-sponsored research and to reduce teaching and other university obligations.	12.9	18.8	18.9‡*	9.6

Table 12.2 continued

Statement	Industry Not Involved (n ≥ 65)	Industry Involved (n ≥ 137)	University Involved (n ≥ 289)	University Not Involved (n ≥ 131)
An academic fails to disclose to the university a substantial interest in any decision, contract, sale, purchase or service related to her/his professional activities.	10.0	6.4	9.7	5.1
An academic fails to disclose patentable information to the university.	7.2	16.3	17.2	18.8

†Indicates significantly different responses between involved university and involved industry respondents (at the .05 level).
‡Indicates significantly different responses between involved university and noninvolved university respondents (at the .05 level).
*Indicates significantly different responses between noninvolved university and involved industry (at the .05 level).

might be beneficial to the academic discipline and the institution. The lukewarm support for this statement made it difficult to determine whether this is an area of increased acceptance of conduct that strays from academic tradition, but the data suggest an emerging climate in which academics must choose between activities that benefit academe and those that offer personal advantages.

Results—Potential Conflict over Internal Equity

Summary Scale

The scale for potential conflict over internal equity (see table 12.3) consisted of statements related to academics' daily work activities, such as teaching and interaction with students, and organizational members' ability to garner significant rewards from within their university or firm (Campbell, 1997). Respondents' views toward these statements were fairly ambivalent, showing neither support nor disapproval. In fact, the most consistent pattern of response demonstrated distinct perspectives between all academics and all industry representatives, particularly when they responded to questions that described the appropriate functions and activities of the opposite sector. The implications for potential difficulties in this area remain unclear, given that responses to these statements were fairly neutral.

Individual Statements

Generally, there were no statistically significant differences in response between involved and noninvolved academics for statements related to considerations of equity within an organization. Only with regard to item 7 did noninvolved academics indicate that they believed that disciplines such as science, medicine, and engineering would be able to sustain their research activities without industry support; this view was significantly different from that of involved academics. The positive view toward this statement suggests that industrial relationships are highly valued and that academics are likely to continue to pursue them. While these findings do not necessarily imply a climate of increased opportunities for misconduct, they do suggest that the academic climate will continue to be one in which concerns of the commercial marketplace are entwined with those of traditional academic norms and duties.

IMPLICATIONS FOR POLICY

At first glance, the recent federal recommendations (U.S. Public Health Service, 1995) to hold institutions accountable for monitoring, admonishing, and minimizing misconduct appear to successfully minimize the potential for misconduct. However, our study points out the possible disconnect in the new approach. Survey responses indicate that mechanisms for collaboration that are created and sanctioned by the institution are supported; they are viewed as appropriate mechanisms for fostering mutually beneficial relations. Faculty members are likely to respond intelligently to these incentives in a manner that provides revenue to the university, their department, students, and themselves. Given this scenario, the organization may find itself in a potential conflict-of-interest situation, since it stands to make money but is also responsible for policing itself. In response to coercive pressures, and to comply with federal regulations, universities are likely to continue supporting separate offices or committees that investigate allegations of misconduct. However, they are also interested in sustaining a relatively constant stream of revenues, and they may decide that it is in their best interest to monitor faculty loosely and handle cases with leniency. This perspective is quite consistent with Turner's contention, in chapter 5 of this book, that such revenues create a reluctance on the part of universities to vigorously pursue allegations of scientific misbehavior. By pushing accountability onto the institutions and relying on occasional audits and the whistleblower industry to point out cases in which institutional systems are inadequate, federal agencies may have inadvertently implemented regulations that provide increased opportunities to obscure misconduct allegations, instead of creating conditions in which institutions can be monitored with greater scrutiny.

CONCLUSION

Respondents supported our hypothesis of isomorphism among individuals across industry and academe who interact regularly with regard to potential conflict of interest only. Academics and businesspersons involved in partnerships offered similar responses toward the issues in the conflict-of-interest scale; these were distinct from the views of those not involved. However, substantively, this simply means that industry-interactive individuals want the university to delve deeper into revenue-generating opportunities. Nevertheless, in the main, all respondents support the notion that universities should gain financially from increased interaction with industry.

Our study did not reveal misconduct per se; instead, four groups of respondents reported their views on university-industry partnerships through items that tapped areas of potential misconduct. What we found was not increased or decreased instances of misconduct but a climate that makes misconduct increasingly possible, given the logic outlined in the introduction to this chapter. While developing ways to meet each other's needs and accepting the new approaches as appropriate, academic conduct may stray from key traditional norms such as objectivity, replicability, and openness, thus multiplying the possibilities for misconduct.

The strength of our study was examining the responses of *all* parties

Table 12.3: Potential Conflict over Internal Equity: Percentage of Respondents Indicating a More Positive View of Statements

Statement	Industry Not Involved (n ≥ 65)	Industry Involved (n ≥ 137)	University Involved (n ≥ 289)	University Not Involved (n ≥ 131)
Company representatives involved in university-industry collaborative activities should be held less accountable to the profitability of the firm than individuals not involved.	17.4	18.4	42.6†*	51.8
Company departments whose employees are involved in university-industry collaborative activities should receive larger budget increases from the firm than departments that are not involved in university-industry activities.	17.3	14.9	43.6†*	32.8
Academics should be able to reduce their course loads as a result of high productivity.	47.1	35.8	72.4†*	63.9
A department does not admit a foreign student to a program because s/he may take sponsored research knowledge to her/his home country upon graduation.	57.1	49.6	31.1†*	26.8
Other members of an academic department should absorb most of an industry-sponsored academic's *public service* responsibilities that are not related to interaction with the sponsoring firm.	32.8	19.1	23.4	18.1
When selecting students to work on university-industry collaborative activities, academics should give primary consideration to the students' ability to hold the study confidential when necessary.	68.0	62.9	45.9†	54.6
Academic units such as science, engineering, and medicine would not be able to conduct significant research without some form of industry sponsorship.	58.9	65.3	70.3‡	53.2

Table 12.3 continued

Statement	Industry Not Involved (n ≥ 65)	Industry Involved (n ≥ 137)	University Involved (n ≥ 289)	University Not Involved (n ≥ 131)
Other members of an academic department should absorb most of an industry-sponsored academic's *teaching* responsibilities.	18.5	12.0	22.8	10.7
Academics involved in university-industry collaborative activities should spend less time with students who are not involved in the project.	25.7	11.3	27.4	19.4

†Indicates significantly different responses between involved university and involved industry respondents (at the .05 level).
‡Indicates significantly different responses between involved university and noninvolved university respondents (at the .05 level).
*Indicates significantly different responses between noninvolved university and involved industry (at the .05 level).

directly or indirectly engaged in university-industry relations (academic involved and not involved, industry involved and noninvolved) to the items on our questionnaire. By studying all four groups, we were able to see points of convergence and divergence within the two types of organizations—universities and corporations—that are not revealed when the aggregate data are studied. We found evidence of isomorphism on the part of academics and businesspersons involved in university-industry partnerships on issues related to conflict of interest but not on issues related to conflict of commitment or conflict over internal equity. We highlighted areas in which the opportunities for misconduct are multiplied. At this point, qualitative case studies may be needed to further our understanding of these increasingly complex issues.

Notes

This research was supported in part by a grant from the National Science Foundation, and we express appreciation to the Research on Science and Technology Program. However, the opinions, findings, conclusions, and recommendations contained in this paper are our own and do not necessarily reflect the views of the National Science Foundation.

    1. Louis et al. (1995) found a higher incidence of misconduct than expected, although they did not have empirical evidence from earlier days to serve as a basis for comparison. In addition, a recent barrage of articles has highlighted numerous cases of alleged misconduct (Blumenstyk, 1993a, 1993b, 1993c, 1993d; Carey, 1992, 1994; Cordes, 1992, 1993a, 1993b, 1993c, 1993d, 1993e, 1993f, 1994; Gross, 1993; Jaschik, 1993; Marshall, 1995; Nicklin, 1993; Ponce, 1994; Solomon, 1993; Wheeler, 1993).
    2. The SPSS statistical package was used for all analyses in this study.
    3. Academics who were involved with firms and/or industry representatives who worked with universities were identified as participating in partnerships, or termed "collaborative," if, in response to the statement "I am currently involved in activities related to the following (please check all that apply)," they checked one or more of the following:

___ Consulting with a company
___ Contractual activities with a company
___ Collaborative research activity with a company
___ Negotiations regarding the licensing of university discoveries
___ Economic development
___ Industrial advisory board(s)
___ Industrial affiliates program(s)
___ University-industry research center(s)
___ Incubator(s)
___ Industrial park(s)

___ University-based institute(s)
___ Joint ownership of facilities with a university
___ Researcher exchange programs between universities and industry

This view of involvement embraces the broad spectrum of university-industry relationships that is discussed in the literature.

4. The term *coercive* is used, not in the negative sense of inappropriate influence, but to describe the federal, state, and local pressures to which an organization is required to respond.

5. It should be noted that private universities, proprietary schools, and community colleges were not included in this study. Private universities are often established for an expressed purpose (e.g., explicit goals of interaction with firms and economic development, religious purposes, or support of the causes of particular benefactors), thus complicating the potential responses of individuals from these institutions. To keep the focus on universities supported by taxpayer dollars expected to uphold the public's trust, and to be very clear in this initial exploration of potential conflicts topics, we included only public institutions in this study.

6. This total of 86 colleges and universities reflects the fact that fewer than 12 public institutions fell under some of the Carnegie classifications (e.g., Liberal Arts II).

7. In this study, institutional differences were not tested, which may be a limitation of the study.

8. For more information about disciplinary differences, see Braxton and Hargens (1997).

9. Evaluating responses at one point in time compared with responses received at a later point in time is a widely used method to check for potential errors in measurement (Rossi, Wright, & Anderson, 1989). To ensure that the results were reliable, wave 1 and wave 2 respondents were compared using cross tabulation and chi-squared statistics for a number of key characteristics, including involvement in collaborative activity, income level, age range, position in the organization, and field of specialization. No substantive differences were found, thus verifying that the resulting sample is representative of the targeted population and is reliable. These analyses also demonstrated that further solicitation of responses through additional waves would not yield a different set of responses.

10. For a copy of the survey instruments, please refer to Campbell (1995) or Campbell and Slaughter (1995).

11. Since this was the first attempt at developing scales for potential conflicts, and since the literature frequently addresses a diverse array of potential conflicts issues in tandem, we felt it was most appropriate to allow the statements to be somewhat correlated, rather than requiring them to be independent (in which case they would have been rotated orthogonally). We were more interested in explaining the different potential conflict constructs than in developing a measurement tool to be used in regression or other parametric analyses.

12. Nunnally (1978) supports the acceptability of these alphas.

13. In an endeavor to capture specific aspects of isomorphism that might

explain perspectives related to conflicts, several questions were included in the survey. A factor analysis was conducted to develop a summary scale of the responses to these questions. These measures proved to be problematic, despite best efforts to develop a summary scale for isomorphism. The reliabilities for industry respondents were not sufficiently strong to justify the use of the summary scale. Therefore, this study relied heavily on the lack of a statistically significant difference in response at the .05 level as an indicator of isomorphism.

References

America's most valuable companies. (1993, April 2). *Business Week* (Special Bonus Issue), pp. 118–163.

Barber, B. (1952). *Science and the social order*. New York: Free Press.

Blumenstyk, G. (1993a, March 31). Business and philanthropy notes. *Chronicle of Higher Education, 39*, A26.

Blumenstyk, G. (1993b, February 10). Boston U's president and trustees face questions about business practices and conflicts of interest. *Chronicle of Higher Education, 39*, A27.

Blumenstyk, G. (1993c, February 24). Colleges eye more-rigorous policies to guard against conflicts of interest. *Chronicle of Higher Education, 39*, A29.

Blumenstyk, G. (1993d, January 27). Financial relationships at Boston U. said to be subject of investigation. *Chronicle of Higher Education, 39*, A25.

Blumenthal, D., Causino, N., & Louis, K. S. (1996, February 8). Relationships between academic institutions and industry in the life sciences: An industry survey. *New England Journal of Medicine, 334*, 368–373.

Blumenthal, D., Gluck, M., Seashore Louis, K., & Wise, D. (1986a). Industrial support of university research in biotechnology. *Science, 23*, 242–246.

Blumenthal, D., Gluck, M., Seashore Louis, K., & Wise, D. (1986b). University-industry research relationships in biotechnology: Implications for the university. *Science, 23*, 1361–1366.

Bok, D. (1982). *Beyond the ivory tower: Social responsibilities of the modern university*. Cambridge, MA: Harvard University Press.

Bok, D. (1993). University professors. In D. Bok, *The cost of talent* (pp. 155–177). New York: Free Press.

Braxton, J. M. (1986). The normative structure of science: Social control in the academic profession. In J. C. Smart (Ed.), *Higher education: Handbook of theory and research* (Vol. 2, pp. 309–357). New York: Agathon.

Braxton, J. M., & Hargens, L. E. (1997). Variation among academic disciplines: Analytical frameworks and research. In J. C. Smart (Ed.), *Higher education: Handbook of theory and research* (Vol. 3, pp. 1–46). New York: Agathon.

Business-Higher Education Forum. (1983). *America's competitive challenge: The need for a national response*. Washington, DC: Author.

Business-Higher Education Forum. (1986, January). *An action agenda for American competitiveness*. Washington, DC: Author.

Business-Higher Education Forum. (1988). *Beyond the rhetoric: Evaluating university-industry cooperation in research and technology exchange*. Washington, DC: Author.

Buzzelli, D. E. (1996, May 17). Letter to the editor. *Science, 272*, 937.
Campbell, T. I. D. (1995). Protecting the public's trust: A search for balance among benefits and conflicts in university-industry relationships. *Dissertation Abstracts International.* UMI Order Number: AAC 9531129.
Campbell, T. I. D. (1997, Summer). Public policy for the 21st century: Addressing potential conflicts in university-industry relationships. *Review of Higher Education, 20*, 357–379.
Campbell, T. I. D., & Slaughter, S. (1995). *Final technical report to the National Science Foundation.* (Available upon request from the Center for the Study of Higher Education, University of Arizona, Education 327, Tucson, AZ 85721, 520–621–7951.)
Campbell, T. I. D., & Slaughter, S. (Forthcoming). Faculty and administrators' attitudes toward potential conflicts of interest, commitment, and equity in university-industry relationships. *Journal of Higher Education.*
Carey, J. (1992, April 20). A think tank for, er, "competitiveness." *Business Week,* p. 90.
Carey, J. (1994, March 7). Could America afford the transistor today? *Business Week,* pp. 80–84.
Carnegie Foundation for the Advancement of Teaching. (1987). *A classification of institutions of higher education.* Lawrenceville, NJ: Princeton University Press.
Chomsky, N. (1994). *World orders old and new.* New York: Columbia University Press.
Cordes, C. (1992, September 16). Debate flares over growing pressures on academe for ties with industry. *Chronicle of Higher Education, 39,* A26.
Cordes, C. (1993a, September 8). As chairman of key house committee restates his vision, scientists worry. *Chronicle of Higher Education, 40,* A26.
Cordes, C. (1993b, June 23). NIH to develop guidelines for research agreements that universities sign with private companies. *Chronicle of Higher Education, 39,* A21.
Cordes, C. (1993c, September 1). President Clinton's support encourages experiments in government-industry efforts to promote technology. *Chronicle of Higher Education, 40,* A32.
Cordes, C. (1993d, January 20). A quiet debate emerges: Can a college's financial ties skew research backed by U.S.? *Chronicle of Higher Education, 39,* A22.
Cordes, C. (1993e, March 3). Research project on ear infections dramatizes challenge of conflicts. *Chronicle of Higher Education, 39,* A23.
Cordes, C. (1993f, September 22). Universities angered by U.S. proposal to deny them patents on some research. *Chronicle of Higher Education, 40,* A26.
Cordes, C. (1994, January 19). University patents barred. *Chronicle of Higher Education, 40,* A29.
Dickson, D. (1984). *The new politics of science.* Cambridge: MIT Press.
DiMaggio, P. J. & Powell, W. W. (1983, April). The iron cage revisited: Institutional isomorphism and collective rationality in organizational fields. *American Sociological Review, 48,* 147–160.
Etzkowitz, H. (1983). Entrepreneurial scientists and entrepreneurial universities in American academic science. *Minerva, 21,* 198–233.

Fairweather, J. S. (1988). *Entrepreneurship and higher education: Lessons for colleges, universities, and industry* (ASHE-ERIC Higher Education Rep. No. 6). Washington, DC: Association for the Study of Higher Education.

Fassin, Y. (1991). Academic ethos versus business ethics. *International Journal of Technology Management, 6*, 533–546.

Geisler, E., & Rubenstein, A. H. (1989). University-industry relations: A review of major issues. In A. N. Link & G. Tassey (Eds.), *Cooperative research and development: The industry, university, government relationship* (pp. 43–62). Boston: Kluwer.

Government-University-Industry Research Roundtable (GUIRR) & Industrial Research Institute (IRI). (1991, February). *Industrial perspectives on innovation and interactions with universities.* Washington, DC: National Academy Press.

Grinnel, F. (1996, April 19). Ambiguity in the practice of science. *Science, 272*, 333.

Gross, N. (1993, May 24). Patent showdown pending. *Business Week*, pp. 96–100.

Hackett, E. J. (1990, May-June). Science as a vocation in the 1990s: The changing organizational culture of academic science. *Journal of Higher Education, 61*, 241–277.

Halstead, K. (1990). *Higher education revenues and expenditures.* Washington, DC: Research Associates of Washington.

Jaschik, S. (1993, February 24). Administration plans upper limit on overhead charges. *Chronicle of Higher Education, 40*, A24.

Kaiser, J. (1995, December 1). Panel urges new approach to inquiries. *Science, 270*, 1431.

Kenney, M. (1986a). Chaos and opportunity: The universities respond. In M. Kenney (Ed.), *Biotechnology: The university-industrial complex* (pp. 73–89). New Haven, CT: Yale University Press.

Kenney, M. (1986b). Professors as entrepreneurs. In M. Kenney (Ed.), *Biotechnology: The university-industrial complex* (pp. 90–106). New Haven, CT: Yale University Press.

Krimsky, S., Ennis, J., & Weissman, R. (1991). Academic-corporate ties in biotechnology: A quantitative study. *Science, Technology, and Human Values, 16*, 275–287.

Lee, Y. (Forthcoming). "Technology transfer" and the research university: A search for the boundaries of university-industry collaboration. *Research Policy.*

Leslie, L. L., & Brinkman, P. T. (1988). *The economic value of higher education.* New York: Macmillan.

Letcher, M. A., & Lang, S. (1991). *Intellectual property handbook.* Phoenix, AZ: Streich-Lang Professional Attorneys Association.

Louis, K. S., Anderson, M. S., & Rosenberg, L. (1995, Summer). Academic misconduct and values: The department's influence. *Review of Higher Education, 18*, 393–422.

Luton, L., & Zinke, R. (1989, Fall). The costs of competitiveness: A reminder. *Policy Studies Journal, 18*, 203–212.

Mangelsdorf, M. E. (1992, October). The 1992 Inc. 500. *Inc.*, pp. 71–143.

Marshall, E. (1995, December). Suit alleges misuse of peer review. *Science, 270,* 1912–1914.
Merton, R. K. (1957). *Social theory and social structure* (rev. ed.). New York: Free Press.
Merton, R. K., & Barber, E. (1963). Sociological ambivalence. In E. A. Tiryakian (Ed.), *Sociological theory, values and sociocultural change* (pp. 91–120). Glencoe, IL: Free Press.
Mervis, J. (1995, March 17). Walker tells universities to look for help from industry. *Science, 267,* 1590.
Mitroff, I. (1974, August). Norms and counternorms in a select group of Apollo moon scientists. *American Sociological Review, 39,* 579–595.
National Science Foundation. (1993). *Federal funds for research and development: Federal obligations for research by agency and detailed field of science and engineering, fiscal years 1971–1993.* Washington, DC: Author.
Nicklin, J. L. (1993, May 26). Many Fortune 500 companies curtail donations to higher education. *Chronicle of Higher Education, 39,* A25.
Nunnally, J. C. (1978). *Psychometric theory.* New York: McGraw-Hill.
Olson, S. (1995). *On being a scientist: Responsible conduct in research* (2nd ed.). Washington, DC: National Academy Press.
Peters, L. S., & Etzkowitz, H. (1990). University-industry connections and academic values. *Technology in Society, 12,* 427–440.
Peters, L. S., & Fusfeld, H. I., et al. (1983). Current U.S. university/industry research connections. In National Science Board, *University-industry research relationships: Selected studies.* Washington, DC: National Science Foundation.
Ponce, P. E. (1994, January 19). State legislator's financial ties to Ohio state university rekindle debate. *Chronicle of Higher Education, 40,* A29.
R&D scoreboard. (1993, June 28). *Business Week,* pp. 105–127.
Reams, B. D., Jr. (1986). *University-industry research partnerships: The major legal issues in research and development agreements.* Westport, CT: Quorum.
Rossi, P. H., Wright, J. D., & Anderson, A. B. (Eds.). (1989). *Handbook of survey research.* New York: Academic Press.
Sanford, T. (1982). The university and technology: New paths and new perspectives. In R. Goldscheider & T. Arnold (Eds.), *The law of business and licensing* (pp. 1–67). New York: Clark Boardman.
Seashore Louis, K., Blumenthal, D., Gluck, M. E., & Stoto, M. A. (1989). Entrepreneurs in academe: An exploration of behaviors among life scientists. *Administrative Science Quarterly, 34,* 110–131.
Schaffer, E. (1990, Winter). The university in service to technocracy. *Educational Theory, 30*(1), 47–52.
Slaughter, S. (1988). Academic freedom in the modern university. In P. G. Altback & R. O. Berdahl (Eds.), *Higher education in American society* (pp. 77–105). Buffalo, NY: Prometheus.
Slaughter, S. (1990). *The higher learning and high technology: Dynamics of higher education policy formation.* Albany: State University of New York Press.
Slaughter, S. (1993a, Summer). Beyond basic science: Research university presi-

dents' narratives of science policy. *Science, Technology, and Human Values, 18,* 278–302.

Slaughter, S. (1993b, May/June). Retrenchment in the 1980s: The politics of prestige and gender. *Journal of Higher Education, 64,* 250–282.

Slaughter, S., & Leslie, L. L. (1997). *Academic capitalism.* Baltimore: Johns Hopkins University Press.

Slaughter, S., & Rhoades, G. (1990). Re-norming the social relations of science: Technology transfer. *Educational Policy, 4,* 341–361.

Slaughter, S., & Rhoades, G. (1991a, April). Professors, administrators, and patents: the negotiation of technology transfer. *Sociology of Education, 64,* 65–77.

Slaughter, S., & Rhoades, G. (1991b). The public interest and professional labor: Research universities. In W. Tierney (Ed.), *Culture and ideology in higher education* (pp. 187–211). New York: Praeger.

Slaughter, S., & Rhoades, G. (1996, Summer). The emergence of a competitiveness research and development policy coalition and the commercialization of academic science and technology. *Science, Technology, and Human Values, 54,* 303–339.

Solomon, J. (1993, June 7). The grand pilferer? *Newsweek,* pp. 38–39.

Stewart, G. H., & Gibson, D. V. (1990). University and industry linkages: The Austin, Texas study. In F. Williams & D. V. Gibson (Eds.), *Technology transfer: A communication perspective* (pp. 109–129). Newbury Park, CA: Sage.

Stone, R. S. (1995, January 27). Federal panel recommends universities play bigger role. *Science, 267,* 449.

Storer, N. W. (1966). *The social system of science.* New York: Holt, Rinehart & Winston.

U.S. Public Health Service. (1989, August 8). Responsibilities of awardee and applicant institutions for dealing with and reporting possible misconduct in science. *Federal Register, 54,* 32446.

U.S. Public Health Service. (1995). *Integrity and misconduct in research: Report of the Commission on Research Integrity.* Washington, DC: U.S. Department of Health and Human Services.

Webster, A. (1991). *Science, technology, and society: New directions.* New York: Macmillan.

Wheeler, D. L. (1993, February 24). A case study: One scientist's ties to a biotechnology company. *Chronicle of Higher Education, 39,* A29.

Wood, F. Q. (1992). The commercialisation of university research in Australia: Issues and problems. *Comparative Education, 28,* 293–313.

Zinberg, D. (1985). The legacy of success: Changing relationships in university-based scientific research in the United States. In M. Gibbons & B. Wittrock (Ed.), *Science as a commodity* (pp. 107–127). Essex, UK: Longman.

Zuckerman, D. (1993, October 13). Why has NIH done nothing to minimize conflict of interest? *Chronicle of Higher Education, 49,* B1-B2.

CHAPTER THIRTEEN

Uncovering the Covert: Research on Academic Misconduct

Melissa S. Anderson

The literature on academic misconduct is dominated by essays and exposés, with relatively little empirical analysis. In the essays, by far the most common complaint is that we do not know much about the extent or prevalence of misconduct, even though it is probably impossible to get satisfactory estimates. The exposés tend to detail such flagrant misconduct that it is easy to dismiss the perpetrators as mentally imbalanced (Broad & Wade, 1982). The academic community tends not to find much relevance in such literature, which emphasizes the unknowable and the fantastic.

This chapter suggests some directions for *empirical* research on misconduct, with the aim of encouraging not only more empirical analysis but, more importantly, analysis that has direct relevance to the academy and its affiliates and usefulness for those who struggle with issues related to misconduct in academic settings. The chapter begins with a review of misconduct and related issues, with attention to their rich potential as topics of empirical research. It then presents an expanded view of misconduct to suggest more complex relationships for analysis, which is followed by a consideration of the difficulties involved in pursuing research on these relationships. It concludes with recommendations for a research agenda on misconduct and related issues.[1]

ELEMENTS OF THE STUDY OF MISCONDUCT

Most instances of academic misconduct become known through stories, published or told. This section uses the elements of these stories as the basis for a simple model of misconduct in relation to other issues. The focal point

Context → Misconduct → Exposure → Consequences

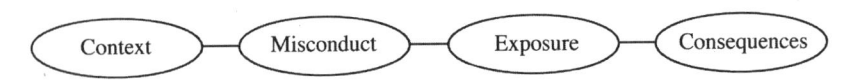

Figure 13.1 A Simple Model of Misconduct

of stories about academic misconduct is the misconduct itself: we find out what the perpetrator did. Next comes some basic information about the context of the misconduct—that is, the relevant facts about the field of study, the institution, the kind of work in which the perpetrator was involved, and the circumstances surrounding the incident or pattern of misconduct. There may follow a discussion of the way the misconduct was exposed: who blew the whistle or how it became known through other means. Finally, if the storyteller does not indicate something about the consequences, the listeners will surely follow up with "So, what happened?" Putting these four elements in their logical order produces the simple misconduct model shown in figure 13.1. It represents in a general way the effects that context has on various aspects of misconduct, which in turn affect the way the misconduct is exposed, which then leads to certain consequences. The remainder of this section addresses the research potential of each separate element of this simple model, beginning with misconduct itself.

Misconduct

There are differing views as to what misconduct should or does signify or encompass (Buzzelli, 1993a, 1993b; Culliton, 1994; Schachman, 1993; Woolf, 1991; Zwolenik, 1992). The Public Health Service definition of misconduct in science is "fabrication, falsification, plagiarism, [FFP] or other practices that seriously deviate from those that are commonly accepted within the scientific community for proposing, conducting, or reporting research" (U.S. Department of Health and Human Services, 1989, p. 32447). Some would confine scientific misconduct to FFP as relatively easily identified, confirmed, and sanctioned (Kaiser, 1995; Schachman, 1993). Others argue that the special focus on FFP is too narrow because many other forms of misbehavior have at least as much potential to damage the research enterprise (Buzzelli, 1993a). Still others maintain that the mention of deviations from commonly accepted practices is too vague, especially because such deviations may be appropriate or even laudable aspects of creative research efforts, without which little progress in science would occur (Committee on Science, Engineering, and Public Policy, 1995, p. 18; Goodstein, 1991, p. 509). The Report of the Panel on Scientific Responsibility and the Conduct of Research (Panel, 1992) identified three categories of concern: misconduct as FFP, questionable research practices, and other misconduct (pp. 24–30).

Another definition is presented in the report of the Commission on Research Integrity (1995): "Research misconduct is significant misbehavior that improperly appropriates the intellectual property or contributions of others, that intentionally impedes the progress of research, or that risks corrupting the scientific record or compromising the integrity of scientific practices" (p. 13). This definition introduces the condition of intention, which is somewhat problematic in practice. Marcel LaFollette (1992) argued that intention is a critical aspect of misconduct (p. 36; see also Pallone & Hennessy, 1995, pp. 12–14), but intention to deceive or injure others can be very difficult to prove (Panel, 1992, p. 25).

Complaints that we do not know how much academic misconduct exists abound (Knoll, 1992). The matter of prevalence is not dismissed by Daniel Koshland's (1987) famous statement that "99.9999 percent of [scientific] reports are accurate and truthful" (p. 141); no more useful is the argument some have made that science is completely untainted because whatever is untruthful lies, by definition, outside the realm of science (David, 1993, p. 177; LaFollette, 1992, p. 17). Paul Friedman (1992) claimed that disagreement about the meaning of misconduct is the main reason why we do not know how much of it exists, and Fox and Braxton (1994) noted that such ambiguity attenuates social control of the ethical aspects of academic work (p. 378). Donald Buzzelli (1992) pointed out the difficulties involved in measuring misconduct (see also Woolf, 1988). However, even restricting attention to only one or two of the most readily identifiable forms of misconduct leaves major problems in the analysis of incidence and prevalence of misconduct (Panel, 1992, chap. 4; see Lee, 1993, p. 46, on the difference between incidence and prevalence). In Zuckerman's (1988) oft-quoted words: "The absence of data on the incidence of deviance means that there is no social epidemiology of deviance in science—no systematic analysis of its distribution, sources, or control" (p. 523; see also Pallone & Hennessy, 1995, p. 8; Panel, 1992, p. 95). Both the low-prevalence ("bad apple") and high-prevalence ("tip of the iceberg") views have their proponents (Woolf, 1988), but it is likely that actual prevalence reflects some intermediate level that no one has yet been able to identify.

Many people wring their hands over this state of affairs, and others try to get empirical data about the scope of misconduct. A few survey-based studies have sought information from academic researchers on experiences with or exposure to misconduct (American Association for the Advancement of Science, 1991; Davis, 1989; Gillespie, Chubin, & Kurzon, 1985; Lock, 1988; St. James-Roberts, 1976; Sigma Xi, 1989; Swazey, Anderson, & Louis, 1993; Tangney, 1987), and there have also been studies based on surveys of students (e.g., Daniel, Adams, & Smith, 1994; Kalichman & Friedman, 1992). Another approach is represented in the Commission on Research Integrity's report, which reflects Drummond Rennie's (1989) call for "data audits" in recommending that funded research for scholarship, teaching, and research in scientific ethics include "an experimental audit of the prevalence of data misrepresentation" (Commission, 1995, p. 36). Perhaps more useful than counts or rates of misconduct would be analyses of distributions and trends of particular kinds of misconduct (Mazur, 1989). Even such basic information is not easily come by, though, given the covert nature of misconduct. Paul Friedman (1992) argued that the prevalence of misconduct is "known to within an order of magnitude" (p. 154), which suffices for all practical purposes (see chapter 4 of this volume for a rejoinder; see also Mosteller, 1977). As the Panel on Scientific Responsibility and the Conduct of Research (1992) noted, however, "Every case of misconduct in science is serious and requires action" (p. 9; see also LaFollette, 1994, p. 7). It does not take many publicized cases to damage science's credibility with the public (Broad & Wade, 1982, p. 12).

A different approach to misconduct is suggested by the link between misconduct and appropriate conduct. Thinking about misconduct as a violation of a standard, rule, law, or other behavioral imperative links it explicitly and usefully to the evolving normative bases of academic research. Consider Ivor Pritchard's (1993) perspective:

> A conception of *good* scientific conduct logically precedes that of scientific *mis*conduct. Scientific misconduct consists of violations of standards of good scientific behavior, and ignorance of those standards makes it impossible to form consistent and reliable judgments about when and how they are transgressed. Furthermore, misconduct does not possess the same kind of internal coherence as good conduct, making it much more difficult—or perhaps impossible—to provide a manageable set of criteria for directly identifying instances of misconduct. The relationship between good and bad scientific conduct is *asymmetrical:* There are many more ways to do science badly than there are to do it well. (p. S68)

But even as Pritchard referred misconduct back to rules (see also List, 1985), J. D. Douglas (1993) pointed out that rules necessarily imply violations: "One of the crucial facts about deviance is that wherever you have rules you have violations. . . . Societies and social groups do not teach and invoke rules that are not violated" (p. S82). Perhaps the best inference we can draw is that the critical locus for research is at the margin, in the gray areas where right behavior and misconduct are not so easily separated. We need to understand more about the *process* by which academic researchers distinguish between acceptable and unacceptable actions and deal with the ambiguity between them in the course of normal, everyday research. As Friedman (1992) put it, we need "a broader perspective on how good scientists make the decisions that they do" (p. 156).

But what kind of research does this perspective suggest? The focus on process suggests that the appropriate site for investigation is the place where these issues come up, in laboratories or offices or field locations—in short, in the messy and turbulent world of academic work. Here one can study the wide variety of things that go wrong at the frontier of knowledge and the ways in which researchers cope with such problems. The advancement of knowledge does not normally proceed smoothly. Zuckerman (1977) quoted Peter Medawar's blunt assessment: "if one wants to find out what scientists actually do, with all the episodes of fumblings, errors, and faulty reasoning that often occur before the work is written up for publication, it is no use looking to scientific 'papers,' for they not merely conceal but actively misrepresent the reasoning that goes into the work they describe" (p. 124). Goodstein (1991) cited a number of standard euphemisms (such as "owing to difficulties in sample handling," meaning "we dropped it on the floor"; p. 514) that reflect the turbulence of the research process.

Misconduct and Error in the Research Process

	Intentional	Not Intentional
Not Acceptable	Misconduct	Avoidable Error
Acceptable	Minor Hypocrisies	Inadvertent Error

Here, then, is a key point for those who would study misconduct in the research process: research unavoidably involves error. As Leibel (1991) put it, "Finally, science, the process, needs to concede not just that scientists will sometimes make mistakes, but that inadvertent error is a normal part of the process no matter how careful one tries to be, and that it is not necessarily shameful to be wrong. I don't mean sloppy or shoddy, just plain incorrect" (p. 604). Such inadvertent errors (what Chubin & Hackett, 1990, p. 128, referred to as "honest errors") differ from misconduct in two important respects. First, they are not intentional but are the kind of mistakes of which researchers are not aware and that, when found, researchers are eager to correct. In contrast, misconduct generally involves some degree of intentionality, even if intention appears only obliquely—for example, as a wanton disregard for proper procedures. Second, inadvertent errors are acceptable in the sense that they are unavoidable and expected, albeit demanding of immediate correction, while real misconduct is never acceptable. In a strict sense, it is only intentional, unacceptable behavior that qualifies as misconduct.

Consider, however, the other possibilities characterized by intention and acceptability as illustrated in the chart above. Misconduct and "inadvertent error" (Leibel, 1991) appear in opposite corners of the diagram. Incompetence or carelessness can lead to actions that are not necessarily intentional but are not acceptable either, labeled here as "avoidable error." This kind of error may arise, for example, when researchers rely on methodologies whose details they do not fully understand. Finally, intentional misbehavior that falls in the generally acceptable category is called, to use Goodstein's (1991) phrase, "minor hypocrisies." To illustrate, an experienced researcher may realize that he or she has computed certain statistics from a large data set that includes three cases that should have been omitted. Knowing that removing the three cases would change the statistics minutely and would in no way affect the results, the researcher might not rerun the statistical analyses with the three cases omitted.

In this intention/acceptability scheme, intention distinguishes misbehavior from error. Within the error category, there is the further distinction between acceptable and unacceptable error, or what Zuckerman (1977) has called "reputable" versus "disreputable" error (p. 110; see also Zuckerman, 1988, p. 521). The difference between minor hypocrisies and misconduct lies largely in the seriousness of the offense, from what Goodstein (1991) referred to as "harmless fudging" (p. 514) to full-scale fabrication of data.

What is the relevance of these other categories to the analysis of misconduct? Obviously, extending observation and analysis to these categories expands the potential for research, since errors and minor misrepresentations are far more common than genuine misconduct, but there is no advantage here if misconduct is entirely distinct from the other activities. The point is that these other activities are not only directly relevant but particularly valuable for the study of misconduct, for the following reasons.

First, distinctions between intentional and unintentional actions are often blurred, and intentionality of another's actions is notoriously difficult to establish, particularly in research settings. Investigations of some of the most famous cases of alleged misconduct (e.g., the Baltimore case) have been complicated by inconclusive evidence of intentional wrongdoing as opposed to incompetence, represented here as avoidable error. In cases of grossly unacceptable behavior, the relative contributions of intentionality and incompetence may be entirely irrelevant. Acceptability is likewise indeterminate, not only subject to interpretation but also affected by disciplinary standards and other contextual factors. Thus, misconduct of various forms occupies no established position, as figure 13.2 might suggest, but ranges along the two continua of intentionality and acceptability, subject to interpretation and contextual norms. Investigation of less flagrant forms of misconduct, even those that merge into the realms of error or acceptability, will shed light on the process by which misconduct emerges and develops.

Second, from a process perspective, all of the categories of action in the error and responsibility chart have to be dealt with in appropriate ways for the integrity of science to be maintained. Science is compromised by both error and misconduct. Indeed, in the early stages of investigation, misconduct is often treated as error, giving the perpetrator the benefit of the doubt

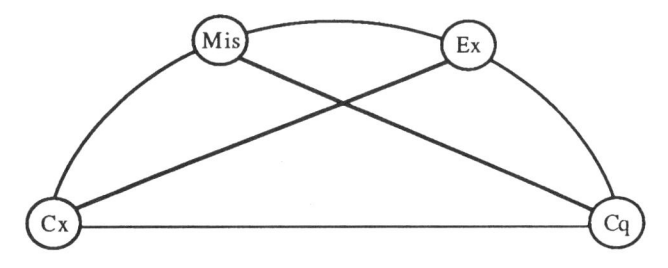

Figure 13.2 Interactive Effects among Context, Misconduct, Exposure, and Consequences

(see, e.g., Broad & Wade, 1982, chaps. 4 and 5), and the process of ongoing misconduct and exposure may not be substantially different from the process of ongoing error and correction, at least from the standpoint of everyone but the perpetrator. Much can be learned, therefore, from observation of processes that fall short of strict characterizations of misconduct.

Third, locating misconduct in a space defined by the two continua of intentionality and acceptability links it to the normal process of academic research. At the opposite extreme is inadvertent error, which is pervasive in research, at least in its minor forms. Nearly all researchers are very good at identifying and dealing with problems at this extreme; indeed, they do so routinely. Researchers and administrators alike, however, are notoriously inept at addressing genuine misconduct at the other extreme. One of the reasons is that it is viewed as something completely foreign, incomprehensible, and dissociated from normal academic work. It is easy to understand why scholars with integrity would want to dissociate themselves and their work from the worst cases of fraud, and indeed their everyday errors are many steps removed from full-blown misconduct. But it is not helpful, either in the abstract or in the critical administrative/policy deliberative arenas, to ignore the full range of problems in the research process, of which presumably rare misconduct and pervasive inadvertent error represent the extremes.

Consider, for example, the value of investigations of the research process that would focus on the ways in which academics identify and deal with error, mistakes, and other problems; determine the difference between acceptable and unacceptable courses of action; decide how much of a given problem has to be fixed to make the outcome acceptable to the scholarly community; develop working understandings of standards and margins of error in project or research groups; negotiate rationales for specific actions in the face of ethically ambiguous circumstances; interpret the norms and standards of a disciplinary field in the context of a given project; work out inconsistencies between ideals of conduct in research and demands of external funders; extend principles of research behavior to previously unimagined research contexts; transmit normative assumptions implicitly and directly to students and other apprentices; and otherwise cope with the indeterminacies of ethical action as a natural part of the research process. This kind of process-oriented research agenda would make a considerable contribution to the study of misconduct and many related issues.

Another research direction related to misconduct itself is suggested by the general principle that deception begets deception (J. D. Douglas, 1993, p. S82; Downes & Rock, 1982, p. 27). The perpetrator must maintain a stream of deceptions as well as a parallel stream of behaviors that preserve a front of legitimacy and conformity (D. J. Douglas, 1972). Analyses of such parallel streams might suggest weak points, opportunities for exposure, or characteristic clues of misconduct, not to benefit future perpetrators but to alert others who might be in a position to observe similar cases.

Context

The second element in a typical misconduct story is the immediate context of the incident. The most basic contextual elements are academic discipline, institution, nature of the research task, and the immediate circumstances. In the story, the role of context is to clarify what actually happened and to describe the situation in which it was possible for the misconduct to arise. In research on misconduct, the role of these contextual elements becomes critical in addressing such questions as "What factors permit or encourage misconduct of various kinds?" or even "What causes misconduct?"

There is evidence that context affects the way academic work is carried out and the incentives or risks associated with misconduct of various kinds. Disciplinary context matters (Fox, 1990): fields with laboratory-based research offer different opportunities for misconduct than, say, disciplines that employ field-based methods (Zuckerman, 1977, 1988). There are considerable differences among institutions in level of regulatory oversight and administrative support. Departmental climate, networks of colleagues, and power and status hierarchies are all part of the complex role played by context in situations of academic misconduct (Anderson, Louis, & Earle, 1994; Zuckerman, 1988). On the basis of their analyses of misconduct cases, Broad and Wade (1982) argued that context is a critical element in misconduct: "The roots of fraud lie in the barrel, not in the bad apples that occasionally roll into public view" (p. 87).

Most analyses of contextual effects, however, have been based on ex post facto reconstructions of the circumstances surrounding a research project. Observers are generally not on hand to document major cases of misconduct as they unfold. The problem with latter-day studies is that it is difficult to determine which contextual elements were really relevant to a particular misconduct episode. Comparative analyses of misconduct in different disciplines, institutions, or types of research may suggest connections between contextual factors and misconduct but may leave out some of the most critical aspects of context for particular misconduct episodes.

On-site studies of scientific work are likely to prove valuable in sorting out contextual effects in that the role of context can be examined more closely. Such studies might focus on the ways in which certain methodologies lend themselves to misconduct, on the influence of departmental or institutional standards or culture on ethical behavior, or on the effects of specific procedures and forms of accountability on research decisions that have ethical dimensions. It would take many such studies and careful comparative analyses to draw reliable conclusions about actual contextual effects.

Exposure

Stories about misconduct always include the element of exposure, since undiscovered misconduct cannot be a subject of discussion. Misconduct is sometimes recognized directly—that is, by those who are close enough to the situation to witness it or who are familiar enough with the process or products of the research to discover telltale discrepancies or patterns (e.g., through the mechanisms of peer review or replication; Ben-Yehuda, 1986; Chubin & Hackett, 1990). It can also become known indirectly, through the reports of whistle-blowers, as in most widely publicized cases.

Whenever a major misconduct incident becomes known, a window of opportunity for the analysis of exposure opens. Unfortunately, such opportunities seem to show up all too often. The same kind of inquiry can be pursued, however, with reference to less sensational cases of misconduct that are subject to local, internal whistle-blowing. Here the exposés of big cases are instructive in that the best ones address many interrelated issues such as the steps from neutrality about the research to suspicion and confirmation of misconduct; the process by which those who learn about the misconduct take on roles of accomplices, enablers, reluctant witnesses, or whistle-blowers; and institutional responses to exposure.

Discussions of exposure of misconduct in higher education (e.g., Sprague, 1987; Swazey, 1991) and in other fields (Miceli, Dozier & Near, 1991; Miethe & Rothschild, 1994; Near, Dworkin, & Miceli, 1993; Near & Miceli, 1995) suggest that it is useful to conceptualize exposure as a process, not as one grand opening of the curtain (Taubes, 1993). In a general way, exposure exerts a deterrent effect before the fact, but it also begins to operate specifically at the very initiation of misconduct because misconduct develops against the tension of potential exposure. The protective fronts that accompany deception are strongest when the possibility of detection is greatest, and exposure is often the result of a perpetrator's miscalculation as to these risks. The process of exposure generally involves many people over a long period of time, not the least of whom is the perpetrator, whose actions and redoubled efforts to conceal the misconduct interact with the exposure process.

Another promising research direction concerns the role of exposure in academic research. Its deterrent role is clear, but what role does exposure, particularly whistle-blowing, play in the academy at large? Exposure is a correction mechanism that is vital for ensuring the integrity and legitimacy of academic research (Ben-Yehuda, 1986) and consequently its support from society (Meyer & Rowan, 1977; Pfeffer & Salancik, 1978). In effect, however, it exhibits the failures of the system (Smith & Reynolds, 1990, pp. 22–23), which is one reason why whistle-blowers often find themselves regarded within the system as more deviant than the perpetrators (Bok, 1980; Swazey, 1991, p. 586; Swazey & Scher, 1982, pp. 184–185). The system cannot entirely escape blame in the face of evidence that one of its own members has been engaged in misconduct. Exposure is the system's smoke detector, but it is calibrated to detect in-house arsonists. Therefore, to continue the analogy, given that the fires of misconduct do occasionally flare up and given that the academy relies on the mechanism of exposure, it has a vital interest in maintaining an alarm loud enough to signal arson internally but not loud enough for anyone else to hear: such smoke detectors are rare.

Given the incentives for keeping exposure quiet, we might say that the dominant mode of exposing misconduct is not whistle-blowing but whispering. Consider the following phrases that Swazey (1991) used in descriptions of misconduct cases and their exposure:

- "our professor quietly let him . . . know that we knew, and would be on guard henceforth" (p. 583)
- "the doctor who, many people whispered, clearly was envious" (p. 584)
- "the funding agency in Washington . . . clearly signaled they did not want to know any more about it, and preferred that it all be handled quietly and decorously in-house" (p. 584)
- "everyone . . . hoped it would just be forgotten and certainly not become known outside the institution" (p. 584)
- "off-the-record conversations, usually prefaced with a 'don't quote me, but . . .'" (p. 585)
- "the justifiability of the experiment also was questioned, in private" (p. 587)
- "the reluctance of knowledgeable, senior physicians . . . to openly criticize fellow-physicians" (p. 587)

The quiet handling of misconduct begins with discussions among researchers or others who find anomalies in papers or procedures (Braxton & Bayer, 1996). These anomalies often emerge as suspiciously intractable puzzles (Panel, 1992, p. 57). In accordance with the rules of professional etiquette (Freidson, 1975), more quiet conversations are held, often including the perpetrator. Eventually the discussions involve people in positions of authority, who then may conduct further discussions that result in a scolding, some negotiated restitution, or some internal sanctions detailed in sealed agreements.

This description suggests a different direction for studies of exposure. Consistent with the suggestions above for process-oriented analysis, studies of quiet exposure and correction of misconduct would seem warranted. Whistle-blowing is even rarer than misconduct and more difficult to locate for analysis; whispering is common.

After all, whispering, as the quiet correction of error or misbehavior, is entirely consonant with both the instructional role of higher education and academics' sense of collective responsibility for the conduct of their peers and their students (Swazey et al., 1993). It ranges all the way from the constant corrections and suggestions offered by faculty to students to the internal resolution of rather serious misconduct. Conceptualizing whispering as the spread of knowledge about error or misconduct suggests the possible usefulness of models of knowledge diffusion (e.g., Greve, 1996; Zander & Kogut, 1995) or network analyses (Wasserman & Galaskiewicz, 1994). Such analyses can be used to track the spread of information through a group and the influence of various other factors on the direction and speed of the diffusion process. One might, for example, look at how widely and how quickly known instances of misconduct become under various conditions, or one might identify the factors most likely to contribute to truncation in the exposure process, as opposed to further exposure or full-blown whistle-blowing.

Consequences

The fourth and final element of the misconduct story is the consequences or outcome of the incident at hand (Panel, 1992, pp. 118–119). Studies of consequences might focus on formal and informal sanctions, the processes by which they are imposed, and their deterrent effects (Dresser, 1993; Greene, Durch, Horwitz, & Hooper, 1985; Hollinger & Clark, 1982, 1983; Mishkin, 1988; Parilla, Hollinger, & Clark, 1988; Parrish, 1994; Shore, 1993). Academic researchers' autonomy complicates the matter of sanctioning, since it is not clear in general or in specific cases who has the authority and responsibility to judge or sanction. John Braxton's (1991) work suggests that departmental quality is related to sanctioning, and other departmental effects are likely. Studies of the differential application of sanctions and other responses to misconduct in relation to such faculty characteristics as reputation, power, productivity, and mobility would be useful (Broad & Wade, 1982, chap. 5; Mazur, 1989, pp. 190–191).

Actual consequences are seldom detailed in stories; indeed, the full consequences of a particular instance of misconduct may never be known. For example, fraudulent papers "have a life of their own" (Broad & Wade, 1982, p. 51) and may continue to influence research long after the fraud has been exposed. When the victims of misconduct are difficult to identify or the negative consequences apply to a diffuse group, it may be particularly difficult to evaluate the outcomes of misconduct (Lee, 1993, p. 44). If consequences are mentioned at all in stories, they usually focus on the fate of the perpetrator. There can be many other victims of misconduct, of course, including the whistle-blower (Sprague, 1987), colleagues, students, administrators, research subjects or subjects of subsequent studies that are based on fraudulent research (Rennie, 1994), competitors who are unfairly delayed by the apparent but fraudulent success of the perpetrator, former collaborators or teachers of the perpetrator, and the perpetrator's family. Though ambitious, a study that aimed to trace the extent of damage wrought by one instance of misconduct or a series of misconduct episodes would illustrate the potential impact of misconduct, particularly in contrast to the usually modest benefits to the perpetrator or others. One relatively manageable approach would be the tracking of citations to fraudulent publications through the literature.

One of the more interesting outcomes to study might be subsequent misconduct. If everyday instances of error and misconduct were tracked, it would be relatively easy to observe patterns of misconduct in the course of academic research, representing a failure of learning and correction. It would be interesting to tie these to both the context of the research and the manner in which the misconduct was handled, to see where correction was most and least likely to take effect.

A MORE EXPANSIVE VIEW OF THE STUDY OF MISCONDUCT

Even the simple model presented in the previous section suggests a wide range of directions for research on misconduct. This section expands the model to suggest an even broader agenda for the analysis of misconduct. It first extends the simple model to an interactive one, which leads to longitudinal considerations. It then suggests an array of other factors that should be considered in investigations of misconduct and related issues. Like the simple model, the expanded models presented in this section are *not* causal models but rather diagrammatic illustrations of a wide variety of relationships that might be explored in future research on the misconduct and related topics.

INTERACTIVE EFFECTS

The simple model presented above shows some connections among the four elements that were examined separately in the previous section. These relationships (between context and misconduct, between misconduct and exposure, and between exposure and consequences) are rich with investigative possibility. For example, researchers have yet to explore fully the effects of the task and funding environments on misconduct (Panel, 1992, p. 30) or the relationship between the gravity of an offense and the manner in which it is handled (Pallone & Hennessy, 1995, pp. 14–17).

More valuable, perhaps, would be analyses that address the full scope of the simple model, specifically the process it represents. Case studies of misconduct often examine all of these elements and connections among them in detail. These accounts, whether in the journalistic-exposé mode or in more analytic forms, do not usually claim generalizability for their findings, and cross-case analyses, which might draw more robust conclusions, are rare (Silverman, 1994, p. 222; Woolf, 1988, is one of the few cross-case comparisons to appear). Broader studies of the elements of misconduct have usually focused on one or two of the elements of the model. The complete process represented in the model remains unexplored. For example, from the standpoint of professional self-regulation, the roles of context, exposure, and consequences in the misconduct process might be summarized as deterrence, detection, and sanction, but holistic analyses of the misconduct process may reveal that these elements play much more complicated roles (Braxton, 1986; Braxton & Bayer, 1996; Zuckerman, 1988).

The significance of this opportunity for research lies not in the telling of misconduct stories from origins to outcomes, which is far better handled by case-analytic methods of which there are already valuable exemplars (e.g., Broad & Wade, 1982), but rather in the full exploration of all the effects implicit in the model. The simple model presented above reflects the temporal logic of a misconduct incident as represented in a story. It is deficient, however, as a causal model because it does not suggest the full range of interactions among its elements. Context affects not only misconduct but also exposure (timing, nature, extent, and diffusion thereof) and consequences (severity and distribution thereof). Context even affects the relationship between misconduct and exposure. For example, misconduct that in one discipline could have grave effects on people's lives and therefore would typically be susceptible to full exposure could, in another discipline, be a less serious matter that would typically be handled quietly.

There is more. The direction of causality implied in the model is also open to examination. Both misconduct and exposure can be thought of as processes and, as such, are interactive. As suggested above, partial exposure can lead either to further misconduct in the form of cover-up or to changes in the way the misconduct is pursued. Misconduct itself, quite apart from its exposure, can affect context in that the working environment of a research project can be altered by secretive behavior. Such interactive loops in the model suggest complex patterns of association rather than strict causation.

A particularly intriguing effect could be represented by an arrow from consequences back to context: How does the fallout from an episode or pattern of misconduct change a laboratory, an academic department, an institution, or a discipline? This effect expands the simple model in three ways. First, it broadens the meaning of context. In the original model, context was defined with reference only to the misbehavior of one individual: that is, context included only those factors that bear directly on the misconduct itself. Treating context as an interactive part of the model, however, recognizes that context is more than just an immediate backdrop for an instance of misbehavior; it consists of many layers of environmental influence on and consequences of misconduct. Second, it highlights the value of multilevel analyses. Insofar as identifiable groups are affected by misconduct, it appears useful to conceptualize and analyze influences of and effects on groups, so that misconduct becomes an element of a complex individual-group process, not just the story of one person doing something wrong. Such multilevel analyses have become more practicable and sophisticated because of recent advances in hierarchical modeling (see, e.g., Bryk & Raudenbush, 1992). Third, it completes the model in the sense of representing a cyclical process—a misconduct life cycle, so to speak—that admits of the recurrence of misconduct. Opportunities for analysis do not end with the conclusion of a misconduct story, and research that takes a holistic view of misconduct would be valuable.

The complexity of this interactive model, which is represented in figure 13.3, would seem to make it useless for research on misconduct. With so few cases of full-blown misconduct and even fewer instances of exposure and consequences open to investigation, it would seem impossible to study all the effects implied here. However, process-oriented analyses of the kind advocated above appear promising as a means of investigating, if not all the implied effects, at least more of them than have been considered to date. Slips, miscalculations, misunderstandings, carelessness, and the like are all frequent enough to be ready opportunities for examination in relation to contextual features and consequences.

LONGITUDINAL EFFECTS

As suggested in the last section, misconduct can be viewed as one element in a continuing cycle. A discipline may face a series of cases of misconduct on the part of its members. Over time, a department or university may have to deal with a number of situations involving misconduct or "questionable research practices" (Panel, 1992, p. 25). The longitudinal and, particularly, cumulative effects of misconduct and its interaction with the other elements are seldom considered. Of special interest in this regard would be studies that would examine the effects of one instance or a series of misconduct episodes on the emergence and handling of subsequent cases. Such research might make use of institutions that have relatively large numbers of miscon-

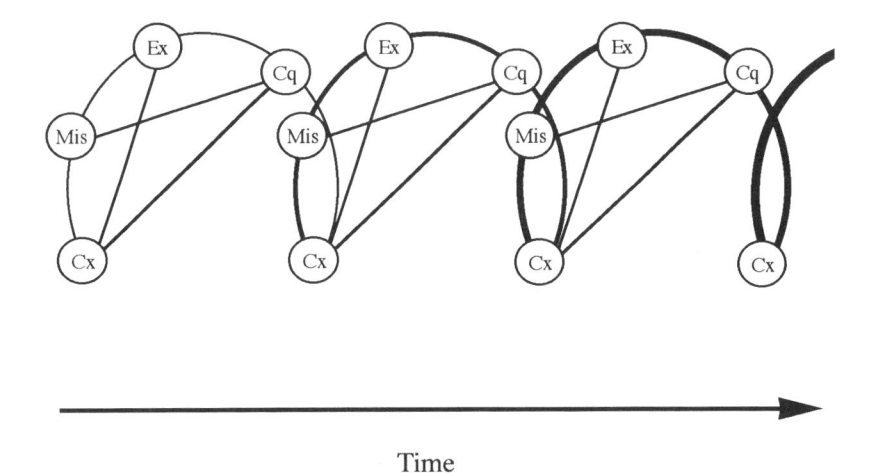

Figure 13.3 Longitudinal Effects among Context, Misconduct, Exposure, and Consequences

duct cases to examine institutional patterns over time. Figure 13.3 represents longitudinal effects by showing a spiral of linkages over time between successive instances of misconduct: the consequences of misconduct in one cycle affect the context of any subsequent misconduct, thereby creating a new context.

Not enough attention has been paid to the career path of the perpetrator either before or after an incident of misconduct. With particular reference to faculty, J. D. Douglas (1993) described deviants as good scouts gone bad: "The person who violates consensus values normally becomes a clearly definable deviant only by taking very small steps over a prolonged time" (p. S81). The consequences of an act of misconduct may not be as severe as some would suppose. Perpetrators often move on without any ill effects—sometimes even prospering—particularly when exposure takes place by whispering rather than whistle-blowing (Ben Yehuda, 1986), as in the case of the confirmed plagiarizer who was allowed to resign quietly, provided with a year's salary upon termination, hired by another institution, and quickly promoted to department chair (Pallone & Hennessy, 1995, p. 14).

Longitudinal studies are suited to the study of process and change. The misconduct life cycle is typically played out over a long period of time, and all of the relationships among all of the variables considered thus far can change over time. Observational analyses (Knorr-Cetina & Mulkay, 1983; Latour & Woolgar, 1986; Sutton, 1984) and longitudinal hierarchical models (Bryk & Raudenbush, 1992) both offer promise as approaches to a process-oriented study of misconduct, particularly in their potential for capturing contextual effects.

298 · *Melissa S. Anderson*

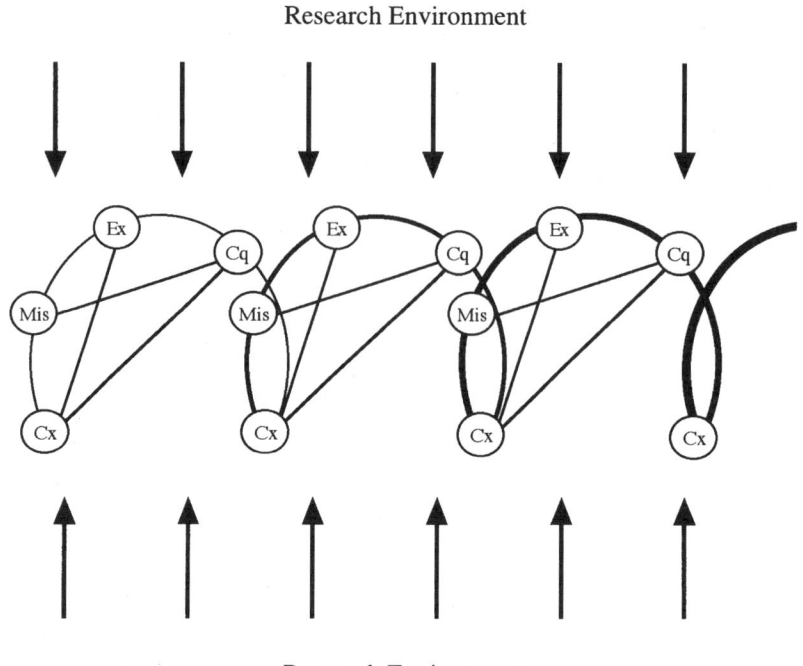

Figure 13.4 Broader Contextual Effects on Context, Misconduct, Exposure, and Consequences

BROADER CONTEXTUAL EFFECTS

The first extension of the simple model above connected its basic elements to each other (interactive effects), and the second extension set the model spinning over time (longitudinal effects). To make the model really complicated, we can add dozens of other variables, any one of which might be examined in terms of its interaction with other variables or in its effects over time. The following list is suggestive of the kinds of additional factors that could be considered in relation to misconduct. These other effects are represented in figure 13.4.

The research environment is increasingly complicated by arrangements with or influence by external agencies or groups (what Fox & Braxton, 1994, have called the "trans-scientific community"; see also Hackett, 1990; Panel, 1992, chap. 3). Funding arrangements involve the federal government, with its policies and regulations (Gold, 1993); industry, with its potential concerns for exclusivity and secrecy derived from the profit motive; or both. Interested and organized publics can exert substantial pressure on certain kinds of research endeavors (Anderson & Louis, 1991), and the composition of such interested groups fluctuates in sometimes unpredictable ways, depending on the issues at stake (Fox & Braxton, 1994). Certain academic societies or journals may have rules or policies that influence the research process: for example, the *Journal of the American Medical Association* requires that original data on which its articles are based be made available upon request (Rennie, 1993). Such external influences affect opportunities for and risks of academic misconduct, and many of these effects remain unexplored.

The imperatives of current academic research also introduce a number of complicating factors. Much of the research done in universities, particularly in the sciences, involves collaboration among many researchers and support personnel. Large teams linked by national or international networks preclude complete oversight by any individual. The scale and complexity of the projects undertaken by these teams stretch traditional control mechanisms of accountability, socialization, and self-regulation to extremes (Braxton, 1986; Huth, 1990; Woolf, 1981). Consider, for example, the matter of credit and blame for published reports. The extent of an author's responsibility for a publication is not always clear when he or she has contributed in only minor ways: Marcel LaFollette (1992, p. 204) likened the publications of big research teams to "allographic" art, inscribed by others on behalf of the artist, in contrast to "autographic" art, completed personally by the artist. Also, increasing collaboration suggests that academic misconduct may involve not just deviant individuals or "loners" (Best & Luckenbill, 1980) but groups of people who support the misconduct actively or passively.

Big projects increase the volume of research by nearly every measure, and the effects of this increase on deterrence and detection mechanisms have not been fully explored (Panel, 1992, p. 72). New technologies raise new ethical issues that cannot always be afforded the careful consideration they deserve, and they also expand the possibilities for circumventing traditional controls (LaFollette, 1992, pp. 202–205). Task environments can be made exceedingly complex by the demands of the research itself, and they can put administrative and management pressures on faculty who may not have sufficient time, commitment, or training to handle the responsibility. The resulting competition for funding and pressure to publish have often been cited as contributing to academic misconduct. Universities, perpetually facing fiscal pressures, may not provide adequate support for the administration of the research enterprise itself or its financial aspects, and inadequate administrative protocols may not provide faculty with enough protection from societal pressures (Laney, 1990, p. 58). All of these pressures can affect relationships among researchers as well as the climate of laboratories, departments, and other research sites. There is evidence, for example, that the climate of academic departments has significant effects on faculty and doctoral students' exposure to misconduct: the Acadia Institute's Project on Professional Values and Ethical Issues in the Graduate Education of Scientists and Engineers found that competition and conflict are associated with higher levels of exposure to misconduct in a department, while a sense of community has the opposite effect (Anderson, in press).

Finally, there are the less tangible but very influential effects of the normative structure or ethic of research (Braxton, 1986; Gaston, 1978; Panel, 1992, pp. 40–46; Reece & Siegal, 1986, p. 62; Zuckerman, 1977, 1988). This ethic can be spelled out specifically as in Robert Merton's (1942) norms of science, or it can be as vague as Richard Feynman's idea of scientific integrity: "a principle of scientific thought that corresponds to a kind of utter honesty" (quoted in Panel, 1992, pp. 36–37). The importance of normative environment is evident in John Braxton's (1990) finding that while an individual's deviance from the Mertonian norms of science is negatively related to the extent to which the individual has internalized the norms, an even stronger negative relationship exists between deviance from the norms and the extent to which the individual's colleagues conform to the norms. Normative environment has also been associated with faculty and students' exposure to misconduct: the Acadia study found that in departments where faculty and students subscribe strongly to the Mertonian norms, significantly fewer faculty and students see colleagues engaging in misconduct (Louis, Anderson, & Rosenberg, 1995). Normative assumptions about academic research and the research process can be conveyed formally, through instruction and policies, or informally, through socialization, mentoring, or, as Richard Feynman put it, the hope that students will "catch on by all the examples of scientific investigation" (quoted in Panel, 1992, p. 37). The increasing internationalization of academic units may affect normative orientations, since students from abroad "may not find it as easy to understand the unspoken transmission of values that somehow is supposed to take place between student and mentor in a scientific graduate education" (Goodstein, 1991, p. 515). Indeed, the Acadia project found evidence that international doctoral students were significantly less likely to subscribe to the Mertonian norms than their U.S. peers (Anderson & Louis, 1994).

This list suggests only some of the factors that appear worth pursuing in research on misconduct. Since all of these factors can be considered in relation to all the elements of the misconduct life cycle, the possibilities for research are staggering.

PROBLEMS IN THE STUDY OF MISCONDUCT

As promising and intriguing as the research directions suggested above are, empirical research on misconduct usually involves special difficulties. Some of the problems are due to the covert nature of misconduct and its sensitive nature as a topic of analysis, while others relate to the peculiarities of the academic setting as a site for research on misconduct.

Various forms of misconduct are illegal, immoral or, at the very least, unacceptable, and as such they are hidden roughly in direct proportion to their seriousness (J. D. Douglas, 1993, p. S82; see also Pallone & Hennessy, 1995, pp. 14–17). Experienced researchers refer to the need to "wrench the truth" (J. D. Douglas, 1976, p. 176) from informants. As Downes and Rock (1982) put it with regard to criminological evidence in general, "Except for a few instances of indirect evidence, data are rarely *given*. They should more appropriately be called *capta*, items which are seized with difficulty" (pp. 47–48). It would stand to reason that those who know the most about misconduct are least likely to reveal information to researchers. The exceptions are those who are "marginal, frustrated, or malcontented . . . [and others who are] too secure, too naive, or have too little stake in what is going on to feel inhibited about revealing potentially discreditable information" (Lee, 1993, p. 135).

In pursuing the study of misconduct, perhaps the most critical imperative is to avoid the mistakes and wrongdoing in which the subjects of the inquiry have engaged. The issue is how to do good research on bad research, or how to follow appropriately the standards and norms of academic research in analyzing deviance from those same standards and norms.

PROBLEMS IN THE STUDY OF SENSITIVE TOPICS

Research on misconduct is usually considered highly sensitive, since the informants and subjects of the study often fear being identified, stigmatized, or incriminated (Lee & Renzetti, 1993, 6). Several good analyses of the problems associated with sensitive research and recommended solutions have appeared (e.g., Beauchamp, Faden, Wallace, & Walters, 1982; Homan, 1991; Kimmel, 1981; Lee, 1993; Reece & Siegal, 1986; Renzetti & Lee, 1993; Reynolds, 1979, 1982; Sieber, 1982, 1992; Sieber & Stanley, 1988). This section reviews some of the most common problems associated with research on misconduct as a particular form of sensitive inquiry.

One of the first difficulties has to do with access to information, sites, and people. It can be very difficult to find informants, such as perpetrators of misconduct, who are scattered relatively sparsely through a larger population (Rothbart, Fine, & Sudman, 1982; Sudman, Sirken, & Cowan, 1988; Waterman & Kosmin, 1986). In field-based research, gaining access is often contingent on having detailed knowledge about a setting, which can only be acquired once access has been granted (Lee, 1993, p. 121). Moreover, access is a problem that is not solved just once at the beginning of a study: "Instead, it is best seen as involving an ongoing, if often implicit, process, in which the researcher's right to be present is continually renegotiated. Looked at in this way the access career can be thought of as both continuous and precarious" (Lee, 1993, p. 122). This negotiation involves not only the subjects of the research but also gatekeepers who have the power, formal or informal, to restrict access at any point (Broadhead & Rist, 1976; Renzetti & Lee, 1993, p. 27). Data may be protected in confidential institutional reports, particularly if the case in question is subject to litigation or private settlement (Panel, 1992, p. 24). Access to individuals or sites is complicated by the subtleties of "social access" (Lee, 1993, pp. 133–140), which is compromised by distrust, subversion, fronts, grudging cooperation, misrepresentation, tests of researcher sympathy, and the social order of the site.

Problems of access are minimized when researchers rely on public information or various forms of aggregate data, but such strategies are not without problems of their own (Starr, 1987). Document analysis is subject to errors and distortions introduced by bureaucratic or political selectivity at the time the documents are created. Lee (1993) cautioned researchers about the "dark figure": "that part of what the statistics purport to measure which goes unreported or unrecorded. Official statistics . . . notoriously underestimate the size of hidden populations and the extent of deviant activities" (p. 45). Indeed, Galliher (1980) went so far as to say that research based on official documents, such as government reports, is "laughable" (p. 303). When the focus of a misconduct study is on extent or prevalence, collecting data directly from individuals through randomized response techniques appears preferable to document analysis (Thomas, 1993, pp. 63–66; see also Lee, 1993, pp. 83–86). These techniques provide a statistically accurate estimate of prevalence without the researcher's being in any way able to link any particular information with an individual. Alternatively, when a study's research question addresses the distribution of misconduct or factors that contribute to misconduct, it might be possible to apply some variation of soft modeling (Thomas, 1993, pp. 52–70; see also Lee, 1993, pp. 54–55). This indirect, macro-level technique relies on inferences about misbehavior that are derived from readily available information, as, for example, one might make inferences about the spread or distribution of the underground economy from changes in the ratio of cash transactions to total deposits

(Thomas, 1993, pp. 56–58). In studies of misconduct, such an approach would depend on creatively but plausibly attributing changes in measurable variables to unobserved misconduct.

Some analyses of misconduct demand more direct approaches to data gathering. When people who have actual experience with misconduct are involved, data can be gathered through either covert or overt methods. Most, if not all, research on academic misconduct has been done overtly, though Roth (cited in Levin, 1981, p. 49) maintained that research always involves some level of secrecy, since researchers never tell their subjects everything about their study and often do not know exactly what they are looking for as they begin their research. Levin (1981) noted that full disclosure is particularly problematic in participant-observer situations or exploratory research, concluding that "the question therefore becomes not whether research should be secret but how much secrecy there shall be with which respondents in which circumstances" (p. 50). It is very difficult, though, to justify genuinely covert research, particularly from the perspective of proving that the benefits outweigh the risks, and it is subject to many practical problems of implementation (Lee, 1993, pp. 143–147). For some researchers, covert methods are tantamount to misconduct itself. While it can be argued that elites, such as senior faculty, are less likely to permit access to observers and therefore might be approachable only through covert methods, there is some question as to whether or not covert research would yield anything more than overt methods. For example, Galliher (1980) reported, with reference to his studies of elites, "I have found few refusals and little hostility . . . even when the details of such interviews are discrediting to respondents. . . . Powerful people seem so convinced of their own righteousness and so sure of their power that they usually talk freely" (pp. 302–303).

Whether the researcher's identity and the purposes of the study are known or unknown, the identity of the subjects remains problematic. Privacy, confidentiality, anonymity, identifiability, and consent are all critically important issues in research on misconduct (Boruch, 1982; Boruch & Cecil, 1979; Lee, 1993, pp. 31, 164–183; Office for Protection from Research Risks, 1993, pp. 3/4, 3/30–3/31; Pinkard, 1982; Sommer & Sommer, 1991, p. 20). Especially in the kinds of longitudinal studies that appear promising in tracking relationships among misconduct, context, and consequences, identification and consent must be handled with great care. It is helpful to view consent, like the access that it represents, as an ongoing process, subject to renegotiation at any time (Office for Protection from Research Risks, 1993, p. 3/11; Wax, 1980).

Even when a study on misconduct is done overtly and confidentiality is scrupulously maintained, researchers can face difficult situations as they become privy to sensitive or even criminal activity. Klockars (1979), addressing "the dirty hands problem" in studies of deviance, asked, "What if, by the very nature of the work, certain research, like politics, requires stepping into situations from which it is impossible to emerge innocent of wrongdoing?" (p. 264) and later claimed that it is impossible to do good fieldwork with deviant subjects without, so to speak, getting one's hands dirty (p. 265). Others take a less extreme view but still admit the likelihood of attaining "guilty knowledge" about wrongdoing or the somewhat less critical "intimate knowledge": that is, familiarity with the details of the subjects' lives (Henslin, 1972, p. 60). Clearly, surveys in which respondents' identities are not linked at any point to their responses provide no actionable guilty knowledge, but field research often demands that the investigator and subjects reach some kind of working agreement on the handling of incriminating information. Experienced researchers have described such agreements as implicit research bargains (Lee, 1993, p. 190), which may involve a use of "small social deceptions" that "smacks of hypocrisy" (Cassell, 1988, 98). Misconduct is one of the research topics that can lead to certain strains on the researcher, who may come to regret being involved in the study but have no way to turn back (Homan, 1991, p. 166). At the conclusion of a study, a researcher may experience an "ethical hangover" (Lofland & Lofland, 1984, p. 154), or guilt at having betrayed the subjects of the study to some extent.

All of these problems are intensified when research on misconduct leads to legal or media attention. Subpoenas become a very real possibility when researchers gain access to information about criminal acts (Sagarin & Moneymaker, 1979), and compliance with one subpoena can lead to further demands ("creeping subpoenas"; Lee, 1993, p. 165). Even the threat of subpoenas can be enough to lead a researcher to self-censorship (Adler & Adler, 1993), though the Public Health Service Act (#301(d)) offers some protection of subjects' privacy, even against subpoena, if the researcher takes appropriate action in advance of data collection (Office for Protection from Research Risks, 1993, pp. 3/37, 3/32). Media attention to so "hot" a topic as academic misconduct may prove even more difficult to control (Channels, 1993, p. 267). Noting that publicity attracted to a research report can be more than the research team, their institution, or their colleagues care to handle, Homan (1991) advised that "it would be irresponsible for a supervisor to take a year's sabbatical leave ... on the eve of publishing a sensitive report" (p. 154). Sometimes publicity is exactly what a researcher wants to make the research findings widely known, but it can also lead to frustration and disappointment: "Research on the accuracy of science reporting in the print media indicates that errors of *fact* are less frequent than errors of *emphasis*. Typically, the headline is flashy and misleading; what is unique about the research is overemphasized, and essential contextual information is omitted" (Sieber, 1993, p. 24). Such omissions are critical in light of the complexity of the elaborated model for misconduct research presented above.

PROBLEMS PECULIAR TO THE STUDY OF ACADEMIC MISCONDUCT

Studies of academic misconduct often involve special problems beyond the usual difficulties of research on sensitive topics. These problems derive from academics' role, the nature of academic work, and the academy as the joint setting for both researchers and those researched.

First, academics are members of society's intellectual elite. Their world exhibits some of the impenetrability, inscrutability, and complexity that complicate all research on elites (Bechtel & Pearson, 1985; Moyser, 1988; Moyser & Wagstaffe, 1987; Spencer, 1973). Their elitism is based, however, on specialized knowledge and expertise that make investigations into misconduct problematic. Academic misconduct often occurs at the frontier of knowledge, and a researcher who studies misconduct is faced with a choice between acquiring enough knowledge in an academic specialty to recognize misconduct when it shows up or relying on information from perpetrators and informants. The latter strategy, which is the only practical one in most cases, leaves the identification and interpretation of instances of misconduct in the hands of the research subjects. This problem suggests the value of the kinds of studies recommended above: investigations of the process by which particular actions in the course of academic research are judged to be acceptable or not.

Second, academic autonomy tends to promote rather isolated working conditions. Even when academics work in large teams of researchers, individuals are often responsible for certain phases of the work that are not reviewed or verified by anyone else. This tendency probably contributes to both the covertness and prevalence of misconduct. Few people are close enough to any particular academic to know how his or her research is being performed. Such isolation may decrease the face value of evidence of the extent of misconduct. To relate a personal example, when the Acadia Institute's study on misconduct was released (Swazey et al., 1993), I received a call from a faculty member who said that he and other department chairs had discussed our report at a meeting and had concluded that probably none of their departments had been included in our study, since none of the department chairs was aware of any of the kinds of reported misconduct going on in his or her own department. When I described our department selection criteria to the caller, it was clear to him that virtually all of the departments included in our study were represented by chairs at the meeting.

Third, academics who study misconduct may, in effect, create disturbances on their own home turf (Chubin, 1988). As LaFollette (1992) noted, "No one likes to be accused of wrongdoing, of course, and scientists are no exception. The leadership of the scientific community does not react cheerfully to either negative mass media attention or legislative scrutiny; they often complain that all scientists are being held accountable for the moral lapses of a few" (pp. 15–16). Such reactions are not exclusive to the study of misconduct. Levin (1981) cited Becker's claim that "a good sociological study will inevitably make someone angry by revealing that a community or organization is less than it claims to be—that there is a gap between the social reality and the ideal to which community representatives are committed" (p. 52; see also Rossi, 1987). Sommer and Sommer (1991) cautioned, "Don't expect to be regarded as a hero because you have identified problems" (p. 26) and warned that resistance to such findings can involve denial, sarcasm, discredit, or trivialization of the results. In effect, a researcher might be subject to whistle-blower sanctions. Academics are an intelligent and eloquent lot who can respond forcefully to bad news. After all, the researcher who studies misconduct is playing by the same rules that have been violated by the misconduct; his or her own work can be subjected to the same scrutiny and held to the same, if not higher, standards.

CONCLUSION

This chapter has presented a variety of suggestions for empirical research on misconduct and related issues. The following recommendations for further research highlight some of the most promising dimensions of a research agenda to make future studies relevant to the concerns of members of the academy and useful to people who are charged with the responsibility of dealing with misconduct.

First, research on misconduct should be empirically based. There is an important role for surveys, especially broad-scale (e.g., national or international) surveys about misconduct, but some of the potentially most illuminating research can best be done by observations, interviews, and other data collection in the laboratories and offices of universities. Interestingly, the Panel on Scientific Responsibility and the Conduct of Research (1992) noted, "An examination of empirical studies on research behaviors yielded few significant insights" (p. 24), and the references cited in this connection include exemplary studies of the very kind advocated here. It is likely, however, that these studies were not particularly informative because they were not designed specifically to address questions of misconduct and ethical behavior. Site-based studies that used observation or other data collection, together with analyses of academic researchers' interpretations of their behavior, specifically to study the complex process by which appropriate and inappropriate actions were distinguished from each other and dealt with on an everyday basis, would be valuable.

Second, rather than focusing on the question of prevalence or on the major cases of misconduct, empirical research should turn to process-oriented analyses of error and misbehavior and their correlates. Error is an integral part of academic research (Panel, 1992, p. 57). As Goodstein (1991) put it, "Because science is a very human activity, hypocrisies and misrepresentations are built into the way we do it" (p. 514). By recognizing this fact, we might move beyond a "gasp—tsk, tsk" approach to misconduct to focus on how academic researchers handle the ethical dimensions of ubiquitous errors, decisions, and conundrums of research. We might find out how misconduct can begin, what mechanisms promote or halt it, and, more generally, how academic researchers deal with the ethically ambiguous aspects of their work.

Third, research on misconduct should explicitly recognize that misconduct is embedded in the complex environment of academic work. The extended model presented in this chapter is only one way among many of representing this complexity. But in representing a maze of interactive, longitudinal, and external effects, it suggests how far research on misconduct has to go.

NOTES

I gratefully acknowledge the helpful comments of John M. Braxton and Judith P. Swazey on earlier drafts of this chapter, but I retain full responsibility for any deficiencies that may remain.

1. This chapter uses the terms *academic misconduct* and *scientific misconduct* interchangeably. Both refer here to misconduct in research in institutions of higher education. Much of the literature uses the phrase *scientific misconduct*, but *academic misconduct* suggests broader applicability in the academy.

REFERENCES

Adler, P. A., & Adler, P. (1993). Ethical issues in self-censorship: Ethnographic research on sensitive topics. In C. M. Renzetti & R. M. Lee (Eds.), *Researching sensitive topics* (pp. 249–266). Newbury Park, CA: Sage.

American Association for the Advancement of Science. (1991). *Professional Ethics Report*, 5(1), 2–3.

Anderson, M. S. (1996). Misconduct and departmental context: Evidence from the Acadia Institute's Graduate Education Project. *Journal of Information Ethics*, 5(1), 15–33.

Anderson, M. S., & Louis, K. S. (1991). The changing locus of control over faculty research: From self-regulation to dispersed influence. In J. C. Smart, (Ed.), *Higher education: Handbook of theory and research* (Vol. 7, pp. 57–101). New York: Agathon.

Anderson, M. S., & Louis, K. S. (1994). The graduate student experience and subscription to the norms of science. *Research in Higher Education, 35,* 273–299.

Anderson, M. S., Louis, K. S., & Earle, J. (1994). Disciplinary and departmental effects on observations of faculty and graduate student misconduct. *Journal of Higher Education, 65,* 331–350.

Beauchamp, T. L., Faden, R. R., Wallace, R. J., Jr., & Walters, L. (Eds.). (1982). *Ethical issues in social science research.* Baltimore: Johns Hopkins University Press.

Bechtel, H. K., Jr., & Pearson, W., Jr. (1985). Deviant scientists and scientific deviance. *Deviant Behavior, 6,* 237-252.

Ben-Yehuda, N. (1986). Deviance in science. *British Journal of Criminology, 26*(1), 1–27.

Best, J., & Luckenbill, D. F. (1980). The social organizational of deviants. *Social Problems, 28*(1), 14–31.

Bok, S. (1980). Whistleblowing and professional responsibilities. In D. Callahan & S. Bok (Eds.), *Ethics teaching in higher education* (pp. 277–295). New York: Plenum.

Boruch, R. F. (1982). Methods for resolving privacy problems in social research. In T. L. Beauchamp, R. R. Faden, R. J. Wallace, Jr., & L. Walters (Eds.), *Ethical issues in social science research* (pp. 292–314). Baltimore: Johns Hopkins University Press.

Boruch, R. F., & Cecil, J. S. (1979). *Assuring the confidentiality of social research data.* Philadelphia: University of Pennsylvania Press.

Braxton, J. M. (1986). The normative structure of science: Social control in the academic profession. In J. C. Smart (Ed.), *Higher education: Handbook of theory and research* (Vol. 2, pp. 309–357). New York: Agathon.

Braxton, J. M. (1990). Deviancy from the norms of science: A test of control theory. *Research in Higher Education, 31,* 461–476.

Braxton, J. M. (1991). The influence of graduate department quality on the sanctioning of scientific misconduct. *Journal of Higher Education, 62,* 87–108.

Braxton, J. M., & Bayer, A. E. (1996). Personal experiences of research misconduct and the response of individual academic scientists. *Science, Technology, and Human Values, 21,* 198–213.

Broad, W., & Wade, N. (1982). *Betrayers of the truth: Fraud and deceit in the halls of science.* New York: Simon & Schuster.

Broadhead, R. S., & Rist, R. C. (1976). Gatekeepers and the social control of social research. *Social Problems, 23,* 325–336.

Bryk, A. S., & Raudenbush, S. W. (1992). *Hierarchical linear models.* Newbury Park, CA: Sage.

Buzzelli, D. E. (1992). The measurement of misconduct. *Knowledge: Creation, Diffusion, Utilization, 14,* 205–211.

Buzzelli, D. E. (1993a). The definition of misconduct in science: A view from NSF. *Science, 259,* 584–585, 647–648.

Buzzelli, D. E. (1993b). Some considerations in defining misconduct in science. In *Ethics, values, and the promise of science: Forum proceedings, February 25–*

26, 1993. Research Triangle Park, NC: Sigma Xi, the Scientific Research Society.

Cassell, J. (1988). The relationship of observer to observed when studying up. In R. G. Burgess (Ed.), *Studies in qualitative methodology: Vol. 1. Conducting qualitative research* (pp. 89–108). Greenwich, CT: JAI.

Channels, N. L. (1993). Anticipating media coverage: Methodological decisions in criminal justice research. In C. M. Renzetti & R. M. Lee (Eds.), *Researching sensitive topics* (pp. 267–280). Newbury Park, CA: Sage.

Chubin, D. E. (1988). Allocating credit and blame in science. *Science, Technology, and Human Values, 13*, 53–63.

Chubin, D. E., & Hackett, E. J. (1990). *Peerless science: Peer review and U.S. science policy.* Albany: State University of New York Press.

Commission on Research Integrity. (1995). *Integrity and misconduct in research.* Washington, DC: U.S. Department of Health and Human Services.

Committee on Science, Engineering, and Public Policy. (1995). *On being a scientist: Responsible conduct in research.* Washington, DC: National Academy Press.

Culliton, B. J. (1994). "Misconduct" definitions still prove elusive. *Nature, 369*, 513.

Daniel, L. G., Adams, B. N., & Smith, N. M. (1994). Academic misconduct among nursing students: A multivariate investigation. *Journal of Professional Nursing, 10*, 278–288.

David, E. E., Jr. (1993). Ethics and values in science: The NAS-COSEPUP report on scientific responsibility and the conduct of research. In *Ethics, values, and the promise of science: Forum proceedings, February 25–26, 1993.* Research Triangle Park, NC: Sigma Xi, the Scientific Research Society.

Davis, M. S. (1989). *The perceived seriousness and incidence of ethical misconduct in academic science.* Unpublished doctoral dissertation, Ohio State University.

Douglas, D. J. (1972). Managing fronts in observing deviance. In J. D. Douglas (Ed.), *Research on deviance.* New York: Random House.

Douglas, J. D. (1976). *Investigative social research.* Beverly Hills, CA: Sage.

Douglas, J. D. (1993). Deviance in the practice of science. *Academic Medicine, 68*(9, Suppl.), S77-S83.

Downes, D., & Rock, P. (1982). *Understanding deviance.* New York: Oxford University Press.

Dresser, R. (1993). Sanctions for research misconduct: A legal perspective. *Academic Medicine, 68*(9, Suppl.), S39-S43.

Fox, M. F. (1990). Fraud, ethics and the disciplinary contexts of science and scholarship. *American Sociologist, 21*(1), 67–71.

Fox, M. F., & Braxton, J. M. (1994). Misconduct and social control in science: Issues, problems, solutions. *Journal of Higher Education, 65*, 373–383.

Freidson, E. (1975). *Doctoring together: A study of professional social control.* New York: Elsevier.

Friedman, P. J. (1992). On misunderstanding scientific misconduct. *Knowledge: Creation, Diffusion, Utilization, 14*, 153–156.

Galliher, J. F. (1980). Social scientists' ethical responsibilities to superordinates: Looking upward meekly. *Social Problems, 27,* 298–308.

Gaston, J. (1978). *The reward system in British and American science.* New York: John Wiley.

Gillespie, G. W., Chubin, D. E., & Kurzon, G. M. (1985). Experience with NIH peer review: Researchers' cynicism and desire for change. *Science, Technology, and Human Values, 10*(3), 44–54.

Gold, B. D. (1993). Congressional activities regarding misconduct and integrity in science. In Panel on Scientific Responsibility and the Conduct of Research (Ed.), *Responsible science: Ensuring the integrity of the research process* (Vol. 2, pp. 90–115). Washington, DC: National Academy Press.

Goodstein, D. (1991). Scientific fraud. *American Scholar, 60,* 505–515.

Greene, P. J., Durch, J. S., Horwitz, W., & Hooper, V. S. (1985). Policies for responding to allegations of fraud in research. *Minerva, 23,* 203–115.

Greve, H. R. (1996). Patterns of competition: The diffusion of a market position in radio broadcasting. *Administrative Science Quarterly, 41*(1), 29–60.

Hackett, E. J. (1990). Science as a vocation in the 1990s: The changing organizational culture of academic science. *Journal of Higher Education, 61,* 241–279.

Hackett, E. J. (1994). A social control perspective on scientific misconduct. *Journal of Higher Education, 65,* 242–260.

Henslin, J. M. (1972). Studying deviance in four settings: Research experiences with cabbies, suicides, drug users, and abortionees. In J. D. Douglas (Ed.), *Research on deviance* (pp. 35–70). New York: Random House.

Hollinger, R. C., & Clark, J. P. (1982). Formal and informal social controls of employee deviance. *Sociological Quarterly, 23,* 333–343.

Hollinger, R. C., & Clark, J. P. (1983). Deterrence in the workplace: Perceived certainty, perceived severity, and employee theft. *Social Forces, 62,* 398–418.

Homan, R. (1991). *The ethics of social research.* London: Longman.

Huth, E. J. (1990). Editors and the problems of authorship: Rulemakers or gatekeepers? In J. C. Bailar, III, M. Angell, S. Boots, E. S. Myers, N. Palmer, M. Shipley, & P. Woolf (Eds.), *Ethics and policy in scientific publication* (pp. 175–180). Bethesda, MD: Council of Biology Editors.

Kaiser, J. (1995). Commission proposes new definition of misconduct. *Science, 269,* 1811.

Kalichman, M. W., & Friedman, P. J. (1992). A pilot study of biomedical trainees' perceptions concerning research ethics. *Academic Medicine, 67,* 769–775.

Kimmel, A. J. (Ed.). (1981). *Ethics of human subject research.* San Francisco: Jossey-Bass.

Klockars, C. B. (1979). Dirty hands and deviant subjects. In C. B. Klockars & F. W. O'Connor (Eds.), *Deviance and decency: The ethics of research with human subjects* (pp. 261–282). Beverly Hills, CA: Sage.

Knoll, E. (1992). What is scientific misconduct? *Knowledge: Creation, Diffusion, Utilization, 14,* 174-180.

Knorr-Cetina, K. D., & Mulkay, M. (Eds.). (1983). *Science observed: Perspectives on the social study of science.* Beverly Hills, CA: Sage.

Koshland, D. E. (1987). Fraud in science. *Science, 235,* 141.

LaFollette, M. C. (1992). *Stealing into print: Fraud, plagiarism, and misconduct in scientific publishing.* Berkeley: University of California Press.
LaFollette, M. C. (1994). Research misconduct. *Society, 31*(3), 6–10.
Laney, J. T. (1990). Through thick and thin: Two ways of talking about the academy and moral responsibility. In W. W. May (Ed.), *Ethics and higher education* (pp. 49–66). New York: American Council on Education.
Latour, B., & Woolgar, S. (1986). *Laboratory life: The construction of scientific facts.* Princeton, NJ: Princeton University Press.
Lee, R. M. (1993). *Doing research on sensitive topics.* Newbury Park, CA: Sage.
Lee, R. M., & Renzetti, C. M. (1993). The problems of researching sensitive topics: An overview and introduction. In C. M. Renzetti & R. M. Lee (Eds.), *Researching sensitive topics* (pp. 3–13). Newbury Park, CA: Sage.
Leibel, W. (1991). When scientists are wrong: Admitting inadvertent error in research. *Journal of Business Ethics, 10,* 601–604.
Levin, J. (1981). Ethical problems in sociological research. In A. J. Kimmel (Ed.), *New directions for methodology of social and behavioral science: Ethics of human subjects research* (pp. 49–54). San Francisco: Jossey-Bass.
List, C. J. (1985). Scientific fraud: Social deviance or the failure of virtue? *Science, Technology, and Human Values, 10*(4), 27–36.
Lock, S. P. (1988). Scientific misconduct. *British Medical Journal, 297,* 1531–1535.
Lofland, J., & Lofland, L. H. (1984). *Analyzing social settings: A guide. Qualitative observation and analysis* (2nd ed.). Belmont, CA: Wadsworth.
Louis, K. S., Anderson, M. S., & Rosenberg, L. (1995). Academic misconduct and values: The department's influence. *Review of Higher Education, 18,* 393–422.
Mazur, A. (1989). Allegations of dishonesty in research and their treatment by American universities. *Minerva, 27,* 177–194.
Merton, R. K. (1942). A note on science and democracy. *Journal of Legal and Political Sociology, 1*(1–2), 115–126.
Meyer, J. W., & Rowan, B. (1977). Institutionalized organizations: Formal structure as myth and ceremony. *American Journal of Sociology, 83,* 340–363.
Miceli, M. P., Dozier, J. B., & Near, J. P. (1991). Blowing the whistle on data fudging: A controlled field experiment. *Journal of Applied Social Psychology, 21,* 271–295.
Miethe, T. D., & Rothschild, J. (1994). Whistleblowing and the control of organizational misconduct. *Sociological Inquiry, 64,* 322–347.
Mishkin, B. (1988). Responding to scientific misconduct: Due process and prevention. *Journal of the American Medical Association, 260,* 1932–1936.
Mosteller, F. (1977). Assessing unknown numbers: Order of magnitude estimation. In W. B. Fairley & F. Mosteller (Eds.), *Statistics and public policy* (pp. 163–184). Reading, MA: Addison-Wesley.
Moyser, G. (1988). Non-standard interviewing in élite research. In R. G. Burgess (Ed.), *Studies in qualitative methodology: Vol. 1. Conducting qualitative research* (pp. 109–136). Greenwich, CT: JAI.
Moyser, G., & Wagstaffe, M. (Eds.). (1987). *Research methods for elite studies.* London: Allen & Unwin.
Near, J. P., Dworkin, T. M., & Miceli, M. P. (1993). Explaining the whistle-

blowing process: Suggestions from power theory and justice theory. *Organization Science, 4,* 393–411.

Near, J. P., & Miceli, M. (1995). Effective whistle-blowing. *Academy of Management Review, 20,* 679–708.

Office for Protection from Research Risks. (1993). *Protecting human research subjects: Institutional review board guidebook.* Washington, DC: Government Printing Office.

Pallone, N. J., & Hennessy, J. J. (1995). Deception, fraud, and fallible judgment. In N. J. Pallone & J. J. Hennessy (Eds.), *Fraud and fallible judgment: Varieties of deception in the social and behavioral sciences* (pp. 3–20). New Brunswick, NJ: Transaction.

Panel on Scientific Responsibility and the Conduct of Research. (1992). *Responsible science: Ensuring the integrity of the research process* (Vol. 1). Washington, DC: National Academy Press.

Parilla, P. F., Hollinger, R. C., & Clark, J. P. (1988). Organizational control of deviant behavior: The case of employee theft. *Social Science Quarterly, 69,* 261–280.

Parrish, D. (1994). Scientific misconduct and the plagiarism cases. *Journal of College and University Law, 21,* 517–554.

Pfeffer, J., & Salancik, G. R. (1978). *The external control of organizations: A resource dependence perspective.* New York: Harper & Row.

Pinkard, T. (1982). Invasions of privacy in social science research. In T. L. Beauchamp, R. R. Faden, R. J. Wallace, Jr., & L. Walters (Eds.), *Ethical issues in social science research* (pp. 257–273). Baltimore: Johns Hopkins University Press.

Pritchard, I. A. (1993). Integrity versus misconduct: Learning the difference between right and wrong. *Academic Medicine, 68*(9, Suppl.), S67-S71.

Reece, R. D., & Siegal, H. A. (1986). *Studying people: A primer in the ethics of social research.* Macon, GA: Mercer University Press.

Rennie, D. (1989). Editors and auditors. *Journal of the American Medical Association, 266,* 2543–2545.

Rennie, D. (1993). Accountability, audit, and reverence for the publication process. *Journal of the American Medical Association, 270,* 495–496.

Rennie, D. (1994). Breast cancer: How to mishandle misconduct. *Journal of the American Medical Association, 271,* 1205–1207.

Renzetti, C. M., & Lee, R. M. (Eds.). 1993. *Researching sensitive topics.* Newbury Park, CA: Sage.

Reynolds, P. D. (1979). *Ethical dilemmas and social science research.* San Francisco: Jossey-Bass.

Reynolds, P. D. (1982). *Ethics and social science research.* Englewood Cliffs, NJ: Prentice Hall.

Rossi, P. H. (1987). No good applied social research goes unpunished. *Society, 25,* 73–80.

Rothbart, G. S., Fine, M., & Sudman, S. (1982). On finding and interviewing the needles in the haystack: The use of multiplicity sampling. *Public Opinion Quarterly, 46,* 408–421.

Sagarin, E., & Moneymaker, J. (1979). The dilemma of researcher immunity. In C. B. Klockars & F. W. O'Connor (Eds.), *Deviance and decency: The ethics of research with human subjects* (pp. 175–193). Beverly Hills, CA: Sage.

St. James-Roberts, I. (1976). Cheating in science. *New Scientist, 72,* 98–101.

Schachman, H. K. (1993). What is misconduct in science? *Science, 261,* 148.

Shore, E. G. (1993). Sanctions and remediation for research misconduct: Differential diagnosis, treatment, and prevention. *Academic Medicine, 68*(9, Suppl.), S44-S48.

Sieber, J. E. (Ed.). (1982). *The ethics of social research: Fieldwork, regulation, and publication.* New York: Springer.

Sieber, J. E. (1992). *Planning ethically responsible research.* Newbury Park, CA: Sage.

Sieber, J. E. (1993). The ethics and politics of sensitive research. In C. M. Renzetti & R. M. Lee (Eds.), *Researching sensitive topics* (pp. 14–26). Newbury Park, CA: Sage.

Sieber, J. E., & Stanley, B. (1988). Ethical and professional dimensions of socially sensitive research. *American Psychologist, 43*(1), 49–55.

Sigma Xi. (1989). *Sketches of the American scientist.* New Haven, CT: Author.

Silverman, S. (1994). Process and detection in fraud and deceit. *Ethics and Behavior, 4,* 219–228.

Smith, D. D., & Reynolds, C. H. (1990). Institutional culture and ethics. In W. W. May (Ed.), *Ethics and higher education* (pp. 21–31). New York: American Council on Education.

Sommer, B., & Sommer, R. (1991). *A practical guide to behavioral research* (3rd ed.). New York: Oxford University Press.

Spencer, G. (1973). Methodological issues in the study of bureaucratic elites: A case study of West Point. *Social Problems, 21,* 90–103.

Sprague, R. L. (1987, December 14). I trusted the research system. *Scientist, 1,* 11–12.

Starr, P. (1987). The sociology of official statistics. In W. Alonso & P. Starr (Eds.), *The politics of numbers* (pp. 7–57). New York: Sage.

Sudman, S., Sirken, M. G., & Cowan, C. D. (1988). Sampling rare and elusive populations. *Science, 240,* 991–996.

Sutton, J. R. (1984). Organizational autonomy and professional norms in science: A case study of the Lawrence Livermore Laboratory. *Social Studies of Science, 14,* 197–224.

Swazey, J. P. (1991). Are physicians a "delinquent community"?: Issues in professional competence, conduct, and self-regulation. *Journal of Business Ethics, 10,* 581–590.

Swazey, J. P., Anderson, M. S., & Louis, K. S. (1993). Ethical problems in academic research. *American Scientist, 81,* 542–553.

Swazey, J. P., & Scher, S. R. (Eds.). (1982). *Whistleblowing in biomedical research: Policies and procedures for responding to reports of misconduct.* Washington, DC: Government Printing Office.

Tangney, J. P. (1987, August 6). Fraud will out—or will it? *New Scientist, 115,* pp. 62–63.

Taubes, G. (1993). Misconduct: Views from the trenches. *Science, 261,* 1108–1111.

Thomas, J. J. (1993). Measuring the underground economy: A suitable case for interdisciplinary treatment?. In C. M. Renzetti & R. M. Lee (Eds.), *Researching sensitive topics* (pp. 52–70). Newbury Park, CA: Sage.

U.S. Department of Health and Human Services. (1989, August 8). Responsibilities of PHS awardee and applicant institutions for dealing with and reporting possible misconduct in science: Final rule. *Federal Register, 54,* 32446–32451.

Wasserman, S., & Galaskiewicz, J. (1994). *Advances in social network analysis: Research in the social and behavioral sciences.* Thousand Oaks, CA: Sage.

Waterman, S., & Kosmin, B. (1986). Mapping an unenumerated ethnic population: Jews in London. *Ethnic and Racial Studies, 9,* 484–501.

Wax, M. L. (1980). Paradoxes of "consent" to the practice of fieldwork. *Social Problems, 27,* 272–283.

Woolf, P. (1981, October). Fraud in science: How much, how serious? *Hastings Center Report, 11,* 9–14.

Woolf, P. K. (1988, Fall). Deception in scientific research. *Jurimetrics Journal, 29,* 67–95.

Woolf, P. K. (1991). Accountability and responsibility in research. *Journal of Business Ethics, 10,* 595–600.

Zander, U., & Kogut, B. (1995). Knowledge and the speed of the transfer and imitation of organizational capabilities: An empirical test. *Organization Science,* 6(1), 76–92.

Zuckerman, H. (1977). Deviant behavior and social control in science. In E. Sagarin (Ed.), *Deviance and social change* (pp. 87–138). Beverly Hills, CA: Sage.

Zuckerman, H. (1988). The sociology of science. In N. J. Smelser (Ed.), *Handbook of sociology* (pp. 511–574). Newbury Park, CA: Sage.

Zwolenik, J. J. (1992). New definitions of misconduct: Priorities for the 1990s. *Knowledge: Creation, Diffusion, Utilization, 14,* 168–173.

CONCLUSION

Self-Regulation and Social Control of Scientific Misconduct: Roles, Patterns, and Constraints

Mary Frank Fox and John M. Braxton

Authority, autonomy, and sanctioning of the larger community are features that define a profession. A profession has the mandate to decide what is or is not in the interests of clients, the capacity to make decisions and exercise judgment without interference from those outside the profession, and the community's approval of the right to govern itself and set its own standards of behavior (Carr-Saunders & Wilson, 1933).

These core features are unified by concepts of "dominance" and "control"—of the profession and by the profession. The hallmarks of dominance and control have been reshaped in analyses as asymmetric relationships between professional members and clients (and other professional members) and later in analyses as economic monopoly—both hallmarks resting upon professional expertise and knowledge (Abbott, 1988, p. 5). Because science, in particular, is grounded in abstract and systematic theory, it has been regarded as a prototype for a profession's claim to authoritative knowledge. In fact, other occupations (from law to librarianship) have tried to mimic scientific rationality and practice in their moves for dominance and control (Derber, Schwartz, & Magrass, 1990, p. 33).

In science, professional self-regulation of conduct is exceptionally important for two reasons. First, self-regulation is a premise of the "social contract for science," an arrangement originally outlined by Vannevar Bush (1945/1990). Under this contract, the federal government provides funds for basic research and scientific training in academia and agrees not to interfere with scientific decision making in exchange for unspecified benefits to the public good that are expected to result ultimately from science (see Guston, 1994). Thus, professional self-regulation protects the public support that underlies science. Further, professional self-regulation of conduct is said to safeguard the practice of science, the validity of scientific findings according to methodological canon (Zuckerman, 1988, p. 524). In this way, self-regulation is regarded as fundamental to the very activity of the scientific enterprise.

The social contract for science assumed self-regulation of science by scientists. However, the contract did not articulate or even suggest mechanisms needed for monitoring or certifying integrity other than fiscal accountability at the institutional level. Rather, the contract relied upon "mutual assurances of trust" between Congress, funding agencies, universities, and individual scientists (see chapter 1 of this volume) and upon regulation of conduct by unspecified means internal to the scientific community, such as processes of peer review, largely unstated codes of professional ethics, and individual responsibility of scientists.[1]

In analyzing conduct, misconduct, and control of illegitimate behavior in science, the boundaries between legitimate and illegitimate behavior are debatable and are to some extent variable by discipline and research areas (Fox, 1990; see also chapters 4, 7, and 13 of this volume). By general statement, however, misconduct encompasses acts of deception: alteration of data or materials, false representation of authorship or originality, and misrepresentation to advance oneself or to hurt the career or position of another (see LaFollette, 1992).

We argue that efforts toward control have been exercised not just by individual scientists but by institutional arrangements—federal agencies and bodies, professional associations, universities, and scientific journals—which, together, form a *trans-scientific community* that is not stably constituted or crystallized over time and concerns but that varies in its alliances depending upon the issues and interests at stake (Fox & Braxton, 1994). The questions of this concluding chapter are these: In exercising control of misconduct, what are the roles of these segments constituting the scientific community? How effective are they? What are the limitations upon control—and the implications for professional self-regulation? In addressing these questions, we draw upon the foregoing chapters in this volume as well as other theory and research.[2]

THE EXERCISE OF CONTROL

Federal Government

By arguing that the scientific research and training would provide technological innovation, health, prosperity, and better living conditions in exchange for funding and autonomy, the post–World War II leadership of the scientific community "secured a remarkable arrangement," as LaFollette puts it in chapter 1 of this book. At the same time, *because* science is funded through public monies, it rests upon public confidence in the integrity and usefulness of its activity (Fox & Firebaugh, 1992). Thus, the incidents of scientific misconduct that have come to the fore in the past 20 years especially have threatened public trust in science and aroused involvement of the federal government, as LaFollette (chapter 1), Steneck (chapter 3), and Hackett (chapter 4) show in this book.

The U.S. Congress has wielded social control of scientific misconduct through its power of oversight and legislation. Under the rubric of oversight are the high-profile congressional investigations in the 1980s. As LaFollette characterizes these investigations, the remarkable aspect is their shift in tone—from benign, polite questioning in 1981 to antagonism and threats of subpoena in 1988. The early message, conveyed at the 1981 and subsequent hearings held in response to publicity surrounding the Darsee case and other cases of misconduct in biomedicine, was simply this: "Scientists should do everything possible to prevent unethical conduct in their ranks, but if fraud did occur, then it should be investigated and resolved quickly by scientists, lest it deter scientific progress. And scientists should not . . . sweep problems under the rug" (LaFollette, chapter 1 of this book). In the years following, the scientific leadership did not embrace this logic and tended to reject the demands of "politics" and the complaints of "nonscientists." This ultimately had consequences for increased federal control and reduced professional self-regulation of misconduct.

The watershed year in hearings was 1988: the House Committee on Energy and Commerce's Subcommittee on Oversight and Investigations, chaired by Congressman John Dingell, began the inquiry of the alleged misconduct of National Institutes of Health (NIH)-supported research by Thereza Imanishi-Kari, reported in a paper coauthored with Nobel laureate David Baltimore and other authors. For eight more years, investigation of the "Baltimore case" continued. By the time of resolution in 1996,[3] "everyone lost something," and, most significantly, the illusion was dispelled that "science and the universities had things under control" (LaFollette, chapter 1 of this book). The hearings and the fallout revealed a side of science that did not correspond to a "self-regulating model" and, in the process, shook congressional confidence in the social contract for science (Guston, 1994, p. 225).

The Office of the Inspector General of the National Science Foundation (NSF), the Office of Research Integrity, and the appeals panel of the U.S. Department of Health and Human Services (USDHHS) have also been established through powers of oversight. These offices have means of investigating, adjudicating, and sanctioning charges of misconduct. As funding agencies, the most severe sanction of NSF and the Public Health Service (PHS) is debarment of scientists from receiving federal research grant monies for a specified period of time (which can bring their research to a halt). The agencies have also stepped into the arena of defining deviance by setting boundaries between appropriate conduct and misconduct that serve as guides to investigations by their offices (Price, 1994) and by university-based committees.

Debarment from federal funds serves as both sanction for offenders and deterrence for potential offenders. Standards of behavior, however, live or die by enactment and enforcement. These, in turn, depend upon the parties who report misconduct and upon the institutions (professional associations and especially universities) that do or do not create a climate for attentiveness to misconduct and complaints of it.

Professional Associations

In his account of academic and scientific associations' response to misconduct, Johnson (chapter 2 of this book) chronicles a pattern "from denial to action." Associations changed their stance in part because of pressure by Congress and the American public and concerns that funding and freedom in research rely upon public support and good will.

Yet associations remain unclear about their stance toward misconduct: Should it be "measured response" or "aggressive action"? Should the approach be low key and collegial or legalistic, with both the accuser and the accused examining the evidence and preparing arguments and counterarguments? The practices of science and those of law are blending, Johnson argues, with some adherence to confidentiality and trust but also with aspects of due process, including systems of appeal.

Johnson reports that two factors influence the likelihood that a professional association will have a more rather than less detailed code of conduct: size and makeup of membership. Large associations and those with direct impact upon the public, such as those containing both scientists and practitioners or significant applied domains, are likely to have the most extensive ethical codes. These include the American Psychological Association, the American Academy of Forensic Studies, and the Association for Computing Machinery—which are large enough to defend themselves and have members whose actions, proper or improper, have an effect upon the public. Differences between disciplines in their professional cultures, research practices, and publication norms have made it difficult to coordinate, much less standardize, codes of ethics and responses to misconduct. Limits on coordination, in turn, restrict the prospects of the associations to take concerted action against misconduct, and this reduces professional self-regulation.

Universities

In response to requirements established by NSF and PHS, the majority of research universities have policies and procedures for investigating allegations of misconduct. But their surveillance and investigation are open to question. Steneck's review of university policies in chapter 3 of this book reveals that most policies extol "general normative statements and lofty goals" but do not provide "realistic guidance that is needed by individuals or committees" for undertaking investigations of misconduct. As Steneck emphasizes, universities are subject to "many competing interests": they are often employers of both the accused and the accuser; they are subject to government funding; they are dependent upon active research and training programs; they are wary of internal working relationships and subject to internal hierarchies, and at the same time are obligated to maintain public reputations. Whether universities can manage such conflicting interests has been questioned in meetings, reports, and publications. Universities' investigations of allegations of misconduct are fraught with issues with which universities largely have been unable to grapple (Greene, Durch, Horwitz, & Hooper, 1985): How should policies be distributed? What are appropriate sanctions? Should parties in direct contact with alleged misconduct be involved in investigation? Should participants outside the university undertake the investigation? What are the requirements of due process? Should funding agencies be notified and when? Should information be released to the public and when?

In chapter 5 on universities and the regulation of scientific morals, Turner analyzes the main conflicts that create obstacles within the university and that shape the university's stance toward rules of conduct or monitoring of misconduct. The central concepts used are power, interests, and the channeling of interests. Applied to the university's role in regulation of misconduct, the question becomes this: In the university, are there *collective interests* represented by competent bodies that can effectively deal with misconduct?

The answer, Turner argues, is no. Research misconduct committees are weak instruments, used only at a certain stage in a dispute, and with very limited powers even at the stage at which they function. The practices of university administrators are to "deal with the issues informally—that is, to suppress them" (chapter 5). The response—or nonresponse—derives from a constellation of interests produced by research, research funding, and indirect overhead costs. Administration is largely about finance, and to understand this, Turner argues, is to understand the interests of administrators and faculties' powers in relation to administrators as they connect to science. The key areas in which administrators can exercise power are those in which funds exist that are not subject to constraints—and the chief source of such discretionary funds is overhead (indirect) costs generated by externally funded research. In the harsh light of this political analysis, "handling matters" and "suppressing problems," including misconduct, become basic administrative "career skills" and "simply the price of getting things done" (chapter 5).

Yet despite serious conflicting interests and unsolved issues, as the major employer of doctoral-level scientists, universities retain strong sanctioning *potential* through salary, appointments, and resources of laboratories, materials, and assistantships. Universities not only have the strongest potential sanctions for control of misconduct but also may be a source or determinant of behavior. First, doctoral training takes place in universities. While norms acquired through socialization are not enough to ensure conformity, as Anderson, Louis, and Earle (chapter 10 of this book) and others (Zuckerman, 1988, p. 524) indicate, such norms may nonetheless influence scientists' attitudes, values, and beliefs regarding professional self-regulation (Braxton, 1991).

Beyond scientists' experience in their graduate training, their current workplaces set the stage for standards of conduct. Organizational research demonstrates that the prevailing moral atmosphere of a workplace represents the norms of the group, not simply individual levels of moral development (Victor & Cullen, 1988). Ethical or unethical standards of behavior have an organizational basis that is separate from individual evaluations (Victor & Cullen, 1988, p. 102). Such a social context of ethical or unethical behavior has been reflected in legal judgments against corporations—for example, in corporate crime (Clinard & Yeager, 1980). For science particularly, however, the problem is that the workplace is composed of concentric environmental spheres (Fox, 1998), and it is unclear which of these is most important as an organizational context governing standards of conduct: the university, department, the research group, or even collaborative teams within research groups.

Scientific Journals

Because journal publication is so important to the normative conduct of science, it is understandable that it is also thought to be a means of addressing misconduct through detection or sanctioning of fraudulent work in the editorial and peer review process. However, the corrective role of scientific journals is limited by structural problems inherent in the editorial and peer review, as Fox emphasizes in chapter 7 of this book. Reviewers lack information such as laboratory notes or raw data needed to ascertain misconduct. Further, reviewers are disinclined to acknowledge fraud; they (as well as editors in the editorial relationships) rely upon trust and tend to assume honest error rather than deceit in research (Chubin & Hackett, 1990).

When misconduct is detected, reviewers have been reluctant to alert editors (Banner, 1988), and for a number of reasons it is difficult for editors to take action even when alerted. A basic problem is that editors work apart from authors' employing institutions and funding agencies, and it is unclear to them where their responsibility lies and what financial costs they can incur in responding to misconduct.

To the extent that both detection and sanctioning of misconduct are constrained in editorial and peer review, so is the potential of the process for deterring misconduct. If potential offenders are aware of the limited corrective role of scientific journals in misconduct, they may figure that chances are good for fraudulent work to make its way through the review process.

Individual Scientists

Misconduct becomes socially defined in the process of a complaint, an inquiry, and action taken or not taken. The process usually begins with an individual observation of alleged wrongdoing, followed by discussion between the accuser and accused or a third party, which may grow into investigation, assessment, or adjudication.

Hence, some argue that the reporting of misconduct is the ultimate responsibility of individual scientists and that the problem is that "peers do not speak out" (Chubin, 1983, p. 187). Yet the action of individuals is a response to social and organizational conditions. First, the high degree of research specialization makes it difficult for those outside of a highly defined and narrow subfield to differentiate error from deception (Weinstein, 1979). Second, in such matters of misconduct, individuals act in response to the requirements of their environments (Elliston, Keenan, Lockhart, & van Schaick, 1985). As Braxton and Bayer suggest in chapter 11 of this book, without protection from retaliation, individuals fear being labeled a whistleblower and fear incurring social isolation or discredit in, or dismissal from, their workplace. Although scientists with certain career advantages—high rank, seniority, and administrative appointments such as chair—enjoy a security that permits them to report or take action on misconduct, they too can be pulled toward inaction or leniency by uncertainty about appropriate behavior and by institutional pressures for professional solidarity within their units.

Theories of organizational power and the "resource dependence perspective" (Pfeffer & Salancik, 1978) in particular provide a model for understanding the control of behavior within organizations, with implications for the likelihood that participants will "speak out" about misconduct. From the resource dependence perspective, power in organizations centers on "critical and scarce resources," both material and human. The organization's power over participants varies with their level of dependence upon the organizational resources—financial, social, psychological—and the availability to participants of alternative sources of support. By implication, members are more likely to "speak out" when employment alternatives are perceived to be available and acceptable (Farrell & Petersen, 1982). In science, this is compounded by the extensive investment that scientists make in education and training and by the nature of membership in the larger community of science. The investment potentially increases the dependence of scientists and the power of the organization, as does the salience of membership in the larger community of science—if alternative employment is scarce.[4]

At present, a role of surveillance of misconduct is not institutionalized in science (Weinstein, 1979; Zuckerman, 1977a), and individual scientists have not been inclined to assume the role on their own. Continuing reluctance of scientists to take action on misconduct has broadened the spectrum of federal control, as LaFollette shows in chapter 1 of this book.

OTHER ISSUES IN THE EXERCISE OF SOCIAL CONTROL

Universities and federal funding agencies potentially share a role in sanctioning misconduct—by retaining, promoting, and rewarding scientists in the case of universities and by debarring scientists from research funding in the case of the funding agencies. But what about the connections between segments of the trans-scientific community, the concurrence of their action, and the implications for control of misconduct and the prospects for professional self-regulation?

To the extent that university committees on scientific integrity formed in response to the presence of federal investigatory bodies, and to the extent that the loss of research funds (through debarment of funding) is against the interests of universities, federal agencies and universities are connected in their roles. But the two groups do not necessarily act out of a concurrence of interests. Universities, as we have seen, are subject to particular conflicts with respect to investigation of alleged misconduct. Among these are conflicts of employing both the accused and accuser, wariness of internal working relationships and internal hierarchies, and interests in maintaining and increasing research overhead costs—which can temper concerns of ethical conduct. Further, as shown by LaFollette's account of the federal hearings on scientific misconduct in chapter 1 of this book, administrative linkages *between* research universities have been weak and fragmented, and universities have not united in producing codes of ethics that articulate common expectations for conduct.

Scientific journals have a loose relationship or no relationship with employing institutions of authors and their funding agencies. Journals are not structurally positioned to act in concert with universities or funding agencies in response to misconduct. They often operate on a weak or marginal financial basis, such that concerns of financial gain or loss loom large—and response to fraud incurs costs of time, money, and resources that journals can ill afford (LaFollette, 1992).

In cases of scientific misconduct, and in other matters relevant to science, various segments of the trans-scientific community may act in concert, or they may not. As in other (nonscientific) pluralistic constellations or constituencies, alliances between segments can shift depending upon the particular issue, the case, or the interests at stake. Where the segments act in concert in control of misconduct, potential impact is concentrated and more certain; where they do not, impact is fragmented, as is, in fact, the intent of the segments when their respective perceptions and interests diverge rather than converge.

In understanding actions and interests of the trans-scientific community, it is also important to consider that science has changed over the past decades. An increase in interdisciplinary and multi-institutional research, often with industrial partners, has resulted in "different set[s] of expectations and disciplinary or organizational standards," as LaFollette points out in chapter 1 of this book. When scientists collaborate with different researchers within different institutions, sorting out the "who, what, where, and when" of actions and responsibilities becomes thorny if disputes of misconduct arise. In addition, rewards—both professional and financial—from research are higher than in the days when Bush developed the contract for science. Changing boundaries between industry and universities, and more specifically research partnerships between them, heighten interests in the "profitability" of research. With increased attention to entrepreneurial research activity, a concern is whether resulting values and interests accelerate conditions for misconduct, as Campbell and Slaughter discuss in chapter 12.

Another issue in misconduct and social control is the unknown incidence of misconduct. The relationship between the reported or known cases of misconduct and the actual or underlying distribution from which they are drawn remains as unknown now as it was when Zuckerman (1977a) emphasized this point over 20 years ago (p. 98). Scientists themselves tend to maintain that fraudulent behavior is rare and act in accordance with the trust that belief entails by assuming error rather than fraud when implausible results appear (Zuckerman, 1988, p. 523). The beliefs of other groups, such as science policy analysts and science journalists, may lead them to estimates of scientific misconduct varying from high or low, with consequences for levels of trust and for vigilance about misconduct. For purposes here, however, of understanding misconduct and corresponding policy, the unknown (or questionably estimated) data on incidence of misconduct means, as Zuckerman (1988) boldly put it, that "there is no social epidemiology of deviance in science—no systematic analysis of its distribution, sources, or control" (p. 523).

When the social control of misconduct is raised, replication is often offered as a mechanism for both detecting and deterring misconduct (see, e.g., Franklin, 1984). The reasoning is that if results are fraudulent, they will be detected when research is repeated by others and that if scientists know that their work may be replicated, they have extra cause to abide by norms of research conduct.

Intentional replication is unusual, however. Because of the premium on originality in the reward structure of science, inducements for replication are low (Weinstein, 1979; Zuckerman, 1988). As a practical matter, when intentional replication occurs, it is likely to take place in highly competitive, intensely active research areas where significant recognition is at stake (Fox, 1990; Zuckerman, 1977a). Or replication occurs unintentionally, as a by-product of using scientific contributions (Zuckerman, 1977a, 1988). In such cases, scientists working in an area of research related to another may identify inconsistencies between their results and others' work and thus raise questions about validity of the prior work (Zuckerman, 1988). This does not distinguish fraud from error, but it is a corrective mechanism for scientific knowledge (Zuckerman, 1988, pp. 524–525).

Further, not all research is equally reproducible. Social science research, for example, depends upon interpretation, and fieldwork, in particular, may be "unique" and unreplicable (Ben-Yehuda, 1985, p. 175). Laboratory science, as well, has variable potential for replication: research areas subject to maturation effects, testing effects, and social change, and those with expensive research designs, are less likely to be reproduced fully (Zuckerman, 1988, p. 525). Thus, from these perspectives (Ben-Yehuda, 1985; Fox, 1990; Zuckerman 1977a, 1988), replication is infrequent and uneven across research and disciplinary areas.

Other observers take a more relativist position about replication and control of scientific conduct. Constructivists such as Knorr-Cetina (1981) argue that scientific findings are not a snapshot of nature but rather a social construction that reflects social exchange and interaction in the laboratory. Under these conditions, then, knowledge is a reflection of the social context from which it derives and as such is not constituted by invariable natural facts to be validated in another setting.

Finally, two factors—ambiguity in definitions of misconduct and ambivalence in responding to misconduct—constrain its regulation. Defining misconduct is an enactment of social control. However, arriving at definitions of misconduct is problematic, and ambiguity in definition attenuates control by making it difficult to label or identify behavior as legitimate or illegitimate and to respond to it as such. The National Academy of Science, PHS, and NSF have each attempted to define misconduct, with depictions that are more and less inclusive and more and less stringent (see chapter 3 of this book).

Anderson argues in chapter 13 that attention should be focused on how, in fact, scientists distinguish between acceptable and unacceptable behavior and how they manage ambiguity between the two in day-to-day activities. A critical locus for research on misconduct is then behavior "at the margins," and this has implications for what is assessed—intentional misconduct and avoidable as well as inadvertent error—and where it is assessed—in laboratories, offices, and field locations.

Professional self-regulation of misconduct is also plagued by ambivalence[5]—values of individual and institutional reputation and resources that may conflict with standards of research conduct. Under such conditions of ambivalence, individuals and universities fear that taking action on misconduct will result in loss of reputation and research resources (see chapter 11 of this book). Any tendencies of scientists to view misconduct as a rare event, to delay reporting of incidents of misconduct, and to be reluctant to speak out about misconduct may result from this ambivalence.[6]

Taken together, these issues indicate that control of misconduct in the scientific community is not a naturally occurring process—that is, a process that can be expected to emerge as a matter of course in scientific practice. Rather, throughout types of collectivities (societies and organizations within them), control of misconduct is established through social structures—patterns and mechanisms—that guide behavior, repress deviance, and create mutual expectations.[7] However, existing means of control in science are underdeveloped, lack coordination, and are invoked haphazardly. The policy recommendations that follow are designed to strengthen responsibility for control of misconduct.

POLICY FOR CONTROL OF MISCONDUCT

The formulations of misconduct, professional self-regulation, and social control discussed here lead us to eight policy recommendations, both general and specific.

1. Mechanisms need be put into place to heighten the visibility of the issue of conduct and to acknowledge incidents of misconduct when they occur. Examples of such mechanisms include the open availability and access to data logs, data books, and computer printouts by laboratories and academic departments (Chubin, 1983). Ultimately, effectiveness of mechanisms of control depends upon the scientific community regarding them as matters of professional self-interest—integral to the validity of research and the preservation of research autonomy.

2. Sanctions function as deterrents to the extent that potential offenders know what sanctions operate (Ben-Yehuda, 1985; Tittle, 1980). With the exception of debarment of federal funds, types of sanctions of misconduct are unknown in the scientific community. The system of allocating punishments is informal, and unclarity exists in matching offense with punishment (see Zuckerman, 1988). In consequence, potential offenders do not anticipate punishment for misconduct, and social control is limited.

Professional associations and universities need to develop sanctions for types and levels of misconduct, and the severity of sanctions should be commensurate with the harm done to various individuals in the scholarly community and/or to the validity of knowledge produced. To be effective, sanctions must be known, communicated, and, moreover, evident through enactment.

3. Relatedly, organizational research demonstrates that the moral atmosphere of a group reflects the norms of the group and that there is an organizational basis for behavior that is separate from that of individual evaluations and perceptions. Thus, a climate about standards of conduct and sanctions for conduct should be conveyed through messages and signals from university presidents, chief academic officers, deans, department chairs, and laboratory chiefs. The messages can take the form of public speeches, speeches to university assemblies, memoranda, and day-to-day conversation among officials, but the action of due and attentive process in cases of alleged misconduct is a louder signal. While the particular associations of climate and misconduct are not known and have yet to be investigated (chapter 7), science exists in organizational settings, the work is done within organizational policies and procedures, and it requires organizational resources, human and material (Fox, 1992). Because of the organizational context of scientific work and behavior, the university, as the major employer of doctoral-level scientists, may be the proximate point of policy for social control of misconduct.

4. To partially counterbalance the constellation of interests—research, research funding, and indirect costs—identified by Turner (chapter 5) as mitigating universities' response to misconduct, we suggest two mechanisms. First, the sources and levels of indirect costs should be taken from the shadows numberless (to quote Keats) and made available. Second, the composition of university research integrity committees should be subject to election by the faculty at large, and their decisions should be binding upon actions of the university. Put differently, the actions of such committees should not be simply advisory to university administrators.

5. Despite the limitations of audits of raw data as a means of addressing the roots of scientific misconduct, random audits of raw data by journals and by university and research integrity offices of NSF and PHS-NIH provide a mechanism for estimating the incidence of misconduct and for monitoring it. In universities, all published research could be subject to random audits, whereas only research projects supported by grants from NSF and NIH could be subject to inspections of the funding agencies. When audits are random, no individuals are singled out, and elements of trust are preserved.

6. Because misconduct is sometimes best observed by parties external to that of the employing institution of the accused, university research integrity committees should establish procedures that allow means for filing of complaints from outside the university in question. This would provide a means by which journal editors, for example, might submit complaints of plagiarism or other research misconduct detected in editorial and peer review.

Although confidentiality during investigations should be afforded the accused, utmost effort should be expended to protect the accuser. University research integrity committees, the research integrity arms of federal granting agencies, and other parties should be assiduous in maintaining confidentiality of the accuser throughout investigations. In fact, the NSF has provided lead in this area by specifying retaliation against whistle-blowers as a form of scientific misconduct.

7. Doctoral training is an impressionable stage in the life course of scientists (see Zuckerman, 1977b). The NIH (1990, 1992) requirement that doctoral students and postdoctoral fellows receiving financial support from the agency acquire formal training in ethics reinforces the potential of doctoral education as a stage and means for transmission of standards of conduct. However, as Bird points out in chapter 8 of this book, most senior scientists have had no formal or specific training in scientific ethics, and ethics courses can be marginalized if taught by faculty outside the department. Further, because self-regulation of conduct is not a naturally occurring process, scientists do not necessarily share a sense of mechanisms of control toward self-regulation. Doctoral training needs to focus not only upon standards of conduct but also upon preparation of students as participants in the social control and self-regulation of misconduct.

8. Replication has been advanced by some as the classic antidote to fraudulent research. As a practical matter, replication has been limited, as discussed earlier. The potential of replication as a means of detecting and deterring misconduct might be enhanced, however, if replicated work were better rewarded and supported. As it is, grants and publications do not accrue to replication unless someone else's work is judged highly significant and something in it has been found to be incorrect or unless a researcher is working in an area sensitive to issues of experimenter reliability (Weinstein, 1979, pp. 645–646).

CONCLUSION

In the control of misconduct, institutions are better positioned than individuals, and universities and federal agencies have stronger sanctioning potential than do journals. The control of misconduct, however, is subject to constraints: shifting connections between segments of the trans-scientific community, an unknown incidence of misconduct, problems with replication as a means of correction, variable definitions of misconduct, and both individual and institutional ambivalence ensuing from conflicting values and interests in identifying and responding to misconduct. Our policy recommendations—for heightening visibility of the issue of misconduct, having sanctions that are known, communicated, and enacted, addressing the organizational basis of behavior and its control, assessing the incidence of misconduct, integrating training in ethics to doctoral education, and bolstering replication in science—are designed to help overcome the constraints to regulation and to strengthen professional responsibility for deterring, detecting, and sanctioning misconduct.

NOTES

1. In a general sense, social control of misconduct in professions entails and depends upon patterns and mechanisms of deterrence, detection, and sanctioning (see Introduction to this book).

2. Of the 13 preceding chapters in this volume, six appeared in earlier forms in *Perspectives on Research Misconduct,* a special issue of *The Journal of Higher Education* (May/June 1994). Parts of the final article (Fox & Braxton, 1994) in that issue are incorporated into this concluding chapter.

3. On June 21, 1996, an appeals panel of the U.S. Department of Health and Human Services handed down a decision that the "preponderance of the evidence" indicated that Imanishi-Kari was cleared of charges of misconduct in connection with the 1986 paper in *Cell.* After 10 years of controversy, the dispute had driven deep rifts in the scientific community. Donald Kennedy, a scientist at Stanford University, commented in the *New York Times* (1996) that the decision marked "the end of the sorriest chapter in American science that I can think of" (Kolata, 1996, p. B-10).

4. In Sarasohn's (1993) account of the Baltimore case, O'Toole, the accuser, speaks with a certain compassion about the ease with which professionals can lose sight of ideals, thus illustrating the relationship between investment, dependence, and reluctance to acknowledge misconduct: "By the time we are expert enough to spot something wrong, we have become insiders. We have spent our lives working to become part of the group, finding a niche suited to talents and aspirations.... It is very difficult to take actions which could adversely affect one's friends and colleagues" (p. 270).

5. Ambivalence—potentially contradictory norms—in science was posed by Merton (1976, pp. 35–36) in his discussion, specifically, of tension between norms of originality and of priority in scientific discovery.

6. These responses are similar to those that Merton (1976) discussed as expressions of "resistance to the systematic study of multiple discoveries and associated conflicts over policy" (pp. 35–36), but his discussion does not refer to misconduct and should not be construed as such.

7. In the society at large, social control is exercised through the government, police, courts, schools, and the media, and by both the common beliefs and values and the powers of force and manipulation underlying them.

REFERENCES

Abbott, A. (1988). *The system of professions.* Chicago: University of Chicago Press.

Banner, J. (1988). Preserving the integrity of peer review. *Scholarly Publishing, 19,* 109-115.
Ben-Yehuda, N. (1985). *Deviance and moral boundaries.* Chicago: University of Chicago Press.
Braxton, J. M. (1991). The influence of graduate department quality on the sanctioning of scientific misconduct. *Journal of Higher Education, 62,* 87–108.
Bush, V. (1990). *Science: The endless frontier.* Washington, DC: National Science Foundation. (Original work published 1945)
Carr-Saunders, A. P., & Wilson, P. A. (1933). *The professions.* Oxford, UK: Oxford University Press.
Chubin, D. (1983). Misconduct in research: An issue of science policy and practice. *Minerva, 23,* 175–202.
Chubin, D., & Hackett, E. J. (1990). *Peerless science: Peer review and U.S. science policy.* Albany: State University of New York.
Clinard, M., & Yeager, P. (1980). *Corporate crime.* New York: Free Press.
Derber, C., Schwartz, W., & Magrass, Y. (1990). *Power in the highest degree: Professionals and the rise of a new mandarin order.* New York: Oxford University Press.
Elliston, F., Keenan, J., Lockhart, P., & van Schaick, J. (1985). *Whistleblowing research: Methodological and moral issues.* New York: Praeger.
Farrell, D., & Petersen, J. C. (1982). Patterns of political behavior in organizations. *Academy of Management Review, 7,* 403–412.
Fox, M. F. (1990). Fraud, ethics, and the disciplinary contexts of science and scholarship. *American Sociologist, 21,* 67–71.
Fox, M. F. (1992). Research productivity and the environmental context. In T. Whiston & R. Geiger (Eds.), *Research and higher education* (pp. 103–111). Buckingham, UK: Society for Research into Higher Education/Open University Press.
Fox, M. F. (1998). Women in science and engineering: Theory, practice, and policy in programs. *Signs: Journal of Women in Culture and Society, 24,* 201–223.
Fox, M. F., & Braxton, J. M. (1994). Misconduct and social control in science. *Journal of Higher Education, 65,* 373–383.
Fox, M. F., & Firebaugh, G. (1992). Confidence in science: The gender gap. *Social Science Quarterly, 73,* 101–113.
Franklin, A. (1984). Forging, cooking, trimming, and riding on the bandwagon. *American Journal of Physics, 52,* 786–793.
Greene, P., Durch, J., Horwitz, W., & Hooper, V. (1985). Policies for responding to allegations of fraud in research. *Minerva, 23,* 203–215.
Guston, D. H. (1994). The demise of the social contract for science: Misconduct in science and the nonmodern world. *Centennial Review, 38,* 215-248.
Knorr-Cetina, K. (1981). *The manufacture of knowledge.* New York: Pergamon.
Kolata, G. (1996, June 25). Decision in scientific misconduct case raises new issues. *New York Times,* p. B-10.
LaFollette, M. (1992). *Stealing into print.* Berkeley: University of California Press.
Merton, R. K. (1976). The ambivalence of scientists. In R. K. Merton, *Sociological ambivalence and other essays* (pp. 32–55). New York: Free Press.

National Institutes of Health. (1990, August 17). Reminder and update: Requirement for programs on the responsible conduct of research in National Research Service Award institutional training programs. *NIH Guide for Grants and Contracts, 19*, 9.

National Institutes of Health. (1992, November 27). Reminder and update: Requirement for programs on the responsible conduct of research in National Research Service Award institutional training programs. *NIH Guide for Grants and Contracts, 21*, 2–3.

Pfeffer, J., & Salancik, G. R. (1978). *The external control of organizations: A resource dependence perspective.* New York: Harper & Row.

Price, A. (1994). Definitions and boundaries of research misconduct: Perspectives from a federal government viewpoint, with particular reference to plagiarism. *Journal of Higher Education, 65*, 286–297.

Sarasohn, J. (1993). *Science on trial: The whistle-blower, the accused, and the nobel laureate.* New York: St. Martin's.

Tittle, C. R. (1980). *Sanctions and social deviance: The question of deterrence.* New York: Praeger.

Victor, B., & Cullen, J. (1988). The organizational bases of ethical work climates. *Administrative Science Quarterly, 33*, 101–125.

Weinstein, D. (1979). Fraud in science. *Social Science Quarterly, 59*, 639–652.

Zuckerman, H. (1977a). Deviant behavior and social control in science. In E. Sagarin (Ed.), *Deviance and social change* (pp. 87–139). Beverly Hills, CA: Sage.

Zuckerman, H. (1977b). *Scientific elite: Nobel laureates in the United States.* New York: Free Press.

Zuckerman, H. (1988). The sociology of science. In N. J. Smelser (Ed.), *Handbook of sociology* (pp. 511–574). Newbury Park, CA: Sage.

CONTRIBUTORS

Melissa S. Anderson is Associate Professor of Higher Education at the University of Minnesota. She was a member of the Acadia Institute's research team for the project Professional Values and Ethical Issues in the Graduate Education of Scientists and Engineers. Her current research focus is graduate education, and she is the director of the Academic Life Project, a longitudinal study of doctoral education. She is the editor of *The Experience of Being in Graduate School: An Exploration.*

Alan Bayer is Professor of Sociology, Adjunct Professor of Science Studies, and Director of the Center for Survey Research at Virginia Tech University. He is author of more than a hundred articles, book chapters, and monographs. His primary books are *Human Resources in Higher Education* (with John K. Folger and Helen S. Astin), *The Power of Protest: A National Study of Student and Faculty Disruptions* (with Alexander W. Astin, Helen S. Astin, and Ann S. Bisconti), and *Faculty Misconduct in Collegiate Teaching* (with John M. Braxton).

Stephanie J. Bird is Special Assistant to the Provost of the Massachusetts Institute of Technology, where she works on the development of educational programs that address the professional responsibilities of scientists, and ethical issues in research practice and in science more generally. She has written numerous articles on issues in the responsible conduct of research and on mentoring and other responsibilities of science professionals. She is coeditor of the journal *Science and Engineering Ethics.*

John M. Braxton is an associate professor of education in the Department of Leadership and Organizations at Peabody College, Vanderbilt University.

His research interests include the sociology of the academic profession with a particular focus on the social control of professional role performance: detection, deterrence, and sanctioning of research and teaching misconduct. His research on these topics has been published in many journals, and he was the guest editor for the special issue of the *Journal of Higher Education* entitled *Perspectives on Research Misconduct*. He is also the coauthor (with Alan E. Bayer) of *Faculty Misconduct in Collegiate Teaching*.

Teresa Isabelle Daza Campbell is an assistant research professor in the Department of Management and Policy at the University of Arizona College of Business. Her areas of research interest focus on university-industry relationships, particularly organizational relations, the operationalization of ideals/norms/values, and the reward/incentive structures related to organizational goals.

Jason Earle is an associate professor at John Carroll University, where he teaches Foundations of Education courses. His most recent publication is *Organizational Literacy for Educators* (coauthored with Sharon D. Kruse).

Mary Frank Fox is Professor of Sociology in the School of History, Technology, and Society at the Georgia Institute of Technology. Her research focuses on gender, science, and professions. Her publications, appearing in over thirty journals and collections, include analyses of salary, publication productivity, research conduct, and educational and career patterns among scientists and academics.

Edward J. Hackett is a professor in the Department of Sociology at Arizona State University. He has written about various aspects of science, technology, and society, including peer review, research misconduct, science and the law, technological change in the workplace, and the social organization of research. He is currently involved in two major projects, a longitudinal study of the dynamics of academic research groups and an examination of the social distribution and understanding of environmental hazards.

David Johnson is Director of the Federation of Behavioral, Psychological, and Cognitive Sciences, a group of 18 scientific societies and some 150 university graduate departments.

Marcel C. Lafollette is a writer and a consultant in science communication and policy in Washington, DC, and is affiliated with the Graduate Program in Public Policy at George Washington University. She is the author of *Stealing into Print: Fraud, Plagiarism, and Misconduct in Scientific Publishing* (1992) and *Making Science Our Own: Public Images of Science, 1910–1955* (1990).

Barbara A. Lee is Professor and Chair of the Department of Human Resource Management at the School of Management and Labor Relations,

Rutgers University. She is the author of numerous books and articles on higher education law, employment law, personnel practices, and legal issues related to scientific misconduct. She is the author of *The Law of Higher Education*, 3d ed. (with William A. Kaplin), and *Academics in Court* (with George LaNoue).

Karen Seashore Louis is currently Director of the Center for Applied Research and Educational Improvement and Professor of Educational Policy and Administration at the University of Minnesota. Her research and teaching interests focus on educational reform, knowledge use in schools and universities, and educational institutions as workplaces.

Sheila Slaughter is Professor at the Center for the Study of Higher Education and Director of the Science and Technology Policy Initiative at the University of Arizona. Her specialties include academic science and technology policy. Her most recent publications include *Academic Capitalism: Politics, Policies and the Entrepreneurial University* (with Larry Leslie, 1997) and "The Emergence of a Competitiveness Research and Development Policy Coalition and the Commercialization of Academic Science and Technology" (with Gary Rhoades, 1996).

Nicholas H. Steneck is Professor of History in LSA and Ethics in Engineering at the University of Michigan. His published works range from discussions of medieval (*Science and Creation*, 1976) and early modern science to post–World War II science policy in the United States (*The Microwave Debate*, 1984). He publishes and lectures widely on research policy and ethics.

Stephen Turner is Graduate Research Professor of Philosophy at the University of South Florida. He has written extensively on expertise and patronage in the history of science, especially nineteenth-century geology and twentieth-century social science. His books include *The Impossible Science: An Institutional Analysis of American Sociology* (1990, with Jonathan Turner).

INDEX

AAAS. *See* American Association for the Advancement of Science
AAAS–ABA National Conference of Lawyers and Scientists, 49, 56, 116; and codes of ethics, 60; creation of, 51; *Project on Scientific Fraud and Misconduct,* 51–52
AAMC. *See* Association of American Medical Colleges
AAU. *See* Association of American Universities
AAUP (American Association of University Professors), 200
ABA. *See* American Bar Association
academic associations: and code of ethics, 156, 157; and response to peer silence, 156; sanctions available to, 148, 153; and scientific misconduct, 42–71 passim
academic departments: cohesion in, 240; effect on graduate students' professional values, 214–15, 220–25
Acadia Institute's Project on Professional Values and Ethical Issues in the Graduate Education of Scientists and Engineers, 215, 232n1, 300
adjudication, defined, 85
administration: financial issues in, 119–23; view of misconduct issues, 129–30
administrators: advisory committees and, 118; response of, 319
advisory committees, usefulness to administrators, 118
AHA. *See* American Historical Association

Alberts, Bruce, on ethics instruction, 177
Alfred P. Sloan Foundation, 51
alienation, as explanation for misconduct, 99, 104–6
allegations: assessment of, 84–85; institutional responsibility to manage, 47
Alsabati, Elias, 162; plagiarism case of, 77
American Academy of Forensic Studies, 61; ethical code of, 318
American Association for the Advancement of Science (AAAS): allegation statistics, 101; Committee on Scientific Freedom and Responsibility, 54, 56, 57; *The Dark Side of Science,* 51; listserv for ethics teachers, 57–58; *Professional Ethics Report,* 57, 61; Professional Society Ethics Group (PSEG), 57; *Project on Scientific Fraud and Misconduct,* 51–52; *Science,* 54; Scientific Freedom, Responsibility, and Law Program, 56, 57; survey on media coverage, 236
American Association of University Professors (AAUP), 200
American Bar Association (ABA), 51; *Project on Scientific Fraud and Misconduct,* 51–52
American Chemical Society, *Chemical and Engineering News,* 55
American Council on Education, 46, 49
American Historical Association (AHA), and Sokolow case, 166–67
American Psychological Association

• *335*

(APA): and Burt case, 168; ethical code of, 61–65, 318; Ethical Principles and Code of Conduct, 62
American Society for Microbiology, 49
animal research, oversight committees for, 77
anomie, as explanation for misconduct, 99, 103–4
APA. *See* American Psychological Association
appeal process, 48, 49
archiving, as function of publication, 163
Arroyo v. Rosen, 203
Association for Computing Machinery, 61; code of ethics, 65, 318
Association of Academic Health Centers, 49
Association of American Medical Colleges (AAMC): Ad Hoc Committee on the Maintenance of High Ethical Standards in the Conduct of Research (1982), 45; committee recommendations, 46–47; *The Maintenance of High Ethical Standards in the Conduct of Research*, 91n6; on self-regulation, 78–79
Association of American Universities (AAU), 49; Committee on the Integrity of Research, 46; on policies of ethical behavior, 78
Atomic Energy Commission, 21
authorship credit, Commission on Research Integrity on, 128
autonomy, and isolation, 305

Baltimore, David, 27–28, 33, 35, 171n1, 317; damage to career of, 132; response to Dingell hearings, 29
"Baltimore case," 27–28, 317, 328nn3, 4; Secret Service testimony in, 29
Barber, Albert, on *Science*, 54
Betrayers of the Truth (Broad and Wade), 78
Black, Donald, 106, 107
Bolling Committee (1974), 23
Breuning, Stephen J., 162; indictment of, 28
Burt, Cyril, 168
Bush, Vannevar, 12, 13; *Science: The Endless Frontier*, 87
Bush model, 36, 37
Bush report, 11, 12–15, 21, 22
Buzzelli, Donald, 260; on measuring misconduct, 285

California Institute of Technology, misconduct policy at, 82

Cattell, James McKeen, 164
CBE. *See* Council of Biology Editors
Cell, and "Baltimore case," 171n1
Chemical and Engineering News, 55
Chu, Paul, 171
Chubin, Daryl E., on policies for research conduct, 145
coauthorship, responsibility in, 167, 168
codes of conduct, formal and informal, 141
codes of ethics, 237; of APA, 61–65, 318; of Association for Computing Machinery, 65; and CSSP survey, 59–61; resources for developing, 56–57; University of Michigan, 79
cold fusion case, 131; University of Utah's response, 123–24
collaboration, 299; and employment misconduct, 221–24, 226; and isomorphism, 270
collective responsibility, in universities, 117
Columbia University, and Soman case, 77
Commission on Research Integrity: on authorship credit, 128; creation of, 30; definitions of scientific misconduct, 140, 285; *Integrity and Misconduct in Research*, 209n3; of NIH, 26; on self-regulation of universities, 116
Committee on Agriculture, 21
Committee on Commerce, 21
Committee on Commerce, Science, and Transportation, 21
Committee on Government Reform and Oversight (1994), 18–19
Committee on National Security, 21
Committee on Science (also, Committee on Science and Astronautics), 21, 23
Committee on Scientific Freedom and Responsibility (AAAS), creation of, 54
Committee System Reorganization Amendments (1977), 21
competition: effect on levels of misconduct, 220, 300; and employment misconduct, 221–24, 226; and personal misconduct, 224
computer printouts, availability of, 145, 152, 325
confidentiality, 81, 302; guarantee of, 191
Congressional Budget Office, evaluation reports from, 20
congressional oversight, 11–37 passim; Health Research Extension Act (1985), 79; improving quality of, 34–35; investigative techniques used in, 19–21; types of, 19

Congressional Research Service (CRS), evaluation reports from, 20
Conscientious Employee Protection Act (New Jersey), 204
consequences, of misconduct, 293–94
context, for misconduct, 290–91, 295–96
copyright law: damages under, 193; fair use doctrine, 193, 193–94; *Weismann v. Freeman,* 193–94
Council of Biology Editors (CBE): Editorial Policy Committee, 67–68; *Ethics and Policy in Scientific Publication,* 68
Council of Graduate Schools, 49; allegation statistics, 101
Council of Scientific Society Presidents (CSSP): and codes of ethics, 59–61; Ethics in Science Committee, 59; *Society Policies on Ethics Issues,* 61
Council on Government Relations, 49
criminal false claims statute, 196
CRS. *See* Congressional Research Service
CSSP. *See* Council of Scientific Society Presidents

damages: under copyright law, 193; under patent law, 194
Danforth, William, 46
Dark Side of Science, The (Kilbourne and Kilbourne), 51
Darsee, John, 24–25, 162, 169, 170
Darsee case, 25, 78, 165, 317
data logs, availability of, 145, 152, 325
data suppression, 152
data trimming, sanctions for, 148, 153
Daubert v. Merrell-Dow Pharmaceuticals, 113n2
defamation, as cause of action, 202–4
definitions: in misconduct investigations, 82–84; of scientific misconduct, 99–100
department climate: as context, 290; effect on graduate students' professional values, 215, 220–25
Department of Health and Human Services (DHHS), 19, 49, 317; Departmental Appeals Board, 192; Inspector General of, 24; regulations for investigating fraud, 26. *See also* Office of Research Integrity; Office of Scientific Integrity Review
Department of Justice, 192; and *qui tam* lawsuits, 197
department structure, effect on graduate students' professional values, 214–15, 225
detection, 142; in dissemination stage, 154–55; in evaluation stage, 156–57; in production stage, 145–48; in reporting stage, 152
deterrence, 142; in dissemination stage, 154–55; in evaluation stage, 156–57; in production stage, 145–48; in reporting stage, 152; use of replication, 145–48
deviance, connection to anomie, 103
DHHS. *See* Department of Health and Human Services
DiMaggio, P. J., theory of institutional isomorphism, 259, 261
Dingell, John, 15; role in "Baltimore case" inquiry, 27–28, 29, 33, 317
direct costs, federal grants and, 119
dissemination, four substages of, 153
doctoral study: as socialization process, 142–43; training in ethics, 327
Douglas, J. D., on rules, 286
"dry run" seminars, for deterrence, 152, 154, 155
due process, 49, 51, 81, 85, 166, 191, 192; protections under, 199, 200–201
Duesberg, Peter, 103
Durkheim, Emile, origin of *anomie,* 104

editorial and peer review processes, 162–71 passim
editors, position on standardized journal policy, 66
educational reform, 89
elitism, 305; of science, 108
employment misconduct, 217, 221–24
Engineering in Medicine and Biology, 55
ethical standards, recommendations for, 326
ethics: codes of, 56–57, 59–61, 79; in graduate education, 174–86 passim; required teaching of, 57
Ethics and Policy in Scientific Publication (CBE), 68
ethics instruction, 174–86 passim, 236; courses, 180; key elements in, 179; mentoring, 182–85; NIH requirement for, 175, 177, 179, 268, 327; seminars, 180–81; topics in, 185
evaluation reports, for assessing research problems, 19–20
expense, of science, 107–8
exposure, of misconduct, 291–93, 295

fabrication, 100, 165; responsibility for deterrence, 154–55; sanctions for, 148, 153

Fairleigh Dickinson Press, and Sokolow case, 166
fair use doctrine, 193–94
False Claims Act, 196–98, 206
false statements statute, 195–96
falsification, 100, 165
FBI (Federal Bureau of Investigation), 192
FDA (Food and Drug Administration), 209n5
Feder, Ned, 33, 103
Federal Bureau of Investigation (FBI), 192
Federal False Claims Act, 196–98, 206
federal grants: institutional pressure for, 240; and overhead costs, 119, 120; payment of "direct" and "indirect" costs, 119
federal laws: criminal false claims statute, 196; false statements statute, 195–96; Federal False Claims Act, 196–98; governing misconduct, 189–98
federal regulation, effects on funded research, 15–16
Federation of American Societies for Experimental Biology, 49
Federation of Behavioral, Psychological, and Cognitive Sciences, 67; Forum on Research Management, 68
Felig, Philip, 77, 79, 170; on Soman case, 44–45, 75
Feynman, Richard, idea of scientific integrity, 300
financial rewards, redistribution of, 112
Food and Drug Administration (FDA), 209n5
formal investigations, and congressional oversight, 23
Forum on Research Management, 68
fragmentation, 165
fraud: difficulty of defining, 164; "professional" vs. "amateur," 102–3
Fredrickson, Donald S.: on role of university, 45; on self-regulation, 78; on university responsibility, 79
Friedman, Paul, 101, 285, 286; on defining misconduct, 285
funding, suspension of, 126

Gallo case, 162, 170–71
General Accounting Office, evaluation reports from, 20
Gore, Albert, Jr., 35, 88; on aggressive action, 43; on Darsee case, 25; and Soman case, 75
graduate education, ethics in, 174–86 passim. *See also* doctoral study

graduate students, socialization of, 213, 214–15
grants. *See* federal grants

Handler, Philip: on Darsee case, 25; on self-regulation, 43, 78
harm, defining, 158–59
Harvard University, 162; Darsee case at, 25, 78; and pressure to publish, 46
Health Research Extension Act (1985), 26, 79
hierarchical linear modeling (HLM), 220, 232n4
"honest error," vs. misconduct, 83
Honor in Science (Sigma Xi), 53
House Committee on Energy and Commerce, Subcommittee on Oversight and Investigations, 27, 317
House Committee on Government Operations, Human Relations and Intergovernmental Relations Subcommittee, 27
House Committee on Science and Technology: and Darsee case, 24–25; Oversight Subcommittee, 43; Subcommittee on Investigations and Oversight, 29, 35
human subjects research, 77; federal regulation of, 16–17

ICMJE. *See* International Committee of Medical Journal Editors
ideological desensitization: attitudes about, 247; influences on, 251–52
Imanishi-Kari, Thereza, 33, 35, 171n1, 317, 328n3; and "Baltimore case," 27–28; cleared of charges, 29
Indiana University, 84
indirect costs: federal grants and, 119; income from, 121; recommendations for, 326
individualism: effect on levels of misconduct, 220–21; and personal misconduct, 224
industrial relationships, 259–76 passim
industry, science and, 110–11
Inspector General Act (1978), 23
Institute of Electrical and Electronics Engineers, *Engineering in Medicine and Biology*, 55
Institute of Medicine, position on ethics instruction, 177
institutional isomorphism: collaboration and, 270; defined, 261; theory of, 259
institutional review boards (IRBs), for human subjects research, 77
Integrity and Misconduct in Research, 209n3

intellectual freedom, Bush on, 13
intellectual property law, 193–95, 206
intention/intentionality: in definition of misconduct, 83–84, 287–89; standard of, 127–28
International Committee of Medical Journal Editors (ICMJE), development of uniform requirements for manuscripts, 67
Internet, 58–59; and debate on misconduct, 90
intraprofessional status, defined, 239–40
investigation, defined, 85
IRBs. *See* institutional review boards
isomorphism. *See* institutional isomorphism

JAMA. See *Journal of the American Medical Association*
Jewett, Frank, on dangers of federal funding, 14
Johns Hopkins University, Policy on Integrity in Research (1988), 82
Joint Committee on Health Policy, and AAU recommendations, 46
Journal des Scavans, 163
journal editors, role in publication of fraudulent research, 66–67
Journal of the American Medical Association (JAMA), 55; policy on availability of data, 299
Journal of the Early Republic, and Sokolow case, 166
journals: editorial policies, 237, 299; and encouragement of replications, 148; publication practices of, 66–70; relationship with universities, 322; responsibility for deterrence, 154; sanctions available to, 148, 153, 155–56

Kennedy, Donald, 79; on outcome of "Baltimore case," 328n3
Knowledge (later *Science Communication*), 55
Koshland, Daniel, 54, 285
Krevans, Julius R., 45

law, science and, 110
legal proceedings, vs. peer review, 47–49
Legislative Reorganization Act: of 1946, 18; of 1970, 23

Maintenance of High Ethical Standards in the Conduct of Research, The (AAMC), 47, 91n6

Manhattan Project, 12, 14
manuscript review, for deterrence, 152, 154, 155
Maplethorpe, Charles, testimony in "Baltimore case," 27, 28
Massachusetts Institute of Technology, "Baltimore case" at, 27–28
Medawar, Peter, 287; on Summerlin case, 76
media: attention to fraud cases, 27, 28; coverage of "Baltimore case," 33; coverage of congressional oversight, 20; coverage of misconduct hearings, 19, 30–31
mentors: definition of, 182, 186n1; and ethics instruction, 182–83
Merton, Robert K., 118; on ambivalence in science, 329n5; on anomie and social structure, 103–4; norms of science, 300
microbiology, employment misconduct in, 224
Minerva, 55
misconduct: administration view of, 129–30; consequences of, 293–94; context of, 290–91; context for, 295–96; contextual effects of, 298–301; defining, 82–84, 163–64, 199, 284–90, 324; empirical research on, 283–307 passim; employment, 217, 221–24; vs. error, 287–88; estimates of, 100–102; explanations of, 102–6; exposure of, 291–93, 295; intentionality in, 287–89; interactive effects of, 294–96; legal aspects of, 189–208 passim; longitudinal effects of, 296–97; NSF definition of, 190; personal, 217, 224–25; PHS definition of, 190; policy recommendations for, 325–27; problems in study of, 301–7; research, 217, 221; social control of, 106–9, 315–28 passim; statistics, 302; surveillance of, 322
misconduct officers, 85
MIT. *See* Massachusetts Institute of Technology

NASA (National Aeronautics and Space Administration), 21
National Academy of Science and Engineering, position on ethics instruction, 177
National Academy of Sciences, 14, 43; *On Being a Scientist*, 52–53, 177; Committee on the Conduct of Science, 52; and definition of misconduct, 324; response to Darsee case, 25
National Aeronautics and Space Administration (NASA), 21

National Association of College and University Attorneys, 49
National Association of State Universities and Land-Grant Colleges, 46, 49
National Institute of Mental Health (NIMH), and Breuning case, 28
National Institutes of Health (NIH), 21, 24, 44, 190; administration views of fraud, 27; and "Baltimore case," 29, 317; Commission on Research Integrity, 26; policy development for fraud investigations, 26; requirement for ethics instruction, 175, 177, 179, 226, 327; response to Darsee case, 25; Revitalization Act (1993), 30; and teaching ethics, 57. *See also* Office of Research Integrity; Office of Scientific Integrity
National Science and Technology Council, definition of misconduct, 30
National Science Foundation (NSF), 21, 44, 49, 79, 190, 236; allegation statistics, 101; and congressional oversight, 80; definition of misconduct, 190, 324; Ethics and Values Studies Program in the Social, Behavioral, and Economic Sciences Directorate, 55; funding of ethics conference, 68; misconduct policy, 83; Office of the Inspector General, 23–24, 141, 317; and pressure to publish, 46; public attitude surveys of, 31; Truman veto of, 14
National Scientific Conduct Assessment, 242; survey instrument, 241
negative sanctions, use in self-regulation, 143–44
New England Journal of Medicine, position on federal oversight, 28–29
NIH. *See* National Institutes of Health
NIMH. *See* National Institute of Mental Health
Ninnemann, John L., fraud case of, 197–98
Nissenbaum, Stephen, and Sokolow case, 166–67
nominal authorship, 165
NSF. *See* National Science Foundation

Office of Research Integrity (ORI), 19, 50, 101, 141, 191–92, 317; definition of plagiarism, 191; FDA and, 209n5; and Gallo case, 162
Office of Scientific Integrity (OSI), 19, 101, 191. *See also* Office of Research Integrity
Office of Scientific Integrity Review (OSIR), 66–67, 192. *See also* Office of Research Integrity

Office of Technology Assessment (OTA), evaluation reports from, 20
On Being a Scientist (NAS), 52–53, 177
ORI. *See* Office of Research Integrity
O'Toole, Margot, 35, 103; on loss of ideals, 328n4; testimony in "Baltimore case," 27–28
overhead funds: administrative freedom and, 121; defined, 120; federal grants and, 119, 120; for scientific auditors, 134
oversight: congressional, 11–37 passim; as congressional responsibility, 17–18

Panel on Scientific Responsibility and the Conduct of Research, 286, 306
patent law, damages under, 194
patent ownership, university policies on, 195
peer review: adoption at *Science,* 164; as deterrent, 152; vs. legal proceedings, 47–49; processes, 162–71 passim; weaknesses of, 77, 320
peer silence: and occurrence of misconduct, 156; university accountability for, 157
personal misconduct, 217, 224–25
Perspectives on Ethical Issues in Science and Technology (PEIST), 57–58, 59
Ph.D. study. *See* doctoral study
Philosophical Transactions of the Royal Society, 163
PHS. *See* Public Health Service
Physical Review Letters, and Chu papers, 171
plagiarism, 65–66, 83, 100; Alsabati case, 77; defining, 84; ORI definition of, 191; percentage of ORI and NSF cases involving, 191; sanctions for, 148, 152–53
policy recommendations, for control of misconduct, 325–27
positive rewards, use in self-regulation, 143–44
Powell, W. W., theory of institutional isomorphism, 259, 261
preceptors, changing role of, 111. *See also* mentors
pressure to publish, 46; as factor in fraud, 170
prevention, as institutional responsibility, 47
Price, Don K., 14–15
Pritchard, Ivor, on scientific conduct, 286
profession, vs. occupation, 141
Professional Ethics Report (AAAS), 57, 61, 237
professional etiquette: attitudes about, 238,

247; influences on, 251; in misconduct exposure, 292–93
Professional Society Ethics Group (PSEG), creation of, 57
professional solidarity, 240
professional values, development of, 214–15
Project on Scientific Fraud and Misconduct (AAAS-ABA), 51–52
promotion, as reward for replication, 145
psychopathology, as explanation for misconduct, 99, 102–3
Public Health Service (PHS), 24, 47, 262, 317; allegation statistics, 101; and congressional oversight, 80; definition of misconduct, 190, 284, 324; misconduct policy, 83; requirement for ethics instruction, 177. *See also* Office of Research Integrity
Public Health Service Act, 304
public relations, and expense of science, 107
publishing, role in scientific misconduct, 65–70
punishment, scientists' view of, 132–33

qualified privilege, in defamation claims, 202–3
qui tam plaintiff, 196–98

Racker, Efraim, on psychopathology explanation of misconduct, 102–3
random audits, as deterrent, 152
raw data: audits, 152, 155, 169, 326; authors' reluctance to supply, 154–55; availability of, 69, 145, 152, 156, 157, 299, 325; in reporting stage, 152
reappointment, as reward for replication, 145
recombinant DNA technology, oversight for, 77
Rennie, Drummond, 89
replication, 157; as deterrent, 145–48, 166, 323–24; in evaluation stage, 156; recommendations for, 327
Report of the Association of American Universities Committee on the Integrity of Research (1982), 46
reputation, 239; potential for damage to, 48
reputational harm: attitudes about, 243; influences on, 248–50
research community, role in teaching ethics, 175–78
Research Ethics: Cases and Materials, 70
research integrity committees, recommendations for, 326–27

research misconduct, 217, 221
research universities, scientific misconduct and, 75–90 passim
retaliation, 209n9
retractions, 148, 169
review, difficulty of defining, 163–64
Revitalization Act (1993), and creation of Commission on Research Integrity, 30
Roe, Robert A., 29
Ryan, Kenneth, 90

salary freezing, as punishment, 157, 158
salary increase, as reward for replication, 145
sanctions: attitudes about, 243; criteria, 239, 250–51; as deterrents, 325–26; in dissemination stage, 155–56; need for, 141–42; reluctance of universities to use, 148; in reporting stage, 152–53; severity of, 144
science: elitism of, 108; and industry, 110–11; and law, 110; as resource for power, 108; as source of intellectual authority, 108
Science (AAAS): adoption of peer review, 164; as medium for treatment of misconduct, 55; and scientific integrity, 54
Science: The Endless Frontier (Bush), 87
Science and Engineering Ethics, 55; ethics instruction and, 183–84
Science Communication, 55
Science, Technology, and Human Values, 55
scientific auditors, for institutional self-regulation, 134
scientific misconduct policies, 75
scientific societies: indirect influences of, 51; sanctions available to, 148; and scientific misconduct, 42–71 passim; and surveillance mechanisms, 158
scientists, position on formal punishment, 132–33
Select Committee on Committees (1974), 23
self-regulation, 112, 236; in academic community, 139–59 passim; attitudinal problems in, 237–39; defined, 1; Fredrickson on, 78; future research on, 254; Handler on, 78; necessary processes for, 142–44; primary obligation for, 140; in production stage, 145–52; scientific auditors for, 134; and social control of misconduct, 315–28 passim; Woolf on, 78; Zuckerman on, 76–77
Senate Commerce Committee. *See* Committee on Commerce, Science, and Transportation
Shine, Kenneth, on ethics instruction, 177

Sigma Xi, 52; *Honor in Science,* 53
Sloan-Kettering Institute for Cancer Research, Summerlin case at, 43
"sloppy science," vs. misconduct, 83
Slutsky case, 162, 165, 169–70; coauthorship in, 169
social control: defined, 1; by federal government, 316–18; by individual scientists, 321–22; by professional associations, 318; by scientific journals, 320–21; over scientific misconduct, 106–9; self-regulation and, 315–28 passim; by universities, 318–20
socialization: doctoral study as, 142–43; of graduate students, 213, 214–15
social status, of professions, 141
Society for Social Studies of Science, 56; *Science, Technology, and Human Values,* 55
Society Policies on Ethics Issues (CSSP), 61
Sokolow, Jayme, 166, 167
Soman, Vijay, 45, 75, 77, 162, 170
Spector, Mark, 102, 162
state contract law, 201
state laws, whistle-blower, 202, 204–5
Stealing into Print: Fraud, Plagiarism, and Misconduct in Scientific Publishing (LaFollette), 66
Stewart, Walter, 33, 103
Summerlin, William, 43, 76; psychopathology explanation for misconduct, 102
supervisory responsibility, 84
surveillance mechanisms, for self-regulation, 143, 158

tenure, as reward for replication, 145
termination of employment, as sanction, 153
trans-scientific community, 316, 322
Truman, Harry S., and NSF, 14
truth, as defense to defamation claim, 202

U.S. Congress, and social control of misconduct, 317
U.S. Office of Scientific Research and Development, 12
U.S. Patent and Trademark Office, 194

universities: advisory committees, 118; patent ownership policies, 195; power within, 118; self-policing of, 116–17; use of sanctions, 148, 157, 320
university-industry relationships, 259–76 passim; potential conflict of commitment, 271–74; potential conflict of interest, 270–71; potential conflict over internal equity, 274
University of Alabama, 198
University of California-San Diego: and Ninnemann case, 197–98; and Slutsky case, 162, 165, 169
University of Colorado, misconduct assessments at, 85
University of Michigan, Task Force on Integrity in Scholarship (1983), 79
University of Utah: and Ninnemann case, 197–98; response to cold fusion case, 123–24

visibility, of science, 107–8

Walker, Robert, 43
Weber, Max, on alienation in science, 105
Weismann v. Freeman, 194
Weiss, Ted, 27
whistle-blower laws, 204–5; state, 202, 207
Whistleblower Protection Act (1989), 204
whistle-blowers, 27, 84, 103, 132, 190; and federal law, 195; protection of, 81, 82, 127; retaliation against, 83; stigmatization of, 245, 251; treatment of, 51
Wigodsky, Herman, 88; on self-regulation, 79
Woolf, Patricia, 101; on self-regulation, 78
World Wide Web, and debate on misconduct, 90

Yale University: Policy Statement on Collaborative Research (1982), 80–81; and Soman case, 77, 162

Zuckerman, Harriet, 78, 86, 106, 158, 285, 323; on error, 288; on self-regulation in science, 76–77

Q 147 .P47 1999

Perspectives on scholarly
misconduct in the sciences

GAYLORD S